M000118443

Bible Scriptures
by
Topic

A Quick-Reference Guide to Bible Verses

Tony L. Warrick

Over 600 Real Topics
More than 5,000 Life-Changing Scriptures

Bible Scriptures by Topic

Copyright © 2021 by Tony L. Warrick

All rights reserved. This book or parts thereof may not be reproduced in any form, stored in any retrieval system, or transmitted in any form by any means—electronic, mechanical, photocopy, recording, or otherwise—without prior written permission of the author, except for the use of brief quotations in a book review and as provided by United States of America's copyright law. For permission requests, please refer all questions to the author: TonyWarrick.com.

Scripture quotations, unless otherwise noted, are taken from The ESV® Bible (The Holy Bible, English Standard Version®) copyright © 2001 by Crossway Bibles, a publishing ministry of Good News Publishers. ESV Text Edition: 2016. The ESV® text has been reproduced in cooperation with and by the permission of Good News Publishers. Unauthorized reproduction of this publication is prohibited. All rights reserved.

Cover design by Jamar Jones, www.gi-designs.com
Printed in the United States of America

ISBN: 978-1-955253-04-8

We live in a time, both locally and globally, where it seems like confusion is everywhere, and there is even more confusion about how to handle the issues of life. Whether it is political tenseness, relational conflict, or substance abuse, there is no unity on the best approach for help; the confusion can feel suffocating. Nonetheless, I'm thankful we have a heavenly Father who guides us through the turmoil and uncertainty. In cultural darkness, we have a God who provides divine light and guidance.

"The unfolding of your words gives light; it imparts understanding to the simple." Psalm 119:130

God's words speak through the confusion. His words provide us with truth in a world of theory and philosophy. The words our heavenly Father speaks through scriptures are full of energy, light, and more sharply than a two-edged sword. It penetrates the very core of our being, where soul and spirit, flesh, and blood meet.

Therefore, whether it is emotional or relational problems, God speaks through scripture. If there is a question of right or wrong, God speaks through scripture. If there is hopelessness, God speaks through scripture. If there is fear, an enslaving habit, or questions on raising children, God is actively speaking through scripture.

This book, Bible Scriptures by Topic, is an excellent place to start if you want to know what scriptures say about specific issues and topics. This does not mean you should not read the scriptures in context. But this book will help you remember critical verses that are fundamental to your faith and help you feel encouraged on specific subjects and maybe in urgent situations.

A Note of Caution

Learn what the scriptures have to say on different issues affecting your everyday life. Choose from the complete list of topics in the Table of Contents. Always remember, check the context of a verse. The context of a verse might put a very different slant on what the verse seems to say. The scriptures aren't a fortune cookie, so don't treat it like one.

Contents

C

D

E

F

G

H

I

J

N

O

P

Q

R

U

V

W

Y

Z

A Tenth

Malachi 3:8-9
Will man rob God? Yet you are robbing me. But you say, 'How have we robbed you?' In your tithes and contributions. You are cursed with a curse, for you are robbing me, the whole nation of you.

2 Corinthians 9:7
Each one must give as he has decided in his heart, not reluctantly or under compulsion, for God loves a cheerful giver.

Malachi 3:10
Bring the full tithe into the storehouse, that there may be food in my house. And thereby put me to the test, says the Lord of hosts, if I will not open the windows of heaven for you and pour down for you a blessing until there is no more need.

Proverbs 3:9
Honor the Lord with your wealth and with the first fruits of all your produce;

Leviticus 27:30
"Every tithe of the land, whether of the seed of the land or of the fruit of the trees, is the Lord's; it is holy to the Lord.

Abandonment

Psalm 34:18
The Lord is near to the brokenhearted and saves the crushed in spirit.

Psalm 27:10
For my father and my mother have forsaken me, but the Lord will take me in.

Deuteronomy 31:6
Be strong and courageous. Do not fear or be in dread of them, for it is the Lord your God who goes with you. He will not leave you or forsake you."

Joshua 1:9
Have I not commanded you? Be strong and courageous. Do not be frightened, and do not be dismayed, for the Lord your God is with you wherever you go."

Isaiah 49:15-16
"Can a woman forget her nursing child, that she should have no compassion on the son of her womb? Even these may forget, yet I will not forget you. Behold, I have engraved you on the palms of my hands; your walls are continually before me.

Romans 8:38-39
For I am sure that neither death nor life, nor angels nor rulers, nor things present nor things to come, nor powers, nor height nor depth, nor anything else in all creation, will be able to separate us from the love of God in Christ Jesus our Lord.

Hebrews 13:5-6
Keep your life free from love of money, and be content with what you have, for he has said, "I will never leave you nor forsake you." So we can confidently say, "The Lord is my helper; I will not fear; what can man do to me?"

Ability

Philippians 4:13
I can do all things through him who strengthens me.

2 Timothy 1:7
For God gave us a spirit not of fear but of power and love and self-control.

Ephesians 3:20
Now to him who is able to do far more abundantly than all that we ask or think, according to the power at work within us,

Colossians 3:23
Whatever you do, work heartily, as for the Lord and not for men,

Abomination

Leviticus 18:22
You shall not lie with a male as with a woman; it is an abomination.

Leviticus 20:13
If a man lies with a male as with a woman, both of them have committed an abomination; they shall surely be put to death; their blood is upon them.

Deuteronomy 22:5
"A woman shall not wear a man's garment, nor shall a man put on a woman's cloak, for whoever does these things is an abomination to the Lord your God.

Proverbs 12:22
Lying lips are an abomination to the Lord, but those who act faithfully are his delight.

Proverbs 17:15
He who justifies the wicked and he who condemns the righteous are both alike an abomination to the Lord.

Proverbs 16:5
Everyone who is arrogant in heart is an abomination to the Lord; be assured, he will not go unpunished.

Matthew 24:15
"So when you see the abomination of desolation spoken of by the prophet Daniel, standing in the holy place (let the reader understand),

Proverbs 11:20

Those of crooked heart are an abomination to the Lord, but those of blameless ways are his delight.

Proverbs 28:9

If one turns away his ear from hearing the law, even his prayer is an abomination.

Proverbs 20:10

Unequal weights and unequal measures are both alike an abomination to the Lord.

Proverbs 11:1

A false balance is an abomination to the Lord, but a just weight is his delight.

Proverbs 15:26

The thoughts of the wicked are an abomination to the Lord, but gracious words are pure.

Proverbs 15:8

The sacrifice of the wicked is an abomination to the Lord, but the prayer of the upright is acceptable to him.

Abortion

Jeremiah 1:5

"Before I formed you in the womb I knew you, and before you were born I consecrated you; I appointed you a prophet to the nations."

Psalm 139:13-16

For you formed my inward parts; you knitted me together in my mother's womb. I praise you, for I am fearfully and wonderfully made. Wonderful are your works; my soul knows it very well. My frame was not hidden from you, when I was being made in secret, intricately woven in the depths of the earth. Your eyes saw my unformed substance; in your book were written, every one of them, the days that were formed for me, when as yet there was none of them.

Job 31:15

Did not he who made me in the womb make him? And did not one fashion us in the womb?

Psalm 127:3-5

Behold, children are a heritage from the Lord, the fruit of the womb a reward. Like arrows in the hand of a warrior are the children of one's youth. Blessed is the man who fills his quiver with them! He shall not be put to shame when he speaks with his enemies in the gate.

Isaiah 44:2

Thus says the Lord who made you, who formed you from the womb and will help you: Fear not, O Jacob my servant, Jeshurun whom I have chosen.

Psalm 139:13

For you formed my inward parts; you knitted me together in my mother's womb.

Abounding

1 Corinthians 15:58
Therefore, my beloved brothers, be steadfast, immovable, always abounding in the work of the Lord, knowing that in the Lord your labor is not in vain.

Romans 15:13
May the God of hope fill you with all joy and peace in believing, so that by the power of the Holy Spirit you may abound in hope.

Colossians 2:6-8
Therefore, as you received Christ Jesus the Lord, so walk in him, rooted and built up in him and established in the faith, just as you were taught, abounding in thanksgiving. See to it that no one takes you captive by philosophy and empty deceit, according to human tradition, according to the elemental spirits of the world, and not according to Christ.

Abstinence

1 Thessalonians 4:3-4
For this is the will of God, your sanctification: that you abstain from sexual immorality; that each one of you know how to control his own body in holiness and honor,

Hebrews 13:4
Let marriage be held in honor among all, and let the marriage bed be undefiled, for God will judge the sexually immoral and adulterous.

1 Corinthians 6:18
Flee from sexual immorality. Every other sin a person commits is outside the body, but the sexually immoral person sins against his own body.

2 Timothy 2:22
So flee youthful passions and pursue righteousness, faith, love, and peace, along with those who call on the Lord from a pure heart.

1 Peter 2:11
Beloved, I urge you as sojourners and exiles to abstain from the passions of the flesh, which wage war against your soul.

Abundance

Deuteronomy 28:1-68
"And if you faithfully obey the voice of the Lord your God, being careful to do all his commandments that I command you today, the Lord your God will set you high above all the nations of the earth. And all these blessings shall come upon you and overtake you, if you obey the voice of the Lord your God. Blessed shall you be in the city, and blessed shall you be in the field. Blessed shall be the fruit of your womb and the fruit of your ground and the fruit of your cattle, the increase of your herds and the young of your flock. Blessed shall be your basket and your kneading bowl. ...

Ephesians 3:20
Now to him who is able to do far more abundantly than all that we ask or think, according to the power at work within us,

John 10:10
The thief comes only to steal and kill and destroy. I came that they may have life and have it abundantly.

Psalm 23:5
You prepare a table before me in the presence of my enemies; you anoint my head with oil; my cup overflows.

Psalm 65:11
You crown the year with your bounty; your wagon tracks overflow with abundance.

Matthew 6:33
But seek first the kingdom of God and his righteousness, and all these things will be added to you.

Luke 6:38
Give, and it will be given to you. Good measure, pressed down, shaken together, running over, will be put into your lap. For with the measure you use it will be measured back to you."

James 1:17
Every good gift and every perfect gift is from above, coming down from the Father of lights with whom there is no variation or shadow due to change.

2 Corinthians 9:8
And God is able to make all grace abound to you, so that having all sufficiency in all things at all times, you may abound in every good work.

Psalm 37:11
But the meek shall inherit the land and delight themselves in abundant peace.

Proverbs 3:10
Then your barns will be filled with plenty, and your vats will be bursting with wine.

Abuse

Ephesians 6:4
Fathers, do not provoke your children to anger, but bring them up in the discipline and instruction of the Lord.

Colossians 3:21
Fathers, do not provoke your children, lest they become discouraged.

Galatians 5:19-21

Now the works of the flesh are evident: sexual immorality, impurity, sensuality, idolatry, sorcery, enmity, strife, jealousy, fits of anger, rivalries, dissensions, divisions, envy, drunkenness, orgies, and things like these. I warn you, as I warned you before, that those who do such things will not inherit the kingdom of God.

Proverbs 22:10

Drive out a scoffer, and strife will go out, and quarreling and abuse will cease.
Acceptance

Colossians 3:19

Husbands, love your wives, and do not be harsh with them.

Proverbs 22:24-25

Make no friendship with a man given to anger, nor go with a wrathful man, lest you learn his ways and entangle yourself in a snare.

Proverbs 15:1

A soft answer turns away wrath, but a harsh word stirs up anger.

<u>Accepting Christ</u>

Romans 10:9

Because, if you confess with your mouth that Jesus is Lord and believe in your heart that God raised him from the dead, you will be saved.

John 3:16

"For God so loved the world, that he gave his only Son, that whoever believes in him should not perish but have eternal life.

Acts 2:38

And Peter said to them, "Repent and be baptized every one of you in the name of Jesus Christ for the forgiveness of your sins, and you will receive the gift of the Holy Spirit.

Romans 6:23

For the wages of sin is death, but the free gift of God is eternal life in Christ Jesus our Lord.

Romans 3:23

For all have sinned and fall short of the glory of God,

John 1:12

But to all who did receive him, who believed in his name, he gave the right to become children of God,

1 John 1:9

If we confess our sins, he is faithful and just to forgive us our sins and to cleanse us from all unrighteousness.

John 14:6

Jesus said to him, "I am the way, and the truth, and the life. No one comes to the Father except through me.

Acts 4:12

And there is salvation in no one else, for there is no other name under heaven given among men by which we must be saved."

Revelation 3:20

Behold, I stand at the door and knock. If anyone hears my voice and opens the door, I will come in to him and eat with him, and he with me.

Romans 10:13

For "everyone who calls on the name of the Lord will be saved."

Romans 5:8

But God shows his love for us in that while we were still sinners, Christ died for us.

Acts 16:31

And they said, "Believe in the Lord Jesus, and you will be saved, you and your household."

Accepting Others

Romans 14:1-4

As for the one who is weak in faith, welcome him, but not to quarrel over opinions. One person believes he may eat anything, while the weak person eats only vegetables. Let not the one who eats despise the one who abstains, and let not the one who abstains pass judgment on the one who eats, for God has welcomed him. Who are you to pass judgment on the servant of another? It is before his own master that he stands or falls. And he will be upheld, for the Lord is able to make him stand.

Romans 2:11

For God shows no partiality.

Romans 15:5-7

May the God of endurance and encouragement grant you to live in such harmony with one another, in accord with Christ Jesus, that together you may with one voice glorify the God and Father of our Lord Jesus Christ. Therefore welcome one another as Christ has welcomed you, for the glory of God.

Leviticus 5:1

"If anyone sins in that he hears a public adjuration to testify, and though he is a witness, whether he has seen or come to know the matter, yet does not speak, he shall bear his iniquity;

Luke 6:37

"Judge not, and you will not be judged; condemn not, and you will not be condemned; forgive, and you will be forgiven;

John 6:37

All that the Father gives me will come to me, and whoever comes to me I will never cast out.

Accountability

Romans 14:12
So then each of us will give an account of himself to God.

Galatians 6:1-5
Brothers, if anyone is caught in any transgression, you who are spiritual should restore him in a spirit of gentleness. Keep watch on yourself, lest you too be tempted. Bear one another's burdens, and so fulfill the law of Christ. For if anyone thinks he is something, when he is nothing, he deceives himself. But let each one test his own work, and then his reason to boast will be in himself alone and not in his neighbor. For each will have to bear his own load.

James 5:16
Therefore, confess your sins to one another and pray for one another, that you may be healed. The prayer of a righteous person has great power as it is working.

1 Thessalonians 5:11
Therefore encourage one another and build one another up, just as you are doing.

Proverbs 27:17
Iron sharpens iron, and one man sharpens another.

Luke 17:3
Pay attention to yourselves! If your brother sins, rebuke him, and if he repents, forgive him,

Matthew 12:36-37
I tell you, on the day of judgment people will give account for every careless word they speak, for by your words you will be justified, and by your words you will be condemned."

Hebrews 4:13
And no creature is hidden from his sight, but all are naked and exposed to the eyes of him to whom we must give account.

Ecclesiastes 4:9-12
Two are better than one, because they have a good reward for their toil. For if they fall, one will lift up his fellow. But woe to him who is alone when he falls and has not another to lift him up! Again, if two lie together, they keep warm, but how can one keep warm alone? And though a man might prevail against one who is alone, two will withstand him—a threefold cord is not quickly broken.

Jeremiah 17:10
"I the Lord search the heart and test the mind, to give every man according to his ways, according to the fruit of his deeds."

Luke 12:47-48
And that servant who knew his master's will but did not get ready or act according to his will, will receive a severe beating. But the one who did not know, and did what deserved a beating, will receive a light

beating. Everyone to whom much was given, of him much will be required, and from him to whom they entrusted much, they will demand the more.

Matthew 7:3-5

Why do you see the speck that is in your brother's eye, but do not notice the log that is in your own eye? Or how can you say to your brother, 'Let me take the speck out of your eye,' when there is the log in your own eye? You hypocrite, first take the log out of your own eye, and then you will see clearly to take the speck out of your brother's eye.

Acknowledging God

Proverbs 3:5-6

Trust in the Lord with all your heart, and do not lean on your own understanding. In all your ways acknowledge him, and he will make straight your paths.

Revelation 4:11

"Worthy are you, our Lord and God, to receive glory and honor and power, for you created all things, and by your will they existed and were created."

Romans 1:28-31

And since they did not see fit to acknowledge God, God gave them up to a debased mind to do what ought not to be done. They were filled with all manner of unrighteousness, evil, covetousness, malice. They are full of envy, murder, strife, deceit, maliciousness. They are gossips, slanderers, haters of God, insolent, haughty, boastful, inventors of evil, disobedient to parents, foolish, faithless, heartless, ruthless.
Acts of Kindness

Addiction

1 Corinthians 10:13

No temptation has overtaken you that is not common to man. God is faithful, and he will not let you be tempted beyond your ability, but with the temptation he will also provide the way of escape, that you may be able to endure it.

1 Peter 5:8

Be sober-minded; be watchful. Your adversary the devil prowls around like a roaring lion, seeking someone to devour.

James 1:12-15

Blessed is the man who remains steadfast under trial, for when he has stood the test he will receive the crown of life, which God has promised to those who love him. Let no one say when he is tempted, "I am being tempted by God," for God cannot be tempted with evil, and he himself tempts no one. But each person is tempted when he is lured and enticed by his own desire. Then desire when it has conceived gives birth to sin, and sin when it is fully grown brings forth death.

1 Corinthians 15:33

Do not be deceived: "Bad company ruins good morals."

1 John 2:16
For all that is in the world—the desires of the flesh and the desires of the eyes and pride in possessions—is not from the Father but is from the world.

1 Peter 5:10
And after you have suffered a little while, the God of all grace, who has called you to his eternal glory in Christ, will himself restore, confirm, strengthen, and establish you.

James 4:7
Submit yourselves therefore to God. Resist the devil, and he will flee from you.

1 Corinthians 6:12
"All things are lawful for me," but not all things are helpful. "All things are lawful for me," but I will not be enslaved by anything.

Galatians 5:19-21
Now the works of the flesh are evident: sexual immorality, impurity, sensuality, idolatry, sorcery, enmity, strife, jealousy, fits of anger, rivalries, dissensions, divisions, envy, drunkenness, orgies, and things like these. I warn you, as I warned you before, that those who do such things will not inherit the kingdom of God.

1 Peter 2:11
Beloved, I urge you as sojourners and exiles to abstain from the passions of the flesh, which wage war against your soul.

Proverbs 20:1
Wine is a mocker, strong drink a brawler, and whoever is led astray by it is not wise.
Admonition

Adultery

Exodus 20:14
"You shall not commit adultery.

Hebrews 13:4
Let marriage be held in honor among all, and let the marriage bed be undefiled, for God will judge the sexually immoral and adulterous.

Proverbs 6:32
He who commits adultery lacks sense; he who does it destroys himself.

Matthew 19:9
And I say to you: whoever divorces his wife, except for sexual immorality, and marries another, commits adultery."

Matthew 5:27-28

"You have heard that it was said, 'You shall not commit adultery.' But I say to you that everyone who looks at a woman with lustful intent has already committed adultery with her in his heart.

1 Corinthians 6:18

Flee from sexual immorality. Every other sin a person commits is outside the body, but the sexually immoral person sins against his own body.

Leviticus 20:10

"If a man commits adultery with the wife of his neighbor, both the adulterer and the adulteress shall surely be put to death.

Luke 16:18

"Everyone who divorces his wife and marries another commits adultery, and he who marries a woman divorced from her husband commits adultery.

Deuteronomy 22:22

"If a man is found lying with the wife of another man, both of them shall die, the man who lay with the woman, and the woman. So you shall purge the evil from Israel.

Matthew 5:32

But I say to you that everyone who divorces his wife, except on the ground of sexual immorality, makes her commit adultery, and whoever marries a divorced woman commits adultery.

1 Corinthians 6:9-10

Or do you not know that the unrighteous will not inherit the kingdom of God? Do not be deceived: neither the sexually immoral, nor idolaters, nor adulterers, nor men who practice homosexuality, nor thieves, nor the greedy, nor drunkards, nor revilers, nor swindlers will inherit the kingdom of God.

Adversity

2 Corinthians 4:8-9

We are afflicted in every way, but not crushed; perplexed, but not driven to despair; persecuted, but not forsaken; struck down, but not destroyed;

1 Peter 5:10

And after you have suffered a little while, the God of all grace, who has called you to his eternal glory in Christ, will himself restore, confirm, strengthen, and establish you.

Proverbs 24:10

If you faint in the day of adversity, your strength is small.

Philippians 4:12-13

I know how to be brought low, and I know how to abound. In any and every circumstance, I have learned the secret of facing plenty and hunger, abundance and need. I can do all things through him who strengthens me.

2 Corinthians 12:9

But he said to me, "My grace is sufficient for you, for my power is made perfect in weakness." Therefore, I will boast all the more gladly of my weaknesses, so that the power of Christ may rest upon me.

Joshua 1:9

Have I not commanded you? Be strong and courageous. Do not be frightened, and do not be dismayed, for the Lord your God is with you wherever you go."

James 1:2-4

Count it all joy, my brothers, when you meet trials of various kinds, for you know that the testing of your faith produces steadfastness. And let steadfastness have its full effect, that you may be perfect and complete, lacking in nothing.

Proverbs 3:4-6

So you will find favor and good success in the sight of God and man. Trust in the Lord with all your heart, and do not lean on your own understanding. In all your ways acknowledge him, and he will make straight your paths.

Romans 8:28

And we know that for those who love God all things work together for good, for those who are called according to his purpose.

1 Peter 5:8

Be sober-minded; be watchful. Your adversary the devil prowls around like a roaring lion, seeking someone to devour.

2 Chronicles 15:7

But you, take courage! Do not let your hands be weak, for your work shall be rewarded."

Revelation 21:4

He will wipe away every tear from their eyes, and death shall be no more, neither shall there be mourning, nor crying, nor pain anymore, for the former things have passed away."

Advice

Proverbs 11:14

Where there is no guidance, a people falls, but in an abundance of counselors there is safety.

Proverbs 19:20

Listen to advice and accept instruction, that you may gain wisdom in the future.

Proverbs 24:6

For by wise guidance you can wage your war, and in abundance of counselors there is victory.

Proverbs 12:15

The way of a fool is right in his own eyes, but a wise man listens to advice.

Affliction

Psalm 34:17-20

When the righteous cry for help, the Lord hears and delivers them out of all their troubles. The Lord is near to the brokenhearted and saves the crushed in spirit. Many are the afflictions of the righteous, but the Lord delivers him out of them all. He keeps all his bones; not one of them is broken.

2 Corinthians 12:9

But he said to me, "My grace is sufficient for you, for my power is made perfect in weakness." Therefore I will boast all the more gladly of my weaknesses, so that the power of Christ may rest upon me.

1 Corinthians 10:13

No temptation has overtaken you that is not common to man. God is faithful, and he will not let you be tempted beyond your ability, but with the temptation he will also provide the way of escape, that you may be able to endure it.

Romans 8:18

For I consider that the sufferings of this present time are not worth comparing with the glory that is to be revealed to us.

Romans 5:3-4

More than that, we rejoice in our sufferings, knowing that suffering produces endurance, and endurance produces character, and character produces hope,

2 Corinthians 4:16

So we do not lose heart. Though our outer self is wasting away, our inner self is being renewed day by day.

Philippians 4:13

I can do all things through him who strengthens me.

Psalm 119:71

It is good for me that I was afflicted, that I might learn your statutes.

Afraid

John 14:27

Peace I leave with you; my peace I give to you. Not as the world gives do I give to you. Let not your hearts be troubled, neither let them be afraid.

Joshua 1:9

Have I not commanded you? Be strong and courageous. Do not be frightened, and do not be dismayed, for the Lord your God is with you wherever you go."

Psalm 34:4

I sought the Lord, and he answered me and delivered me from all my fears.

Deuteronomy 31:6
Be strong and courageous. Do not fear or be in dread of them, for it is the Lord your God who goes with you. He will not leave you or forsake you."

After Life

John 3:16
"For God so loved the world, that he gave his only Son, that whoever believes in him should not perish but have eternal life.

Matthew 25:46
And these will go away into eternal punishment, but the righteous into eternal life."

Revelation 21:8
But as for the cowardly, the faithless, the detestable, as for murderers, the sexually immoral, sorcerers, idolaters, and all liars, their portion will be in the lake that burns with fire and sulfur, which is the second death."

Luke 23:43
And he said to him, "Truly, I say to you, today you will be with me in Paradise."

John 14:2
In my Father's house are many rooms. If it were not so, would I have told you that I go to prepare a place for you?

Aggressive

James 1:19
Know this, my beloved brothers: let every person be quick to hear, slow to speak, slow to anger;

Matthew 5:9
"Blessed are the peacemakers, for they shall be called sons of God.

Matthew 26:52
Then Jesus said to him, "Put your sword back into its place. For all who take the sword will perish by the sword.

Aging

1 Timothy 4:12
Let no one despise you for your youth, but set the believers an example in speech, in conduct, in love, in faith, in purity.

2 Corinthians 4:16
So we do not lose heart. Though our outer self is wasting away, our inner self is being renewed day by day.

Psalm 71:18

So even to old age and gray hairs, O God, do not forsake me, until I proclaim your might to another generation, your power to all those to come.

Proverbs 20:29

The glory of young men is their strength, but the splendor of old men is their gray hair.

Psalm 71:9

Do not cast me off in the time of old age; forsake me not when my strength is spent.

Proverbs 16:31

Gray hair is a crown of glory; it is gained in a righteous life.

Job 12:12

Wisdom is with the aged, and understanding in length of days.

Agnosticism

Jude 1:22

And have mercy on those who doubt;

James 2:24

You see that a person is justified by works and not by faith alone.

Romans 12:2

Do not be conformed to this world, but be transformed by the renewal of your mind, that by testing you may discern what is the will of God, what is good and acceptable and perfect.

Agreement

Matthew 18:19

Again I say to you, if two of you agree on earth about anything they ask, it will be done for them by my Father in heaven.

Amos 3:3

"Do two walk together, unless they have agreed to meet?

Alcohol Abuse

Ephesians 5:18

And do not get drunk with wine, for that is debauchery, but be filled with the Spirit,

Proverbs 23:29-33

Who has woe? Who has sorrow? Who has strife? Who has complaining? Who has wounds without cause? Who has redness of eyes? Those who tarry long over wine; those who go to try mixed wine. Do not look at wine when it is red, when it sparkles in the cup and goes down smoothly. In the end it bites like a serpent and stings like an adder. Your eyes will see strange things, and your heart utter perverse things.

1 Peter 5:8

Be sober-minded; be watchful. Your adversary the devil prowls around like a roaring lion, seeking someone to devour.

1 Corinthians 6:10

Nor thieves, nor the greedy, nor drunkards, nor revilers, nor swindlers will inherit the kingdom of God.

Proverbs 20:1

Wine is a mocker, strong drink a brawler, and whoever is led astray by it is not wise.

Isaiah 5:22

Woe to those who are heroes at drinking wine, and valiant men in mixing strong drink,

Isaiah 5:11

Woe to those who rise early in the morning, that they may run after strong drink, who tarry late into the evening as wine inflames them!

Galatians 5:21

Envy, drunkenness, orgies, and things like these. I warn you, as I warned you before, that those who do such things will not inherit the kingdom of God.

Ambassadors

2 Corinthians 5:20

Therefore, we are ambassadors for Christ, God making his appeal through us. We implore you on behalf of Christ, be reconciled to God.

Ambition

Luke 9:25

For what does it profit a man if he gains the whole world and loses or forfeits himself?

Matthew 6:33

But seek first the kingdom of God and his righteousness, and all these things will be added to you.

Matthew 23:12

Whoever exalts himself will be humbled, and whoever humbles himself will be exalted.

1 Timothy 6:9

But those who desire to be rich fall into temptation, into a snare, into many senseless and harmful desires that plunge people into ruin and destruction.

1 John 2:16

For all that is in the world—the desires of the flesh and the desires of the eyes and pride in possessions—is not from the Father but is from the world.
Ancestral Worship

Angels

Psalm 91:11

For he will command his angels concerning you to guard you in all your ways.

Hebrews 13:2

Do not neglect to show hospitality to strangers, for thereby some have entertained angels unawares.

Hebrews 1:14

Are they not all ministering spirits sent out to serve for the sake of those who are to inherit salvation?

Psalm 103:20

Bless the Lord, O you his angels, you mighty ones who do his word, obeying the voice of his word!

Psalm 34:7

The angel of the Lord encamps around those who fear him, and delivers them.

Jude 1:6

And the angels who did not stay within their own position of authority, but left their proper dwelling, he has kept in eternal chains under gloomy darkness until the judgment of the great day—

Isaiah 6:2

Above him stood the seraphim. Each had six wings: with two he covered his face, and with two he covered his feet, and with two he flew.

Revelation 19:10

Then I fell down at his feet to worship him, but he said to me, "You must not do that! I am a fellow servant with you and your brothers who hold to the testimony of Jesus. Worship God." For the testimony of Jesus is the spirit of prophecy.

Matthew 24:31

And he will send out his angels with a loud trumpet call, and they will gather his elect from the four winds, from one end of heaven to the other.

Jude 1:9

But when the archangel Michael, contending with the devil, was disputing about the body of Moses, he did not presume to pronounce a blasphemous judgment, but said, "The Lord rebuke you."

Anger Management

Psalm 37:8
Refrain from anger, and forsake wrath! Fret not yourself; it tends only to evil.

Proverbs 14:29
Whoever is slow to anger has great understanding, but he who has a hasty temper exalts folly.

James 1:20
For the anger of man does not produce the righteousness of God.

Proverbs 15:1
A soft answer turns away wrath, but a harsh word stirs up anger.

Proverbs 19:11
Good sense makes one slow to anger, and it is his glory to overlook an offense.

Ecclesiastes 7:9
Be not quick in your spirit to become angry, for anger lodges in the bosom of fools.

Ephesians 4:31
Let all bitterness and wrath and anger and clamor and slander be put away from you, along with all malice.

James 1:19-20
Know this, my beloved brothers: let every person be quick to hear, slow to speak, slow to anger; for the anger of man does not produce the righteousness of God.

Proverbs 29:11
A fool gives full vent to his spirit, but a wise man quietly holds it back.

Ephesians 4:26-27
Be angry and do not sin; do not let the sun go down on your anger, and give no opportunity to the devil.

Proverbs 16:32
Whoever is slow to anger is better than the mighty, and he who rules his spirit than he who takes a city.

Proverbs 15:18
A hot-tempered man stirs up strife, but he who is slow to anger quiets contention.

Colossians 3:8
But now you must put them all away: anger, wrath, malice, slander, and obscene talk from your mouth.

Animal Cruelty

Proverbs 12:10
Whoever is righteous has regard for the life of his beast, but the mercy of the wicked is cruel.

Ecclesiastes 3:19

For what happens to the children of man and what happens to the beasts is the same; as one dies, so dies the other. They all have the same breath, and man has no advantage over the beasts, for all is vanity.

Proverbs 27:23

Know well the condition of your flocks, and give attention to your herds,

Exodus 23:5

If you see the donkey of one who hates you lying down under its burden, you shall refrain from leaving him with it; you shall rescue it with him.

Deuteronomy 25:4

"You shall not muzzle an ox when it is treading out the grain.

Psalm 145:9

The Lord is good to all, and his mercy is over all that he has made.

Anorexia

1 Corinthians 6:19-20

Or do you not know that your body is a temple of the Holy Spirit within you, whom you have from God? You are not your own, for you were bought with a price. So glorify God in your body.

1 Samuel 16:7

But the Lord said to Samuel, "Do not look on his appearance or on the height of his stature, because I have rejected him. For the Lord sees not as man sees: man looks on the outward appearance, but the Lord looks on the heart."

Song of Solomon 4:7

You are altogether beautiful, my love; there is no flaw in you.

Matthew 6:25

"Therefore, I tell you, do not be anxious about your life, what you will eat or what you will drink, nor about your body, what you will put on. Is not life more than food, and the body more than clothing?

1 Corinthians 3:16

Do you not know that you are God's temple and that God's Spirit dwells in you?

Antichrist

2 John 1:7

For many deceivers have gone out into the world, those who do not confess the coming of Jesus Christ in the flesh. Such a one is the deceiver and the antichrist.

1 John 2:22

Who is the liar but he who denies that Jesus is the Christ? This is the antichrist, he who denies the Father and the Son.

2 Thessalonians 2:3-12

Let no one deceive you in any way. For that day will not come, unless the rebellion comes first, and the man of lawlessness is revealed, the son of destruction, who opposes and exalts himself against every so-called god or object of worship, so that he takes his seat in the temple of God, proclaiming himself to be God. Do you not remember that when I was still with you I told you these things? And you know what is restraining him now so that he may be revealed in his time. For the mystery of lawlessness is already at work. Only he who now restrains it will do so until he is out of the way. And then the lawless one will be revealed, whom the Lord Jesus will kill with the breath of his mouth and bring to nothing by the appearance of his coming. The coming of the lawless one is by the activity of Satan with all power and false signs and wonders, and with all wicked deception for those who are perishing, because they refused to love the truth and so be saved. Therefore, God sends them a strong delusion, so that they may believe what is false, in order that all may be condemned who did not believe the truth but had pleasure in unrighteousness.

1 John 4:3

And every spirit that does not confess Jesus is not from God. This is the spirit of the antichrist, which you heard was coming and now is in the world already.

1 John 2:18

Children, it is the last hour, and as you have heard that antichrist is coming, so now many antichrists have come. Therefore, we know that it is the last hour.

Mark 13:22

For false christs and false prophets will arise and perform signs and wonders, to lead astray, if possible, the elect.

Anxiety

Philippians 4:6-7

Do not be anxious about anything, but in everything by prayer and supplication with thanksgiving let your requests be made known to God. And the peace of God, which surpasses all understanding, will guard your hearts and your minds in Christ Jesus.

1 Peter 5:7

Casting all your anxieties on him, because he cares for you.

Matthew 6:25-34

"Therefore I tell you, do not be anxious about your life, what you will eat or what you will drink, nor about your body, what you will put on. Is not life more than food, and the body more than clothing? Look at the birds of the air: they neither sow nor reap nor gather into barns, and yet your heavenly Father feeds them. Are you not of more value than they? And which of you by being anxious can add a single hour to his span of life? And why are you anxious about clothing? Consider the lilies of the field, how they grow: they neither toil nor spin, yet I tell you, even Solomon in all his glory was not arrayed like one of these. But if God so clothes the grass of the field, which today is alive and tomorrow is thrown into the oven, will he not much more clothe you, O you of little faith? Therefore do not be anxious, saying, 'What shall we eat?' or 'What shall we drink?' or 'What shall we wear?' For the Gentiles seek after all these things, and your heavenly Father knows that you need them all. But seek first the kingdom of God and his righteousness, and all these things will be added to you.

"Therefore do not be anxious about tomorrow, for tomorrow will be anxious for itself. Sufficient for the day is its own trouble.

Philippians 4:13
I can do all things through him who strengthens me.

1 Peter 5:6-7
Humble yourselves, therefore, under the mighty hand of God so that at the proper time he may exalt you, casting all your anxieties on him, because he cares for you.

John 14:27
Peace I leave with you; my peace I give to you. Not as the world gives do I give to you. Let not your hearts be troubled, neither let them be afraid.

Hebrews 13:6
So we can confidently say, "The Lord is my helper; I will not fear; what can man do to me?"

Apathy

Revelation 3:16
So, because you are lukewarm, and neither hot nor cold, I will spit you out of my mouth.

Romans 12:11
Do not be slothful in zeal, be fervent in spirit, serve the Lord.

Zephaniah 1:12-13
At that time, I will search Jerusalem with lamps, and I will punish the men who are complacent, those who say in their hearts, 'The Lord will not do good, nor will he do ill.' Their goods shall be plundered, and their houses laid waste. Though they build houses, they shall not inhabit them; though they plant vineyards, they shall not drink wine from them."

Apologizing

Ephesians 4:32
Be kind to one another, tenderhearted, forgiving one another, as God in Christ forgave you.

Luke 11:4
And forgive us our sins, for we ourselves forgive everyone who is indebted to us. And lead us not into temptation."

Colossians 3:13
Bearing with one another and, if one has a complaint against another, forgiving each other; as the Lord has forgiven you, so you also must forgive.

1 Peter 5:5

Likewise, you who are younger, be subject to the elders. Clothe yourselves, all of you, with humility toward one another, for "God opposes the proud but gives grace to the humble."

Apostasy

1 Timothy 4:1

Now the Spirit expressly says that in later times some will depart from the faith by devoting themselves to deceitful spirits and teachings of demons,

2 Thessalonians 2:3

Let no one deceive you in any way. For that day will not come, unless the rebellion comes first, and the man of lawlessness is revealed, the son of destruction,

2 Peter 2:20-22

For if, after they have escaped the defilements of the world through the knowledge of our Lord and Savior Jesus Christ, they are again entangled in them and overcome, the last state has become worse for them than the first. For it would have been better for them never to have known the way of righteousness than after knowing it to turn back from the holy commandment delivered to them. What the true proverb says has happened to them: "The dog returns to its own vomit, and the sow, after washing herself, returns to wallow in the mire."

Appreciation

Ruth 2:12

The Lord repay you for what you have done, and a full reward be given you by the Lord, the God of Israel, under whose wings you have come to take refuge!"

Colossians 3:16

Let the word of Christ dwell in you richly, teaching and admonishing one another in all wisdom, singing psalms and hymns and spiritual songs, with thankfulness in your hearts to God.

Hebrews 13:5

Keep your life free from love of money, and be content with what you have, for he has said, "I will never leave you nor forsake you."

1 Thessalonians 1:2

We give thanks to God always for all of you, constantly mentioning you in our prayers,

1 Timothy 5:17

Let the elders who rule well be considered worthy of double honor, especially those who labor in preaching and teaching.

Approval

Galatians 1:10
For am I now seeking the approval of man, or of God? Or am I trying to please man? If I were still trying to please man, I would not be a servant of Christ.

John 12:43
For they loved the glory that comes from man more than the glory that comes from God.

2 Timothy 2:15
Do your best to present yourself to God as one approved, a worker who has no need to be ashamed, rightly handling the word of truth.

Psalm 118:6-9
The Lord is on my side; I will not fear. What can man do to me? The Lord is on my side as my helper; I shall look in triumph on those who hate me. It is better to take refuge in the Lord than to trust in man. It is better to take refuge in the Lord than to trust in princes.

1 Thessalonians 2:4
But just as we have been approved by God to be entrusted with the gospel, so we speak, not to please man, but to please God who tests our hearts.

Arguing

2 Timothy 2:23-24
Have nothing to do with foolish, ignorant controversies; you know that they breed quarrels. And the Lord's servant must not be quarrelsome but kind to everyone, able to teach, patiently enduring evil,

Proverbs 15:1
A soft answer turns away wrath, but a harsh word stirs up anger.

Philippians 2:14
Do all things without grumbling or questioning,

Romans 12:19
Beloved, never avenge yourselves, but leave it to the wrath of God, for it is written, "Vengeance is mine, I will repay, says the Lord."

Titus 3:1-2
Remind them to be submissive to rulers and authorities, to be obedient, to be ready for every good work, to speak evil of no one, to avoid quarreling, to be gentle, and to show perfect courtesy toward all people.

Romans 14:19
So then let us pursue what makes for peace and for mutual upbuilding.

Proverbs 26:4
Answer not a fool according to his folly, lest you be like him yourself.

Proverbs 3:30
Do not contend with a man for no reason, when he has done you no harm.

Armor of God

Ephesians 6:10-18
Finally, be strong in the Lord and in the strength of his might. Put on the whole armor of God, that you may be able to stand against the schemes of the devil. For we do not wrestle against flesh and blood, but against the rulers, against the authorities, against the cosmic powers over this present darkness, against the spiritual forces of evil in the heavenly places. Therefore, take up the whole armor of God, that you may be able to withstand in the evil day, and having done all, to stand firm. Stand therefore, having fastened on the belt of truth, and having put on the breastplate of righteousness, and, as shoes for your feet, having put on the readiness given by the gospel of peace. In all circumstances take up the shield of faith, with which you can extinguish all the flaming darts of the evil one; and take the helmet of salvation, and the sword of the Spirit, which is the word of God, praying at all times in the Spirit, with all prayer and supplication. To that end, keep alert with all perseverance, making supplication for all the saints,

1 Thessalonians 5:8
But since we belong to the day, let us be sober, having put on the breastplate of faith and love, and for a helmet the hope of salvation.

Arrogance

1 Samuel 2:3
Talk no more so very proudly, let not arrogance come from your mouth; for the Lord is a God of knowledge, and by him actions are weighed.

Romans 12:3
For by the grace given to me I say to everyone among you not to think of himself more highly than he ought to think, but to think with sober judgment, each according to the measure of faith that God has assigned.

Proverbs 8:13
The fear of the Lord is hatred of evil. Pride and arrogance and the way of evil and perverted speech I hate.

Isaiah 13:11
I will punish the world for its evil, and the wicked for their iniquity; I will put an end to the pomp of the arrogant, and lay low the pompous pride of the ruthless.

Proverbs 27:2
Let another praise you, and not your own mouth; a stranger, and not your own lips.

1 Timothy 5:8

But if anyone does not provide for his relatives, and especially for members of his household, he has denied the faith and is worse than an unbeliever.

Proverbs 16:18

Pride goes before destruction, and a haughty spirit before a fall.

Ashamed

2 Timothy 2:15

Do your best to present yourself to God as one approved, a worker who has no need to be ashamed, rightly handling the word of truth.

Romans 1:16

For I am not ashamed of the gospel, for it is the power of God for salvation to everyone who believes, to the Jew first and also to the Greek.

Mark 8:38

For whoever is ashamed of me and of my words in this adulterous and sinful generation, of him will the Son of Man also be ashamed when he comes in the glory of his Father with the holy angels."

Assurance of Salvation

John 5:24

Truly, truly, I say to you, whoever hears my word and believes him who sent me has eternal life. He does not come into judgment, but has passed from death to life.

John 3:36

Whoever believes in the Son has eternal life; whoever does not obey the Son shall not see life, but the wrath of God remains on him.

Matthew 24:11-13

And many false prophets will arise and lead many astray. And because lawlessness will be increased, the love of many will grow cold. But the one who endures to the end will be saved.

Ephesians 2:8-9

For by grace you have been saved through faith. And this is not your own doing; it is the gift of God, not a result of works, so that no one may boast.

Hebrews 10:26-27

For if we go on sinning deliberately after receiving the knowledge of the truth, there no longer remains a sacrifice for sins, but a fearful expectation of judgment, and a fury of fire that will consume the adversaries.

Matthew 7:21

"Not everyone who says to me, 'Lord, Lord,' will enter the kingdom of heaven, but the one who does the will of my Father who is in heaven.

John 10:28

I give them eternal life, and they will never perish, and no one will snatch them out of my hand.

John 8:31-32

So Jesus said to the Jews who had believed in him, "If you abide in my word, you are truly my disciples, and you will know the truth, and the truth will set you free."

1 John 5:11-13

And this is the testimony, that God gave us eternal life, and this life is in his Son. Whoever has the Son has life; whoever does not have the Son of God does not have life. I write these things to you who believe in the name of the Son of God that you may know that you have eternal life.

Romans 10:9

Because, if you confess with your mouth that Jesus is Lord and believe in your heart that God raised him from the dead, you will be saved.

1 John 5:13

I write these things to you who believe in the name of the Son of God that you may know that you have eternal life.

Atheism

Jude 1:22

And have mercy on those who doubt;

Psalm 14:1

To the choirmaster. Of David. The fool says in his heart, "There is no God." They are corrupt, they do abominable deeds, there is none who does good.

Ephesians 4:18

They are darkened in their understanding, alienated from the life of God because of the ignorance that is in them, due to their hardness of heart.

Atonement

1 Peter 2:24

He himself bore our sins in his body on the tree, that we might die to sin and live to righteousness. By his wounds you have been healed.

Leviticus 17:11

For the life of the flesh is in the blood, and I have given it for you on the altar to make atonement for your souls, for it is the blood that makes atonement by the life.

1 John 2:2

He is the propitiation for our sins, and not for ours only but also for the sins of the whole world.

Hebrews 9:12

He entered once for all into the holy places, not by means of the blood of goats and calves but by means of his own blood, thus securing an eternal redemption.

Revelation 5:9

And they sang a new song, saying, "Worthy are you to take the scroll and to open its seals, for you were slain, and by your blood you ransomed people for God from every tribe and language and people and nation,

Attention Seekers

Matthew 6:1

"Beware of practicing your righteousness before other people in order to be seen by them, for then you will have no reward from your Father who is in heaven.

Romans 2:8

But for those who are self-seeking and do not obey the truth, but obey unrighteousness, there will be wrath and fury.

James 4:6

But he gives more grace. Therefore it says, "God opposes the proud, but gives grace to the humble."

Philippians 2:3-5

Do nothing from rivalry or conceit, but in humility count others more significant than yourselves. Let each of you look not only to his own interests, but also to the interests of others. Have this mind among yourselves, which is yours in Christ Jesus,

Romans 12:3

For by the grace given to me I say to everyone among you not to think of himself more highly than he ought to think, but to think with sober judgment, each according to the measure of faith that God has assigned.

Attitude

Philippians 2:14-15

Do all things without grumbling or questioning, that you may be blameless and innocent, children of God without blemish in the midst of a crooked and twisted generation, among whom you shine as lights in the world,

Proverbs 17:22

A joyful heart is good medicine, but a crushed spirit dries up the bones.

Philippians 4:8-9

Finally, brothers, whatever is true, whatever is honorable, whatever is just, whatever is pure, whatever is lovely, whatever is commendable, if there is any excellence, if there is anything worthy of praise, think about these things. What you have learned and received and heard and seen in me—practice these things, and the God of peace will be with you.

Philippians 2:5

Have this mind among yourselves, which is yours in Christ Jesus,

Romans 12:2

Do not be conformed to this world, but be transformed by the renewal of your mind, that by testing you may discern what is the will of God, what is good and acceptable and perfect.

Colossians 3:23

Whatever you do, work heartily, as for the Lord and not for men,

Philippians 2:14

Do all things without grumbling or questioning,

Authority

Romans 13:1

Let every person be subject to the governing authorities. For there is no authority except from God, and those that exist have been instituted by God.

Matthew 28:18

And Jesus came and said to them, "All authority in heaven and on earth has been given to me.

Acts 5:29

But Peter and the apostles answered, "We must obey God rather than men.

Hebrews 13:17

Obey your leaders and submit to them, for they are keeping watch over your souls, as those who will have to give an account. Let them do this with joy and not with groaning, for that would be of no advantage to you.

Luke 10:19

Behold, I have given you authority to tread on serpents and scorpions, and over all the power of the enemy, and nothing shall hurt you.

2 John 1:9

Everyone who goes on ahead and does not abide in the teaching of Christ, does not have God. Whoever abides in the teaching has both the Father and the Son.

Autism

John 9:1-3

As he passed by, he saw a man blind from birth. And his disciples asked him, "Rabbi, who sinned, this man or his parents, that he was born blind?" Jesus answered, "It was not that this man sinned, or his parents, but that the works of God might be displayed in him.

Exodus 4:11

Then the Lord said to him, "Who has made man's mouth? Who makes him mute, or deaf, or seeing, or blind? Is it not I, the Lord?

Isaiah 54:13

All your children shall be taught by the Lord, and great shall be the peace of your children.

1 Corinthians 12:18

But as it is, God arranged the members in the body, each one of them, as he chose.

Awakening

Ephesians 5:14

For anything that becomes visible is light. Therefore, it says, "Awake, O sleeper, and arise from the dead, and Christ will shine on you."

Romans 13:11

Besides this you know the time, that the hour has come for you to wake from sleep. For salvation is nearer to us now than when we first believed.

John 11:11-14

After saying these things, he said to them, "Our friend Lazarus has fallen asleep, but I go to awaken him." The disciples said to him, "Lord, if he has fallen asleep, he will recover." Now Jesus had spoken of his death, but they thought that he meant taking rest in sleep. Then Jesus told them plainly, "Lazarus has died,

Isaiah 52:1

Awake, awake, put on your strength, O Zion; put on your beautiful garments, O Jerusalem, the holy city; for there shall no more come into you the uncircumcised and the unclean.

Backbiting

Proverbs 16:28
A dishonest man spreads strife, and a whisperer separates close friends.

Romans 16:17-18
I appeal to you, brothers, to watch out for those who cause divisions and create obstacles contrary to the doctrine that you have been taught; avoid them. For such persons do not serve our Lord Christ, but their own appetites, and by smooth talk and flattery they deceive the hearts of the naive.

Proverbs 25:23
The north wind brings forth rain, and a backbiting tongue, angry looks.

Psalm 15:1-3
A Psalm of David. O Lord, who shall sojourn in your tent? Who shall dwell on your holy hill? He who walks blamelessly and does what is right and speaks truth in his heart; who does not slander with his tongue and does no evil to his neighbor, nor takes up a reproach against his friend;

James 4:11-12
Do not speak evil against one another, brothers. The one who speaks against a brother or judges his brother, speaks evil against the law and judges the law. But if you judge the law, you are not a doer of the law but a judge. There is only one lawgiver and judge, he who is able to save and to destroy. But who are you to judge your neighbor?

2 Corinthians 12:20
For I fear that perhaps when I come I may find you not as I wish, and that you may find me not as you wish—that perhaps there may be quarreling, jealousy, anger, hostility, slander, gossip, conceit, and disorder.

Proverbs 17:9
Whoever covers an offense seeks love, but he who repeats a matter separates close friends.

Proverbs 26:20
For lack of wood the fire goes out, and where there is no whisperer, quarreling ceases.

Leviticus 19:16
You shall not go around as a slanderer among your people, and you shall not stand up against the life of your neighbor: I am the Lord.

Backsliding

1 John 1:9
If we confess our sins, he is faithful and just to forgive us our sins and to cleanse us from all unrighteousness.

Hebrews 6:4-6

For it is impossible, in the case of those who have once been enlightened, who have tasted the heavenly gift, and have shared in the Holy Spirit, and have tasted the goodness of the word of God and the powers of the age to come, and then have fallen away, to restore them again to repentance, since they are crucifying once again the Son of God to their own harm and holding him up to contempt.

Jeremiah 3:12

Go, and proclaim these words toward the north, and say, "'Return, faithless Israel, declares the Lord. I will not look on you in anger, for I am merciful, declares the Lord; I will not be angry forever.

Jeremiah 3:22

"Return, O faithless sons; I will heal your faithlessness." "Behold, we come to you, for you are the Lord our God.

Proverbs 14:14

The backslider in heart will be filled with the fruit of his ways, and a good man will be filled with the fruit of his ways.

2 Corinthians 13:5

Examine yourselves, to see whether you are in the faith. Test yourselves. Or do you not realize this about yourselves, that Jesus Christ is in you? — unless indeed you fail to meet the test!

Jeremiah 8:5

Why then has this people turned away in perpetual backsliding? They hold fast to deceit; they refuse to return.

Proverbs 24:16

For the righteous falls seven times and rises again, but the wicked stumble in times of calamity.

Jeremiah 14:7

"Though our iniquities testify against us, act, O Lord, for your name's sake; for our backslidings are many; we have sinned against you.

Backstabbing

Proverbs 16:28

A dishonest man spreads strife, and a whisperer separates close friends.

2 Corinthians 12:20

For I fear that perhaps when I come I may find you not as I wish, and that you may find me not as you wish—that perhaps there may be quarreling, jealousy, anger, hostility, slander, gossip, conceit, and disorder.

Proverbs 20:19

Whoever goes about slandering reveals secrets; therefore, do not associate with a simple babbler.

John 8:7

And as they continued to ask him, he stood up and said to them, "Let him who is without sin among you be the first to throw a stone at her."

Proverbs 20:20

If one curses his father or his mother, his lamp will be put out in utter darkness.

Romans 1:18

For the wrath of God is revealed from heaven against all ungodliness and unrighteousness of men, who by their unrighteousness suppress the truth.

Romans 1:30

Slanderers, haters of God, insolent, haughty, boastful, inventors of evil, disobedient to parents,

Ephesians 4:26

Be angry and do not sin; do not let the sun go down on your anger,

Balance in Life

Ecclesiastes 3:1-8

For everything there is a season, and a time for every matter under heaven: a time to be born, and a time to die; a time to plant, and a time to pluck up what is planted; a time to kill, and a time to heal; a time to break down, and a time to build up; a time to weep, and a time to laugh; a time to mourn, and a time to dance; a time to cast away stones, and a time to gather stones together; a time to embrace, and a time to refrain from embracing; a time to seek, and a time to lose; a time to keep, and a time to cast away; a time to tear, and a time to sew; a time to keep silence, and a time to speak; a time to love, and a time to hate; a time for war, and a time for peace.

Matthew 6:33-34

But seek first the kingdom of God and his righteousness, and all these things will be added to you. "Therefore do not be anxious about tomorrow, for tomorrow will be anxious for itself. Sufficient for the day is its own trouble.

Proverbs 11:1

A false balance is an abomination to the Lord, but a just weight is his delight.

2 Peter 3:17

You therefore, beloved, knowing this beforehand, take care that you are not carried away with the error of lawless people and lose your own stability.

Philippians 4:8

Finally, brothers, whatever is true, whatever is honorable, whatever is just, whatever is pure, whatever is lovely, whatever is commendable, if there is any excellence, if there is anything worthy of praise, think about these things.

1 Peter 5:7

Casting all your anxieties on him, because he cares for you.

Hebrews 13:5

Keep your life free from love of money, and be content with what you have, for he has said, "I will never leave you nor forsake you."

Philippians 4:11

Not that I am speaking of being in need, for I have learned in whatever situation I am to be content.

2 Timothy 1:7

For God gave us a spirit not of fear but of power and love and self-control.

1 Corinthians 10:13

No temptation has overtaken you that is not common to man. God is faithful, and he will not let you be tempted beyond your ability, but with the temptation he will also provide the way of escape, that you may be able to endure it.

Isaiah 41:13

For I, the Lord your God, hold your right hand; it is I who say to you, "Fear not, I am the one who helps you."

Ephesians 5:15

Look carefully then how you walk, not as unwise but as wise,

Baptism

Acts 2:38

And Peter said to them, "Repent and be baptized every one of you in the name of Jesus Christ for the forgiveness of your sins, and you will receive the gift of the Holy Spirit.

Acts 22:16

And now why do you wait? Rise and be baptized and wash away your sins, calling on his name.'

1 Peter 3:21

Baptism, which corresponds to this, now saves you, not as a removal of dirt from the body but as an appeal to God for a good conscience, through the resurrection of Jesus Christ,

Mark 16:16

Whoever believes and is baptized will be saved, but whoever does not believe will be condemned.

John 3:5

Jesus answered, "Truly, truly, I say to you, unless one is born of water and the Spirit, he cannot enter the kingdom of God.

Matthew 28:19

Go therefore and make disciples of all nations, baptizing them in the name of the Father and of the Son and of the Holy Spirit,

Romans 6:4

We were buried therefore with him by baptism into death, in order that, just as Christ was raised from the dead by the glory of the Father, we too might walk in newness of life.

1 Corinthians 12:13

For in one Spirit we were all baptized into one body—Jews or Greeks, slaves or free—and all were made to drink of one Spirit.

Ephesians 4:5

One Lord, one faith, one baptism,

Galatians 3:27

For as many of you as were baptized into Christ have put on Christ.

Romans 6:3-4

Do you not know that all of us who have been baptized into Christ Jesus were baptized into his death? We were buried therefore with him by baptism into death, in order that, just as Christ was raised from the dead by the glory of the Father, we too might walk in newness of life.

Acts 2:41

So those who received his word were baptized, and there were added that day about three thousand souls.

Matthew 3:11

"I baptize you with water for repentance, but he who is coming after me is mightier than I, whose sandals I am not worthy to carry. He will baptize you with the Holy Spirit and fire.

Barren Women

Psalm 113:9

He gives the barren woman a home, making her the joyous mother of children. Praise the Lord!

Luke 23:29

For behold, the days are coming when they will say, 'Blessed are the barren and the wombs that never bore and the breasts that never nursed!'

Genesis 25:21

And Isaac prayed to the Lord for his wife, because she was barren. And the Lord granted his prayer, and Rebekah his wife conceived.

Hebrews 11:11

By faith Sarah herself received power to conceive, even when she was past the age, since she considered him faithful who had promised.

Psalm 128:3-6

Your wife will be like a fruitful vine within your house; your children will be like olive shoots around your table. Behold, thus shall the man be blessed who fears the Lord. The Lord bless you from Zion! May you see the prosperity of Jerusalem all the days of your life! May you see your children's children! Peace be upon Israel!

Psalm 127:3-5
Behold, children are a heritage from the Lord, the fruit of the womb a reward. Like arrows in the hand of a warrior are the children of one's youth. Blessed is the man who fills his quiver with them! He shall not be put to shame when he speaks with his enemies in the gate.

Battlefield of the Mind

Romans 12:2
Do not be conformed to this world, but be transformed by the renewal of your mind, that by testing you may discern what is the will of God, what is good and acceptable and perfect.

2 Corinthians 10:3-5
For though we walk in the flesh, we are not waging war according to the flesh. For the weapons of our warfare are not of the flesh but have divine power to destroy strongholds. We destroy arguments and every lofty opinion raised against the knowledge of God, and take every thought captive to obey Christ,

Isaiah 26:3
You keep him in perfect peace whose mind is stayed on you, because he trusts in you.

Ephesians 6:12
For we do not wrestle against flesh and blood, but against the rulers, against the authorities, against the cosmic powers over this present darkness, against the spiritual forces of evil in the heavenly places.

Philippians 4:6-8
Do not be anxious about anything, but in everything by prayer and supplication with thanksgiving let your requests be made known to God. And the peace of God, which surpasses all understanding, will guard your hearts and your minds in Christ Jesus. Finally, brothers, whatever is true, whatever is honorable, whatever is just, whatever is pure, whatever is lovely, whatever is commendable, if there is any excellence, if there is anything worthy of praise, think about these things.

James 4:7
Submit yourselves therefore to God. Resist the devil, and he will flee from you.

Beauty

Song of Solomon 4:7
You are altogether beautiful, my love; there is no flaw in you.

1 Peter 3:3-4
Do not let your adorning be external—the braiding of hair and the putting on of gold jewelry, or the clothing you wear— but let your adorning be the hidden person of the heart with the imperishable beauty of a gentle and quiet spirit, which in God's sight is very precious.

Proverbs 31:30

Charm is deceitful, and beauty is vain, but a woman who fears the Lord is to be praised.

Psalm 139:14

I praise you, for I am fearfully and wonderfully made. Wonderful are your works; my soul knows it very well.

1 Samuel 16:7

But the Lord said to Samuel, "Do not look on his appearance or on the height of his stature, because I have rejected him. For the Lord sees not as man sees: man looks on the outward appearance, but the Lord looks on the heart."

Ecclesiastes 3:11

He has made everything beautiful in its time. Also, he has put eternity into man's heart, yet so that he cannot find out what God has done from the beginning to the end.

Isaiah 40:8

The grass withers, the flower fades, but the word of our God will stand forever.

Genesis 1:27

So God created man in his own image, in the image of God he created him; male and female he created them.

1 Timothy 2:9

Likewise also that women should adorn themselves in respectable apparel, with modesty and self-control, not with braided hair and gold or pearls or costly attire,

Ezekiel 28:17

Your heart was proud because of your beauty; you corrupted your wisdom for the sake of your splendor. I cast you to the ground; I exposed you before kings, to feast their eyes on you.

Psalm 45:11

And the king will desire your beauty. Since he is your lord, bow to him.

Behavior

Galatians 5:22-23

But the fruit of the Spirit is love, joy, peace, patience, kindness, goodness, faithfulness, gentleness, self-control; against such things there is no law.

Hebrews 10:26

For if we go on sinning deliberately after receiving the knowledge of the truth, there no longer remains a sacrifice for sins,

Romans 3:23

For all have sinned and fall short of the glory of God,

Titus 2:12

Training us to renounce ungodliness and worldly passions, and to live self-controlled, upright, and godly lives in the present age,

Proverbs 3:5-6

Trust in the Lord with all your heart, and do not lean on your own understanding. In all your ways acknowledge him, and he will make straight your paths.

Colossians 3:5

Put to death therefore what is earthly in you: sexual immorality, impurity, passion, evil desire, and covetousness, which is idolatry.

Romans 1:26-27

For this reason, God gave them up to dishonorable passions. For their women exchanged natural relations for those that are contrary to nature; and the men likewise gave up natural relations with women and were consumed with passion for one another, men committing shameless acts with men and receiving in themselves the due penalty for their error.

Proverbs 16:28

A dishonest man spreads strife, and a whisperer separates close friends.

Luke 16:13

No servant can serve two masters, for either he will hate the one and love the other, or he will be devoted to the one and despise the other. You cannot serve God and money."

1 Corinthians 6:9

Or do you not know that the unrighteous will not inherit the kingdom of God? Do not be deceived: neither the sexually immoral, nor idolaters, nor adulterers, nor men who practice homosexuality

Belief

John 20:29

Jesus said to him, "Have you believed because you have seen me? Blessed are those who have not seen and yet have believed."

John 14:12-14

"Truly, truly, I say to you, whoever believes in me will also do the works that I do; and greater works than these will he do, because I am going to the Father. Whatever you ask in my name, this I will do, that the Father may be glorified in the Son. If you ask me anything in my name, I will do it.

John 3:16

"For God so loved the world, that he gave his only Son, that whoever believes in him should not perish but have eternal life.

John 14:1

"Let not your hearts be troubled. Believe in God; believe also in me.

Romans 10:9-10

Because, if you confess with your mouth that Jesus is Lord and believe in your heart that God raised him from the dead, you will be saved. For with the heart one believes and is justified, and with the mouth one confesses and is saved.

Mark 16:15-16

And he said to them, "Go into all the world and proclaim the gospel to the whole creation. Whoever believes and is baptized will be saved, but whoever does not believe will be condemned.

Mark 9:24

Immediately the father of the child cried out and said, "I believe; help my unbelief!"

Benevolence

John 3:16

"For God so loved the world, that he gave his only Son, that whoever believes in him should not perish but have eternal life.

Galatians 6:10

So then, as we have opportunity, let us do good to everyone, and especially to those who are of the household of faith.

James 1:27

Religion that is pure and undefiled before God, the Father, is this: to visit orphans and widows in their affliction, and to keep oneself unstained from the world.

1 Corinthians 7:3

The husband should give to his wife her conjugal rights, and likewise the wife to her husband.

Proverbs 28:27

Whoever gives to the poor will not want, but he who hides his eyes will get many a curse.

Exodus 21:10

If he takes another wife to himself, he shall not diminish her food, her clothing, or her marital rights.

Galatians 5:22

But the fruit of the Spirit is love, joy, peace, patience, kindness, goodness, faithfulness,

Ephesians 4:32

Be kind to one another, tenderhearted, forgiving one another, as God in Christ forgave you.

Betrayal

Proverbs 19:5

A false witness will not go unpunished, and he who breathes out lies will not escape.

Matthew 6:14-15

For if you forgive others their trespasses, your heavenly Father will also forgive you, but if you do not forgive others their trespasses, neither will your Father forgive your trespasses.

Genesis 12:3

I will bless those who bless you, and him who dishonors you I will curse, and in you all the families of the earth shall be blessed."

Matthew 24:10

And then many will fall away and betray one another and hate one another.

Luke 22:48

But Jesus said to him, "Judas, would you betray the Son of Man with a kiss?"

Psalm 41:9

Even my close friend in whom I trusted, who ate my bread, has lifted his heel against me.

Mark 11:25

And whenever you stand praying, forgive, if you have anything against anyone, so that your Father also who is in heaven may forgive you your trespasses."

Matthew 7:12

"So whatever you wish that others would do to you, do also to them, for this is the Law and the Prophets.

Bible Reliability

2 Timothy 3:16-17

All Scripture is breathed out by God and profitable for teaching, for reproof, for correction, and for training in righteousness, that the man of God may be competent, equipped for every good work.

Hebrews 4:12

For the word of God is living and active, sharper than any two-edged sword, piercing to the division of soul and of spirit, of joints and of marrow, and discerning the thoughts and intentions of the heart.

Psalm 19:7-11

The law of the Lord is perfect, reviving the soul; the testimony of the Lord is sure, making wise the simple; the precepts of the Lord are right, rejoicing the heart; the commandment of the Lord is pure, enlightening the eyes; the fear of the Lord is clean, enduring forever; the rules of the Lord are true, and righteous altogether. More to be desired are they than gold, even much fine gold; sweeter also than honey and drippings of the honeycomb. Moreover, by them is your servant warned; in keeping them there is great reward.

Matthew 4:4

But he answered, "It is written, "'Man shall not live by bread alone, but by every word that comes from the mouth of God.'"

Psalm 119:105

Your word is a lamp to my feet and a light to my path.

Psalm 119:11

I have stored up your word in my heart, that I might not sin against you.

Bigamy

Deuteronomy 17:17

And he shall not acquire many wives for himself, lest his heart turn away, nor shall he acquire for himself excessive silver and gold.

1 Corinthians 7:2

But because of the temptation to sexual immorality, each man should have his own wife and each woman her own husband.

Genesis 4:19

And Lamech took two wives. The name of the one was Adah, and the name of the other Zillah.

Ephesians 5:31

"Therefore a man shall leave his father and mother and hold fast to his wife, and the two shall become one flesh."

Bigotry

Galatians 3:28

There is neither Jew nor Greek, there is neither slave nor free, there is no male and female, for you are all one in Christ Jesus.

Proverbs 10:12

Hatred stirs up strife, but love covers all offenses.

Bipolar

1 Peter 5:6-7

Humble yourselves, therefore, under the mighty hand of God so that at the proper time he may exalt you, casting all your anxieties on him, because he cares for you.

Isaiah 41:10

Fear not, for I am with you; be not dismayed, for I am your God; I will strengthen you, I will help you, I will uphold you with my righteous right hand.

Proverbs 3:5

Trust in the Lord with all your heart, and do not lean on your own understanding.

John 16:33

I have said these things to you, that in me you may have peace. In the world you will have tribulation. But take heart; I have overcome the world."

Romans 8:38-39

For I am sure that neither death nor life, nor angels nor rulers, nor things present nor things to come, nor powers, nor height nor depth, nor anything else in all creation, will be able to separate us from the love of God in Christ Jesus our Lord.

Psalm 62:6

He only is my rock and my salvation, my fortress; I shall not be shaken.

Micah 7:8

Rejoice not over me, O my enemy; when I fall, I shall rise; when I sit in darkness, the Lord will be a light to me.

Ephesians 6:12-13

For we do not wrestle against flesh and blood, but against the rulers, against the authorities, against the cosmic powers over this present darkness, against the spiritual forces of evil in the heavenly places. Therefore, take up the whole armor of God, that you may be able to withstand in the evil day, and having done all, to stand firm.

Birth - Physical

Jeremiah 1:5

"Before I formed you in the womb I knew you, and before you were born I consecrated you; I appointed you a prophet to the nations."

Psalm 139:13-16

For you formed my inward parts; you knitted me together in my mother's womb. I praise you, for I am fearfully and wonderfully made. Wonderful are your works; my soul knows it very well. My frame was not hidden from you, when I was being made in secret, intricately woven in the depths of the earth. Your eyes saw my unformed substance; in your book were written, every one of them, the days that were formed for me, when as yet there was none of them.

John 16:21

When a woman is giving birth, she has sorrow because her hour has come, but when she has delivered the baby, she no longer remembers the anguish, for joy that a human being has been born into the world.

Isaiah 9:6

For to us a child is born, to us a son is given; and the government shall be upon his shoulder, and his name shall be called Wonderful Counselor, Mighty God, Everlasting Father, Prince of Peace.

Psalm 127:3

Behold, children are a heritage from the Lord, the fruit of the womb a reward.

Isaiah 7:14
Therefore, the Lord himself will give you a sign. Behold, the virgin shall conceive and bear a son, and shall call his name Immanuel.

Bisexual

1 Corinthians 6:9-11
Or do you not know that the unrighteous will not inherit the kingdom of God? Do not be deceived: neither the sexually immoral, nor idolaters, nor adulterers, nor men who practice homosexuality, nor thieves, nor the greedy, nor drunkards, nor revilers, nor swindlers will inherit the kingdom of God. And such were some of you. But you were washed, you were sanctified, you were justified in the name of the Lord Jesus Christ and by the Spirit of our God.

Leviticus 18:22
You shall not lie with a male as with a woman; it is an abomination.

Bitterness

Ephesians 4:31-32
Let all bitterness and wrath and anger and clamor and slander be put away from you, along with all malice. Be kind to one another, tenderhearted, forgiving one another, as God in Christ forgave you.

Acts 8:23
For I see that you are in the gall of bitterness and in the bond of iniquity."

Ephesians 4:26
Be angry and do not sin; do not let the sun go down on your anger,

Romans 3:14
"Their mouth is full of curses and bitterness."

Matthew 6:14-15
For if you forgive others their trespasses, your heavenly Father will also forgive you, but if you do not forgive others their trespasses, neither will your Father forgive your trespasses.

Job 10:1
"I loathe my life; I will give free utterance to my complaint; I will speak in the bitterness of my soul.

Hebrews 12:14-15
Strive for peace with everyone, and for the holiness without which no one will see the Lord. See to it that no one fails to obtain the grace of God; that no "root of bitterness" springs up and causes trouble, and by it many become defiled;

Job 7:11
"Therefore I will not restrain my mouth; I will speak in the anguish of my spirit; I will complain in the bitterness of my soul.

Proverbs 14:10

The heart knows its own bitterness, and no stranger shares its joy.

Proverbs 17:25

A foolish son is a grief to his father and bitterness to her who bore him.

Proverbs 10:12

Hatred stirs up strife, but love covers all offenses.

Colossians 3:8

But now you must put them all away: anger, wrath, malice, slander, and obscene talk from your mouth.

Blame shifting

Matthew 7:3-5

Why do you see the speck that is in your brother's eye, but do not notice the log that is in your own eye? Or how can you say to your brother, 'Let me take the speck out of your eye,' when there is the log in your own eye? You hypocrite, first take the log out of your own eye, and then you will see clearly to take the speck out of your brother's eye.

Romans 2:1

Therefore, you have no excuse, O man, every one of you who judges. For in passing judgment on another you condemn yourself, because you, the judge, practice the very same things.

Proverbs 28:13

Whoever conceals his transgressions will not prosper, but he who confesses and forsakes them will obtain mercy.

Genesis 3:12-13

The man said, "The woman whom you gave to be with me, she gave me fruit of the tree, and I ate." Then the Lord God said to the woman, "What is this that you have done?" The woman said, "The serpent deceived me, and I ate."

Blasphemy

Luke 12:10

And everyone who speaks a word against the Son of Man will be forgiven, but the one who blasphemes against the Holy Spirit will not be forgiven.

Matthew 12:31-32

Therefore I tell you, every sin and blasphemy will be forgiven people, but the blasphemy against the Spirit will not be forgiven. And whoever speaks a word against the Son of Man will be forgiven, but whoever speaks against the Holy Spirit will not be forgiven, either in this age or in the age to come.

Mark 3:29

But whoever blasphemes against the Holy Spirit never has forgiveness, but is guilty of an eternal sin.

Blended Family

Galatians 3:28
There is neither Jew nor Greek, there is neither slave nor free, there is no male and female, for you are all one in Christ Jesus.

Blessing

Philippians 4:19
And my God will supply every need of yours according to his riches in glory in Christ Jesus.

James 1:17
Every good gift and every perfect gift is from above, coming down from the Father of lights with whom there is no variation or shadow due to change.

Luke 6:38
Give, and it will be given to you. Good measure, pressed down, shaken together, running over, will be put into your lap. For with the measure you use it will be measured back to you."

Numbers 6:24-26
The Lord bless you and keep you; the Lord make his face to shine upon you and be gracious to you; the Lord lift up his countenance upon you and give you peace.

Isaiah 41:10
Fear not, for I am with you; be not dismayed, for I am your God; I will strengthen you, I will help you, I will uphold you with my righteous right hand.

3 John 1:2
Beloved, I pray that all may go well with you and that you may be in good health, as it goes well with your soul.

2 Corinthians 9:8
And God is able to make all grace abound to you, so that having all sufficiency in all things at all times, you may abound in every good work.

John 1:16
And from his fullness we have all received, grace upon grace.

Blindness

Matthew 15:14
Let them alone; they are blind guides. And if the blind lead the blind, both will fall into a pit."

Blood of Jesus

Hebrews 9:22
Indeed, under the law almost everything is purified with blood, and without the shedding of blood there is no forgiveness of sins.

Hebrews 9:14
How much more will the blood of Christ, who through the eternal Spirit offered himself without blemish to God, purify our conscience from dead works to serve the living God.

Romans 5:9
Since, therefore, we have now been justified by his blood, much more shall we be saved by him from the wrath of God.

1 John 1:7-9
But if we walk in the light, as he is in the light, we have fellowship with one another, and the blood of Jesus his Son cleanses us from all sin. If we say we have no sin, we deceive ourselves, and the truth is not in us. If we confess our sins, he is faithful and just to forgive us our sins and to cleanse us from all unrighteousness.

Revelation 12:11
And they have conquered him by the blood of the Lamb and by the word of their testimony, for they loved not their lives even unto death.

Revelation 1:5
And from Jesus Christ the faithful witness, the firstborn of the dead, and the ruler of kings on earth. To him who loves us and has freed us from our sins by his blood

Acts 20:28
Pay careful attention to yourselves and to all the flock, in which the Holy Spirit has made you overseers, to care for the church of God, which he obtained with his own blood.

Ephesians 1:7
In him we have redemption through his blood, the forgiveness of our trespasses, according to the riches of his grace,

Boasting

James 4:16
As it is, you boast in your arrogance. All such boasting is evil.

Proverbs 27:2
Let another praise you, and not your own mouth; a stranger, and not your own lips.

Jeremiah 9:23
Thus says the Lord: "Let not the wise man boast in his wisdom, let not the mighty man boast in his might, let not the rich man boast in his riches,

2 Timothy 3:1-5

But understand this, that in the last days there will come times of difficulty. For people will be lovers of self, lovers of money, proud, arrogant, abusive, disobedient to their parents, ungrateful, unholy, heartless, unappeasable, slanderous, without self-control, brutal, not loving good, treacherous, reckless, swollen with conceit, lovers of pleasure rather than lovers of God, having the appearance of godliness, but denying its power. Avoid such people.

Proverbs 27:1

Do not boast about tomorrow, for you do not know what a day may bring.

1 Corinthians 4:7

For who sees anything different in you? What do you have that you did not receive? If then you received it, why do you boast as if you did not receive it?

Ephesians 2:8

For by grace you have been saved through faith. And this is not your own doing; it is the gift of God,

Psalm 94:4

They pour out their arrogant words; all the evildoers boast.

2 Corinthians 11:30

If I must boast, I will boast of the things that show my weakness.

James 3:5

So also the tongue is a small member, yet it boasts of great things. How great a forest is set ablaze by such a small fire!

Ephesians 2:9

Not a result of works, so that no one may boast.

Body Image

1 Samuel 16:7

But the Lord said to Samuel, "Do not look on his appearance or on the height of his stature, because I have rejected him. For the Lord sees not as man sees: man looks on the outward appearance, but the Lord looks on the heart."

Psalm 139:14

I praise you, for I am fearfully and wonderfully made. Wonderful are your works; my soul knows it very well.

1 Peter 3:3-4

Do not let your adorning be external—the braiding of hair and the putting on of gold jewelry, or the clothing you wear— but let your adorning be the hidden person of the heart with the imperishable beauty of a gentle and quiet spirit, which in God's sight is very precious.

1 Corinthians 6:19-20
Or do you not know that your body is a temple of the Holy Spirit within you, whom you have from God? You are not your own, for you were bought with a price. So glorify God in your body.

Proverbs 31:30
Charm is deceitful, and beauty is vain, but a woman who fears the Lord is to be praised.

Genesis 1:26-27
Then God said, "Let us make man in our image, after our likeness. And let them have dominion over the fish of the sea and over the birds of the heavens and over the livestock and over all the earth and over every creeping thing that creeps on the earth." So God created man in his own image, in the image of God he created him; male and female he created them.

Boldness

Acts 28:31
Proclaiming the kingdom of God and teaching about the Lord Jesus Christ with all boldness and without hindrance.

Proverbs 28:1
The wicked flee when no one pursues, but the righteous are bold as a lion.

Ephesians 3:12
In whom we have boldness and access with confidence through our faith in him.

Acts 4:31
And when they had prayed, the place in which they were gathered together was shaken, and they were all filled with the Holy Spirit and continued to speak the word of God with boldness.

Acts 4:29
And now, Lord, look upon their threats and grant to your servants to continue to speak your word with all boldness,

2 Corinthians 3:12
Since we have such a hope, we are very bold,

Acts 4:13
Now when they saw the boldness of Peter and John, and perceived that they were uneducated, common men, they were astonished. And they recognized that they had been with Jesus.

Born Again

John 3:3
Jesus answered him, "Truly, truly, I say to you, unless one is born again he cannot see the kingdom of God."

2 Corinthians 5:17

Therefore, if anyone is in Christ, he is a new creation. The old has passed away; behold, the new has come.

1 Peter 1:23

Since you have been born again, not of perishable seed but of imperishable, through the living and abiding word of God;

John 3:36

Whoever believes in the Son has eternal life; whoever does not obey the Son shall not see life, but the wrath of God remains on him.

John 3:16

"For God so loved the world, that he gave his only Son, that whoever believes in him should not perish but have eternal life.

Romans 6:23

For the wages of sin is death, but the free gift of God is eternal life in Christ Jesus our Lord.

John 3:7

Do not marvel that I said to you, 'You must be born again.'

John 1:12

But to all who did receive him, who believed in his name, he gave the right to become children of God,

Borrowing Money

Psalm 37:21

The wicked borrows but does not pay back, but the righteous is generous and gives;

Romans 13:8

Owe no one anything, except to love each other, for the one who loves another has fulfilled the law.

Proverbs 22:26-27

Be not one of those who give pledges, who put up security for debts. If you have nothing with which to pay, why should your bed be taken from under you?

Exodus 22:25-27

"If you lend money to any of my people with you who is poor, you shall not be like a moneylender to him, and you shall not exact interest from him. If ever you take your neighbor's cloak in pledge, you shall return it to him before the sun goes down, for that is his only covering, and it is his cloak for his body; in what else shall he sleep? And if he cries to me, I will hear, for I am compassionate.

Proverbs 3:27-28

Do not withhold good from those to whom it is due, when it is in your power to do it. Do not say to your neighbor, "Go, and come again, tomorrow I will give it"—when you have it with you.

Luke 6:35

But love your enemies, and do good, and lend, expecting nothing in return, and your reward will be great, and you will be sons of the Most High, for he is kind to the ungrateful and the evil.

Deuteronomy 28:12

The Lord will open to you his good treasury, the heavens, to give the rain to your land in its season and to bless all the work of your hands. And you shall lend to many nations, but you shall not borrow.

Boundaries

Galatians 6:5

For each will have to bear his own load.

Colossians 4:6

Let your speech always be gracious, seasoned with salt, so that you may know how you ought to answer each person.

2 Corinthians 6:14

Do not be unequally yoked with unbelievers. For what partnership has righteousness with lawlessness? Or what fellowship has light with darkness?

Proverbs 25:17

Let your foot be seldom in your neighbor's house, lest he have his fill of you and hate you.

Acts 17:26

And he made from one man every nation of mankind to live on all the face of the earth, having determined allotted periods and the boundaries of their dwelling place,

Psalm 16:5-9

The Lord is my chosen portion and my cup; you hold my lot. The lines have fallen for me in pleasant places; indeed, I have a beautiful inheritance. I bless the Lord who gives me counsel; in the night also my heart instructs me. I have set the Lord always before me; because he is at my right hand, I shall not be shaken. Therefore my heart is glad, and my whole being rejoices; my flesh also dwells secure.

Proverbs 15:1

A soft answer turns away wrath, but a harsh word stirs up anger.

Bravery

2 Timothy 1:7

For God gave us a spirit not of fear but of power and love and self-control.

1 Corinthians 16:13

Be watchful, stand firm in the faith, act like men, be strong.

1 Chronicles 28:20

Then David said to Solomon his son, "Be strong and courageous and do it. Do not be afraid and do not be dismayed, for the Lord God, even my God, is with you. He will not leave you or forsake you, until all the work for the service of the house of the Lord is finished.

Deuteronomy 31:6

Be strong and courageous. Do not fear or be in dread of them, for it is the Lord your God who goes with you. He will not leave you or forsake you."

Joshua 1:9

Have I not commanded you? Be strong and courageous. Do not be frightened, and do not be dismayed, for the Lord your God is with you wherever you go."

Philippians 1:28

And not frightened in anything by your opponents. This is a clear sign to them of their destruction, but of your salvation, and that from God.

Bribery

Exodus 23:8

And you shall take no bribe, for a bribe blinds the clear-sighted and subverts the cause of those who are in the right.

Proverbs 17:23

The wicked accepts a bribe in secret to pervert the ways of justice.

Proverbs 15:27

Whoever is greedy for unjust gain troubles his own household, but he who hates bribes will live.

Proverbs 17:8

A bribe is like a magic stone in the eyes of the one who gives it; wherever he turns he prospers.

Amos 5:12

For I know how many are your transgressions and how great are your sins— you who afflict the righteous, who take a bribe, and turn aside the needy in the gate.

Ecclesiastes 7:7

Surely oppression drives the wise into madness, and a bribe corrupts the heart.

Psalm 26:10

In whose hands are evil devices, and whose right hands are full of bribes.

Proverbs 21:14

A gift in secret averts anger, and a concealed bribe, strong wrath.

Deuteronomy 16:19

You shall not pervert justice. You shall not show partiality, and you shall not accept a bribe, for a bribe blinds the eyes of the wise and subverts the cause of the righteous.

Isaiah 5:23

Who acquit the guilty for a bribe, and deprive the innocent of his right!

Proverbs 10:2

Treasures gained by wickedness do not profit, but righteousness delivers from death.

Broken Hearted

Psalm 147:3

He heals the brokenhearted and binds up their wounds.

Psalm 34:17-20

When the righteous cry for help, the Lord hears and delivers them out of all their troubles. The Lord is near to the brokenhearted and saves the crushed in spirit. Many are the afflictions of the righteous, but the Lord delivers him out of them all. He keeps all his bones; not one of them is broken.

1 Peter 5:7

Casting all your anxieties on him, because he cares for you.

Isaiah 61:1

The Spirit of the Lord God is upon me, because the Lord has anointed me to bring good news to the poor; he has sent me to bind up the brokenhearted, to proclaim liberty to the captives, and the opening of the prison to those who are bound;

John 14:27

Peace I leave with you; my peace I give to you. Not as the world gives do I give to you. Let not your hearts be troubled, neither let them be afraid.

Proverbs 3:5-6

Trust in the Lord with all your heart, and do not lean on your own understanding. In all your ways acknowledge him, and he will make straight your paths.

Psalm 73:26

My flesh and my heart may fail, but God is the strength of my heart and my portion forever.

Bulimia

1 Corinthians 6:19-20

Or do you not know that your body is a temple of the Holy Spirit within you, whom you have from God? You are not your own, for you were bought with a price. So glorify God in your body.

Romans 12:2

Do not be conformed to this world, but be transformed by the renewal of your mind, that by testing you may discern what is the will of God, what is good and acceptable and perfect.

1 Corinthians 3:16

Do you not know that you are God's temple and that God's Spirit dwells in you?

Bullying

Leviticus 19:18

You shall not take vengeance or bear a grudge against the sons of your own people, but you shall love your neighbor as yourself: I am the Lord.

2 Timothy 1:7

For God gave us a spirit not of fear but of power and love and self-control.

Romans 12:19-20

Beloved, never avenge yourselves, but leave it to the wrath of God, for it is written, "Vengeance is mine, I will repay, says the Lord." To the contrary, "if your enemy is hungry, feed him; if he is thirsty, give him something to drink; for by so doing you will heap burning coals on his head."

Deuteronomy 31:6

Be strong and courageous. Do not fear or be in dread of them, for it is the Lord your God who goes with you. He will not leave you or forsake you."

Burdens

Matthew 11:28-30

Come to me, all who labor and are heavy laden, and I will give you rest. Take my yoke upon you, and learn from me, for I am gentle and lowly in heart, and you will find rest for your souls. For my yoke is easy, and my burden is light."

Psalm 55:22

Cast your burden on the Lord, and he will sustain you; he will never permit the righteous to be moved.

Galatians 6:2

Bear one another's burdens, and so fulfill the law of Christ.

1 Corinthians 10:13

No temptation has overtaken you that is not common to man. God is faithful, and he will not let you be tempted beyond your ability, but with the temptation he will also provide the way of escape, that you may be able to endure it.

1 Peter 5:6-7

Humble yourselves, therefore, under the mighty hand of God so that at the proper time he may exalt you, casting all your anxieties on him, because he cares for you.

John 16:33

I have said these things to you, that in me you may have peace. In the world you will have tribulation. But take heart; I have overcome the world."

Acts 20:35

In all things I have shown you that by working hard in this way we must help the weak and remember the words of the Lord Jesus, how he himself said, 'It is more blessed to give than to receive.'"

Burial

Genesis 49:29

Then he commanded them and said to them, "I am to be gathered to my people; bury me with my fathers in the cave that is in the field of Ephron the Hittite,

Romans 6:3-4

Do you not know that all of us who have been baptized into Christ Jesus were baptized into his death? We were buried therefore with him by baptism into death, in order that, just as Christ was raised from the dead by the glory of the Father, we too might walk in newness of life.

Colossians 2:12

Having been buried with him in baptism, in which you were also raised with him through faith in the powerful working of God, who raised him from the dead.

Revelation 11:9

For three and a half days some from the peoples and tribes and languages and nations will gaze at their dead bodies and refuse to let them be placed in a tomb,

Acts 8:2

Devout men buried Stephen and made great lamentation over him.

Revelation 21:4

He will wipe away every tear from their eyes, and death shall be no more, neither shall there be mourning, nor crying, nor pain anymore, for the former things have passed away."

Business Ethics

Leviticus 19:11

"You shall not steal; you shall not deal falsely; you shall not lie to one another.

Proverbs 22:1

A good name is to be chosen rather than great riches, and favor is better than silver or gold.

Romans 12:2

Do not be conformed to this world, but be transformed by the renewal of your mind, that by testing you may discern what is the will of God, what is good and acceptable and perfect.

Proverbs 11:1

A false balance is an abomination to the Lord, but a just weight is his delight.

Mark 8:36

For what does it profit a man to gain the whole world and forfeit his soul?

Colossians 3:23

Whatever you do, work heartily, as for the Lord and not for men,

Proverbs 19:17

Whoever is generous to the poor lends to the Lord, and he will repay him for his deed.

Isaiah 1:17-19

Learn to do good; seek justice, correct oppression; bring justice to the fatherless, plead the widow's cause. "Come now, let us reason together, says the Lord: though your sins are like scarlet, they shall be as white as snow; though they are red like crimson, they shall become like wool. If you are willing and obedient, you shall eat the good of the land;

Colossians 3:17

And whatever you do, in word or deed, do everything in the name of the Lord Jesus, giving thanks to God the Father through him.

Called by God

2 Timothy 1:9
Who saved us and called us to a holy calling, not because of our works but because of his own purpose and grace, which he gave us in Christ Jesus before the ages began,

Matthew 22:14
For many are called, but few are chosen."

Romans 8:28-30
And we know that for those who love God all things work together for good, for those who are called according to his purpose. For those whom he foreknew he also predestined to be conformed to the image of his Son, in order that he might be the firstborn among many brothers. And those whom he predestined he also called, and those whom he called he also justified, and those whom he justified he also glorified.

John 6:44
No one can come to me unless the Father who sent me draws him. And I will raise him up on the last day.

Philippians 1:6
And I am sure of this, that he who began a good work in you will bring it to completion at the day of Jesus Christ.

1 Corinthians 1:26
For consider your calling, brothers: not many of you were wise according to worldly standards, not many were powerful, not many were of noble birth.

Jeremiah 33:3
Call to me and I will answer you, and will tell you great and hidden things that you have not known.

Ephesians 4:1-3
I therefore, a prisoner for the Lord, urge you to walk in a manner worthy of the calling to which you have been called, with all humility and gentleness, with patience, bearing with one another in love, eager to maintain the unity of the Spirit in the bond of peace.

Romans 11:29
For the gifts and the calling of God are irrevocable.

2 Peter 1:10
Therefore, brothers, be all the more diligent to make your calling and election sure, for if you practice these qualities you will never fall.

Calm

2 Timothy 1:7
For God gave us a spirit not of fear but of power and love and self-control.

Mark 11:24

Therefore I tell you, whatever you ask in prayer, believe that you have received it, and it will be yours.

Matthew 5:44

But I say to you, Love your enemies and pray for those who persecute you,

Isaiah 43:2

When you pass through the waters, I will be with you; and through the rivers, they shall not overwhelm you; when you walk through fire you shall not be burned, and the flame shall not consume you.

Psalm 16:11

You make known to me the path of life; in your presence there is fullness of joy; at your right hand are pleasures forevermore.

2 Peter 3:9

The Lord is not slow to fulfill his promise as some count slowness, but is patient toward you, not wishing that any should perish, but that all should reach repentance.

Cancer

2 Corinthians 4:16-18

So we do not lose heart. Though our outer self is wasting away, our inner self is being renewed day by day. For this light momentary affliction is preparing for us an eternal weight of glory beyond all comparison, as we look not to the things that are seen but to the things that are unseen. For the things that are seen are transient, but the things that are unseen are eternal.

Jeremiah 30:17

For I will restore health to you, and your wounds I will heal, declares the Lord, because they have called you an outcast: 'It is Zion, for whom no one cares!'

Isaiah 53:4

Surely he has borne our griefs and carried our sorrows; yet we esteemed him stricken, smitten by God, and afflicted.

Joshua 1:9

Have I not commanded you? Be strong and courageous. Do not be frightened, and do not be dismayed, for the Lord your God is with you wherever you go."

Psalm 107:20

He sent out his word and healed them, and delivered them from their destruction.

James 5:15

And the prayer of faith will save the one who is sick, and the Lord will raise him up. And if he has committed sins, he will be forgiven.

Proverbs 4:20-22
My son, be attentive to my words; incline your ear to my sayings. Let them not escape from your sight; keep them within your heart. For they are life to those who find them, and healing to all their flesh. Capability

Capital Punishment

Genesis 9:6
"Whoever sheds the blood of man, by man shall his blood be shed, for God made man in his own image.

Exodus 21:12
"Whoever strikes a man so that he dies shall be put to death.

Leviticus 24:17
"Whoever takes a human life shall surely be put to death.

Acts 25:11
If then I am a wrongdoer and have committed anything for which I deserve to die, I do not seek to escape death. But if there is nothing to their charges against me, no one can give me up to them. I appeal to Caesar."

Numbers 35:30-31
"If anyone kills a person, the murderer shall be put to death on the evidence of witnesses. But no person shall be put to death on the testimony of one witness. Moreover, you shall accept no ransom for the life of a murderer, who is guilty of death, but he shall be put to death.

Exodus 20:13
"You shall not murder.

Exodus 21:16
"Whoever steals a man and sells him, and anyone found in possession of him, shall be put to death.

Caring

1 Peter 5:7
Casting all your anxieties on him, because he cares for you.

Philippians 2:4
Let each of you look not only to his own interests, but also to the interests of others.

Hebrews 13:8
Jesus Christ is the same yesterday and today and forever.

James 1:27
Religion that is pure and undefiled before God, the Father, is this: to visit orphans and widows in their affliction, and to keep oneself unstained from the world.

Ephesians 4:32

Be kind to one another, tenderhearted, forgiving one another, as God in Christ forgave you.

Proverbs 27:23

Know well the condition of your flocks, and give attention to your herds,

3 John 1:2

Beloved, I pray that all may go well with you and that you may be in good health, as it goes well with your soul.

Ezekiel 16:49

Behold, this was the guilt of your sister Sodom: she and her daughters had pride, excess of food, and prosperous ease, but did not aid the poor and needy.

1 Corinthians 6:19-20

Or do you not know that your body is a temple of the Holy Spirit within you, whom you have from God? You are not your own, for you were bought with a price. So glorify God in your body.

Job 12:7-10

"But ask the beasts, and they will teach you; the birds of the heavens, and they will tell you; or the bushes of the earth, and they will teach you; and the fish of the sea will declare to you. Who among all these does not know that the hand of the Lord has done this? In his hand is the life of every living thing and the breath of all mankind.

Proverbs 21:13

Whoever closes his ear to the cry of the poor will himself call out and not be answered.

Ephesians 4:2

With all humility and gentleness, with patience, bearing with one another in love,

Caregiving

John 13:34-35

A new commandment I give to you, that you love one another: just as I have loved you, you also are to love one another. By this all people will know that you are my disciples, if you have love for one another."

Galatians 6:10

So then, as we have opportunity, let us do good to everyone, and especially to those who are of the household of faith.

James 2:14-17

What good is it, my brothers, if someone says he has faith but does not have works? Can that faith save him? If a brother or sister is poorly clothed and lacking in daily food, and one of you says to them, "Go in peace, be warmed and filled," without giving them the things needed for the body, what good is that? So also faith by itself, if it does not have works, is dead.

Philippians 2:4

Let each of you look not only to his own interests, but also to the interests of others.

1 Timothy 5:8

But if anyone does not provide for his relatives, and especially for members of his household, he has denied the faith and is worse than an unbeliever.

1 Corinthians 13:1-2

If I speak in the tongues of men and of angels, but have not love, I am a noisy gong or a clanging cymbal. And if I have prophetic powers, and understand all mysteries and all knowledge, and if I have all faith, so as to remove mountains, but have not love, I am nothing.

Luke 6:31

And as you wish that others would do to you, do so to them.

Carnality

Romans 8:6

For to set the mind on the flesh is death, but to set the mind on the Spirit is life and peace.

1 Corinthians 3:3

For you are still of the flesh. For while there is jealousy and strife among you, are you not of the flesh and behaving only in a human way?

1 Corinthians 2:14

The natural person does not accept the things of the Spirit of God, for they are folly to him, and he is not able to understand them because they are spiritually discerned.

1 Corinthians 15:33

Do not be deceived: "Bad company ruins good morals."

1 John 1:9

If we confess our sins, he is faithful and just to forgive us our sins and to cleanse us from all unrighteousness.

2 Corinthians 13:5

Examine yourselves, to see whether you are in the faith. Test yourselves. Or do you not realize this about yourselves, that Jesus Christ is in you?—unless indeed you fail to meet the test!

2 Timothy 3:16

All Scripture is breathed out by God and profitable for teaching, for reproof, for correction, and for training in righteousness,

1 Timothy 6:20

O Timothy, guard the deposit entrusted to you. Avoid the irreverent babble and contradictions of what is falsely called "knowledge,"

Romans 8:7

For the mind that is set on the flesh is hostile to God, for it does not submit to God's law; indeed, it cannot.

James 4:7

Submit yourselves therefore to God. Resist the devil, and he will flee from you.

1 Corinthians 3:1

But I, brothers, could not address you as spiritual people, but as people of the flesh, as infants in Christ.

Ephesians 2:3

Among whom we all once lived in the passions of our flesh, carrying out the desires of the body and the mind, and were by nature children of wrath, like the rest of mankind.

Galatians 5:19

Now the works of the flesh are evident: sexual immorality, impurity, sensuality,

Celebration

1 Corinthians 10:31

So, whether you eat or drink, or whatever you do, do all to the glory of God.

1 Corinthians 5:8

Let us therefore celebrate the festival, not with the old leaven, the leaven of malice and evil, but with the unleavened bread of sincerity and truth.

Luke 15:23-24

And bring the fattened calf and kill it, and let us eat and celebrate. For this my son was dead, and is alive again; he was lost, and is found.' And they began to celebrate.

Ecclesiastes 3:4

A time to weep, and a time to laugh; a time to mourn, and a time to dance;

Ecclesiastes 3:13

Also that everyone should eat and drink and take pleasure in all his toil—this is God's gift to man.

Psalm 118:24

This is the day that the Lord has made; let us rejoice and be glad in it.

Celibacy

1 Corinthians 7:7-9

I wish that all were as I myself am. But each has his own gift from God, one of one kind and one of another. To the unmarried and the widows I say that it is good for them to remain single as I am. But if they cannot exercise self-control, they should marry. For it is better to marry than to burn with passion.

1 Corinthians 6:18-20

Flee from sexual immorality. Every other sin a person commits is outside the body, but the sexually immoral person sins against his own body. Or do you not know that your body is a temple of the Holy Spirit within you, whom you have from God? You are not your own, for you were bought with a price. So glorify God in your body.

1 Corinthians 7:2

But because of the temptation to sexual immorality, each man should have his own wife and each woman her own husband.

1 Timothy 3:2

Therefore an overseer must be above reproach, the husband of one wife, sober-minded, self-controlled, respectable, hospitable, able to teach,

Matthew 19:10-12

The disciples said to him, "If such is the case of a man with his wife, it is better not to marry." But he said to them, "Not everyone can receive this saying, but only those to whom it is given. For there are eunuchs who have been so from birth, and there are eunuchs who have been made eunuchs by men, and there are eunuchs who have made themselves eunuchs for the sake of the kingdom of heaven. Let the one who is able to receive this receive it."

1 Timothy 4:1-3

Now the Spirit expressly says that in later times some will depart from the faith by devoting themselves to deceitful spirits and teachings of demons, through the insincerity of liars whose consciences are seared, who forbid marriage and require abstinence from foods that God created to be received with thanksgiving by those who believe and know the truth.

Challenges

James 1:2-4

Count it all joy, my brothers, when you meet trials of various kinds, for you know that the testing of your faith produces steadfastness. And let steadfastness have its full effect, that you may be perfect and complete, lacking in nothing.

Philippians 4:6

Do not be anxious about anything, but in everything by prayer and supplication with thanksgiving let your requests be made known to God.

2 Corinthians 4:8-9

We are afflicted in every way, but not crushed; perplexed, but not driven to despair; persecuted, but not forsaken; struck down, but not destroyed;

Philippians 4:13
I can do all things through him who strengthens me.

1 Corinthians 10:13

No temptation has overtaken you that is not common to man. God is faithful, and he will not let you be tempted beyond your ability, but with the temptation he will also provide the way of escape, that you may be able to endure it.

Hebrews 13:5

Keep your life free from love of money, and be content with what you have, for he has said, "I will never leave you nor forsake you."

1 Peter 5:10

And after you have suffered a little while, the God of all grace, who has called you to his eternal glory in Christ, will himself restore, confirm, strengthen, and establish you.

1 John 4:18

There is no fear in love, but perfect love casts out fear. For fear has to do with punishment, and whoever fears has not been perfected in love.

Chance

Proverbs 16:33

The lot is cast into the lap, but its every decision is from the Lord.

Ecclesiastes 9:11

Again I saw that under the sun the race is not to the swift, nor the battle to the strong, nor bread to the wise, nor riches to the intelligent, nor favor to those with knowledge, but time and chance happen to them all.

Romans 8:28-30

And we know that for those who love God all things work together for good, for those who are called according to his purpose. For those whom he foreknew he also predestined to be conformed to the image of his Son, in order that he might be the firstborn among many brothers. And those whom he predestined he also called, and those whom he called he also justified, and those whom he justified he also glorified.

Isaiah 46:9-10

Remember the former things of old; for I am God, and there is no other; I am God, and there is none like me, declaring the end from the beginning and from ancient times things not yet done, saying, 'My counsel shall stand, and I will accomplish all my purpose,'

Ephesians 1:11

In him we have obtained an inheritance, having been predestined according to the purpose of him who works all things according to the counsel of his will,

Change

Hebrews 13:8

Jesus Christ is the same yesterday and today and forever.

Joshua 1:9

Have I not commanded you? Be strong and courageous. Do not be frightened, and do not be dismayed, for the Lord your God is with you wherever you go."

Jeremiah 29:11

For I know the plans I have for you, declares the Lord, plans for welfare and not for evil, to give you a future and a hope.

Ecclesiastes 3:1

For everything there is a season, and a time for every matter under heaven:

Romans 12:1-2

I appeal to you therefore, brothers, by the mercies of God, to present your bodies as a living sacrifice, holy and acceptable to God, which is your spiritual worship. Do not be conformed to this world, but be transformed by the renewal of your mind, that by testing you may discern what is the will of God, what is good and acceptable and perfect.

Philippians 4:6-7

Do not be anxious about anything, but in everything by prayer and supplication with thanksgiving let your requests be made known to God. And the peace of God, which surpasses all understanding, will guard your hearts and your minds in Christ Jesus.

Deuteronomy 31:6

Be strong and courageous. Do not fear or be in dread of them, for it is the Lord your God who goes with you. He will not leave you or forsake you."

2 Corinthians 4:16-18

So we do not lose heart. Though our outer self is wasting away, our inner self is being renewed day by day. For this light momentary affliction is preparing for us an eternal weight of glory beyond all comparison, as we look not to the things that are seen but to the things that are unseen. For the things that are seen are transient, but the things that are unseen are eternal.

2 Corinthians 5:17

Therefore, if anyone is in Christ, he is a new creation. The old has passed away; behold, the new has come.

James 1:17

Every good gift and every perfect gift is from above, coming down from the Father of lights with whom there is no variation or shadow due to change.

1 Corinthians 15:51

Behold! I tell you a mystery. We shall not all sleep, but we shall all be changed,

Malachi 3:6

"For I the Lord do not change; therefore you, O children of Jacob, are not consumed.

Proverbs 18:15

An intelligent heart acquires knowledge, and the ear of the wise seeks knowledge.

2 Peter 3:9

The Lord is not slow to fulfill his promise as some count slowness, but is patient toward you, not wishing that any should perish, but that all should reach repentance.

Proverbs 19:2

Desire without knowledge is not good, and whoever makes haste with his feet misses his way.

2 Timothy 3:16-17

All Scripture is breathed out by God and profitable for teaching, for reproof, for correction, and for training in righteousness, that the man of God may be competent, equipped for every good work.

Numbers 23:19

God is not man, that he should lie, or a son of man, that he should change his mind. Has he said, and will he not do it? Or has he spoken, and will he not fulfill it?

Ephesians 4:22-24

To put off your old self, which belongs to your former manner of life and is corrupt through deceitful desires, and to be renewed in the spirit of your minds, and to put on the new self, created after the likeness of God in true righteousness and holiness.

Changed Heart

Ezekiel 11:19

And I will give them one heart, and a new spirit I will put within them. I will remove the heart of stone from their flesh and give them a heart of flesh,

2 Corinthians 5:17

Therefore, if anyone is in Christ, he is a new creation. The old has passed away; behold, the new has come.

Ezekiel 36:25-27

I will sprinkle clean water on you, and you shall be clean from all your uncleannesses, and from all your idols I will cleanse you. And I will give you a new heart, and a new spirit I will put within you. And I will remove the heart of stone from your flesh and give you a heart of flesh. And I will put my Spirit within you, and cause you to walk in my statutes and be careful to obey my rules.

Psalm 51:10

Create in me a clean heart, O God, and renew a right spirit within me.

Psalm 37:4

Delight yourself in the Lord, and he will give you the desires of your heart.

Romans 2:29

But a Jew is one inwardly, and circumcision is a matter of the heart, by the Spirit, not by the letter. His praise is not from man but from God.

Ezekiel 36:26
And I will give you a new heart, and a new spirit I will put within you. And I will remove the heart of stone from your flesh and give you a heart of flesh.

Chaos

1 Corinthians 14:33
For God is not a God of confusion but of peace. As in all the churches of the saints,

John 14:27
Peace I leave with you; my peace I give to you. Not as the world gives do I give to you. Let not your hearts be troubled, neither let them be afraid.

Proverbs 25:28
A man without self-control is like a city broken into and left without walls.

Proverbs 11:14
Where there is no guidance, a people falls, but in an abundance of counselors there is safety.

1 Corinthians 14:40
But all things should be done decently and in order.

Isaiah 32:17-18
And the effect of righteousness will be peace, and the result of righteousness, quietness and trust forever. My people will abide in a peaceful habitation, in secure dwellings, and in quiet resting places.

Matthew 11:28-30
Come to me, all who labor and are heavy laden, and I will give you rest. Take my yoke upon you, and learn from me, for I am gentle and lowly in heart, and you will find rest for your souls. For my yoke is easy, and my burden is light."

Philippians 4:6-7
Do not be anxious about anything, but in everything by prayer and supplication with thanksgiving let your requests be made known to God. And the peace of God, which surpasses all understanding, will guard your hearts and your minds in Christ Jesus.

Isaiah 41:10
Fear not, for I am with you; be not dismayed, for I am your God; I will strengthen you, I will help you, I will uphold you with my righteous right hand.

John 16:33
I have said these things to you, that in me you may have peace. In the world you will have tribulation. But take heart; I have overcome the world."

Isaiah 26:3
You keep him in perfect peace whose mind is stayed on you, because he trusts in you.

Character

1 Samuel 16:7
But the Lord said to Samuel, "Do not look on his appearance or on the height of his stature, because I have rejected him. For the Lord sees not as man sees: man looks on the outward appearance, but the Lord looks on the heart."

Romans 5:1-5
Therefore, since we have been justified by faith, we have peace with God through our Lord Jesus Christ. Through him we have also obtained access by faith into this grace in which we stand, and we rejoice in hope of the glory of God. More than that, we rejoice in our sufferings, knowing that suffering produces endurance, and endurance produces character, and character produces hope, and hope does not put us to shame, because God's love has been poured into our hearts through the Holy Spirit who has been given to us.

Philippians 2:12-16
Therefore, my beloved, as you have always obeyed, so now, not only as in my presence but much more in my absence, work out your own salvation with fear and trembling, for it is God who works in you, both to will and to work for his good pleasure. Do all things without grumbling or questioning, that you may be blameless and innocent, children of God without blemish in the midst of a crooked and twisted generation, among whom you shine as lights in the world, holding fast to the word of life, so that in the day of Christ I may be proud that I did not run in vain or labor in vain.

Philippians 4:8
Finally, brothers, whatever is true, whatever is honorable, whatever is just, whatever is pure, whatever is lovely, whatever is commendable, if there is any excellence, if there is anything worthy of praise, think about these things.

Romans 12:2
Do not be conformed to this world, but be transformed by the renewal of your mind, that by testing you may discern what is the will of God, what is good and acceptable and perfect.

Proverbs 10:9
Whoever walks in integrity walks securely, but he who makes his ways crooked will be found out.

Galatians 5:22-23
But the fruit of the Spirit is love, joy, peace, patience, kindness, goodness, faithfulness, gentleness, self-control; against such things there is no law.

Character of God

1 John 4:8
Anyone who does not love does not know God, because God is love.

Hebrews 13:8
Jesus Christ is the same yesterday and today and forever.

2 Peter 3:9

The Lord is not slow to fulfill his promise as some count slowness, but is patient toward you, not wishing that any should perish, but that all should reach repentance.

1 John 1:5

This is the message we have heard from him and proclaim to you, that God is light, and in him is no darkness at all.

James 1:17

Every good gift and every perfect gift is from above, coming down from the Father of lights with whom there is no variation or shadow due to change.

Isaiah 40:28

Have you not known? Have you not heard? The Lord is the everlasting God, the Creator of the ends of the earth. He does not faint or grow weary; his understanding is unsearchable.

Psalm 30:5

For his anger is but for a moment, and his favor is for a lifetime. Weeping may tarry for the night, but joy comes with the morning.

John 3:16

"For God so loved the world, that he gave his only Son, that whoever believes in him should not perish but have eternal life.

Psalm 18:30

This God—his way is perfect; the word of the Lord proves true; he is a shield for all those who take refuge in him.

Galatians 5:22

But the fruit of the Spirit is love, joy, peace, patience, kindness, goodness, faithfulness,

John 14:6

Jesus said to him, "I am the way, and the truth, and the life. No one comes to the Father except through me.

John 4:24

God is spirit, and those who worship him must worship in spirit and truth."

John 14:26

But the Helper, the Holy Spirit, whom the Father will send in my name, he will teach you all things and bring to your remembrance all that I have said to you.

Isaiah 41:10

Fear not, for I am with you; be not dismayed, for I am your God; I will strengthen you, I will help you, I will uphold you with my righteous right hand.

Charity

Acts 20:35
In all things I have shown you that by working hard in this way we must help the weak and remember the words of the Lord Jesus, how he himself said, 'It is more blessed to give than to receive.'"

Hebrews 13:16
Do not neglect to do good and to share what you have, for such sacrifices are pleasing to God.

Matthew 6:1-4
"Beware of practicing your righteousness before other people in order to be seen by them, for then you will have no reward from your Father who is in heaven. "Thus, when you give to the needy, sound no trumpet before you, as the hypocrites do in the synagogues and in the streets, that they may be praised by others. Truly, I say to you, they have received their reward. But when you give to the needy, do not let your left hand know what your right hand is doing, so that your giving may be in secret. And your Father who sees in secret will reward you.

Proverbs 19:17
Whoever is generous to the poor lends to the Lord, and he will repay him for his deed.

Luke 21:1-4
Jesus looked up and saw the rich putting their gifts into the offering box, and he saw a poor widow put in two small copper coins. And he said, "Truly, I tell you, this poor widow has put in more than all of them. For they all contributed out of their abundance, but she out of her poverty put in all she had to live on."

1 John 3:17
But if anyone has the world's goods and sees his brother in need, yet closes his heart against him, how does God's love abide in him?

2 Corinthians 9:7
Each one must give as he has decided in his heart, not reluctantly or under compulsion, for God loves a cheerful giver.

Luke 12:33
Sell your possessions, and give to the needy. Provide yourselves with moneybags that do not grow old, with a treasure in the heavens that does not fail, where no thief approaches and no moth destroys.

Luke 6:38
Give, and it will be given to you. Good measure, pressed down, shaken together, running over, will be put into your lap. For with the measure you use it will be measured back to you."

Cheating

James 4:17
So whoever knows the right thing to do and fails to do it, for him it is sin.

Proverbs 12:22

Lying lips are an abomination to the Lord, but those who act faithfully are his delight.

Hebrews 13:4

Let marriage be held in honor among all, and let the marriage bed be undefiled, for God will judge the sexually immoral and adulterous.

Matthew 5:27-28

"You have heard that it was said, 'You shall not commit adultery.' But I say to you that everyone who looks at a woman with lustful intent has already committed adultery with her in his heart.

Proverbs 19:1

Better is a poor person who walks in his integrity than one who is crooked in speech and is a fool.

Proverbs 10:9

Whoever walks in integrity walks securely, but he who makes his ways crooked will be found out.

Proverbs 6:32

He who commits adultery lacks sense; he who does it destroys himself.

Galatians 6:7-8

Do not be deceived: God is not mocked, for whatever one sows, that will he also reap. For the one who sows to his own flesh will from the flesh reap corruption, but the one who sows to the Spirit will from the Spirit reap eternal life.

Proverbs 20:22

Do not say, "I will repay evil"; wait for the Lord, and he will deliver you.

Proverbs 28:6

Better is a poor man who walks in his integrity than a rich man who is crooked in his ways.

Joshua 1:9

Have I not commanded you? Be strong and courageous. Do not be frightened, and do not be dismayed, for the Lord your God is with you wherever you go."

Luke 6:31

And as you wish that others would do to you, do so to them.

Luke 16:10-12

"One who is faithful in a very little is also faithful in much, and one who is dishonest in a very little is also dishonest in much. If then you have not been faithful in the unrighteous wealth, who will entrust to you the true riches? And if you have not been faithful in that which is another's, who will give you that which is your own?

James 1:26

If anyone thinks he is religious and does not bridle his tongue but deceives his heart, this person's religion is worthless.

Child Abuse

Ephesians 6:4
Fathers, do not provoke your children to anger, but bring them up in the discipline and instruction of the Lord.

Mark 9:42
"Whoever causes one of these little ones who believe in me to sin, it would be better for him if a great millstone were hung around his neck and he were thrown into the sea.

Proverbs 19:18
Discipline your son, for there is hope; do not set your heart on putting him to death.

Psalm 137:9
Blessed shall he be who takes your little ones and dashes them against the rock!

Colossians 3:21
Fathers, do not provoke your children, lest they become discouraged.

Matthew 18:6
But whoever causes one of these little ones who believe in me to sin, it would be better for him to have a great millstone fastened around his neck and to be drowned in the depth of the sea.

Mark 10:14
But when Jesus saw it, he was indignant and said to them, "Let the children come to me; do not hinder them, for to such belongs the kingdom of God.

Proverbs 22:15
Folly is bound up in the heart of a child, but the rod of discipline drives it far from him.

Exodus 21:22
"When men strive together and hit a pregnant woman, so that her children come out, but there is no harm, the one who hit her shall surely be fined, as the woman's husband shall impose on him, and he shall pay as the judges determine.

Revelation 21:8
But as for the cowardly, the faithless, the detestable, as for murderers, the sexually immoral, sorcerers, idolaters, and all liars, their portion will be in the lake that burns with fire and sulfur, which is the second death."

Proverbs 13:24
Whoever spares the rod hates his son, but he who loves him is diligent to discipline him.

Proverbs 22:6
Train up a child in the way he should go; even when he is old he will not depart from it.

Psalm 127:3-5

Behold, children are a heritage from the Lord, the fruit of the womb a reward. Like arrows in the hand of a warrior are the children of one's youth. Blessed is the man who fills his quiver with them! He shall not be put to shame when he speaks with his enemies in the gate.

Child Dedication

Proverbs 22:6

Train up a child in the way he should go; even when he is old he will not depart from it.

Deuteronomy 6:5-7

You shall love the Lord your God with all your heart and with all your soul and with all your might. And these words that I command you today shall be on your heart. You shall teach them diligently to your children, and shall talk of them when you sit in your house, and when you walk by the way, and when you lie down, and when you rise.

Psalm 127:3

Behold, children are a heritage from the Lord, the fruit of the womb a reward.

1 Samuel 1:27-28

For this child I prayed, and the Lord has granted me my petition that I made to him. Therefore I have lent him to the Lord. As long as he lives, he is lent to the Lord." And he worshiped the Lord there.

Mark 10:13-16

And they were bringing children to him that he might touch them, and the disciples rebuked them. But when Jesus saw it, he was indignant and said to them, "Let the children come to me; do not hinder them, for to such belongs the kingdom of God. Truly, I say to you, whoever does not receive the kingdom of God like a child shall not enter it." And he took them in his arms and blessed them, laying his hands on them.

Jeremiah 1:5

"Before I formed you in the womb I knew you, and before you were born I consecrated you; I appointed you a prophet to the nations."

Luke 2:22

And when the time came for their purification according to the Law of Moses, they brought him up to Jerusalem to present him to the Lord

Child Labor

Matthew 19:14

But Jesus said, "Let the little children come to me and do not hinder them, for to such belongs the kingdom of heaven."

2 Corinthians 12:14

Here for the third time I am ready to come to you. And I will not be a burden, for I seek not what is yours but you. For children are not obligated to save up for their parents, but parents for their children.

John 16:21

When a woman is giving birth, she has sorrow because her hour has come, but when she has delivered the baby, she no longer remembers the anguish, for joy that a human being has been born into the world.

Philippians 4:13

I can do all things through him who strengthens me.

Isaiah 41:10

Fear not, for I am with you; be not dismayed, for I am your God; I will strengthen you, I will help you, I will uphold you with my righteous right hand.

Colossians 3:23

Whatever you do, work heartily, as for the Lord and not for men,

Luke 18:15-17

Now they were bringing even infants to him that he might touch them. And when the disciples saw it, they rebuked them. But Jesus called them to him, saying, "Let the children come to me, and do not hinder them, for to such belongs the kingdom of God. Truly, I say to you, whoever does not receive the kingdom of God like a child shall not enter it."

Ephesians 4:28

Let the thief no longer steal, but rather let him labor, doing honest work with his own hands, so that he may have something to share with anyone in need.

Genesis 3:16

To the woman he said, "I will surely multiply your pain in childbearing; in pain you shall bring forth children. Your desire shall be for your husband, and he shall rule over you."

Child of God

John 1:12

But to all who did receive him, who believed in his name, he gave the right to become children of God,

Proverbs 22:6

Train up a child in the way he should go; even when he is old he will not depart from it.

Galatians 3:26

For in Christ Jesus you are all sons of God, through faith.

Ephesians 6:4

Fathers, do not provoke your children to anger, but bring them up in the discipline and instruction of the Lord.

Psalm 127:3-5

Behold, children are a heritage from the Lord, the fruit of the womb a reward. Like arrows in the hand of a warrior are the children of one's youth. Blessed is the man who fills his quiver with them! He shall not be put to shame when he speaks with his enemies in the gate.

Romans 8:16

The Spirit himself bears witness with our spirit that we are children of God,

1 John 3:1

See what kind of love the Father has given to us, that we should be called children of God; and so we are. The reason why the world does not know us is that it did not know him.

John 3:16

"For God so loved the world, that he gave his only Son, that whoever believes in him should not perish but have eternal life.

Mark 10:13-16

And they were bringing children to him that he might touch them, and the disciples rebuked them. But when Jesus saw it, he was indignant and said to them, "Let the children come to me; do not hinder them, for to such belongs the kingdom of God. Truly, I say to you, whoever does not receive the kingdom of God like a child shall not enter it." And he took them in his arms and blessed them, laying his hands on them.

Matthew 18:10

"See that you do not despise one of these little ones. For I tell you that in heaven their angels always see the face of my Father who is in heaven.

Matthew 5:9

"Blessed are the peacemakers, for they shall be called sons of God.

Romans 8:14

For all who are led by the Spirit of God are sons of God.

Romans 8:17

And if children, then heirs—heirs of God and fellow heirs with Christ, provided we suffer with him in order that we may also be glorified with him.

1 John 3:10

By this it is evident who are the children of God, and who are the children of the devil: whoever does not practice righteousness is not of God, nor is the one who does not love his brother.

Proverbs 22:15

Folly is bound up in the heart of a child, but the rod of discipline drives it far from him.

2 Timothy 3:14-15

But as for you, continue in what you have learned and have firmly believed, knowing from whom you learned it and how from childhood you have been acquainted with the sacred writings, which are able to make you wise for salvation through faith in Christ Jesus.

Proverbs 17:6
Grandchildren are the crown of the aged, and the glory of children is their fathers.

Psalm 127:3
Behold, children are a heritage from the Lord, the fruit of the womb a reward.

Child Sacrifice

Leviticus 18:21
You shall not give any of your children to offer them to Molech, and so profane the name of your God: I am the Lord.

Deuteronomy 12:31
You shall not worship the Lord your God in that way, for every abominable thing that the Lord hates they have done for their gods, for they even burn their sons and their daughters in the fire to their gods.

Child Support

1 Timothy 5:8
But if anyone does not provide for his relatives, and especially for members of his household, he has denied the faith and is worse than an unbeliever.

2 Corinthians 12:14
Here for the third time I am ready to come to you. And I will not be a burden, for I seek not what is yours but you. For children are not obligated to save up for their parents, but parents for their children.

Child Training

Proverbs 22:6
Train up a child in the way he should go; even when he is old he will not depart from it.

Proverbs 23:13-14
Do not withhold discipline from a child; if you strike him with a rod, he will not die. If you strike him with the rod, you will save his soul from Sheol.

Ephesians 6:4
Fathers, do not provoke your children to anger, but bring them up in the discipline and instruction of the Lord.

Proverbs 13:24
Whoever spares the rod hates his son, but he who loves him is diligent to discipline him.

Deuteronomy 6:6-7

And these words that I command you today shall be on your heart. You shall teach them diligently to your children, and shall talk of them when you sit in your house, and when you walk by the way, and when you lie down, and when you rise.

3 John 1:4

I have no greater joy than to hear that my children are walking in the truth.

Children

Proverbs 22:6

Train up a child in the way he should go; even when he is old he will not depart from it.

Psalm 127:3-5

Behold, children are a heritage from the Lord, the fruit of the womb a reward. Like arrows in the hand of a warrior are the children of one's youth. Blessed is the man who fills his quiver with them! He shall not be put to shame when he speaks with his enemies in the gate.

Matthew 18:10

"See that you do not despise one of these little ones. For I tell you that in heaven their angels always see the face of my Father who is in heaven.

Proverbs 17:6

Grandchildren are the crown of the aged, and the glory of children is their fathers.

Isaiah 54:13

All your children shall be taught by the Lord, and great shall be the peace of your children.

Mark 10:13-16

And they were bringing children to him that he might touch them, and the disciples rebuked them. But when Jesus saw it, he was indignant and said to them, "Let the children come to me; do not hinder them, for to such belongs the kingdom of God. Truly, I say to you, whoever does not receive the kingdom of God like a child shall not enter it." And he took them in his arms and blessed them, laying his hands on them.

John 16:21

When a woman is giving birth, she has sorrow because her hour has come, but when she has delivered the baby, she no longer remembers the anguish, for joy that a human being has been born into the world.

Matthew 19:14

But Jesus said, "Let the little children come to me and do not hinder them, for to such belongs the kingdom of heaven."

Proverbs 20:11

Even a child makes himself known by his acts, by whether his conduct is pure and upright.

Colossians 3:20

Children, obey your parents in everything, for this pleases the Lord.

Ephesians 6:1-4

Children, obey your parents in the Lord, for this is right. "Honor your father and mother" (this is the first commandment with a promise), "that it may go well with you and that you may live long in the land." Fathers, do not provoke your children to anger, but bring them up in the discipline and instruction of the Lord.

Exodus 20:12

"Honor your father and your mother, that your days may be long in the land that the Lord your God is giving you.

Proverbs 13:24

Whoever spares the rod hates his son, but he who loves him is diligent to discipline him.

Proverbs 1:8-9

Hear, my son, your father's instruction, and forsake not your mother's teaching, for they are a graceful garland for your head and pendants for your neck.

Deuteronomy 6:7

You shall teach them diligently to your children, and shall talk of them when you sit in your house, and when you walk by the way, and when you lie down, and when you rise.

Choice

Ephesians 1:4-5

Even as he chose us in him before the foundation of the world, that we should be holy and blameless before him. In love he predestined us for adoption as sons through Jesus Christ, according to the purpose of his will,

Romans 8:28-30

And we know that for those who love God all things work together for good, for those who are called according to his purpose. For those whom he foreknew he also predestined to be conformed to the image of his Son, in order that he might be the firstborn among many brothers. And those whom he predestined he also called, and those whom he called he also justified, and those whom he justified he also glorified.

John 15:16

You did not choose me, but I chose you and appointed you that you should go and bear fruit and that your fruit should abide, so that whatever you ask the Father in my name, he may give it to you.

Proverbs 16:16

How much better to get wisdom than gold! To get understanding is to be chosen rather than silver.

Choose Life

Deuteronomy 30:19-20
I call heaven and earth to witness against you today, that I have set before you life and death, blessing and curse. Therefore choose life, that you and your offspring may live, loving the Lord your God, obeying his voice and holding fast to him, for he is your life and length of days, that you may dwell in the land that the Lord swore to your fathers, to Abraham, to Isaac, and to Jacob, to give them."

Psalm 139:13-16
For you formed my inward parts; you knitted me together in my mother's womb. I praise you, for I am fearfully and wonderfully made. Wonderful are your works; my soul knows it very well. My frame was not hidden from you, when I was being made in secret, intricately woven in the depths of the earth. Your eyes saw my unformed substance; in your book were written, every one of them, the days that were formed for me, when as yet there was none of them.

John 10:10
The thief comes only to steal and kill and destroy. I came that they may have life and have it abundantly.

Jeremiah 1:5
"Before I formed you in the womb I knew you, and before you were born I consecrated you; I appointed you a prophet to the nations."

Romans 6:23
For the wages of sin is death, but the free gift of God is eternal life in Christ Jesus our Lord.

2 Peter 3:9
The Lord is not slow to fulfill his promise as some count slowness, but is patient toward you, not wishing that any should perish, but that all should reach repentance.

John 3:16
"For God so loved the world, that he gave his only Son, that whoever believes in him should not perish but have eternal life.

1 Peter 2:9
But you are a chosen race, a royal priesthood, a holy nation, a people for his own possession, that you may proclaim the excellencies of him who called you out of darkness into his marvelous light.

Joshua 24:15
And if it is evil in your eyes to serve the Lord, choose this day whom you will serve, whether the gods your fathers served in the region beyond the River, or the gods of the Amorites in whose land you dwell. But as for me and my house, we will serve the Lord."

Christ

2 Corinthians 5:17
Therefore, if anyone is in Christ, he is a new creation. The old has passed away; behold, the new has come.

1 John 5:20

And we know that the Son of God has come and has given us understanding, so that we may know him who is true; and we are in him who is true, in his Son Jesus Christ. He is the true God and eternal life.

Romans 6:3

Do you not know that all of us who have been baptized into Christ Jesus were baptized into his death?

Acts 4:12

And there is salvation in no one else, for there is no other name under heaven given among men by which we must be saved."

John 1:14

And the Word became flesh and dwelt among us, and we have seen his glory, glory as of the only Son from the Father, full of grace and truth.

1 John 2:2

He is the propitiation for our sins, and not for ours only but also for the sins of the whole world.

Matthew 28:18-20

And Jesus came and said to them, "All authority in heaven and on earth has been given to me. Go therefore and make disciples of all nations, baptizing them in the name of the Father and of the Son and of the Holy Spirit, teaching them to observe all that I have commanded you. And behold, I am with you always, to the end of the age."

Christ-Centered

Matthew 6:33

But seek first the kingdom of God and his righteousness, and all these things will be added to you.

Proverbs 3:5-6

Trust in the Lord with all your heart, and do not lean on your own understanding. In all your ways acknowledge him, and he will make straight your paths.

Psalm 28:7

The Lord is my strength and my shield; in him my heart trusts, and I am helped; my heart exults, and with my song I give thanks to him.

Romans 12:2

Do not be conformed to this world, but be transformed by the renewal of your mind, that by testing you may discern what is the will of God, what is good and acceptable and perfect.

1 Corinthians 11:1-2

Be imitators of me, as I am of Christ. Now I commend you because you remember me in everything and maintain the traditions even as I delivered them to you.

Romans 8:38-39

For I am sure that neither death nor life, nor angels nor rulers, nor things present nor things to come, nor powers, nor height nor depth, nor anything else in all creation, will be able to separate us from the love of God in Christ Jesus our Lord.

Philippians 4:13

I can do all things through him who strengthens me.

Galatians 2:20

I have been crucified with Christ. It is no longer I who live, but Christ who lives in me. And the life I now live in the flesh I live by faith in the Son of God, who loved me and gave himself for me.

Hebrews 13:8

Jesus Christ is the same yesterday and today and forever.

Philippians 1:20-21

As it is my eager expectation and hope that I will not be at all ashamed, but that with full courage now as always Christ will be honored in my body, whether by life or by death. For to me to live is Christ, and to die is gain.

Romans 10:10

For with the heart one believes and is justified, and with the mouth one confesses and is saved.

Colossians 3:1

If then you have been raised with Christ, seek the things that are above, where Christ is, seated at the right hand of God.

Christians

1 Peter 4:16

Yet if anyone suffers as a Christian, let him not be ashamed, but let him glorify God in that name.

Matthew 6:24

"No one can serve two masters, for either he will hate the one and love the other, or he will be devoted to the one and despise the other. You cannot serve God and money.

Acts 11:26

And when he had found him, he brought him to Antioch. For a whole year they met with the church and taught a great many people. And in Antioch the disciples were first called Christians.

Church

Matthew 16:18

And I tell you, you are Peter, and on this rock I will build my church, and the gates of hell shall not prevail against it.

Acts 20:28

Pay careful attention to yourselves and to all the flock, in which the Holy Spirit has made you overseers, to care for the church of God, which he obtained with his own blood.

Ephesians 2:20-22

Built on the foundation of the apostles and prophets, Christ Jesus himself being the cornerstone, in whom the whole structure, being joined together, grows into a holy temple in the Lord. In him you also are being built together into a dwelling place for God by the Spirit.

Hebrews 10:24-25

And let us consider how to stir up one another to love and good works, not neglecting to meet together, as is the habit of some, but encouraging one another, and all the more as you see the Day drawing near.

Colossians 3:16

Let the word of Christ dwell in you richly, teaching and admonishing one another in all wisdom, singing psalms and hymns and spiritual songs, with thankfulness in your hearts to God.

Romans 12:5

So we, though many, are one body in Christ, and individually members one of another.

Acts 2:47

Praising God and having favor with all the people. And the Lord added to their number day by day those who were being saved.

Ephesians 1:22

And he put all things under his feet and gave him as head over all things to the church,

1 Corinthians 3:17

If anyone destroys God's temple, God will destroy him. For God's temple is holy, and you are that temple.

Romans 16:17

I appeal to you, brothers, to watch out for those who cause divisions and create obstacles contrary to the doctrine that you have been taught; avoid them.

Church Disciple

Titus 3:9-11

But avoid foolish controversies, genealogies, dissensions, and quarrels about the law, for they are unprofitable and worthless. As for a person who stirs up division, after warning him once and then twice, have nothing more to do with him, knowing that such a person is warped and sinful; he is self-condemned.

1 Corinthians 5:11

But now I am writing to you not to associate with anyone who bears the name of brother if he is guilty of sexual immorality or greed, or is an idolater, reviler, drunkard, or swindler—not even to eat with such a one.

Galatians 6:1

Brothers, if anyone is caught in any transgression, you who are spiritual should restore him in a spirit of gentleness. Keep watch on yourself, lest you too be tempted.

2 Thessalonians 3:13-15

As for you, brothers, do not grow weary in doing good. If anyone does not obey what we say in this letter, take note of that person, and have nothing to do with him, that he may be ashamed. Do not regard him as an enemy, but warn him as a brother.

1 Corinthians 5:5

You are to deliver this man to Satan for the destruction of the flesh, so that his spirit may be saved in the day of the Lord.

James 5:19-20

My brothers, if anyone among you wanders from the truth and someone brings him back, let him know that whoever brings back a sinner from his wandering will save his soul from death and will cover a multitude of sins.

2 Thessalonians 3:6

Now we command you, brothers, in the name of our Lord Jesus Christ, that you keep away from any brother who is walking in idleness and not in accord with the tradition that you received from us.

Codependency

Galatians 1:10

For am I now seeking the approval of man, or of God? Or am I trying to please man? If I were still trying to please man, I would not be a servant of Christ.

Galatians 6:1-5

Brothers, if anyone is caught in any transgression, you who are spiritual should restore him in a spirit of gentleness. Keep watch on yourself, lest you too be tempted. Bear one another's burdens, and so fulfill the law of Christ. For if anyone thinks he is something, when he is nothing, he deceives himself. But let each one test his own work, and then his reason to boast will be in himself alone and not in his neighbor. For each will have to bear his own load.

Proverbs 3:5

Trust in the Lord with all your heart, and do not lean on your own understanding.

1 Thessalonians 2:4

But just as we have been approved by God to be entrusted with the gospel, so we speak, not to please man, but to please God who tests our hearts.

Psalm 118:6

The Lord is on my side; I will not fear. What can man do to me?

Comfort

2 Corinthians 1:3-4

Blessed be the God and Father of our Lord Jesus Christ, the Father of mercies and God of all comfort, who comforts us in all our affliction, so that we may be able to comfort those who are in any affliction, with the comfort with which we ourselves are comforted by God.

Psalm 23:4

Even though I walk through the valley of the shadow of death, I will fear no evil, for you are with me; your rod and your staff, they comfort me.

Matthew 11:28-30

Come to me, all who labor and are heavy laden, and I will give you rest. Take my yoke upon you, and learn from me, for I am gentle and lowly in heart, and you will find rest for your souls. For my yoke is easy, and my burden is light."

Psalm 119:76

Let your steadfast love comfort me according to your promise to your servant.

Psalm 119:50

This is my comfort in my affliction, that your promise gives me life.

Matthew 5:4

"Blessed are those who mourn, for they shall be comforted.

Isaiah 49:13

Sing for joy, O heavens, and exult, O earth; break forth, O mountains, into singing! For the Lord has comforted his people and will have compassion on his afflicted.

Commandments

John 14:15

"If you love me, you will keep my commandments.

Matthew 22:36-38

"Teacher, which is the great commandment in the Law?" And he said to him, "You shall love the Lord your God with all your heart and with all your soul and with all your mind. This is the great and first commandment.

2 John 1:6

And this is love, that we walk according to his commandments; this is the commandment, just as you have heard from the beginning, so that you should walk in it.

1 John 2:4-5

Whoever says "I know him" but does not keep his commandments is a liar, and the truth is not in him, but whoever keeps his word, in him truly the love of God is perfected. By this we may know that we are in him:

Commission

Matthew 28:18-20
And Jesus came and said to them, "All authority in heaven and on earth has been given to me. Go therefore and make disciples of all nations, baptizing them in the name of the Father and of the Son and of the Holy Spirit, teaching them to observe all that I have commanded you. And behold, I am with you always, to the end of the age."

Luke 24:47
And that repentance and forgiveness of sins should be proclaimed in his name to all nations, beginning from Jerusalem.

Isaiah 60:19-20
The sun shall be no more your light by day, nor for brightness shall the moon give you light; but the Lord will be your everlasting light, and your God will be your glory. Your sun shall no more go down, nor your moon withdraw itself; for the Lord will be your everlasting light, and your days of mourning shall be ended.

Commitment

Psalm 37:5
Commit your way to the Lord; trust in him, and he will act.

Proverbs 16:3
Commit your work to the Lord, and your plans will be established.

Numbers 30:2
If a man vows a vow to the Lord, or swears an oath to bind himself by a pledge, he shall not break his word. He shall do according to all that proceeds out of his mouth.

Communication

Colossians 4:6
Let your speech always be gracious, seasoned with salt, so that you may know how you ought to answer each person.

Proverbs 15:1-2
A soft answer turns away wrath, but a harsh word stirs up anger. The tongue of the wise commends knowledge, but the mouths of fools pour out folly.

Ephesians 4:25-29
Therefore, having put away falsehood, let each one of you speak the truth with his neighbor, for we are members one of another. Be angry and do not sin; do not let the sun go down on your anger, and give no opportunity to the devil. Let the thief no longer steal, but rather let him labor, doing honest work with his own hands, so that he may have something to share with anyone in need. Let no corrupting talk come out of your mouths, but only such as is good for building up, as fits the occasion, that it may give grace to those who hear.

1 John 3:18

Little children, let us not love in word or talk but in deed and in truth.

Matthew 15:18-20

But what comes out of the mouth proceeds from the heart, and this defiles a person. For out of the heart come evil thoughts, murder, adultery, sexual immorality, theft, false witness, slander. These are what defile a person. But to eat with unwashed hands does not defile anyone."

1 Thessalonians 5:11

Therefore encourage one another and build one another up, just as you are doing.

James 1:19

Know this, my beloved brothers: let every person be quick to hear, slow to speak, slow to anger;

Communion

1 Corinthians 11:26

For as often as you eat this bread and drink the cup, you proclaim the Lord's death until he comes.

Matthew 26:26-28

Now as they were eating, Jesus took bread, and after blessing it broke it and gave it to the disciples, and said, "Take, eat; this is my body." And he took a cup, and when he had given thanks he gave it to them, saying, "Drink of it, all of you, for this is my blood of the covenant, which is poured out for many for the forgiveness of sins.

1 Corinthians 10:16

The cup of blessing that we bless, is it not a participation in the blood of Christ? The bread that we break, is it not a participation in the body of Christ?

Acts 2:42

And they devoted themselves to the apostles' teaching and the fellowship, to the breaking of bread and the prayers.

Luke 22:19-20

And he took bread, and when he had given thanks, he broke it and gave it to them, saying, "This is my body, which is given for you. Do this in remembrance of me." And likewise the cup after they had eaten, saying, "This cup that is poured out for you is the new covenant in my blood.

1 Corinthians 10:17

Because there is one bread, we who are many are one body, for we all partake of the one bread.

Acts 20:7

On the first day of the week, when we were gathered together to break bread, Paul talked with them, intending to depart on the next day, and he prolonged his speech until midnight.

1 Corinthians 11:24

And when he had given thanks, he broke it, and said, "This is my body which is for you. Do this in remembrance of me."

1 Corinthians 11:25

In the same way also he took the cup, after supper, saying, "This cup is the new covenant in my blood. Do this, as often as you drink it, in remembrance of me."

Community

Hebrews 10:24-25

And let us consider how to stir up one another to love and good works, not neglecting to meet together, as is the habit of some, but encouraging one another, and all the more as you see the Day drawing near.

Galatians 6:2

Bear one another's burdens, and so fulfill the law of Christ.

Acts 2:42-47

And they devoted themselves to the apostles' teaching and the fellowship, to the breaking of bread and the prayers. And awe came upon every soul, and many wonders and signs were being done through the apostles. And all who believed were together and had all things in common. And they were selling their possessions and belongings and distributing the proceeds to all, as any had need. And day by day, attending the temple together and breaking bread in their homes, they received their food with glad and generous hearts, praising God and having favor with all the people. And the Lord added to their number day by day those who were being saved.

Ecclesiastes 4:9-12

Two are better than one, because they have a good reward for their toil. For if they fall, one will lift up his fellow. But woe to him who is alone when he falls and has not another to lift him up! Again, if two lie together, they keep warm, but how can one keep warm alone? And though a man might prevail against one who is alone, two will withstand him—a threefold cord is not quickly broken.

Romans 12:3-13

For by the grace given to me I say to everyone among you not to think of himself more highly than he ought to think, but to think with sober judgment, each according to the measure of faith that God has assigned. For as in one body we have many members, and the members do not all have the same function, so we, though many, are one body in Christ, and individually members one of another. Having gifts that differ according to the grace given to us, let us use them: if prophecy, in proportion to our faith; if service, in our serving; the one who teaches, in his teaching; the one who exhorts, in his exhortation; the one who contributes, in generosity; the one who leads, with zeal; the one who does acts of mercy, with cheerfulness. Let love be genuine. Abhor what is evil; hold fast to what is good. Love one another with brotherly affection. Outdo one another in showing honor. Do not be slothful in zeal, be fervent in spirit, serve the Lord. Rejoice in hope, be patient in tribulation, be constant in prayer. Contribute to the needs of the saints and seek to show hospitality

1 Thessalonians 5:14

And we urge you, brothers, admonish the idle, encourage the fainthearted, help the weak, be patient with them all.

Matthew 18:20

For where two or three are gathered in my name, there am I among them."

Community Service

1 Peter 4:10

As each has received a gift, use it to serve one another, as good stewards of God's varied grace:

James 2:14-17

What good is it, my brothers, if someone says he has faith but does not have works? Can that faith save him? If a brother or sister is poorly clothed and lacking in daily food, and one of you says to them, "Go in peace, be warmed and filled," without giving them the things needed for the body, what good is that? So also faith by itself, if it does not have works, is dead.

Galatians 6:10

So then, as we have opportunity, let us do good to everyone, and especially to those who are of the household of faith.

Matthew 25:35

For I was hungry and you gave me food, I was thirsty and you gave me drink, I was a stranger and you welcomed me,

Romans 12:13-17

Contribute to the needs of the saints and seek to show hospitality. Bless those who persecute you; bless and do not curse them. Rejoice with those who rejoice, weep with those who weep. Live in harmony with one another. Do not be haughty, but associate with the lowly. Never be wise in your own sight. Repay no one evil for evil, but give thought to do what is honorable in the sight of all.

Ephesians 2:10

For we are his workmanship, created in Christ Jesus for good works, which God prepared beforehand, that we should walk in them.

Galatians 6:2

Bear one another's burdens, and so fulfill the law of Christ.

Romans 12:20-21

To the contrary, "if your enemy is hungry, feed him; if he is thirsty, give him something to drink; for by so doing you will heap burning coals on his head." Do not be overcome by evil, but overcome evil with good.

Hebrews 10:24-25

And let us consider how to stir up one another to love and good works, not neglecting to meet together, as is the habit of some, but encouraging one another, and all the more as you see the Day drawing near.

Companionship

Ecclesiastes 4:9-12
Two are better than one, because they have a good reward for their toil. For if they fall, one will lift up his fellow. But woe to him who is alone when he falls and has not another to lift him up! Again, if two lie together, they keep warm, but how can one keep warm alone? And though a man might prevail against one who is alone, two will withstand him—a threefold cord is not quickly broken.

Genesis 2:18
Then the Lord God said, "It is not good that the man should be alone; I will make him a helper fit for him."

Genesis 2:24
Therefore a man shall leave his father and his mother and hold fast to his wife, and they shall become one flesh.

Proverbs 18:22
He who finds a wife finds a good thing and obtains favor from the Lord.

Comparing Ourselves

2 Corinthians 10:12
Not that we dare to classify or compare ourselves with some of those who are commending themselves. But when they measure themselves by one another and compare themselves with one another, they are without understanding.

Galatians 1:10
For am I now seeking the approval of man, or of God? Or am I trying to please man? If I were still trying to please man, I would not be a servant of Christ.

Galatians 6:4
But let each one test his own work, and then his reason to boast will be in himself alone and not in his neighbor.

Philippians 2:3
Do nothing from rivalry or conceit, but in humility count others more significant than yourselves.

Compassion

Ephesians 4:32
Be kind to one another, tenderhearted, forgiving one another, as God in Christ forgave you.

Mark 6:34
When he went ashore he saw a great crowd, and he had compassion on them, because they were like sheep without a shepherd. And he began to teach them many things.

Colossians 3:12-13

Put on then, as God's chosen ones, holy and beloved, compassionate hearts, kindness, humility, meekness, and patience, bearing with one another and, if one has a complaint against another, forgiving each other; as the Lord has forgiven you, so you also must forgive.

2 Corinthians 1:3-4

Blessed be the God and Father of our Lord Jesus Christ, the Father of mercies and God of all comfort, who comforts us in all our affliction, so that we may be able to comfort those who are in any affliction, with the comfort with which we ourselves are comforted by God.

Galatians 6:2

Bear one another's burdens, and so fulfill the law of Christ.

Genesis 6:6

And the Lord was sorry that he had made man on the earth, and it grieved him to his heart.

Matthew 14:14

When he went ashore he saw a great crowd, and he had compassion on them and healed their sick.

Matthew 9:36

When he saw the crowds, he had compassion for them, because they were harassed and helpless, like sheep without a shepherd.

1 Peter 3:8

Finally, all of you, have unity of mind, sympathy, brotherly love, a tender heart, and a humble mind.

1 John 3:17

But if anyone has the world's goods and sees his brother in need, yet closes his heart against him, how does God's love abide in him?

<u>Competition</u>

Philippians 2:3-4

Do nothing from rivalry or conceit, but in humility count others more significant than yourselves. Let each of you look not only to his own interests, but also to the interests of others.

1 Corinthians 9:24

Do you not know that in a race all the runners run, but only one receives the prize? So run that you may obtain it.

Colossians 3:23

Whatever you do, work heartily, as for the Lord and not for men,

2 Timothy 2:5

An athlete is not crowned unless he competes according to the rules.

Galatians 6:4

But let each one test his own work, and then his reason to boast will be in himself alone and not in his neighbor.

Colossians 3:17

And whatever you do, in word or deed, do everything in the name of the Lord Jesus, giving thanks to God the Father through him.

Complaining

James 5:9

Do not grumble against one another, brothers, so that you may not be judged; behold, the Judge is standing at the door.

1 Corinthians 10:10

Nor grumble, as some of them did and were destroyed by the Destroyer.

1 Thessalonians 5:18

Give thanks in all circumstances; for this is the will of God in Christ Jesus for you.

1 Peter 4:9

Show hospitality to one another without grumbling.

Ephesians 4:29

Let no corrupting talk come out of your mouths, but only such as is good for building up, as fits the occasion, that it may give grace to those who hear.

Romans 12:2

Do not be conformed to this world, but be transformed by the renewal of your mind, that by testing you may discern what is the will of God, what is good and acceptable and perfect.

Exodus 16:8

And Moses said, "When the Lord gives you in the evening meat to eat and in the morning bread to the full, because the Lord has heard your grumbling that you grumble against him—what are we? Your grumbling is not against us but against the Lord."

Psalm 106:25

They murmured in their tents, and did not obey the voice of the Lord.

Philippians 2:12-16

Therefore, my beloved, as you have always obeyed, so now, not only as in my presence but much more in my absence, work out your own salvation with fear and trembling, for it is God who works in you, both to will and to work for his good pleasure. Do all things without grumbling or questioning, that you may be blameless and innocent, children of God without blemish in the midst of a crooked and twisted generation, among whom you shine as lights in the world, holding fast to the word of life, so that in the day of Christ I may be proud that I did not run in vain or labor in vain.

Compromise

John 14:15
"If you love me, you will keep my commandments.

Hebrews 10:26
For if we go on sinning deliberately after receiving the knowledge of the truth, there no longer remains a sacrifice for sins,

Romans 14:1-23
As for the one who is weak in faith, welcome him, but not to quarrel over opinions. One person believes he may eat anything, while the weak person eats only vegetables. Let not the one who eats despise the one who abstains, and let not the one who abstains pass judgment on the one who eats, for God has welcomed him. Who are you to pass judgment on the servant of another? It is before his own master that he stands or falls. And he will be upheld, for the Lord is able to make him stand. One person esteems one day as better than another, while another esteems all days alike. Each one should be fully convinced in his own mind. ...

Romans 12:1-21
I appeal to you therefore, brothers, by the mercies of God, to present your bodies as a living sacrifice, holy and acceptable to God, which is your spiritual worship. Do not be conformed to this world, but be transformed by the renewal of your mind, that by testing you may discern what is the will of God, what is good and acceptable and perfect. For by the grace given to me I say to everyone among you not to think of himself more highly than he ought to think, but to think with sober judgment, each according to the measure of faith that God has assigned. For as in one body we have many members, and the members do not all have the same function, so we, though many, are one body in Christ, and individually members one of another. ...

James 4:17
So whoever knows the right thing to do and fails to do it, for him it is sin.

Conceit

Jeremiah 9:23
Thus says the Lord: "Let not the wise man boast in his wisdom, let not the mighty man boast in his might, let not the rich man boast in his riches,

Romans 12:16
Live in harmony with one another. Do not be haughty, but associate with the lowly. Never be wise in your own sight.

Proverbs 3:7
Be not wise in your own eyes; fear the Lord, and turn away from evil.

Proverbs 26:12
Do you see a man who is wise in his own eyes? There is more hope for a fool than for him.

Condemnation

Romans 8:1
There is therefore now no condemnation for those who are in Christ Jesus.

John 3:17
For God did not send his Son into the world to condemn the world, but in order that the world might be saved through him.

1 John 3:20
For whenever our heart condemns us, God is greater than our heart, and he knows everything.

Romans 8:34
Who is to condemn? Christ Jesus is the one who died—more than that, who was raised—who is at the right hand of God, who indeed is interceding for us.

John 8:11
She said, "No one, Lord." And Jesus said, "Neither do I condemn you; go, and from now on sin no more."

Confess

1 John 1:9
If we confess our sins, he is faithful and just to forgive us our sins and to cleanse us from all unrighteousness.

James 5:16
Therefore, confess your sins to one another and pray for one another, that you may be healed. The prayer of a righteous person has great power as it is working.

Proverbs 28:13
Whoever conceals his transgressions will not prosper, but he who confesses and forsakes them will obtain mercy.

Philippians 2:11
And every tongue confess that Jesus Christ is Lord, to the glory of God the Father.

Romans 10:9
Because, if you confess with your mouth that Jesus is Lord and believe in your heart that God raised him from the dead, you will be saved.

Confidence

Proverbs 3:26
For the Lord will be your confidence and will keep your foot from being caught.

Isaiah 41:10

Fear not, for I am with you; be not dismayed, for I am your God; I will strengthen you, I will help you, I will uphold you with my righteous right hand.

2 Corinthians 3:5

Not that we are sufficient in ourselves to claim anything as coming from us, but our sufficiency is from God,

1 John 3:20-21

For whenever our heart condemns us, God is greater than our heart, and he knows everything. Beloved, if our heart does not condemn us, we have confidence before God;

Philippians 4:13

I can do all things through him who strengthens me.

Hebrews 13:6

So we can confidently say, "The Lord is my helper; I will not fear; what can man do to me?"

Conflict Resolution

Proverbs 15:1

A soft answer turns away wrath, but a harsh word stirs up anger.

James 4:1-2

What causes quarrels and what causes fights among you? Is it not this, that your passions are at war within you? You desire and do not have, so you murder. You covet and cannot obtain, so you fight and quarrel. You do not have, because you do not ask.

Matthew 18:15-17

"If your brother sins against you, go and tell him his fault, between you and him alone. If he listens to you, you have gained your brother. But if he does not listen, take one or two others along with you, that every charge may be established by the evidence of two or three witnesses. If he refuses to listen to them, tell it to the church. And if he refuses to listen even to the church, let him be to you as a Gentile and a tax collector.

Ephesians 4:26

Be angry and do not sin; do not let the sun go down on your anger,

1 Corinthians 13:4-7

Love is patient and kind; love does not envy or boast; it is not arrogant or rude. It does not insist on its own way; it is not irritable or resentful; it does not rejoice at wrongdoing, but rejoices with the truth. Love bears all things, believes all things, hopes all things, endures all things.

Matthew 5:38-39

"You have heard that it was said, 'An eye for an eye and a tooth for a tooth.' But I say to you, Do not resist the one who is evil. But if anyone slaps you on the right cheek, turn to him the other also.

Matthew 5:9

"Blessed are the peacemakers, for they shall be called sons of God.

Luke 17:3-4

Pay attention to yourselves! If your brother sins, rebuke him, and if he repents, forgive him, and if he sins against you seven times in the day, and turns to you seven times, saying, 'I repent,' you must forgive him."

Conform

Romans 12:1-2

I appeal to you therefore, brothers, by the mercies of God, to present your bodies as a living sacrifice, holy and acceptable to God, which is your spiritual worship. Do not be conformed to this world, but be transformed by the renewal of your mind, that by testing you may discern what is the will of God, what is good and acceptable and perfect.

1 Peter 1:14

As obedient children, do not be conformed to the passions of your former ignorance,

1 John 2:15-17

Do not love the world or the things in the world. If anyone loves the world, the love of the Father is not in him. For all that is in the world—the desires of the flesh and the desires of the eyes and pride in possessions—is not from the Father but is from the world. And the world is passing away along with its desires, but whoever does the will of God abides forever.

Confrontation

Galatians 6:1

Brothers, if anyone is caught in any transgression, you who are spiritual should restore him in a spirit of gentleness. Keep watch on yourself, lest you too be tempted.

Proverbs 29:11

A fool gives full vent to his spirit, but a wise man quietly holds it back.

Galatians 6:1-2

Brothers, if anyone is caught in any transgression, you who are spiritual should restore him in a spirit of gentleness. Keep watch on yourself, lest you too be tempted. Bear one another's burdens, and so fulfill the law of Christ.

2 Timothy 2:24-26

And the Lord's servant must not be quarrelsome but kind to everyone, able to teach, patiently enduring evil, correcting his opponents with gentleness. God may perhaps grant them repentance leading to a knowledge of the truth, and they may come to their senses and escape from the snare of the devil, after being captured by him to do his will.

Proverbs 15:1

A soft answer turns away wrath, but a harsh word stirs up anger.

Colossians 3:13

Bearing with one another and, if one has a complaint against another, forgiving each other; as the Lord has forgiven you, so you also must forgive.

Philippians 2:3-4

Do nothing from rivalry or conceit, but in humility count others more significant than yourselves. Let each of you look not only to his own interests, but also to the interests of others.

Ephesians 4:29

Let no corrupting talk come out of your mouths, but only such as is good for building up, as fits the occasion, that it may give grace to those who hear.

Matthew 18:15-17

"If your brother sins against you, go and tell him his fault, between you and him alone. If he listens to you, you have gained your brother. But if he does not listen, take one or two others along with you, that every charge may be established by the evidence of two or three witnesses. If he refuses to listen to them, tell it to the church. And if he refuses to listen even to the church, let him be to you as a Gentile and a tax collector.

Confusion

1 Corinthians 14:33

For God is not a God of confusion but of peace. As in all the churches of the saints,

2 Timothy 2:7

Think over what I say, for the Lord will give you understanding in everything.

1 John 4:1

Beloved, do not believe every spirit, but test the spirits to see whether they are from God, for many false prophets have gone out into the world.

1 Peter 5:8

Be sober-minded; be watchful. Your adversary the devil prowls around like a roaring lion, seeking someone to devour.

Philippians 4:8-9

Finally, brothers, whatever is true, whatever is honorable, whatever is just, whatever is pure, whatever is lovely, whatever is commendable, if there is any excellence, if there is anything worthy of praise, think about these things. What you have learned and received and heard and seen in me—practice these things, and the God of peace will be with you.

Psalm 119:169

Let my cry come before you, O Lord; give me understanding according to your word!

Psalm 119:34

Give me understanding, that I may keep your law and observe it with my whole heart.

Matthew 7:7

"Ask, and it will be given to you; seek, and you will find; knock, and it will be opened to you.

John 16:13

When the Spirit of truth comes, he will guide you into all the truth, for he will not speak on his own authority, but whatever he hears he will speak, and he will declare to you the things that are to come.

Conscience

Isaiah 30:21

And your ears shall hear a word behind you, saying, "This is the way, walk in it," when you turn to the right or when you turn to the left.

Romans 2:15

They show that the work of the law is written on their hearts, while their conscience also bears witness, and their conflicting thoughts accuse or even excuse them

Hebrews 10:22

Let us draw near with a true heart in full assurance of faith, with our hearts sprinkled clean from an evil conscience and our bodies washed with pure water.

1 Timothy 1:5

The aim of our charge is love that issues from a pure heart and a good conscience and a sincere faith.

1 Timothy 1:19

Holding faith and a good conscience. By rejecting this, some have made shipwreck of their faith,

1 Peter 3:16

Having a good conscience, so that, when you are slandered, those who revile your good behavior in Christ may be put to shame.

Titus 1:15

To the pure, all things are pure, but to the defiled and unbelieving, nothing is pure; but both their minds and their consciences are defiled.

Consequences

Galatians 6:7-8

Do not be deceived: God is not mocked, for whatever one sows, that will he also reap. For the one who sows to his own flesh will from the flesh reap corruption, but the one who sows to the Spirit will from the Spirit reap eternal life.

James 2:10

For whoever keeps the whole law but fails in one point has become accountable for all of it.

Jeremiah 17:9-10

The heart is deceitful above all things, and desperately sick; who can understand it? "I the Lord search the heart and test the mind, to give every man according to his ways, according to the fruit of his deeds."

Hebrews 12:11

For the moment all discipline seems painful rather than pleasant, but later it yields the peaceful fruit of righteousness to those who have been trained by it.

2 Peter 3:9

The Lord is not slow to fulfill his promise as some count slowness, but is patient toward you, not wishing that any should perish, but that all should reach repentance.

Romans 13:4

For he is God's servant for your good. But if you do wrong, be afraid, for he does not bear the sword in vain. For he is the servant of God, an avenger who carries out God's wrath on the wrongdoer

Consistency

1 Corinthians 15:58

Therefore, my beloved brothers, be steadfast, immovable, always abounding in the work of the Lord, knowing that in the Lord your labor is not in vain.

Galatians 6:9

And let us not grow weary of doing good, for in due season we will reap, if we do not give up.

Luke 16:13

No servant can serve two masters, for either he will hate the one and love the other, or he will be devoted to the one and despise the other. You cannot serve God and money."

Matthew 5:37

Let what you say be simply 'Yes' or 'No'; anything more than this comes from evil.

1 Corinthians 10:21

You cannot drink the cup of the Lord and the cup of demons. You cannot partake of the table of the Lord and the table of demons.

Contentment

Hebrews 13:5

Keep your life free from love of money, and be content with what you have, for he has said, "I will never leave you nor forsake you."

Philippians 4:11-12

Not that I am speaking of being in need, for I have learned in whatever situation I am to be content. I know how to be brought low, and I know how to abound. In any and every circumstance, I have learned the secret of facing plenty and hunger, abundance and need.

1 Timothy 6:6-8

Now there is great gain in godliness with contentment, for we brought nothing into the world, and we cannot take anything out of the world. But if we have food and clothing, with these we will be content.

Luke 12:15

And he said to them, "Take care, and be on your guard against all covetousness, for one's life does not consist in the abundance of his possessions."

Matthew 6:33

But seek first the kingdom of God and his righteousness, and all these things will be added to you.

Philippians 4:11

Not that I am speaking of being in need, for I have learned in whatever situation I am to be content.

Controversy

Titus 3:9-11

But avoid foolish controversies, genealogies, dissensions, and quarrels about the law, for they are unprofitable and worthless. As for a person who stirs up division, after warning him once and then twice, have nothing more to do with him, knowing that such a person is warped and sinful; he is self-condemned.

2 Timothy 2:22-26

So flee youthful passions and pursue righteousness, faith, love, and peace, along with those who call on the Lord from a pure heart. Have nothing to do with foolish, ignorant controversies; you know that they breed quarrels. And the Lord's servant must not be quarrelsome but kind to everyone, able to teach, patiently enduring evil, correcting his opponents with gentleness. God may perhaps grant them repentance leading to a knowledge of the truth, and they may come to their senses and escape from the snare of the devil, after being captured by him to do his will.

Coping

Philippians 4:6-7

Do not be anxious about anything, but in everything by prayer and supplication with thanksgiving let your requests be made known to God. And the peace of God, which surpasses all understanding, will guard your hearts and your minds in Christ Jesus.

James 5:16

Therefore, confess your sins to one another and pray for one another, that you may be healed. The prayer of a righteous person has great power as it is working.

1 John 1:9

If we confess our sins, he is faithful and just to forgive us our sins and to cleanse us from all unrighteousness.

Correction

Proverbs 12:1
Whoever loves discipline loves knowledge, but he who hates reproof is stupid.

Hebrews 12:11
For the moment all discipline seems painful rather than pleasant, but later it yields the peaceful fruit of righteousness to those who have been trained by it.

2 Timothy 3:16
All Scripture is breathed out by God and profitable for teaching, for reproof, for correction, and for training in righteousness,

Proverbs 15:32
Whoever ignores instruction despises himself, but he who listens to reproof gains intelligence.

Proverbs 29:15
The rod and reproof give wisdom, but a child left to himself brings shame to his mother.

Proverbs 8:33
Hear instruction and be wise, and do not neglect it.

Counseling

Proverbs 15:22
Without counsel plans fail, but with many advisers they succeed.

Proverbs 13:10
By insolence comes nothing but strife, but with those who take advice is wisdom.

Proverbs 20:5
The purpose in a man's heart is like deep water, but a man of understanding will draw it out.

John 16:13
When the Spirit of truth comes, he will guide you into all the truth, for he will not speak on his own authority, but whatever he hears he will speak, and he will declare to you the things that are to come.

Proverbs 11:14
Where there is no guidance, a people falls, but in an abundance of counselors there is safety.

Proverbs 12:18
There is one whose rash words are like sword thrusts, but the tongue of the wise brings healing.

2 Timothy 3:16-17
All Scripture is breathed out by God and profitable for teaching, for reproof, for correction, and for training in righteousness, that the man of God may be competent, equipped for every good work.

Galatians 6:2

Bear one another's burdens, and so fulfill the law of Christ.

Proverbs 12:15

The way of a fool is right in his own eyes, but a wise man listens to advice.

Proverbs 27:9

Oil and perfume make the heart glad, and the sweetness of a friend comes from his earnest counsel.

Romans 15:14

I myself am satisfied about you, my brothers, that you yourselves are full of goodness, filled with all knowledge and able to instruct one another.

Courage

Joshua 1:9

Have I not commanded you? Be strong and courageous. Do not be frightened, and do not be dismayed, for the Lord your God is with you wherever you go."

Deuteronomy 31:6

Be strong and courageous. Do not fear or be in dread of them, for it is the Lord your God who goes with you. He will not leave you or forsake you."

2 Timothy 1:7

For God gave us a spirit not of fear but of power and love and self-control.

1 Corinthians 16:13

Be watchful, stand firm in the faith, act like men, be strong.

Psalm 27:14

Wait for the Lord; be strong, and let your heart take courage; wait for the Lord!

Proverbs 28:1

The wicked flee when no one pursues, but the righteous are bold as a lion.

Proverbs 3:5-6

Trust in the Lord with all your heart, and do not lean on your own understanding. In all your ways acknowledge him, and he will make straight your paths.

John 16:33

I have said these things to you, that in me you may have peace. In the world you will have tribulation. But take heart; I have overcome the world."

1 Chronicles 28:20

Then David said to Solomon his son, "Be strong and courageous and do it. Do not be afraid and do not be dismayed, for the Lord God, even my God, is with you. He will not leave you or forsake you, until all the work for the service of the house of the Lord is finished.

Psalm 31:24

Be strong, and let your heart take courage, all you who wait for the Lord!

Philippians 4:13

I can do all things through him who strengthens me.

Mark 5:36

But overhearing what they said, Jesus said to the ruler of the synagogue, "Do not fear, only believe."

Courtship

Proverbs 18:22

He who finds a wife finds a good thing and obtains favor from the Lord.

1 Timothy 4:12

Let no one despise you for your youth, but set the believers an example in speech, in conduct, in love, in faith, in purity.

Matthew 19:5

And said, 'Therefore a man shall leave his father and his mother and hold fast to his wife, and the two shall become one flesh'?

1 Corinthians 7:2

But because of the temptation to sexual immorality, each man should have his own wife and each woman her own husband.

Covenant

Jeremiah 31:31-34

"Behold, the days are coming, declares the Lord, when I will make a new covenant with the house of Israel and the house of Judah, not like the covenant that I made with their fathers on the day when I took them by the hand to bring them out of the land of Egypt, my covenant that they broke, though I was their husband, declares the Lord. But this is the covenant that I will make with the house of Israel after those days, declares the Lord: I will put my law within them, and I will write it on their hearts. And I will be their God, and they shall be my people. And no longer shall each one teach his neighbor and each his brother, saying, 'Know the Lord,' for they shall all know me, from the least of them to the greatest, declares the Lord. For I will forgive their iniquity, and I will remember their sin no more."

Psalm 105:8-11

He remembers his covenant forever, the word that he commanded, for a thousand generations, the covenant that he made with Abraham, his sworn promise to Isaac, which he confirmed to Jacob as a statute, to Israel as an everlasting covenant, saying, "To you I will give the land of Canaan as your portion for an inheritance."

Luke 22:20
And likewise the cup after they had eaten, saying, "This cup that is poured out for you is the new covenant in my blood.

Matthew 26:28
For this is my blood of the covenant, which is poured out for many for the forgiveness of sins.

Hebrews 13:20
Now may the God of peace who brought again from the dead our Lord Jesus, the great shepherd of the sheep, by the blood of the eternal covenant,

Psalm 105:8
He remembers his covenant forever, the word that he commanded, for a thousand generations,

Hebrews 9:15
Therefore, he is the mediator of a new covenant, so that those who are called may receive the promised eternal inheritance, since a death has occurred that redeems them from the transgressions committed under the first covenant.

Exodus 34:28
So he was there with the Lord forty days and forty nights. He neither ate bread nor drank water. And he wrote on the tablets the words of the covenant, the Ten Commandments.

Exodus 19:5
Now therefore, if you will indeed obey my voice and keep my covenant, you shall be my treasured possession among all peoples, for all the earth is mine;

Hebrews 8:6
But as it is, Christ has obtained a ministry that is as much more excellent than the old as the covenant he mediates is better, since it is enacted on better promises.

Cremation

Genesis 3:19
By the sweat of your face you shall eat bread, till you return to the ground, for out of it you were taken; for you are dust, and to dust you shall return."

1 Samuel 31:12
All the valiant men arose and went all night and took the body of Saul and the bodies of his sons from the wall of Beth-shan, and they came to Jabesh and burned them there.

1 Corinthians 13:3
If I give away all I have, and if I deliver up my body to be burned, but have not love, I gain nothing.

Crime

Exodus 21:24-25

Eye for eye, tooth for tooth, hand for hand, foot for foot, burn for burn, wound for wound, stripe for stripe.

Romans 12:19

Beloved, never avenge yourselves, but leave it to the wrath of God, for it is written, "Vengeance is mine, I will repay, says the Lord."

Romans 13:1-4

Let every person be subject to the governing authorities. For there is no authority except from God, and those that exist have been instituted by God. Therefore whoever resists the authorities resists what God has appointed, and those who resist will incur judgment. For rulers are not a terror to good conduct, but to bad. Would you have no fear of the one who is in authority? Then do what is good, and you will receive his approval, for he is God's servant for your good. But if you do wrong, be afraid, for he does not bear the sword in vain. For he is the servant of God, an avenger who carries out God's wrath on the wrongdoer.

Matthew 5:38-39

"You have heard that it was said, 'An eye for an eye and a tooth for a tooth.' But I say to you, Do not resist the one who is evil. But if anyone slaps you on the right cheek, turn to him the other also.

Exodus 20:13

"You shall not murder.

Genesis 9:6

"Whoever sheds the blood of man, by man shall his blood be shed, for God made man in his own image.

Crisis

Psalm 34:17-20

When the righteous cry for help, the Lord hears and delivers them out of all their troubles. The Lord is near to the brokenhearted and saves the crushed in spirit. Many are the afflictions of the righteous, but the Lord delivers him out of them all. He keeps all his bones; not one of them is broken.

2 Corinthians 12:9

But he said to me, "My grace is sufficient for you, for my power is made perfect in weakness." Therefore, I will boast all the more gladly of my weaknesses, so that the power of Christ may rest upon me.

Philippians 4:19

And my God will supply every need of yours according to his riches in glory in Christ Jesus.

John 16:33

I have said these things to you, that in me you may have peace. In the world you will have tribulation. But take heart; I have overcome the world."

Matthew 24:13

But the one who endures to the end will be saved.

Jeremiah 29:11

For I know the plans I have for you, declares the Lord, plans for welfare and not for evil, to give you a future and a hope.

James 4:1-2

What causes quarrels and what causes fights among you? Is it not this, that your passions are at war within you? You desire and do not have, so you murder. You covet and cannot obtain, so you fight and quarrel. You do not have, because you do not ask.

Criticism

Matthew 7:1-5

"Judge not, that you be not judged. For with the judgment you pronounce you will be judged, and with the measure you use it will be measured to you. Why do you see the speck that is in your brother's eye, but do not notice the log that is in your own eye? Or how can you say to your brother, 'Let me take the speck out of your eye,' when there is the log in your own eye? You hypocrite, first take the log out of your own eye, and then you will see clearly to take the speck out of your brother's eye.

James 4:11-12

Do not speak evil against one another, brothers. The one who speaks against a brother or judges his brother, speaks evil against the law and judges the law. But if you judge the law, you are not a doer of the law but a judge. There is only one lawgiver and judge, he who is able to save and to destroy. But who are you to judge your neighbor?

James 1:19-20

Know this, my beloved brothers: let every person be quick to hear, slow to speak, slow to anger; for the anger of man does not produce the righteousness of God.

Galatians 6:1

Brothers, if anyone is caught in any transgression, you who are spiritual should restore him in a spirit of gentleness. Keep watch on yourself, lest you too be tempted.

Romans 14:4

Who are you to pass judgment on the servant of another? It is before his own master that he stands or falls. And he will be upheld, for the Lord is able to make him stand.

Ephesians 4:29

Let no corrupting talk come out of your mouths, but only such as is good for building up, as fits the occasion, that it may give grace to those who hear.

2 Timothy 3:16

All Scripture is breathed out by God and profitable for teaching, for reproof, for correction, and for training in righteousness,

Proverbs 27:6

Faithful are the wounds of a friend; profuse are the kisses of an enemy.

Proverbs 15:31
The ear that listens to life-giving reproof will dwell among the wise.

2 Timothy 2:24-25
And the Lord's servant must not be quarrelsome but kind to everyone, able to teach, patiently enduring evil, correcting his opponents with gentleness. God may perhaps grant them repentance leading to a knowledge of the truth,

Proverbs 29:11
A fool gives full vent to his spirit, but a wise man quietly holds it back.

Hebrews 10:24
And let us consider how to stir up one another to love and good works,

Ecclesiastes 5:2
Be not rash with your mouth, nor let your heart be hasty to utter a word before God, for God is in heaven and you are on earth. Therefore, let your words be few.

Proverbs 27:17
Iron sharpens iron, and one man sharpens another.

Proverbs 8:13
The fear of the Lord is hatred of evil. Pride and arrogance and the way of evil and perverted speech I hate.

Galatians 5:15
But if you bite and devour one another, watch out that you are not consumed by one another.

Proverbs 9:8
Do not reprove a scoffer, or he will hate you; reprove a wise man, and he will love you.

Ecclesiastes 5:2-3
Be not rash with your mouth, nor let your heart be hasty to utter a word before God, for God is in heaven and you are on earth. Therefore, let your words be few. For a dream comes with much business, and a fool's voice with many words.

Cross

Mark 8:34
And calling the crowd to him with his disciples, he said to them, "If anyone would come after me, let him deny himself and take up his cross and follow me.

1 Corinthians 1:18
For the word of the cross is folly to those who are perishing, but to us who are being saved it is the power of God.

John 3:16

"For God so loved the world, that he gave his only Son, that whoever believes in him should not perish but have eternal life.

Galatians 2:20

I have been crucified with Christ. It is no longer I who live, but Christ who lives in me. And the life I now live in the flesh I live by faith in the Son of God, who loved me and gave himself for me.

Matthew 10:38

And whoever does not take his cross and follow me is not worthy of me.

Hebrews 12:2

Looking to Jesus, the founder and perfecter of our faith, who for the joy that was set before him endured the cross, despising the shame, and is seated at the right hand of the throne of God.

Luke 14:27

Whoever does not bear his own cross and come after me cannot be my disciple.

Romans 5:8

But God shows his love for us in that while we were still sinners, Christ died for us.

Colossians 2:14

By canceling the record of debt that stood against us with its legal demands. This he set aside, nailing it to the cross.

Crown

James 1:12

Blessed is the man who remains steadfast under trial, for when he has stood the test he will receive the crown of life, which God has promised to those who love him.

1 Peter 5:4

And when the chief Shepherd appears, you will receive the unfading crown of glory.

Revelation 2:10

Do not fear what you are about to suffer. Behold, the devil is about to throw some of you into prison, that you may be tested, and for ten days you will have tribulation. Be faithful unto death, and I will give you the crown of life.

2 Timothy 4:8

Henceforth there is laid up for me the crown of righteousness, which the Lord, the righteous judge, will award to me on that Day, and not only to me but also to all who have loved his appearing.

Revelation 3:11

I am coming soon. Hold fast what you have, so that no one may seize your crown.

Isaiah 62:3
You shall be a crown of beauty in the hand of the Lord, and a royal diadem in the hand of your God.

Crying

Revelation 21:4
He will wipe away every tear from their eyes, and death shall be no more, neither shall there be mourning, nor crying, nor pain anymore, for the former things have passed away."

Isaiah 41:10
Fear not, for I am with you; be not dismayed, for I am your God; I will strengthen you, I will help you, I will uphold you with my righteous right hand.

John 11:35
Jesus wept.

John 14:1-31
"Let not your hearts be troubled. Believe in God; believe also in me. In my Father's house are many rooms. If it were not so, would I have told you that I go to prepare a place for you? And if I go and prepare a place for you, I will come again and will take you to myself, that where I am you may be also. And you know the way to where I am going." Thomas said to him, "Lord, we do not know where you are going. How can we know the way?" ...

1 Corinthians 12:26
If one member suffers, all suffer together; if one member is honored, all rejoice together.

Luke 7:13
And when the Lord saw her, he had compassion on her and said to her, "Do not weep."

Cults

2 John 1:7-11
For many deceivers have gone out into the world, those who do not confess the coming of Jesus Christ in the flesh. Such a one is the deceiver and the antichrist. Watch yourselves, so that you may not lose what we have worked for, but may win a full reward. Everyone who goes on ahead and does not abide in the teaching of Christ, does not have God. Whoever abides in the teaching has both the Father and the Son. If anyone comes to you and does not bring this teaching, do not receive him into your house or give him any greeting, for whoever greets him takes part in his wicked works.

2 Peter 2:1
But false prophets also arose among the people, just as there will be false teachers among you, who will secretly bring in destructive heresies, even denying the Master who bought them, bringing upon themselves swift destruction.

1 John 4:1

Beloved, do not believe every spirit, but test the spirits to see whether they are from God, for many false prophets have gone out into the world.

Cursing

Ephesians 4:29

Let no corrupting talk come out of your mouths, but only such as is good for building up, as fits the occasion, that it may give grace to those who hear.

Ephesians 5:4

Let there be no filthiness nor foolish talk nor crude joking, which are out of place, but instead let there be thanksgiving.

James 1:26

If anyone thinks he is religious and does not bridle his tongue but deceives his heart, this person's religion is worthless.

James 3:8-10

But no human being can tame the tongue. It is a restless evil, full of deadly poison. With it we bless our Lord and Father, and with it we curse people who are made in the likeness of God. From the same mouth come blessing and cursing. My brothers, these things ought not to be so.

Colossians 3:8

But now you must put them all away: anger, wrath, malice, slander, and obscene talk from your mouth.

Luke 6:28

Bless those who curse you, pray for those who abuse you.

Dance

Psalm 149:3

Let them praise his name with dancing, making melody to him with tambourine and lyre!

Ecclesiastes 3:4

A time to weep, and a time to laugh; a time to mourn, and a time to dance;

Psalm 30:11

You have turned for me my mourning into dancing; you have loosed my sackcloth and clothed me with gladness,

Jeremiah 31:13

Then shall the young women rejoice in the dance, and the young men and the old shall be merry. I will turn their mourning into joy; I will comfort them, and give them gladness for sorrow.

2 Samuel 6:14

And David danced before the Lord with all his might. And David was wearing a linen ephod.

Psalm 150:4

Praise him with tambourine and dance; praise him with strings and pipe!

Danger

Proverbs 22:3

The prudent sees danger and hides himself, but the simple go on and suffer for it.

Dating

2 Timothy 2:22

So flee youthful passions and pursue righteousness, faith, love, and peace, along with those who call on the Lord from a pure heart.

1 Corinthians 15:33

Do not be deceived: "Bad company ruins good morals."

1 Corinthians 13:4-7

Love is patient and kind; love does not envy or boast; it is not arrogant or rude. It does not insist on its own way; it is not irritable or resentful; it does not rejoice at wrongdoing, but rejoices with the truth. Love bears all things, believes all things, hopes all things, endures all things.

2 Corinthians 6:14

Do not be unequally yoked with unbelievers. For what partnership has righteousness with lawlessness? Or what fellowship has light with darkness?

1 Corinthians 6:18

Flee from sexual immorality. Every other sin a person commits is outside the body, but the sexually immoral person sins against his own body.

Genesis 2:18

Then the Lord God said, "It is not good that the man should be alone; I will make him a helper fit for him."

Death

Revelation 21:4

He will wipe away every tear from their eyes, and death shall be no more, neither shall there be mourning, nor crying, nor pain anymore, for the former things have passed away."

Romans 14:8

For if we live, we live to the Lord, and if we die, we die to the Lord. So then, whether we live or whether we die, we are the Lord's.

Ecclesiastes 12:7

And the dust returns to the earth as it was, and the spirit returns to God who gave it.

Luke 23:43

And he said to him, "Truly, I say to you, today you will be with me in Paradise."

John 3:16

"For God so loved the world, that he gave his only Son, that whoever believes in him should not perish but have eternal life.

1 Thessalonians 4:14

For since we believe that Jesus died and rose again, even so, through Jesus, God will bring with him those who have fallen asleep.

John 11:26

And everyone who lives and believes in me shall never die. Do you believe this?"

Romans 6:23

For the wages of sin is death, but the free gift of God is eternal life in Christ Jesus our Lord.

Matthew 10:28

And do not fear those who kill the body but cannot kill the soul. Rather fear him who can destroy both soul and body in hell.

Death Penalty

Genesis 9:6
"Whoever sheds the blood of man, by man shall his blood be shed, for God made man in his own image.

Exodus 21:12
"Whoever strikes a man so that he dies shall be put to death.

Romans 12:19
Beloved, never avenge yourselves, but leave it to the wrath of God, for it is written, "Vengeance is mine, I will repay, says the Lord."

Exodus 20:13
"You shall not murder.

Debate

Titus 3:9
But avoid foolish controversies, genealogies, dissensions, and quarrels about the law, for they are unprofitable and worthless.

1 Peter 3:15-16
But in your hearts honor Christ the Lord as holy, always being prepared to make a defense to anyone who asks you for a reason for the hope that is in you; yet do it with gentleness and respect, having a good conscience, so that, when you are slandered, those who revile your good behavior in Christ may be put to shame.

Romans 14:1
As for the one who is weak in faith, welcome him, but not to quarrel over opinions.

Acts 19:9
But when some became stubborn and continued in unbelief, speaking evil of the Way before the congregation, he withdrew from them and took the disciples with him, reasoning daily in the hall of Tyrannus.

2 Timothy 3:16
All Scripture is breathed out by God and profitable for teaching, for reproof, for correction, and for training in righteousness,

2 Timothy 4:2
Preach the word; be ready in season and out of season; reprove, rebuke, and exhort, with complete patience and teaching.

Debt

Proverbs 22:7
The rich rules over the poor, and the borrower is the slave of the lender.

Romans 13:8
Owe no one anything, except to love each other, for the one who loves another has fulfilled the law.

Romans 13:7
Pay to all what is owed to them: taxes to whom taxes are owed, revenue to whom revenue is owed, respect to whom respect is owed, honor to whom honor is owed.

Psalm 37:21
The wicked borrows but does not pay back, but the righteous is generous and gives;

Luke 14:28
For which of you, desiring to build a tower, does not first sit down and count the cost, whether he has enough to complete it?

Proverbs 22:26-27
Be not one of those who give pledges, who put up security for debts. If you have nothing with which to pay, why should your bed be taken from under you?

1 Timothy 5:8
But if anyone does not provide for his relatives, and especially for members of his household, he has denied the faith and is worse than an unbeliever.

Matthew 6:24
"No one can serve two masters, for either he will hate the one and love the other, or he will be devoted to the one and despise the other. You cannot serve God and money.

Deceit

Psalm 101:7
No one who practices deceit shall dwell in my house; no one who utters lies shall continue before my eyes.

Proverbs 20:17
Bread gained by deceit is sweet to a man, but afterward his mouth will be full of gravel.

Proverbs 6:16-19
There are six things that the Lord hates, seven that are an abomination to him: haughty eyes, a lying tongue, and hands that shed innocent blood, a heart that devises wicked plans, feet that make haste to run to evil, a false witness who breathes out lies, and one who sows discord among brothers.

Proverbs 26:24-26

Whoever hates disguises himself with his lips and harbors deceit in his heart; when he speaks graciously, believe him not, for there are seven abominations in his heart; though his hatred be covered with deception, his wickedness will be exposed in the assembly.

Psalm 120:2

Deliver me, O Lord, from lying lips, from a deceitful tongue.

Romans 16:18

For such persons do not serve our Lord Christ, but their own appetites, and by smooth talk and flattery they deceive the hearts of the naive.

Jeremiah 17:9

The heart is deceitful above all things, and desperately sick; who can understand it?

Psalm 36:3

The words of his mouth are trouble and deceit; he has ceased to act wisely and do good.

Colossians 2:8

See to it that no one takes you captive by philosophy and empty deceit, according to human tradition, according to the elemental spirits of the world, and not according to Christ.

Proverbs 19:9

A false witness will not go unpunished, and he who breathes out lies will perish.

Psalm 43:1

Vindicate me, O God, and defend my cause against an ungodly people, from the deceitful and unjust man deliver me!

1 Peter 3:10

For "Whoever desires to love life and see good days, let him keep his tongue from evil and his lips from speaking deceit;

Mark 7:20-23

And he said, "What comes out of a person is what defiles him. For from within, out of the heart of man, come evil thoughts, sexual immorality, theft, murder, adultery, coveting, wickedness, deceit, sensuality, envy, slander, pride, foolishness. All these evil things come from within, and they defile a person."

Deceivers

Matthew 7:15

"Beware of false prophets, who come to you in sheep's clothing but inwardly are ravenous wolves.

2 John 1:7

For many deceivers have gone out into the world, those who do not confess the coming of Jesus Christ in the flesh. Such a one is the deceiver and the antichrist.

John 8:44

You are of your father the devil, and your will is to do your father's desires. He was a murderer from the beginning, and has nothing to do with the truth, because there is no truth in him. When he lies, he speaks out of his own character, for he is a liar and the father of lies.

2 Timothy 3:5

Having the appearance of godliness, but denying its power. Avoid such people.

1 Timothy 4:1

Now the Spirit expressly says that in later times some will depart from the faith by devoting themselves to deceitful spirits and teachings of demons,

Deception

Galatians 6:7-8

Do not be deceived: God is not mocked, for whatever one sows, that will he also reap. For the one who sows to his own flesh will from the flesh reap corruption, but the one who sows to the Spirit will from the Spirit reap eternal life.

Proverbs 10:9

Whoever walks in integrity walks securely, but he who makes his ways crooked will be found out.

Proverbs 12:22

Lying lips are an abomination to the Lord, but those who act faithfully are his delight.

Psalm 52:2

Your tongue plots destruction, like a sharp razor, you worker of deceit.

Romans 12:2

Do not be conformed to this world, but be transformed by the renewal of your mind, that by testing you may discern what is the will of God, what is good and acceptable and perfect.

James 1:22

But be doers of the word, and not hearers only, deceiving yourselves.

Decision Making

Proverbs 3:5-6

Trust in the Lord with all your heart, and do not lean on your own understanding. In all your ways acknowledge him, and he will make straight your paths.

James 1:5

If any of you lacks wisdom, let him ask God, who gives generously to all without reproach, and it will be given him.

Jeremiah 29:11

For I know the plans I have for you, declares the Lord, plans for welfare and not for evil, to give you a future and a hope.

Philippians 4:6-7

Do not be anxious about anything, but in everything by prayer and supplication with thanksgiving let your requests be made known to God. And the peace of God, which surpasses all understanding, will guard your hearts and your minds in Christ Jesus.

Isaiah 30:21

And your ears shall hear a word behind you, saying, "This is the way, walk in it," when you turn to the right or when you turn to the left.

Proverbs 11:14

Where there is no guidance, a people falls, but in an abundance of counselors there is safety.

1 John 5:14

And this is the confidence that we have toward him, that if we ask anything according to his will he hears us.

Jeremiah 33:3

Call to me and I will answer you, and will tell you great and hidden things that you have not known.

Dedication

Romans 12:1-2

I appeal to you therefore, brothers, by the mercies of God, to present your bodies as a living sacrifice, holy and acceptable to God, which is your spiritual worship. Do not be conformed to this world, but be transformed by the renewal of your mind, that by testing you may discern what is the will of God, what is good and acceptable and perfect.

Colossians 3:17

And whatever you do, in word or deed, do everything in the name of the Lord Jesus, giving thanks to God the Father through him.

1 Peter 1:13

Therefore, preparing your minds for action, and being sober-minded, set your hope fully on the grace that will be brought to you at the revelation of Jesus Christ.

Defiance

James 4:17

So whoever knows the right thing to do and fails to do it, for him it is sin.

Colossians 3:20

Children, obey your parents in everything, for this pleases the Lord.

James 1:14
But each person is tempted when he is lured and enticed by his own desire.

Deliverance

Psalm 34:17
When the righteous cry for help, the Lord hears and delivers them out of all their troubles.

Psalm 107:6
Then they cried to the Lord in their trouble, and he delivered them from their distress.

Psalm 50:15
And call upon me in the day of trouble; I will deliver you, and you shall glorify me."

2 Samuel 22:2
He said, "The Lord is my rock and my fortress and my deliverer,

Psalm 34:4
I sought the Lord, and he answered me and delivered me from all my fears.

James 5:16
Therefore, confess your sins to one another and pray for one another, that you may be healed. The prayer of a righteous person has great power as it is working.

Galatians 5:1
For freedom Christ has set us free; stand firm therefore, and do not submit again to a yoke of slavery.

John 8:32
And you will know the truth, and the truth will set you free."

Delusion

1 Peter 5:8
Be sober-minded; be watchful. Your adversary the devil prowls around like a roaring lion, seeking someone to devour.

Demons

James 2:19
You believe that God is one; you do well. Even the demons believe—and shudder!

Matthew 12:43-45
"When the unclean spirit has gone out of a person, it passes through waterless places seeking rest, but finds none. Then it says, 'I will return to my house from which I came.' And when it comes, it finds the house empty, swept, and put in order. Then it goes and brings with it seven other spirits more evil than

itself, and they enter and dwell there, and the last state of that person is worse than the first. So also will it be with this evil generation."

2 Peter 2:4

For if God did not spare angels when they sinned, but cast them into hell and committed them to chains of gloomy darkness to be kept until the judgment;

1 Peter 5:8

Be sober-minded; be watchful. Your adversary the devil prowls around like a roaring lion, seeking someone to devour.

James 4:7

Submit yourselves therefore to God. Resist the devil, and he will flee from you.

Luke 8:2

And also some women who had been healed of evil spirits and infirmities: Mary, called Magdalene, from whom seven demons had gone out,

Mark 9:29

And he said to them, "This kind cannot be driven out by anything but prayer."

Mark 3:11

And whenever the unclean spirits saw him, they fell down before him and cried out, "You are the Son of God."

Matthew 10:1

And he called to him his twelve disciples and gave them authority over unclean spirits, to cast them out, and to heal every disease and every affliction.

Jude 1:6

And the angels who did not stay within their own position of authority, but left their proper dwelling, he has kept in eternal chains under gloomy darkness until the judgment of the great day.

Denials

1 Timothy 5:8

But if anyone does not provide for his relatives, and especially for members of his household, he has denied the faith and is worse than an unbeliever.

Proverbs 25:26

Like a muddied spring or a polluted fountain is a righteous man who gives way before the wicked.

Luke 9:23

And he said to all, "If anyone would come after me, let him deny himself and take up his cross daily and follow me.

John 14:26

But the Helper, the Holy Spirit, whom the Father will send in my name, he will teach you all things and bring to your remembrance all that I have said to you.

John 14:15

"If you love me, you will keep my commandments.

Deuteronomy 28:47-48

Because you did not serve the Lord your God with joyfulness and gladness of heart, because of the abundance of all things, therefore you shall serve your enemies whom the Lord will send against you, in hunger and thirst, in nakedness, and lacking everything. And he will put a yoke of iron on your neck until he has destroyed you.

Romans 13:4

For he is God's servant for your good. But if you do wrong, be afraid, for he does not bear the sword in vain. For he is the servant of God, an avenger who carries out God's wrath on the wrongdoer.

Denominations

1 Corinthians 1:10

I appeal to you, brothers, by the name of our Lord Jesus Christ, that all of you agree, and that there be no divisions among you, but that you be united in the same mind and the same judgment.

1 Corinthians 1:12-13

What I mean is that each one of you says, "I follow Paul," or "I follow Apollos," or "I follow Cephas," or "I follow Christ." Is Christ divided? Was Paul crucified for you? Or were you baptized in the name of Paul?

Romans 16:17

I appeal to you, brothers, to watch out for those who cause divisions and create obstacles contrary to the doctrine that you have been taught; avoid them.

Ephesians 4:4-5

There is one body and one Spirit—just as you were called to the one hope that belongs to your call— one Lord, one faith, one baptism,

2 John 1:9

Everyone who goes on ahead and does not abide in the teaching of Christ, does not have God. Whoever abides in the teaching has both the Father and the Son.

Denying God

Matthew 10:33

But whoever denies me before men, I also will deny before my Father who is in heaven.

Matthew 10:32

So everyone who acknowledges me before men, I also will acknowledge before my Father who is in heaven,

2 Peter 2:1

But false prophets also arose among the people, just as there will be false teachers among you, who will secretly bring in destructive heresies, even denying the Master who bought them, bringing upon themselves swift destruction.

Jeremiah 17:10

"I the Lord search the heart and test the mind, to give every man according to his ways, according to the fruit of his deeds."

Ephesians 6:11

Put on the whole armor of God, that you may be able to stand against the schemes of the devil.

Romans 10:13

For "everyone who calls on the name of the Lord will be saved."

Dependence

John 15:5

I am the vine; you are the branches. Whoever abides in me and I in him, he it is that bears much fruit, for apart from me you can do nothing.

Psalm 40:3-4

He put a new song in my mouth, a song of praise to our God. Many will see and fear, and put their trust in the Lord. Blessed is the man who makes the Lord his trust, who does not turn to the proud, to those who go astray after a lie!

1 Thessalonians 4:9-12

Now concerning brotherly love you have no need for anyone to write to you, for you yourselves have been taught by God to love one another, for that indeed is what you are doing to all the brothers throughout Macedonia. But we urge you, brothers, to do this more and more, and to aspire to live quietly, and to mind your own affairs, and to work with your hands, as we instructed you, so that you may walk properly before outsiders and be dependent on no one.

John 6:47-50

Truly, truly, I say to you, whoever believes has eternal life. I am the bread of life. Your fathers ate the manna in the wilderness, and they died. This is the bread that comes down from heaven, so that one may eat of it and not die.

2 Corinthians 1:8-9

For we do not want you to be ignorant, brothers, of the affliction we experienced in Asia. For we were so utterly burdened beyond our strength that we despaired of life itself. Indeed, we felt that we had received the sentence of death. But that was to make us rely not on ourselves but on God who raises the dead.

Depression

Psalm 34:17-18
When the righteous cry for help, the Lord hears and delivers them out of all their troubles. The Lord is near to the brokenhearted and saves the crushed in spirit.

Isaiah 41:10
Fear not, for I am with you; be not dismayed, for I am your God; I will strengthen you, I will help you, I will uphold you with my righteous right hand.

1 Peter 5:7
Casting all your anxieties on him, because he cares for you.

Matthew 11:28
Come to me, all who labor and are heavy laden, and I will give you rest.

Jeremiah 29:11
For I know the plans I have for you, declares the Lord, plans for welfare and not for evil, to give you a future and a hope.

Proverbs 3:5-6
Trust in the Lord with all your heart, and do not lean on your own understanding. In all your ways acknowledge him, and he will make straight your paths.

Psalm 143:7-8
Answer me quickly, O Lord! My spirit fails! Hide not your face from me, lest I be like those who go down to the pit. Let me hear in the morning of your steadfast love, for in you I trust. Make me know the way I should go, for to you I lift up my soul.

Psalm 30:5
For his anger is but for a moment, and his favor is for a lifetime. Weeping may tarry for the night, but joy comes with the morning.

Philippians 4:6-7
Do not be anxious about anything, but in everything by prayer and supplication with thanksgiving let your requests be made known to God. And the peace of God, which surpasses all understanding, will guard your hearts and your minds in Christ Jesus.

Psalm 23:4
Even though I walk through the valley of the shadow of death, I will fear no evil, for you are with me; your rod and your staff, they comfort me.

Proverbs 12:25
Anxiety in a man's heart weighs him down, but a good word makes him glad.

Psalm 9:9
The Lord is a stronghold for the oppressed, a stronghold in times of trouble.

Psalm 34:18

The Lord is near to the brokenhearted and saves the crushed in spirit.

Romans 12:2

Do not be conformed to this world, but be transformed by the renewal of your mind, that by testing you may discern what is the will of God, what is good and acceptable and perfect.

2 Timothy 1:7

For God gave us a spirit not of fear but of power and love and self-control.

Revelation 21:4

He will wipe away every tear from their eyes, and death shall be no more, neither shall there be mourning, nor crying, nor pain anymore, for the former things have passed away."

John 10:10

The thief comes only to steal and kill and destroy. I came that they may have life and have it abundantly.

Isaiah 40:31

But they who wait for the Lord shall renew their strength; they shall mount up with wings like eagles; they shall run and not be weary; they shall walk and not faint.

Deuteronomy 31:8

It is the Lord who goes before you. He will be with you; he will not leave you or forsake you. Do not fear or be dismayed."

Psalm 3:3

But you, O Lord, are a shield about me, my glory, and the lifter of my head.

Psalm 30:11

You have turned for me my mourning into dancing; you have loosed my sackcloth and clothed me with gladness,

Isaiah 26:3

You keep him in perfect peace whose mind is stayed on you, because he trusts in you.

Desertion

1 Corinthians 7:15

But if the unbelieving partner separates, let it be so. In such cases the brother or sister is not enslaved. God has called you to peace.

2 Timothy 4:3-4

For the time is coming when people will not endure sound teaching, but having itching ears they will accumulate for themselves teachers to suit their own passions, and will turn away from listening to the truth and wander off into myths.

Acts 17:30

The times of ignorance God overlooked, but now he commands all people everywhere to repent,

1 John 1:9

If we confess our sins, he is faithful and just to forgive us our sins and to cleanse us from all unrighteousness.

Malachi 2:16

"For the man who does not love his wife but divorces her, says the Lord, the God of Israel, covers his garment with violence, says the Lord of hosts. So guard yourselves in your spirit, and do not be faithless."

2 Peter 3:15-16

And count the patience of our Lord as salvation, just as our beloved brother Paul also wrote to you according to the wisdom given him, as he does in all his letters when he speaks in them of these matters. There are some things in them that are hard to understand, which the ignorant and unstable twist to their own destruction, as they do the other Scriptures.

1 Timothy 5:8

But if anyone does not provide for his relatives, and especially for members of his household, he has denied the faith and is worse than an unbeliever.

1 Corinthians 7:11

(but if she does, she should remain unmarried or else be reconciled to her husband), and the husband should not divorce his wife.

Desire

Psalm 37:4

Delight yourself in the Lord, and he will give you the desires of your heart.

Proverbs 10:24

What the wicked dreads will come upon him, but the desire of the righteous will be granted.

Jeremiah 29:13

You will seek me and find me, when you seek me with all your heart.

Matthew 5:6

"Blessed are those who hunger and thirst for righteousness, for they shall be satisfied.

Proverbs 2:3-5

Yes, if you call out for insight and raise your voice for understanding, if you seek it like silver and search for it as for hidden treasures, then you will understand the fear of the Lord and find the knowledge of God.

1 Corinthians 10:13

No temptation has overtaken you that is not common to man. God is faithful, and he will not let you be tempted beyond your ability, but with the temptation he will also provide the way of escape, that you may be able to endure it.

Despair

Psalm 34:17-20
When the righteous cry for help, the Lord hears and delivers them out of all their troubles. The Lord is near to the brokenhearted and saves the crushed in spirit. Many are the afflictions of the righteous, but the Lord delivers him out of them all. He keeps all his bones; not one of them is broken.

2 Corinthians 4:8-9
We are afflicted in every way, but not crushed; perplexed, but not driven to despair; persecuted, but not forsaken; struck down, but not destroyed;

1 Peter 5:7
Casting all your anxieties on him, because he cares for you.

1 Corinthians 10:13
No temptation has overtaken you that is not common to man. God is faithful, and he will not let you be tempted beyond your ability, but with the temptation he will also provide the way of escape, that you may be able to endure it.

Romans 15:13
May the God of hope fill you with all joy and peace in believing, so that by the power of the Holy Spirit you may abound in hope.

Philippians 4:19
And my God will supply every need of yours according to his riches in glory in Christ Jesus.

Revelation 21:4
He will wipe away every tear from their eyes, and death shall be no more, neither shall there be mourning, nor crying, nor pain anymore, for the former things have passed away."

Philippians 4:6-7
Do not be anxious about anything, but in everything by prayer and supplication with thanksgiving let your requests be made known to God. And the peace of God, which surpasses all understanding, will guard your hearts and your minds in Christ Jesus.

2 Corinthians 12:9
But he said to me, "My grace is sufficient for you, for my power is made perfect in weakness." Therefore, I will boast all the more gladly of my weaknesses, so that the power of Christ may rest upon me.

Destiny

Jeremiah 29:11
For I know the plans I have for you, declares the Lord, plans for welfare and not for evil, to give you a future and a hope.

Habakkuk 2:3

For still the vision awaits its appointed time; it hastens to the end—it will not lie. If it seems slow, wait for it; it will surely come; it will not delay.

Psalm 138:8

The Lord will fulfill his purpose for me; your steadfast love, O Lord, endures forever. Do not forsake the work of your hands.

John 16:33

I have said these things to you, that in me you may have peace. In the world you will have tribulation. But take heart; I have overcome the world."

Isaiah 55:11

So shall my word be that goes out from my mouth; it shall not return to me empty, but it shall accomplish that which I purpose, and shall succeed in the thing for which I sent it.

Romans 8:29

For those whom he foreknew he also predestined to be conformed to the image of his Son, in order that he might be the firstborn among many brothers.

Romans 8:28

And we know that for those who love God all things work together for good, for those who are called according to his purpose.

Proverbs 16:3

Commit your work to the Lord, and your plans will be established.

Jeremiah 1:5

"Before I formed you in the womb I knew you, and before you were born I consecrated you; I appointed you a prophet to the nations."

Devil

1 Peter 5:8

Be sober-minded; be watchful. Your adversary the devil prowls around like a roaring lion, seeking someone to devour.

James 4:7

Submit yourselves therefore to God. Resist the devil, and he will flee from you.

2 Corinthians 11:14

And no wonder, for even Satan disguises himself as an angel of light.

1 John 5:18-19

We know that everyone who has been born of God does not keep on sinning, but he who was born of God protects him, and the evil one does not touch him. We know that we are from God, and the whole world lies in the power of the evil one.

Revelation 12:12

Therefore, rejoice, O heavens and you who dwell in them! But woe to you, O earth and sea, for the devil has come down to you in great wrath, because he knows that his time is short!"

John 8:44

You are of your father the devil, and your will is to do your father's desires. He was a murderer from the beginning, and has nothing to do with the truth, because there is no truth in him. When he lies, he speaks out of his own character, for he is a liar and the father of lies.

Ephesians 6:11-12

Put on the whole armor of God, that you may be able to stand against the schemes of the devil. For we do not wrestle against flesh and blood, but against the rulers, against the authorities, against the cosmic powers over this present darkness, against the spiritual forces of evil in the heavenly places.

2 Corinthians 4:4

In their case the god of this world has blinded the minds of the unbelievers, to keep them from seeing the light of the gospel of the glory of Christ, who is the image of God.

John 10:10

The thief comes only to steal and kill and destroy. I came that they may have life and have it abundantly.

Devotion to God

Colossians 3:17

And whatever you do, in word or deed, do everything in the name of the Lord Jesus, giving thanks to God the Father through him.

Philippians 4:13

I can do all things through him who strengthens me.

Romans 12:1

I appeal to you therefore, brothers, by the mercies of God, to present your bodies as a living sacrifice, holy and acceptable to God, which is your spiritual worship.

Acts 20:35

In all things I have shown you that by working hard in this way we must help the weak and remember the words of the Lord Jesus, how he himself said, 'It is more blessed to give than to receive.'"

Luke 16:13

No servant can serve two masters, for either he will hate the one and love the other, or he will be devoted to the one and despise the other. You cannot serve God and money."

Philippians 4:8-9

Finally, brothers, whatever is true, whatever is honorable, whatever is just, whatever is pure, whatever is lovely, whatever is commendable, if there is any excellence, if there is anything worthy of praise, think about these things. What you have learned and received and heard and seen in me—practice these things, and the God of peace will be with you.

Differences

Galatians 3:28
There is neither Jew nor Greek, there is neither slave nor free, there is no male and female, for you are all one in Christ Jesus.

Galatians 3:26
For in Christ Jesus you are all sons of God, through faith.

John 13:34-35
A new commandment I give to you, that you love one another: just as I have loved you, you also are to love one another. By this all people will know that you are my disciples, if you have love for one another.

Different Races

Galatians 3:28
There is neither Jew nor Greek, there is neither slave nor free, there is no male and female, for you are all one in Christ Jesus.

Acts 10:35
But in every nation anyone who fears him and does what is right is acceptable to him.

Revelation 7:9-10
After this I looked, and behold, a great multitude that no one could number, from every nation, from all tribes and peoples and languages, standing before the throne and before the Lamb, clothed in white robes, with palm branches in their hands, and crying out with a loud voice, "Salvation belongs to our God who sits on the throne, and to the Lamb!"

Difficult Times

Philippians 4:6-7
Do not be anxious about anything, but in everything by prayer and supplication with thanksgiving let your requests be made known to God. And the peace of God, which surpasses all understanding, will guard your hearts and your minds in Christ Jesus.

Isaiah 41:10
Fear not, for I am with you; be not dismayed, for I am your God; I will strengthen you, I will help you, I will uphold you with my righteous right hand.

John 16:33
I have said these things to you, that in me you may have peace. In the world you will have tribulation. But take heart; I have overcome the world."

1 Peter 5:7

Casting all your anxieties on him, because he cares for you.

Romans 8:18

For I consider that the sufferings of this present time are not worth comparing with the glory that is to be revealed to us.

Jeremiah 29:11-13

For I know the plans I have for you, declares the Lord, plans for welfare and not for evil, to give you a future and a hope. Then you will call upon me and come and pray to me, and I will hear you. You will seek me and find me, when you seek me with all your heart.

Philippians 4:13

I can do all things through him who strengthens me.

James 1:2-4

Count it all joy, my brothers, when you meet trials of various kinds, for you know that the testing of your faith produces steadfastness. And let steadfastness have its full effect, that you may be perfect and complete, lacking in nothing.

James 1:3-4

For you know that the testing of your faith produces steadfastness. And let steadfastness have its full effect, that you may be perfect and complete, lacking in nothing.

Psalm 9:9-10

The Lord is a stronghold for the oppressed, a stronghold in times of trouble. And those who know your name put their trust in you, for you, O Lord, have not forsaken those who seek you.

2 Corinthians 12:8-10

Three times I pleaded with the Lord about this, that it should leave me. But he said to me, "My grace is sufficient for you, for my power is made perfect in weakness." Therefore, I will boast all the more gladly of my weaknesses, so that the power of Christ may rest upon me. For the sake of Christ, then, I am content with weaknesses, insults, hardships, persecutions, and calamities. For when I am weak, then I am strong.

1 Peter 1:6-7

In this you rejoice, though now for a little while, if necessary, you have been grieved by various trials, so that the tested genuineness of your faith—more precious than gold that perishes though it is tested by fire—may be found to result in praise and glory and honor at the revelation of Jesus Christ.

Disaster

1 Timothy 5:8

But if anyone does not provide for his relatives, and especially for members of his household, he has denied the faith and is worse than an unbeliever.

Romans 12:19

Beloved, never avenge yourselves, but leave it to the wrath of God, for it is written, "Vengeance is mine, I will repay, says the Lord."

Deuteronomy 28:47-48

Because you did not serve the Lord your God with joyfulness and gladness of heart, because of the abundance of all things, therefore you shall serve your enemies whom the Lord will send against you, in hunger and thirst, in nakedness, and lacking everything. And he will put a yoke of iron on your neck until he has destroyed you.

Discernment

1 John 4:1

Beloved, do not believe every spirit, but test the spirits to see whether they are from God, for many false prophets have gone out into the world.

Philippians 1:9-10

And it is my prayer that your love may abound more and more, with knowledge and all discernment, so that you may approve what is excellent, and so be pure and blameless for the day of Christ,

Hebrews 5:14

But solid food is for the mature, for those who have their powers of discernment trained by constant practice to distinguish good from evil.

Hebrews 4:12

For the word of God is living and active, sharper than any two-edged sword, piercing to the division of soul and of spirit, of joints and of marrow, and discerning the thoughts and intentions of the heart.

1 Kings 3:9

Give your servant therefore an understanding mind to govern your people, that I may discern between good and evil, for who is able to govern this your great people?"

Romans 12:2

Do not be conformed to this world, but be transformed by the renewal of your mind, that by testing you may discern what is the will of God, what is good and acceptable and perfect.

James 1:5

If any of you lacks wisdom, let him ask God, who gives generously to all without reproach, and it will be given him.

1 Corinthians 2:14

The natural person does not accept the things of the Spirit of God, for they are folly to him, and he is not able to understand them because they are spiritually discerned.

John 7:24

Do not judge by appearances, but judge with right judgment."

1 Corinthians 14:33

For God is not a God of confusion but of peace. As in all the churches of the saints,

2 Corinthians 11:13-15

For such men are false apostles, deceitful workmen, disguising themselves as apostles of Christ. And no wonder, for even Satan disguises himself as an angel of light. So, it is no surprise if his servants, also, disguise themselves as servants of righteousness. Their end will correspond to their deeds.

1 Thessalonians 5:21

But test everything; hold fast what is good.

Discipleship

Matthew 28:18-20

And Jesus came and said to them, "All authority in heaven and on earth has been given to me. Go therefore and make disciples of all nations, baptizing them in the name of the Father and of the Son and of the Holy Spirit, teaching them to observe all that I have commanded you. And behold, I am with you always, to the end of the age."

Matthew 5:14-16

"You are the light of the world. A city set on a hill cannot be hidden. Nor do people light a lamp and put it under a basket, but on a stand, and it gives light to all in the house. In the same way, let your light shine before others, so that they may see your good works and give glory to your Father who is in heaven.

Luke 14:27

Whoever does not bear his own cross and come after me cannot be my disciple.

2 Timothy 2:2

And what you have heard from me in the presence of many witnesses entrust to faithful men who will be able to teach others also.

Luke 9:23

And he said to all, "If anyone would come after me, let him deny himself and take up his cross daily and follow me.

Acts 2:42

And they devoted themselves to the apostles' teaching and the fellowship, to the breaking of bread and the prayers.

John 8:31-32

So Jesus said to the Jews who had believed in him, "If you abide in my word, you are truly my disciples, and you will know the truth, and the truth will set you free."

Luke 6:40

A disciple is not above his teacher, but everyone when he is fully trained will be like his teacher.

John 13:34-35

A new commandment I give to you, that you love one another: just as I have loved you, you also are to love one another. By this all people will know that you are my disciples, if you have love for one another."

Matthew 16:24-25
Then Jesus told his disciples, "If anyone would come after me, let him deny himself and take up his cross and follow me. For whoever would save his life will lose it, but whoever loses his life for my sake will find it.

Luke 14:26
"If anyone comes to me and does not hate his own father and mother and wife and children and brothers and sisters, yes, and even his own life, he cannot be my disciple.

Discipline

Hebrews 12:11
For the moment all discipline seems painful rather than pleasant, but later it yields the peaceful fruit of righteousness to those who have been trained by it.

Proverbs 12:1
Whoever loves discipline loves knowledge, but he who hates reproof is stupid.

Proverbs 13:24
Whoever spares the rod hates his son, but he who loves him is diligent to discipline him.

1 Corinthians 9:27
But I discipline my body and keep it under control, lest after preaching to others I myself should be disqualified.

Revelation 3:19
Those whom I love, I reprove and discipline, so be zealous and repent.

Proverbs 3:11-12
My son, do not despise the Lord's discipline or be weary of his reproof, for the Lord reproves him whom he loves, as a father the son in whom he delights.

Proverbs 23:13
Do not withhold discipline from a child; if you strike him with a rod, he will not die.

Hebrews 12:5-6
And have you forgotten the exhortation that addresses you as sons? "My son, do not regard lightly the discipline of the Lord, nor be weary when reproved by him. For the Lord disciplines the one he loves, and chastises every son whom he receives."

Proverbs 29:15
The rod and reproof give wisdom, but a child left to himself brings shame to his mother.

Proverbs 29:17
Discipline your son, and he will give you rest; he will give delight to your heart.

Titus 1:8
But hospitable, a lover of good, self-controlled, upright, holy, and disciplined.

Discouragement

Jeremiah 29:11
For I know the plans I have for you, declares the Lord, plans for welfare and not for evil, to give you a future and a hope.

Proverbs 3:5-6
Trust in the Lord with all your heart, and do not lean on your own understanding. In all your ways acknowledge him, and he will make straight your paths.

Joshua 1:9
Have I not commanded you? Be strong and courageous. Do not be frightened, and do not be dismayed, for the Lord your God is with you wherever you go."

2 Corinthians 12:9
But he said to me, "My grace is sufficient for you, for my power is made perfect in weakness." Therefore, I will boast all the more gladly of my weaknesses, so that the power of Christ may rest upon me.

John 16:33
I have said these things to you, that in me you may have peace. In the world you will have tribulation. But take heart; I have overcome the world."

1 Peter 5:7
Casting all your anxieties on him, because he cares for you.

Romans 8:26
Likewise the Spirit helps us in our weakness. For we do not know what to pray for as we ought, but the Spirit himself intercedes for us with groanings too deep for words.

Romans 8:31
What then shall we say to these things? If God is for us, who can be against us?

1 Corinthians 15:58
Therefore, my beloved brothers, be steadfast, immovable, always abounding in the work of the Lord, knowing that in the Lord your labor is not in vain.

Romans 15:13
May the God of hope fill you with all joy and peace in believing, so that by the power of the Holy Spirit you may abound in hope.

James 4:7
Submit yourselves therefore to God. Resist the devil, and he will flee from you.

Discrimination

James 2:2-4
For if a man wearing a gold ring and fine clothing comes into your assembly, and a poor man in shabby clothing also comes in, and if you pay attention to the one who wears the fine clothing and say, "You sit here in a good place," while you say to the poor man, "You stand over there," or, "Sit down at my feet," have you not then made distinctions among yourselves and become judges with evil thoughts?

Galatians 5:14
For the whole law is fulfilled in one word: "You shall love your neighbor as yourself."

Galatians 3:27-29
For as many of you as were baptized into Christ have put on Christ. There is neither Jew nor Greek, there is neither slave nor free, there is no male and female, for you are all one in Christ Jesus. And if you are Christ's, then you are Abraham's offspring, heirs according to promise.

Matthew 5:44
But I say to you, Love your enemies and pray for those who persecute you,

Romans 2:11
For God shows no partiality.

Matthew 7:12
"So, whatever you wish that others would do to you, do also to them, for this is the Law and the Prophets.

Acts 10:34
So, Peter opened his mouth and said: "Truly I understand that God shows no partiality,

Mark 12:31
The second is this: 'You shall love your neighbor as yourself.' There is no other commandment greater than these."

Proverbs 6:16-19
There are six things that the Lord hates, seven that are an abomination to him: haughty eyes, a lying tongue, and hands that shed innocent blood, a heart that devises wicked plans, feet that make haste to run to evil, a false witness who breathes out lies, and one who sows discord among brothers.

Disease

Jeremiah 33:6
Behold, I will bring to it health and healing, and I will heal them and reveal to them abundance of prosperity and security.

Exodus 23:25
You shall serve the Lord your God, and he will bless your bread and your water, and I will take sickness away from among you.

Proverbs 17:22

A joyful heart is good medicine, but a crushed spirit dries up the bones.

Psalm 107:20

He sent out his word and healed them, and delivered them from their destruction.

Exodus 15:26

Saying, "If you will diligently listen to the voice of the Lord your God, and do that which is right in his eyes, and give ear to his commandments and keep all his statutes, I will put none of the diseases on you that I put on the Egyptians, for I am the Lord, your healer."

Psalm 103:2-4

Bless the Lord, O my soul, and forget not all his benefits, who forgives all your iniquity, who heals all your diseases, who redeems your life from the pit, who crowns you with steadfast love and mercy,

2 Corinthians 12:7-10

So to keep me from becoming conceited because of the surpassing greatness of the revelations, a thorn was given me in the flesh, a messenger of Satan to harass me, to keep me from becoming conceited. Three times I pleaded with the Lord about this, that it should leave me. But he said to me, "My grace is sufficient for you, for my power is made perfect in weakness." Therefore, I will boast all the more gladly of my weaknesses, so that the power of Christ may rest upon me. For the sake of Christ, then, I am content with weaknesses, insults, hardships, persecutions, and calamities. For when I am weak, then I am strong.

Dishonesty

Proverbs 6:16-19

There are six things that the Lord hates, seven that are an abomination to him: haughty eyes, a lying tongue, and hands that shed innocent blood, a heart that devises wicked plans, feet that make haste to run to evil, a false witness who breathes out lies, and one who sows discord among brothers.

Proverbs 20:17

Bread gained by deceit is sweet to a man, but afterward his mouth will be full of gravel.

Colossians 3:9-10

Do not lie to one another, seeing that you have put off the old self with its practices and have put on the new self, which is being renewed in knowledge after the image of its creator.

Exodus 20:16

"You shall not bear false witness against your neighbor.

Luke 16:10-12

"One who is faithful in a very little is also faithful in much, and one who is dishonest in a very little is also dishonest in much. If then you have not been faithful in the unrighteous wealth, who will entrust to you the true riches? And if you have not been faithful in that which is another's, who will give you that which is your own?

Proverbs 11:3

The integrity of the upright guides them, but the crookedness of the treacherous destroys them.

Disobedience

John 14:15
"If you love me, you will keep my commandments.

James 1:14-15
But each person is tempted when he is lured and enticed by his own desire. Then desire when it has conceived gives birth to sin, and sin when it is fully grown brings forth death.

Romans 6:23
For the wages of sin is death, but the free gift of God is eternal life in Christ Jesus our Lord.

1 John 1:9
If we confess our sins, he is faithful and just to forgive us our sins and to cleanse us from all unrighteousness.

Luke 6:46
"Why do you call me 'Lord, Lord,' and not do what I tell you?

Acts 5:29
But Peter and the apostles answered, "We must obey God rather than men.

Disrespect

1 Corinthians 15:33
Do not be deceived: "Bad company ruins good morals."

Colossians 3:20
Children, obey your parents in everything, for this pleases the Lord.

Ephesians 5:11
Take no part in the unfruitful works of darkness, but instead expose them.

Romans 12:2
Do not be conformed to this world, but be transformed by the renewal of your mind, that by testing you may discern what is the will of God, what is good and acceptable and perfect.

Distraction

Proverbs 4:25-27
Let your eyes look directly forward, and your gaze be straight before you. Ponder the path of your feet; then all your ways will be sure. Do not swerve to the right or to the left; turn your foot away from evil.

1 Corinthians 10:13

No temptation has overtaken you that is not common to man. God is faithful, and he will not let you be tempted beyond your ability, but with the temptation he will also provide the way of escape, that you may be able to endure it.

Psalm 119:15

I will meditate on your precepts and fix my eyes on your ways.

1 Corinthians 7:35

I say this for your own benefit, not to lay any restraint upon you, but to promote good order and to secure your undivided devotion to the Lord.

Philippians 4:8

Finally, brothers, whatever is true, whatever is honorable, whatever is just, whatever is pure, whatever is lovely, whatever is commendable, if there is any excellence, if there is anything worthy of praise, think about these things.

Division

1 Corinthians 1:10-13

I appeal to you, brothers, by the name of our Lord Jesus Christ, that all of you agree, and that there be no divisions among you, but that you be united in the same mind and the same judgment. For it has been reported to me by Chloe's people that there is quarreling among you, my brothers. What I mean is that each one of you says, "I follow Paul," or "I follow Apollos," or "I follow Cephas," or "I follow Christ." Is Christ divided? Was Paul crucified for you? Or were you baptized in the name of Paul?

Romans 16:17-18

I appeal to you, brothers, to watch out for those who cause divisions and create obstacles contrary to the doctrine that you have been taught; avoid them. For such persons do not serve our Lord Christ, but their own appetites, and by smooth talk and flattery they deceive the hearts of the naive.

Titus 3:9-11

But avoid foolish controversies, genealogies, dissensions, and quarrels about the law, for they are unprofitable and worthless. As for a person who stirs up division, after warning him once and then twice, have nothing more to do with him, knowing that such a person is warped and sinful; he is self-condemned.

Luke 11:17

But he, knowing their thoughts, said to them, "Every kingdom divided against itself is laid waste, and a divided household falls.

Jude 1:16-19

These are grumblers, malcontents, following their own sinful desires; they are loud-mouthed boasters, showing favoritism to gain advantage. But you must remember, beloved, the predictions of the apostles of our Lord Jesus Christ. They said to you, "In the last time there will be scoffers, following their own ungodly passions." It is these who cause divisions, worldly people, devoid of the Spirit.

Ephesians 4:3-6
Eager to maintain the unity of the Spirit in the bond of peace. There is one body and one Spirit—just as you were called to the one hope that belongs to your call— one Lord, one faith, one baptism, one God and Father of all, who is over all and through all and in all.

Divorce

Luke 16:18
"Everyone who divorces his wife and marries another commits adultery, and he who marries a woman divorced from her husband commits adultery.

1 Corinthians 7:10-11
To the married I give this charge (not I, but the Lord): the wife should not separate from her husband (but if she does, she should remain unmarried or else be reconciled to her husband), and the husband should not divorce his wife.

1 Corinthians 7:15
But if the unbelieving partner separates, let it be so. In such cases the brother or sister is not enslaved. God has called you to peace.

Matthew 5:32
But I say to you that everyone who divorces his wife, except on the ground of sexual immorality, makes her commit adultery, and whoever marries a divorced woman commits adultery.

Matthew 19:6
So they are no longer two but one flesh. What therefore God has joined together, let not man separate."

Matthew 19:9
And I say to you: whoever divorces his wife, except for sexual immorality, and marries another, commits adultery."

Romans 7:2
For a married woman is bound by law to her husband while he lives, but if her husband dies she is released from the law of marriage.

Malachi 2:16
"For the man who does not love his wife but divorces her, says the Lord, the God of Israel, covers his garment with violence, says the Lord of hosts. So guard yourselves in your spirit, and do not be faithless."

Mark 10:12
And if she divorces her husband and marries another, she commits adultery."

Matthew 19:8
He said to them, "Because of your hardness of heart Moses allowed you to divorce your wives, but from the beginning it was not so.

Doubt

James 1:6
But let him ask in faith, with no doubting, for the one who doubts is like a wave of the sea that is driven and tossed by the wind.

Proverbs 3:5-8
Trust in the Lord with all your heart, and do not lean on your own understanding. In all your ways acknowledge him, and he will make straight your paths. Be not wise in your own eyes; fear the Lord, and turn away from evil. It will be healing to your flesh and refreshment to your bones.

Matthew 21:21
And Jesus answered them, "Truly, I say to you, if you have faith and do not doubt, you will not only do what has been done to the fig tree, but even if you say to this mountain, 'Be taken up and thrown into the sea,' it will happen.

Matthew 14:31
Jesus immediately reached out his hand and took hold of him, saying to him, "O you of little faith, why did you doubt?"

Mark 11:23
Truly, I say to you, whoever says to this mountain, 'Be taken up and thrown into the sea,' and does not doubt in his heart, but believes that what he says will come to pass, it will be done for him.

James 1:5-8
If any of you lacks wisdom, let him ask God, who gives generously to all without reproach, and it will be given him. But let him ask in faith, with no doubting, for the one who doubts is like a wave of the sea that is driven and tossed by the wind. For that person must not suppose that he will receive anything from the Lord; he is a double-minded man, unstable in all his ways.

Jude 1:22
And have mercy on those who doubt;

Mark 9:24
Immediately the father of the child cried out and said, "I believe; help my unbelief!"

Isaiah 41:10
Fear not, for I am with you; be not dismayed, for I am your God; I will strengthen you, I will help you, I will uphold you with my righteous right hand.

Luke 24:38
And he said to them, "Why are you troubled, and why do doubts arise in your hearts?

John 20:27
Then he said to Thomas, "Put your finger here, and see my hands; and put out your hand, and place it in my side. Do not disbelieve, but believe."

Romans 14:23

But whoever has doubts is condemned if he eats, because the eating is not from faith. For whatever does not proceed from faith is sin.

<u>Dreams</u>

Acts 2:17

"'And in the last days it shall be, God declares, that I will pour out my Spirit on all flesh, and your sons and your daughters shall prophesy, and your young men shall see visions, and your old men shall dream dreams;

Ecclesiastes 5:7

For when dreams increase and words grow many, there is vanity; but God is the one you must fear.

Job 33:14-18

For God speaks in one way, and in two, though man does not perceive it. In a dream, in a vision of the night, when deep sleep falls on men, while they slumber on their beds, then he opens the ears of men and terrifies them with warnings, that he may turn man aside from his deed and conceal pride from a man; he keeps back his soul from the pit, his life from perishing by the sword.

Joel 2:28

"And it shall come to pass afterward, that I will pour out my Spirit on all flesh; your sons and your daughters shall prophesy, your old men shall dream dreams, and your young men shall see visions.

Jeremiah 23:32

Behold, I am against those who prophesy lying dreams, declares the Lord, and who tell them and lead my people astray by their lies and their recklessness, when I did not send them or charge them. So they do not profit this people at all, declares the Lord.

Genesis 40:8

They said to him, "We have had dreams, and there is no one to interpret them." And Joseph said to them, "Do not interpretations belong to God? Please tell them to me."

Numbers 12:6

And he said, "Hear my words: If there is a prophet among you, I the Lord make myself known to him in a vision; I speak with him in a dream.

Luke 10:19

Behold, I have given you authority to tread on serpents and scorpions, and over all the power of the enemy, and nothing shall hurt you.

Genesis 20:3

But God came to Abimelech in a dream by night and said to him, "Behold, you are a dead man because of the woman whom you have taken, for she is a man's wife."

Dream Interpretation

Acts 2:17
"And in the last days it shall be, God declares, that I will pour out my Spirit on all flesh, and your sons and your daughters shall prophesy, and your young men shall see visions, and your old men shall dream dreams;

Matthew 27:19
Besides, while he was sitting on the judgment seat, his wife sent word to him, "Have nothing to do with that righteous man, for I have suffered much because of him today in a dream."

Zechariah 10:2
For the household gods utter nonsense, and the diviners see lies; they tell false dreams and give empty consolation. Therefore the people wander like sheep; they are afflicted for lack of a shepherd.

Drug Abuse

1 Corinthians 6:19-20
Or do you not know that your body is a temple of the Holy Spirit within you, whom you have from God? You are not your own, for you were bought with a price. So glorify God in your body.

1 Peter 5:8
Be sober-minded; be watchful. Your adversary the devil prowls around like a roaring lion, seeking someone to devour.

Proverbs 20:1
Wine is a mocker, strong drink a brawler, and whoever is led astray by it is not wise.

Eating Disorders

1 Corinthians 6:19-20

Or do you not know that your body is a temple of the Holy Spirit within you, whom you have from God? You are not your own, for you were bought with a price. So glorify God in your body.

1 Samuel 16:7

But the Lord said to Samuel, "Do not look on his appearance or on the height of his stature, because I have rejected him. For the Lord sees not as man sees: man looks on the outward appearance, but the Lord looks on the heart."

1 Corinthians 10:13

No temptation has overtaken you that is not common to man. God is faithful, and he will not let you be tempted beyond your ability, but with the temptation he will also provide the way of escape, that you may be able to endure it.

Romans 12:1

I appeal to you therefore, brothers, by the mercies of God, to present your bodies as a living sacrifice, holy and acceptable to God, which is your spiritual worship.

Song of Solomon 4:7

You are altogether beautiful, my love; there is no flaw in you.

Psalm 139:14

I praise you, for I am fearfully and wonderfully made. Wonderful are your works; my soul knows it very well.

Matthew 6:25

"Therefore, I tell you, do not be anxious about your life, what you will eat or what you will drink, nor about your body, what you will put on. Is not life more than food, and the body more than clothing?

James 4:7

Submit yourselves therefore to God. Resist the devil, and he will flee from you.

1 Corinthians 10:31

So, whether you eat or drink, or whatever you do, do all to the glory of God.

Philippians 4:6-7

Do not be anxious about anything, but in everything by prayer and supplication with thanksgiving let your requests be made known to God. And the peace of God, which surpasses all understanding, will guard your hearts and your minds in Christ Jesus.

2 Corinthians 12:9-10

But he said to me, "My grace is sufficient for you, for my power is made perfect in weakness." Therefore, I will boast all the more gladly of my weaknesses, so that the power of Christ may rest upon me. For the sake of Christ, then, I am content with weaknesses, insults, hardships, persecutions, and calamities. For when I am weak, then I am strong.

Economics

2 Thessalonians 3:10
For even when we were with you, we would give you this command: If anyone is not willing to work, let him not eat.

Proverbs 19:17
Whoever is generous to the poor lends to the Lord, and he will repay him for his deed.

Ecclesiastes 5:10
He who loves money will not be satisfied with money, nor he who loves wealth with his income; this also is vanity.

Proverbs 22:16
Whoever oppresses the poor to increase his own wealth, or gives to the rich, will only come to poverty.

Proverbs 22:7
The rich rules over the poor, and the borrower is the slave of the lender.

1 Timothy 6:10
For the love of money is a root of all kinds of evils. It is through this craving that some have wandered away from the faith and pierced themselves with many pangs.

Luke 12:15
And he said to them, "Take care, and be on your guard against all covetousness, for one's life does not consist in the abundance of his possessions."

Luke 6:38
Give, and it will be given to you. Good measure, pressed down, shaken together, running over, will be put into your lap. For with the measure you use it will be measured back to you."

Ego

John 5:30
"I can do nothing on my own. As I hear, I judge, and my judgment is just, because I seek not my own will but the will of him who sent me.

John 5:31
If I alone bear witness about myself, my testimony is not deemed true.

Colossians 4:6
Let your speech always be gracious, seasoned with salt, so that you may know how you ought to answer each person.

John 8:28

So Jesus said to them, "When you have lifted up the Son of Man, then you will know that I am he, and that I do nothing on my own authority, but speak just as the Father taught me.

Mark 10:17-18

And as he was setting out on his journey, a man ran up and knelt before him and asked him, "Good Teacher, what must I do to inherit eternal life?" And Jesus said to him, "Why do you call me good? No one is good except God alone.

Elderly

Leviticus 19:32

"You shall stand up before the gray head and honor the face of an old man, and you shall fear your God: I am the Lord.

1 Timothy 5:1-2

Do not rebuke an older man but encourage him as you would a father, younger men as brothers, older women as mothers, younger women as sisters, in all purity.

Proverbs 23:22

Listen to your father who gave you life, and do not despise your mother when she is old.

Psalm 71:9

Do not cast me off in the time of old age; forsake me not when my strength is spent.

Proverbs 20:29

The glory of young men is their strength, but the splendor of old men is their gray hair.

Exodus 20:12

"Honor your father and your mother, that your days may be long in the land that the Lord your God is giving you.

Proverbs 16:31

Gray hair is a crown of glory; it is gained in a righteous life.

Job 12:12

Wisdom is with the aged, and understanding in length of days.

Isaiah 46:4

Even to your old age I am he, and to gray hairs I will carry you. I have made, and I will bear; I will carry and will save.

1 Timothy 5:8

But if anyone does not provide for his relatives, and especially for members of his household, he has denied the faith and is worse than an unbeliever.

Psalm 71:18

So even to old age and gray hairs, O God, do not forsake me, until I proclaim your might to another generation, your power to all those to come.

Emotional Abuse

Psalm 34:17-20

When the righteous cry for help, the Lord hears and delivers them out of all their troubles. The Lord is near to the brokenhearted and saves the crushed in spirit. Many are the afflictions of the righteous, but the Lord delivers him out of them all. He keeps all his bones; not one of them is broken.

1 Peter 3:7

Likewise, husbands, live with your wives in an understanding way, showing honor to the woman as the weaker vessel, since they are heirs with you of the grace of life, so that your prayers may not be hindered.

Ephesians 6:4

Fathers, do not provoke your children to anger, but bring them up in the discipline and instruction of the Lord.

Psalm 103:6

The Lord works righteousness and justice for all who are oppressed.

2 Corinthians 6:14

Do not be unequally yoked with unbelievers. For what partnership has righteousness with lawlessness? Or what fellowship has light with darkness?

Empathy

Romans 12:15

Rejoice with those who rejoice, weep with those who weep.

Ephesians 4:32

Be kind to one another, tenderhearted, forgiving one another, as God in Christ forgave you.

1 Peter 3:8

Finally, all of you, have unity of mind, sympathy, brotherly love, a tender heart, and a humble mind.

Matthew 7:12

"So whatever you wish that others would do to you, do also to them, for this is the Law and the Prophets.

John 15:12

"This is my commandment, that you love one another as I have loved you.

Ephesians 4:29

Let no corrupting talk come out of your mouths, but only such as is good for building up, as fits the occasion, that it may give grace to those who hear.

Galatians 6:2
Bear one another's burdens, and so fulfill the law of Christ.

1 Corinthians 12:26
If one member suffers, all suffer together; if one member is honored, all rejoice together.

John 11:33-35
When Jesus saw her weeping, and the Jews who had come with her also weeping, he was deeply moved in his spirit and greatly troubled. And he said, "Where have you laid him?" They said to him, "Lord, come and see." Jesus wept.

Colossians 3:12
Put on then, as God's chosen ones, holy and beloved, compassionate hearts, kindness, humility, meekness, and patience,

Hebrews 4:15
For we do not have a high priest who is unable to sympathize with our weaknesses, but one who in every respect has been tempted as we are, yet without sin.

Philippians 2:3
Do nothing from rivalry or conceit, but in humility count others more significant than yourselves.

Matthew 9:36
When he saw the crowds, he had compassion for them, because they were harassed and helpless, like sheep without a shepherd.

Employment

Colossians 3:23
Whatever you do, work heartily, as for the Lord and not for men,

Matthew 6:33
But seek first the kingdom of God and his righteousness, and all these things will be added to you.

Empowerment

2 Corinthians 12:9
But he said to me, "My grace is sufficient for you, for my power is made perfect in weakness." Therefore I will boast all the more gladly of my weaknesses, so that the power of Christ may rest upon me.

Deuteronomy 31:6
Be strong and courageous. Do not fear or be in dread of them, for it is the Lord your God who goes with you. He will not leave you or forsake you."

Acts 1:8

But you will receive power when the Holy Spirit has come upon you, and you will be my witnesses in Jerusalem and in all Judea and Samaria, and to the end of the earth."

1 John 4:4

Little children, you are from God and have overcome them, for he who is in you is greater than he who is in the world.

Luke 10:19-20

Behold, I have given you authority to tread on serpents and scorpions, and over all the power of the enemy, and nothing shall hurt you. Nevertheless, do not rejoice in this, that the spirits are subject to you, but rejoice that your names are written in heaven."

Titus 2:12

Training us to renounce ungodliness and worldly passions, and to live self-controlled, upright, and godly lives in the present age,

2 Peter 1:3-4

His divine power has granted to us all things that pertain to life and godliness, through the knowledge of him who called us to his own glory and excellence, by which he has granted to us his precious and very great promises, so that through them you may become partakers of the divine nature, having escaped from the corruption that is in the world because of sinful desire.

2 Corinthians 4:16-18

So we do not lose heart. Though our outer self is wasting away, our inner self is being renewed day by day. For this light momentary affliction is preparing for us an eternal weight of glory beyond all comparison, as we look not to the things that are seen but to the things that are unseen. For the things that are seen are transient, but the things that are unseen are eternal.

Encouragement

Joshua 1:9

Have I not commanded you? Be strong and courageous. Do not be frightened, and do not be dismayed, for the Lord your God is with you wherever you go."

2 Timothy 1:7

For God gave us a spirit not of fear but of power and love and self-control.

Psalm 37:4

Delight yourself in the Lord, and he will give you the desires of your heart.

Mark 11:24

Therefore I tell you, whatever you ask in prayer, believe that you have received it, and it will be yours.

Proverbs 30:5

Every word of God proves true; he is a shield to those who take refuge in him.

Psalm 34:4

I sought the Lord, and he answered me and delivered me from all my fears.

Psalm 28:7

The Lord is my strength and my shield; in him my heart trusts, and I am helped; my heart exults, and with my song I give thanks to him.

Philippians 4:13

I can do all things through him who strengthens me.

Psalm 55:22

Cast your burden on the Lord, and he will sustain you; he will never permit the righteous to be moved.

Jeremiah 29:11

For I know the plans I have for you, declares the Lord, plans for welfare and not for evil, to give you a future and a hope.

Romans 15:13

May the God of hope fill you with all joy and peace in believing, so that by the power of the Holy Spirit you may abound in hope.

1 Thessalonians 5:9-11

For God has not destined us for wrath, but to obtain salvation through our Lord Jesus Christ, who died for us so that whether we are awake or asleep we might live with him. Therefore encourage one another and build one another up, just as you are doing.

End of Days

2 Timothy 3:1-5

But understand this, that in the last days there will come times of difficulty. For people will be lovers of self, lovers of money, proud, arrogant, abusive, disobedient to their parents, ungrateful, unholy, heartless, unappeasable, slanderous, without self-control, brutal, not loving good, treacherous, reckless, swollen with conceit, lovers of pleasure rather than lovers of God, having the appearance of godliness, but denying its power. Avoid such people.

Matthew 24:36

"But concerning that day and hour no one knows, not even the angels of heaven, nor the Son, but the Father only.

Matthew 24:44

Therefore you also must be ready, for the Son of Man is coming at an hour you do not expect.

Matthew 24:6

And you will hear of wars and rumors of wars. See that you are not alarmed, for this must take place, but the end is not yet.

Endurance

Romans 5:3-4
More than that, we rejoice in our sufferings, knowing that suffering produces endurance, and endurance produces character, and character produces hope,

Hebrews 10:36
For you have need of endurance, so that when you have done the will of God you may receive what is promised.

James 1:2-4
Count it all joy, my brothers, when you meet trials of various kinds, for you know that the testing of your faith produces steadfastness. And let steadfastness have its full effect, that you may be perfect and complete, lacking in nothing.

James 1:12
Blessed is the man who remains steadfast under trial, for when he has stood the test he will receive the crown of life, which God has promised to those who love him.

Colossians 1:11
May you be strengthened with all power, according to his glorious might, for all endurance and patience with joy,

Romans 12:12
Rejoice in hope, be patient in tribulation, be constant in prayer.

1 Corinthians 10:13
No temptation has overtaken you that is not common to man. God is faithful, and he will not let you be tempted beyond your ability, but with the temptation he will also provide the way of escape, that you may be able to endure it.

Enemies

Psalm 109:2-5
For wicked and deceitful mouths are opened against me, speaking against me with lying tongues. They encircle me with words of hate, and attack me without cause. In return for my love they accuse me, but I give myself to prayer. So they reward me evil for good, and hatred for my love.

Romans 12:14
Bless those who persecute you; bless and do not curse them.

Deuteronomy 31:6
Be strong and courageous. Do not fear or be in dread of them, for it is the Lord your God who goes with you. He will not leave you or forsake you."

Proverbs 24:17
Do not rejoice when your enemy falls, and let not your heart be glad when he stumbles,

Psalm 57:6

They set a net for my steps; my soul was bowed down. They dug a pit in my way, but they have fallen into it themselves. Selah

Romans 12:20

To the contrary, "if your enemy is hungry, feed him; if he is thirsty, give him something to drink; for by so doing you will heap burning coals on his head."

Envy

Exodus 34:14

(for you shall worship no other god, for the Lord, whose name is Jealous, is a jealous God),

Proverbs 14:30

A tranquil heart gives life to the flesh, but envy makes the bones rot.

Proverbs 23:17

Let not your heart envy sinners, but continue in the fear of the Lord all the day.

Galatians 5:19-21

Now the works of the flesh are evident: sexual immorality, impurity, sensuality, idolatry, sorcery, enmity, strife, jealousy, fits of anger, rivalries, dissensions, divisions, envy, drunkenness, orgies, and things like these. I warn you, as I warned you before, that those who do such things will not inherit the kingdom of God.

Galatians 5:26

Let us not become conceited, provoking one another, envying one another.

1 Peter 2:1

So put away all malice and all deceit and hypocrisy and envy and all slander.

James 3:16

For where jealousy and selfish ambition exist, there will be disorder and every vile practice.

Proverbs 24:1

Be not envious of evil men, nor desire to be with them,

1 Corinthians 13:4

Love is patient and kind; love does not envy or boast; it is not arrogant

Equal Rights

Galatians 3:28

There is neither Jew nor Greek, there is neither slave nor free, there is no male and female, for you are all one in Christ Jesus.

Proverbs 22:2

The rich and the poor meet together; the Lord is the maker of them all.

Eternal Life

John 3:16

"For God so loved the world, that he gave his only Son, that whoever believes in him should not perish but have eternal life.

Romans 6:23

For the wages of sin is death, but the free gift of God is eternal life in Christ Jesus our Lord.

John 17:3

And this is eternal life, that they know you the only true God, and Jesus Christ whom you have sent.

Matthew 25:46

And these will go away into eternal punishment, but the righteous into eternal life."

Romans 10:13

For "everyone who calls on the name of the Lord will be saved."

John 5:24

Truly, truly, I say to you, whoever hears my word and believes him who sent me has eternal life. He does not come into judgment, but has passed from death to life.

Eternal Security

John 10:27-29

My sheep hear my voice, and I know them, and they follow me. I give them eternal life, and they will never perish, and no one will snatch them out of my hand. My Father, who has given them to me, is greater than all, and no one is able to snatch them out of the Father's hand.

John 6:37

All that the Father gives me will come to me, and whoever comes to me I will never cast out.

John 5:24

Truly, truly, I say to you, whoever hears my word and believes him who sent me has eternal life. He does not come into judgment, but has passed from death to life.

John 3:16

"For God so loved the world, that he gave his only Son, that whoever believes in him should not perish but have eternal life.

Romans 11:29

For the gifts and the calling of God are irrevocable.

Romans 8:38-39

For I am sure that neither death nor life, nor angels nor rulers, nor things present nor things to come, nor powers, nor height nor depth, nor anything else in all creation, will be able to separate us from the love of God in Christ Jesus our Lord.

Jude 1:24

Now to him who is able to keep you from stumbling and to present you blameless before the presence of his glory with great joy,

2 Corinthians 1:22

And who has also put his seal on us and given us his Spirit in our hearts as a guarantee.

1 John 5:13

I write these things to you who believe in the name of the Son of God that you may know that you have eternal life.

Philippians 1:6

And I am sure of this, that he who began a good work in you will bring it to completion at the day of Jesus Christ.

Ephesians 2:8

For by grace you have been saved through faith. And this is not your own doing; it is the gift of God,

Ethics

Proverbs 11:1

A false balance is an abomination to the Lord, but a just weight is his delight.

Psalm 25:21

May integrity and uprightness preserve me, for I wait for you.

Matthew 7:12

"So whatever you wish that others would do to you, do also to them, for this is the Law and the Prophets.

John 13:34-35

A new commandment I give to you, that you love one another: just as I have loved you, you also are to love one another. By this all people will know that you are my disciples, if you have love for one another."

Euthanasia

Ecclesiastes 7:17

Be not overly wicked, neither be a fool. Why should you die before your time?

1 Corinthians 6:19-20

Or do you not know that your body is a temple of the Holy Spirit within you, whom you have from God? You are not your own, for you were bought with a price. So glorify God in your body.

Exodus 20:13

"You shall not murder.

Ecclesiastes 8:8

No man has power to retain the spirit, or power over the day of death. There is no discharge from war, nor will wickedness deliver those who are given to it.

1 Corinthians 3:16-17

Do you not know that you are God's temple and that God's Spirit dwells in you? If anyone destroys God's temple, God will destroy him. For God's temple is holy, and you are that temple.

Genesis 9:6

"Whoever sheds the blood of man, by man shall his blood be shed, for God made man in his own image.

Romans 5:3-5

More than that, we rejoice in our sufferings, knowing that suffering produces endurance, and endurance produces character, and character produces hope, and hope does not put us to shame, because God's love has been poured into our hearts through the Holy Spirit who has been given to us.

Hebrews 9:27

And just as it is appointed for man to die once, and after that comes judgment,

Ecclesiastes 3:1-3

For everything there is a season, and a time for every matter under heaven: a time to be born, and a time to die; a time to plant, and a time to pluck up what is planted; a time to kill, and a time to heal; a time to break down, and a time to build up;

1 Corinthians 10:13

No temptation has overtaken you that is not common to man. God is faithful, and he will not let you be tempted beyond your ability, but with the temptation he will also provide the way of escape, that you may be able to endure it.

Job 1:21

And he said, "Naked I came from my mother's womb, and naked shall I return. The Lord gave, and the Lord has taken away; blessed be the name of the Lord."

Evangelism

Matthew 28:19-20

Go therefore and make disciples of all nations, baptizing them in the name of the Father and of the Son and of the Holy Spirit, teaching them to observe all that I have commanded you. And behold, I am with you always, to the end of the age."

Matthew 9:37-38

Then he said to his disciples, "The harvest is plentiful, but the laborers are few; therefore pray earnestly to the Lord of the harvest to send out laborers into his harvest."

1 Peter 3:15

But in your hearts honor Christ the Lord as holy, always being prepared to make a defense to anyone who asks you for a reason for the hope that is in you; yet do it with gentleness and respect,

1 Corinthians 9:22

To the weak I became weak, that I might win the weak. I have become all things to all people, that by all means I might save some.

Isaiah 6:8

And I heard the voice of the Lord saying, "Whom shall I send, and who will go for us?" Then I said, "Here am I! Send me."

Romans 1:16

For I am not ashamed of the gospel, for it is the power of God for salvation to everyone who believes, to the Jew first and also to the Greek.

Acts 1:8

But you will receive power when the Holy Spirit has come upon you, and you will be my witnesses in Jerusalem and in all Judea and Samaria, and to the end of the earth."

2 Timothy 4:5

As for you, always be sober-minded, endure suffering, do the work of an evangelist, fulfill your ministry.

Mark 16:15-16

And he said to them, "Go into all the world and proclaim the gospel to the whole creation. Whoever believes and is baptized will be saved, but whoever does not believe will be condemned.

Evil

Isaiah 5:20

Woe to those who call evil good and good evil, who put darkness for light and light for darkness, who put bitter for sweet and sweet for bitter!

Proverbs 8:13

The fear of the Lord is hatred of evil. Pride and arrogance and the way of evil and perverted speech I hate.

Psalm 23:4

Even though I walk through the valley of the shadow of death, I will fear no evil, for you are with me; your rod and your staff, they comfort me.

Evil Doers

Proverbs 21:15
When justice is done, it is a joy to the righteous but terror to evildoers.

James 4:17
So whoever knows the right thing to do and fails to do it, for him it is sin.

Matthew 12:36-37
I tell you, on the day of judgment people will give account for every careless word they speak, for by your words you will be justified, and by your words you will be condemned."

Romans 13:4
For he is God's servant for your good. But if you do wrong, be afraid, for he does not bear the sword in vain. For he is the servant of God, an avenger who carries out God's wrath on the wrongdoer.

Luke 6:35
But love your enemies, and do good, and lend, expecting nothing in return, and your reward will be great, and you will be sons of the Most High, for he is kind to the ungrateful and the evil.

Revelation 21:8
But as for the cowardly, the faithless, the detestable, as for murderers, the sexually immoral, sorcerers, idolaters, and all liars, their portion will be in the lake that burns with fire and sulfur, which is the second death."

Example to Other

1 Timothy 4:12
Let no one despise you for your youth, but set the believers an example in speech, in conduct, in love, in faith, in purity.

Titus 2:7
Show yourself in all respects to be a model of good works, and in your teaching show integrity, dignity,

Matthew 5:16
In the same way, let your light shine before others, so that they may see your good works and give glory to your Father who is in heaven.

Ephesians 5:1
Therefore be imitators of God, as beloved children.

1 Corinthians 11:1
Be imitators of me, as I am of Christ.

Philippians 3:17

Brothers, join in imitating me, and keep your eyes on those who walk according to the example you have in us.

1 Thessalonians 1:6

And you became imitators of us and of the Lord, for you received the word in much affliction, with the joy of the Holy Spirit,

Excellence

Daniel 6:3

Then this Daniel became distinguished above all the other presidents and satraps, because an excellent spirit was in him. And the king planned to set him over the whole kingdom.

Philippians 4:8

Finally, brothers, whatever is true, whatever is honorable, whatever is just, whatever is pure, whatever is lovely, whatever is commendable, if there is any excellence, if there is anything worthy of praise, think about these things.

Colossians 3:23

Whatever you do, work heartily, as for the Lord and not for men,

Titus 2:7

Show yourself in all respects to be a model of good works, and in your teaching show integrity, dignity,

2 Corinthians 8:7

But as you excel in everything—in faith, in speech, in knowledge, in all earnestness, and in our love for you—see that you excel in this act of grace also.

Philippians 1:9-10

And it is my prayer that your love may abound more and more, with knowledge and all discernment, so that you may approve what is excellent, and so be pure and blameless for the day of Christ,

Daniel 5:12

Because an excellent spirit, knowledge, and understanding to interpret dreams, explain riddles, and solve problems were found in this Daniel, whom the king named Belteshazzar. Now let Daniel be called, and he will show the interpretation."

Excuses

Romans 2:1

Therefore you have no excuse, O man, every one of you who judges. For in passing judgment on another you condemn yourself, because you, the judge, practice the very same things.

Romans 1:20

For his invisible attributes, namely, his eternal power and divine nature, have been clearly perceived, ever since the creation of the world, in the things that have been made. So they are without excuse.

Exercise

1 Timothy 4:8
For while bodily training is of some value, godliness is of value in every way, as it holds promise for the present life and also for the life to come.

1 Corinthians 6:19
Or do you not know that your body is a temple of the Holy Spirit within you, whom you have from God? You are not your own,

Proverbs 24:5
A wise man is full of strength, and a man of knowledge enhances his might,

Proverbs 31:17
She dresses herself with strength and makes her arms strong.

1 Corinthians 9:24-27
Do you not know that in a race all the runners run, but only one receives the prize? So run that you may obtain it. Every athlete exercises self-control in all things. They do it to receive a perishable wreath, but we an imperishable. So I do not run aimlessly; I do not box as one beating the air. But I discipline my body and keep it under control, lest after preaching to others I myself should be disqualified.

2 Timothy 3:1-5
But understand this, that in the last days there will come times of difficulty. For people will be lovers of self, lovers of money, proud, arrogant, abusive, disobedient to their parents, ungrateful, unholy, heartless, unappeasable, slanderous, without self-control, brutal, not loving good, treacherous, reckless, swollen with conceit, lovers of pleasure rather than lovers of God, having the appearance of godliness, but denying its power. Avoid such people.

2 Timothy 2:5
An athlete is not crowned unless he competes according to the rules.

2 Timothy 4:7
I have fought the good fight, I have finished the race, I have kept the faith.

Exorcism

Mark 16:16-18
Whoever believes and is baptized will be saved, but whoever does not believe will be condemned. And these signs will accompany those who believe: in my name they will cast out demons; they will speak in new tongues; they will pick up serpents with their hands; and if they drink any deadly poison, it will not hurt them; they will lay their hands on the sick, and they will recover."

1 Peter 5:8
Be sober-minded; be watchful. Your adversary the devil prowls around like a roaring lion, seeking someone to devour.

Expectation

Jeremiah 29:11
For I know the plans I have for you, declares the Lord, plans for welfare and not for evil, to give you a future and a hope.

Proverbs 10:28
The hope of the righteous brings joy, but the expectation of the wicked will perish.

Proverbs 23:18
Surely there is a future, and your hope will not be cut off.

Psalm 62:5
For God alone, O my soul, wait in silence, for my hope is from him.

Philippians 1:20
As it is my eager expectation and hope that I will not be at all ashamed, but that with full courage now as always Christ will be honored in my body, whether by life or by death.

Acts 3:5
And he fixed his attention on them, expecting to receive something from them.

Philippians 4:6
Do not be anxious about anything, but in everything by prayer and supplication with thanksgiving let your requests be made known to God.

Failure

2 Corinthians 12:9-10

But he said to me, "My grace is sufficient for you, for my power is made perfect in weakness." Therefore I will boast all the more gladly of my weaknesses, so that the power of Christ may rest upon me. For the sake of Christ, then, I am content with weaknesses, insults, hardships, persecutions, and calamities. For when I am weak, then I am strong.

Romans 5:3-5

More than that, we rejoice in our sufferings, knowing that suffering produces endurance, and endurance produces character, and character produces hope, and hope does not put us to shame, because God's love has been poured into our hearts through the Holy Spirit who has been given to us.

Psalm 73:26

My flesh and my heart may fail, but God is the strength of my heart and my portion forever.

Philippians 4:13

I can do all things through him who strengthens me.

1 John 1:9

If we confess our sins, he is faithful and just to forgive us our sins and to cleanse us from all unrighteousness.

Proverbs 24:16

For the righteous falls seven times and rises again, but the wicked stumble in times of calamity.

Philippians 4:4-7

Rejoice in the Lord always; again I will say, Rejoice. Let your reasonableness be known to everyone. The Lord is at hand; do not be anxious about anything, but in everything by prayer and supplication with thanksgiving let your requests be made known to God. And the peace of God, which surpasses all understanding, will guard your hearts and your minds in Christ Jesus.

Proverbs 28:13

Whoever conceals his transgressions will not prosper, but he who confesses and forsakes them will obtain mercy.

Jeremiah 29:11

For I know the plans I have for you, declares the Lord, plans for welfare and not for evil, to give you a future and a hope.

Galatians 6:7

Do not be deceived: God is not mocked, for whatever one sows, that will he also reap.

2 Corinthians 5:17

Therefore, if anyone is in Christ, he is a new creation. The old has passed away; behold, the new has come.

Proverbs 3:5-6

Trust in the Lord with all your heart, and do not lean on your own understanding. In all your ways acknowledge him, and he will make straight your paths.

Psalm 55:22

Cast your burden on the Lord, and he will sustain you; he will never permit the righteous to be moved.

Faith

Matthew 21:22

And whatever you ask in prayer, you will receive, if you have faith."

Romans 10:17

So faith comes from hearing, and hearing through the word of Christ.

Hebrews 11:6

And without faith it is impossible to please him, for whoever would draw near to God must believe that he exists and that he rewards those who seek him.

Hebrews 11:1

Now faith is the assurance of things hoped for, the conviction of things not seen.

Mark 11:22-24

And Jesus answered them, "Have faith in God. Truly, I say to you, whoever says to this mountain, 'Be taken up and thrown into the sea,' and does not doubt in his heart, but believes that what he says will come to pass, it will be done for him. Therefore I tell you, whatever you ask in prayer, believe that you have received it, and it will be yours.

James 2:19

You believe that God is one; you do well. Even the demons believe—and shudder!

Ephesians 2:8-9

For by grace you have been saved through faith. And this is not your own doing; it is the gift of God, not a result of works, so that no one may boast.

Luke 1:37

For nothing will be impossible with God."

Proverbs 3:5-6

Trust in the Lord with all your heart, and do not lean on your own understanding. In all your ways acknowledge him, and he will make straight your paths.

2 Corinthians 5:7

For we walk by faith, not by sight.

Ephesians 2:8

For by grace you have been saved through faith. And this is not your own doing; it is the gift of God,

1 Corinthians 2:5

That your faith might not rest in the wisdom of men but in the power of God.

Faith in God

Hebrews 11:1

Now faith is the assurance of things hoped for, the conviction of things not seen.

Hebrews 11:6

And without faith it is impossible to please him, for whoever would draw near to God must believe that he exists and that he rewards those who seek him.

Romans 10:17

So faith comes from hearing, and hearing through the word of Christ.

Matthew 17:20

He said to them, "Because of your little faith. For truly, I say to you, if you have faith like a grain of mustard seed, you will say to this mountain, 'Move from here to there,' and it will move, and nothing will be impossible for you."

John 3:16

"For God so loved the world, that he gave his only Son, that whoever believes in him should not perish but have eternal life.

Ephesians 2:8

For by grace you have been saved through faith. And this is not your own doing; it is the gift of God,

Ephesians 2:8-9

For by grace you have been saved through faith. And this is not your own doing; it is the gift of God, not a result of works, so that no one may boast.

2 Corinthians 5:7

For we walk by faith, not by sight.

Faithfulness

Proverbs 28:20

A faithful man will abound with blessings, but whoever hastens to be rich will not go unpunished.

Luke 16:10-12

"One who is faithful in a very little is also faithful in much, and one who is dishonest in a very little is also dishonest in much. If then you have not been faithful in the unrighteous wealth, who will entrust to you the true riches? And if you have not been faithful in that which is another's, who will give you that which is your own?

2 Corinthians 5:7

For we walk by faith, not by sight.

Hebrews 13:8

Jesus Christ is the same yesterday and today and forever.

Galatians 5:22-23

But the fruit of the Spirit is love, joy, peace, patience, kindness, goodness, faithfulness, gentleness, self-control; against such things there is no law.

1 John 1:9

If we confess our sins, he is faithful and just to forgive us our sins and to cleanse us from all unrighteousness.

1 Corinthians 10:13

No temptation has overtaken you that is not common to man. God is faithful, and he will not let you be tempted beyond your ability, but with the temptation he will also provide the way of escape, that you may be able to endure it.

Luke 12:42-44

And the Lord said, "Who then is the faithful and wise manager, whom his master will set over his household, to give them their portion of food at the proper time? Blessed is that servant whom his master will find so doing when he comes. Truly, I say to you, he will set him over all his possessions.

2 Timothy 2:13

If we are faithless, he remains faithful— for he cannot deny himself.

Psalm 91:4

He will cover you with his pinions, and under his wings you will find refuge; his faithfulness is a shield and buckler.

Proverbs 3:3-4

Let not steadfast love and faithfulness forsake you; bind them around your neck; write them on the tablet of your heart. So you will find favor and good success in the sight of God and man.

False Accusations

1 Peter 3:16

Having a good conscience, so that, when you are slandered, those who revile your good behavior in Christ may be put to shame.

Exodus 20:16

"You shall not bear false witness against your neighbor.

Exodus 23:1

"You shall not spread a false report. You shall not join hands with a wicked man to be a malicious witness.

Isaiah 54:17

No weapon that is fashioned against you shall succeed, and you shall confute every tongue that rises against you in judgment. This is the heritage of the servants of the Lord and their vindication from me, declares the Lord."

Deuteronomy 19:18-19

The judges shall inquire diligently, and if the witness is a false witness and has accused his brother falsely, then you shall do to him as he had meant to do to his brother. So you shall purge the evil from your midst.

Matthew 5:11

"Blessed are you when others revile you and persecute you and utter all kinds of evil against you falsely on my account.

Revelation 12:10

And I heard a loud voice in heaven, saying, "Now the salvation and the power and the kingdom of our God and the authority of his Christ have come, for the accuser of our brothers has been thrown down, who accuses them day and night before our God.

False Prophets and Teachers

Matthew 7:15

"Beware of false prophets, who come to you in sheep's clothing but inwardly are ravenous wolves.

1 John 4:1

Beloved, do not believe every spirit, but test the spirits to see whether they are from God, for many false prophets have gone out into the world.

Matthew 24:24

For false christs and false prophets will arise and perform great signs and wonders, so as to lead astray, if possible, even the elect.

2 Peter 2:1

But false prophets also arose among the people, just as there will be false teachers among you, who will secretly bring in destructive heresies, even denying the Master who bought them, bringing upon themselves swift destruction.

2 Corinthians 11:13-15

For such men are false apostles, deceitful workmen, disguising themselves as apostles of Christ. And no wonder, for even Satan disguises himself as an angel of light. So it is no surprise if his servants, also, disguise themselves as servants of righteousness. Their end will correspond to their deeds.

Matthew 24:11

And many false prophets will arise and lead many astray.

Fame

Hebrews 13:5

Keep your life free from love of money, and be content with what you have, for he has said, "I will never leave you nor forsake you."

1 John 2:15-16

Do not love the world or the things in the world. If anyone loves the world, the love of the Father is not in him. For all that is in the world—the desires of the flesh and the desires of the eyes and pride in possessions—is not from the Father but is from the world.

1 Peter 1:24

For "All flesh is like grass and all its glory like the flower of grass. The grass withers, and the flower falls,

Family

Exodus 20:12

"Honor your father and your mother, that your days may be long in the land that the Lord your God is giving you.

Proverbs 22:6

Train up a child in the way he should go; even when he is old he will not depart from it.

Colossians 3:20

Children, obey your parents in everything, for this pleases the Lord.

1 Timothy 5:8

But if anyone does not provide for his relatives, and especially for members of his household, he has denied the faith and is worse than an unbeliever.

1 Timothy 3:5

For if someone does not know how to manage his own household, how will he care for God's church?

Genesis 2:24

Therefore, a man shall leave his father and his mother and hold fast to his wife, and they shall become one flesh.

Psalm 128:3

Your wife will be like a fruitful vine within your house; your children will be like olive shoots around your table.

Joshua 24:15

And if it is evil in your eyes to serve the Lord, choose this day whom you will serve, whether the gods your fathers served in the region beyond the River, or the gods of the Amorites in whose land you dwell. But as for me and my house, we will serve the Lord."

Psalm 127:3-5

Behold, children are a heritage from the Lord, the fruit of the womb a reward. Like arrows in the hand of a warrior are the children of one's youth. Blessed is the man who fills his quiver with them! He shall not be put to shame when he speaks with his enemies in the gate.

Famine

Amos 8:11

"Behold, the days are coming," declares the Lord God, "when I will send a famine on the land— not a famine of bread, nor a thirst for water, but of hearing the words of the Lord.

Luke 21:11

There will be great earthquakes, and in various places famines and pestilences. And there will be terrors and great signs from heaven.

Matthew 24:7

For nation will rise against nation, and kingdom against kingdom, and there will be famines and earthquakes in various places.

Genesis 12:10

Now there was a famine in the land. So Abram went down to Egypt to sojourn there, for the famine was severe in the land.

Fasting

Joel 2:12

"Yet even now," declares the Lord, "return to me with all your heart, with fasting, with weeping, and with mourning;

Psalm 69:10

When I wept and humbled my soul with fasting, it became my reproach.

Matthew 6:18

That your fasting may not be seen by others but by your Father who is in secret. And your Father who sees in secret will reward you.

Daniel 10:3

I ate no delicacies, no meat or wine entered my mouth, nor did I anoint myself at all, for the full three weeks.

Acts 14:23

And when they had appointed elders for them in every church, with prayer and fasting they committed them to the Lord in whom they had believed.

Luke 4:2

For forty days, being tempted by the devil. And he ate nothing during those days. And when they were ended, he was hungry.

Isaiah 58:6

"Is not this the fast that I choose: to loose the bonds of wickedness, to undo the straps of the yoke, to let the oppressed go free, and to break every yoke?

1 Corinthians 7:5

Do not deprive one another, except perhaps by agreement for a limited time, that you may devote yourselves to prayer; but then come together again, so that Satan may not tempt you because of your lack of self-control.

Matthew 4:4

But he answered, "It is written, "'Man shall not live by bread alone, but by every word that comes from the mouth of God.'"

Psalm 35:13

But I, when they were sick— I wore sackcloth; I afflicted myself with fasting; I prayed with head bowed on my chest.

Nehemiah 1:4

As soon as I heard these words I sat down and wept and mourned for days, and I continued fasting and praying before the God of heaven.

Ezra 8:23

So we fasted and implored our God for this, and he listened to our entreaty.

Luke 18:12

I fast twice a week; I give tithes of all that I get.'

Acts 13:2

While they were worshiping the Lord and fasting, the Holy Spirit said, "Set apart for me Barnabas and Saul for the work to which I have called them."

Fathers

Ephesians 6:4

Fathers, do not provoke your children to anger, but bring them up in the discipline and instruction of the Lord.

Psalm 103:13

As a father shows compassion to his children, so the Lord shows compassion to those who fear him.

Colossians 3:21

Fathers, do not provoke your children, lest they become discouraged.

Proverbs 3:11-12

My son, do not despise the Lord's discipline or be weary of his reproof, for the Lord reproves him whom he loves, as a father the son in whom he delights.

Proverbs 22:6

Train up a child in the way he should go; even when he is old he will not depart from it.

Malachi 4:6

And he will turn the hearts of fathers to their children and the hearts of children to their fathers, lest I come and strike the land with a decree of utter destruction."

Psalm 127:3-5

Behold, children are a heritage from the Lord, the fruit of the womb a reward. Like arrows in the hand of a warrior are the children of one's youth. Blessed is the man who fills his quiver with them! He shall not be put to shame when he speaks with his enemies in the gate.

Proverbs 23:24

The father of the righteous will greatly rejoice; he who fathers a wise son will be glad in him.

Proverbs 14:26

In the fear of the Lord one has strong confidence, and his children will have a refuge.

Proverbs 23:22

Listen to your father who gave you life, and do not despise your mother when she is old.

Proverbs 20:7

The righteous who walks in his integrity— blessed are his children after him!

Fatigue

Isaiah 40:29

He gives power to the faint, and to him who has no might he increases strength.

Matthew 11:28-30

Come to me, all who labor and are heavy laden, and I will give you rest. Take my yoke upon you, and learn from me, for I am gentle and lowly in heart, and you will find rest for your souls. For my yoke is easy, and my burden is light."

Favor

Psalm 5:12

For you bless the righteous, O Lord; you cover him with favor as with a shield.

Psalm 90:17

Let the favor of the Lord our God be upon us, and establish the work of our hands upon us; yes, establish the work of our hands!

Psalm 84:11

For the Lord God is a sun and shield; the Lord bestows favor and honor. No good thing does he withhold from those who walk uprightly.

Psalm 30:5

For his anger is but for a moment, and his favor is for a lifetime. Weeping may tarry for the night, but joy comes with the morning.

Genesis 6:8

But Noah found favor in the eyes of the Lord.

Ephesians 1:11

In him we have obtained an inheritance, having been predestined according to the purpose of him who works all things according to the counsel of his will,

Proverbs 3:1-4

My son, do not forget my teaching, but let your heart keep my commandments, for length of days and years of life and peace they will add to you. Let not steadfast love and faithfulness forsake you; bind them around your neck; write them on the tablet of your heart. So you will find favor and good success in the sight of God and man.

Luke 2:52

And Jesus increased in wisdom and in stature and in favor with God and man.

Isaiah 58:11

And the Lord will guide you continually and satisfy your desire in scorched places and make your bones strong; and you shall be like a watered garden, like a spring of water, whose waters do not fail.

Favoritism

James 2:9

But if you show partiality, you are committing sin and are convicted by the law as transgressors.

Romans 2:11

For God shows no partiality.

Acts 10:34

So Peter opened his mouth and said: "Truly I understand that God shows no partiality,

James 2:1

My brothers, show no partiality as you hold the faith in our Lord Jesus Christ, the Lord of glory.

Genesis 37:4

But when his brothers saw that their father loved him more than all his brothers, they hated him and could not speak peacefully to him.

Deuteronomy 10:17

For the Lord your God is God of gods and Lord of lords, the great, the mighty, and the awesome God, who is not partial and takes no bribe.

Galatians 3:28

There is neither Jew nor Greek, there is neither slave nor free, there is no male and female, for you are all one in Christ Jesus.

Fear

Isaiah 41:10

Fear not, for I am with you; be not dismayed, for I am your God; I will strengthen you, I will help you, I will uphold you with my righteous right hand.

2 Timothy 1:7

For God gave us a spirit not of fear but of power and love and self-control.

1 John 4:18

There is no fear in love, but perfect love casts out fear. For fear has to do with punishment, and whoever fears has not been perfected in love.

Psalm 34:4

I sought the Lord, and he answered me and delivered me from all my fears.

Proverbs 29:25

The fear of man lays a snare, but whoever trusts in the Lord is safe.

Joshua 1:9

Have I not commanded you? Be strong and courageous. Do not be frightened, and do not be dismayed, for the Lord your God is with you wherever you go."

Psalm 56:3-4

When I am afraid, I put my trust in you. In God, whose word I praise, in God I trust; I shall not be afraid. What can flesh do to me?

Philippians 4:6

Do not be anxious about anything, but in everything by prayer and supplication with thanksgiving let your requests be made known to God.

Romans 8:15

For you did not receive the spirit of slavery to fall back into fear, but you have received the Spirit of adoption as sons, by whom we cry, "Abba! Father!"

Deuteronomy 31:6

Be strong and courageous. Do not fear or be in dread of them, for it is the Lord your God who goes with you. He will not leave you or forsake you."

Psalm 27:1

Of David. The Lord is my light and my salvation; whom shall I fear? The Lord is the stronghold of my life; of whom shall I be afraid?

Psalm 56:3

When I am afraid, I put my trust in you.

Romans 8:38-39

For I am sure that neither death nor life, nor angels nor rulers, nor things present nor things to come, nor powers, nor height nor depth, nor anything else in all creation, will be able to separate us from the love of God in Christ Jesus our Lord.

John 14:27

Peace I leave with you; my peace I give to you. Not as the world gives do I give to you. Let not your hearts be troubled, neither let them be afraid.

Fear Not

Isaiah 41:10

Fear not, for I am with you; be not dismayed, for I am your God; I will strengthen you, I will help you, I will uphold you with my righteous right hand.

Joshua 1:9

Have I not commanded you? Be strong and courageous. Do not be frightened, and do not be dismayed, for the Lord your God is with you wherever you go."

Psalm 34:4

I sought the Lord, and he answered me and delivered me from all my fears.

2 Timothy 1:7

For God gave us a spirit not of fear but of power and love and self-control.

Psalm 27:1

Of David. The Lord is my light and my salvation; whom shall I fear? The Lord is the stronghold of my life; of whom shall I be afraid?

1 John 4:18

There is no fear in love, but perfect love casts out fear. For fear has to do with punishment, and whoever fears has not been perfected in love.

Deuteronomy 31:6

Be strong and courageous. Do not fear or be in dread of them, for it is the Lord your God who goes with you. He will not leave you or forsake you."

Psalm 23:4

Even though I walk through the valley of the shadow of death, I will fear no evil, for you are with me; your rod and your staff, they comfort me.

Philippians 4:6-

Do not be anxious about anything, but in everything by prayer and supplication with thanksgiving let your requests be made known to God. And the peace of God, which surpasses all understanding, will guard your hearts and your minds in Christ Jesus.

Isaiah 43:1

But now thus says the Lord, he who created you, O Jacob, he who formed you, O Israel: "Fear not, for I have redeemed you; I have called you by name, you are mine.

John 14:27

Peace I leave with you; my peace I give to you. Not as the world gives do I give to you. Let not your hearts be troubled, neither let them be afraid.

Romans 8:15

For you did not receive the spirit of slavery to fall back into fear, but you have received the Spirit of adoption as sons, by whom we cry, "Abba! Father!"

Isaiah 41:13

For I, the Lord your God, hold your right hand; it is I who say to you, "Fear not, I am the one who helps you."

Fellowship

1 Thessalonians 5:11

Therefore encourage one another and build one another up, just as you are doing.

Hebrews 10:25

Not neglecting to meet together, as is the habit of some, but encouraging one another, and all the more as you see the Day drawing near.

Ecclesiastes 4:9-12

Two are better than one, because they have a good reward for their toil. For if they fall, one will lift up his fellow. But woe to him who is alone when he falls and has not another to lift him up! Again, if two lie together, they keep warm, but how can one keep warm alone? And though a man might prevail against one who is alone, two will withstand him—a threefold cord is not quickly broken.

1 John 1:3

That which we have seen and heard we proclaim also to you, so that you too may have fellowship with us; and indeed our fellowship is with the Father and with his Son Jesus Christ.

Proverbs 27:17

Iron sharpens iron, and one man sharpens another.

Matthew 18:20

For where two or three are gathered in my name, there am I among them."

Hebrews 10:24

And let us consider how to stir up one another to love and good works,

1 John 1:7

But if we walk in the light, as he is in the light, we have fellowship with one another, and the blood of Jesus his Son cleanses us from all sin.

Acts 2:42

And they devoted themselves to the apostles' teaching and the fellowship, to the breaking of bread and the prayers.

Galatians 6:2

Bear one another's burdens, and so fulfill the law of Christ.

1 Peter 3:8

Finally, all of you, have unity of mind, sympathy, brotherly love, a tender heart, and a humble mind.

Acts 2:44-47

And all who believed were together and had all things in common. And they were selling their possessions and belongings and distributing the proceeds to all, as any had need. And day by day, attending the temple together and breaking bread in their homes, they received their food with glad and generous hearts, praising God and having favor with all the people. And the Lord added to their number day by day those who were being saved.

Romans 1:12

That is, that we may be mutually encouraged by each other's faith, both yours and mine.

John 17:21-23

That they may all be one, just as you, Father, are in me, and I in you, that they also may be in us, so that the world may believe that you have sent me. The glory that you have given me I have given to them, that they may be one even as we are one, I in them and you in me, that they may become perfectly one, so that the world may know that you sent me and loved them even as you loved me.

1 Corinthians 1:9

God is faithful, by whom you were called into the fellowship of his Son, Jesus Christ our Lord.

Fighting

Matthew 18:15

"If your brother sins against you, go and tell him his fault, between you and him alone. If he listens to you, you have gained your brother.

Matthew 12:36-37

I tell you, on the day of judgment people will give account for every careless word they speak, for by your words you will be justified, and by your words you will be condemned."

Romans 12:17

Repay no one evil for evil, but give thought to do what is honorable in the sight of all.

Proverbs 17:14

The beginning of strife is like letting out water, so quit before the quarrel breaks out.

Psalm 144:1

Of David. Blessed be the Lord, my rock, who trains my hands for war, and my fingers for battle;

Proverbs 28:25

A greedy man stirs up strife, but the one who trusts in the Lord will be enriched.

1 Thessalonians 5:9

For God has not destined us for wrath, but to obtain salvation through our Lord Jesus Christ,

Titus 3:10

As for a person who stirs up division, after warning him once and then twice, have nothing more to do with him,

Ephesians 6:13

Therefore, take up the whole armor of God, that you may be able to withstand in the evil day, and having done all, to stand firm.

Fighting Back

Psalm 144:1

Of David. Blessed be the Lord, my rock, who trains my hands for war, and my fingers for battle;

1 Timothy 6:12

Fight the good fight of the faith. Take hold of the eternal life to which you were called and about which you made the good confession in the presence of many witnesses.

Ecclesiastes 3:8

A time to love, and a time to hate; a time for war, and a time for peace.

Exodus 14:14

The Lord will fight for you, and you have only to be silent."

Romans 13:4

For he is God's servant for your good. But if you do wrong, be afraid, for he does not bear the sword in vain. For he is the servant of God, an avenger who carries out God's wrath on the wrongdoer.

1 John 1:9

If we confess our sins, he is faithful and just to forgive us our sins and to cleanse us from all unrighteousness.

Matthew 12:36-37
I tell you, on the day of judgment people will give account for every careless word they speak, for by your words you will be justified, and by your words you will be condemned."

James 4:7
Submit yourselves therefore to God. Resist the devil, and he will flee from you.

James 4:1-2
What causes quarrels and what causes fights among you? Is it not this, that your passions are at war within you? You desire and do not have, so you murder. You covet and cannot obtain, so you fight and quarrel. You do not have, because you do not ask.

Proverbs 21:15
When justice is done, it is a joy to the righteous but terror to evildoers.

John 16:33
I have said these things to you, that in me you may have peace. In the world you will have tribulation. But take heart; I have overcome the world."

Philippians 3:2
Look out for the dogs, look out for the evildoers, look out for those who mutilate the flesh.

Ephesians 6:12
For we do not wrestle against flesh and blood, but against the rulers, against the authorities, against the cosmic powers over this present darkness, against the spiritual forces of evil in the heavenly places.

Matthew 5:22
But I say to you that everyone who is angry with his brother will be liable to judgment; whoever insults his brother will be liable to the council; and whoever says, 'You fool!' will be liable to the hell of fire.

1 Thessalonians 5:22
Abstain from every form of evil.

Finances

Proverbs 22:7
The rich rules over the poor, and the borrower is the slave of the lender.

Philippians 4:19
And my God will supply every need of yours according to his riches in glory in Christ Jesus.

Hebrews 13:5
Keep your life free from love of money, and be content with what you have, for he has said, "I will never leave you nor forsake you."

1 Timothy 6:10

For the love of money is a root of all kinds of evils. It is through this craving that some have wandered away from the faith and pierced themselves with many pangs.

Proverbs 13:11

Wealth gained hastily will dwindle, but whoever gathers little by little will increase it.

Ecclesiastes 5:10

He who loves money will not be satisfied with money, nor he who loves wealth with his income; this also is vanity.

Proverbs 10:22

The blessing of the Lord makes rich, and he adds no sorrow with it.

Proverbs 13:22

A good man leaves an inheritance to his children's children, but the sinner's wealth is laid up for the righteous.

Luke 6:38

Give, and it will be given to you. Good measure, pressed down, shaken together, running over, will be put into your lap. For with the measure you use it will be measured back to you."

Luke 12:15

And he said to them, "Take care, and be on your guard against all covetousness, for one's life does not consist in the abundance of his possessions."

Proverbs 3:9-10

Honor the Lord with your wealth and with the first fruits of all your produce; then your barns will be filled with plenty, and your vats will be bursting with wine.

Matthew 6:21

For where your treasure is, there your heart will be also.

Matthew 6:24

"No one can serve two masters, for either he will hate the one and love the other, or he will be devoted to the one and despise the other. You cannot serve God and money.

Romans 13:8

Owe no one anything, except to love each other, for the one who loves another has fulfilled the law.

Flattery

Proverbs 29:5

A man who flatters his neighbor spreads a net for his feet.

Proverbs 26:24-28

Whoever hates disguises himself with his lips and harbors deceit in his heart; when he speaks graciously, believe him not, for there are seven abominations in his heart; though his hatred be covered with deception, his wickedness will be exposed in the assembly. Whoever digs a pit will fall into it, and a stone will come back on him who starts it rolling. A lying tongue hates its victims, and a flattering mouth works ruin.

Proverbs 28:23

Whoever rebukes a man will afterward find more favor than he who flatters with his tongue.

Job 32:21-22

I will not show partiality to any man or use flattery toward any person. For I do not know how to flatter, else my Maker would soon take me away.

Following Christ

Matthew 16:24

Then Jesus told his disciples, "If anyone would come after me, let him deny himself and take up his cross and follow me.

John 14:6

Jesus said to him, "I am the way, and the truth, and the life. No one comes to the Father except through me.

Romans 10:10

For with the heart one believes and is justified, and with the mouth one confesses and is saved.

Foolish

Proverbs 1:7

The fear of the Lord is the beginning of knowledge; fools despise wisdom and instruction.

1 Corinthians 2:14

The natural person does not accept the things of the Spirit of God, for they are folly to him, and he is not able to understand them because they are spiritually discerned.

Psalm 14:1

To the choirmaster. Of David. The fool says in his heart, "There is no God." They are corrupt, they do abominable deeds, there is none who does good.

James 1:26

If anyone thinks he is religious and does not bridle his tongue but deceives his heart, this person's religion is worthless.

Romans 14:1

As for the one who is weak in faith, welcome him, but not to quarrel over opinions.

Galatians 6:7-8

Do not be deceived: God is not mocked, for whatever one sows, that will he also reap. For the one who sows to his own flesh will from the flesh reap corruption, but the one who sows to the Spirit will from the Spirit reap eternal life.

1 Corinthians 1:18

For the word of the cross is folly to those who are perishing, but to us who are being saved it is the power of God.

Proverbs 29:11

A fool gives full vent to his spirit, but a wise man quietly holds it back.

Mark 7:20-22

And he said, "What comes out of a person is what defiles him. For from within, out of the heart of man, come evil thoughts, sexual immorality, theft, murder, adultery, coveting, wickedness, deceit, sensuality, envy, slander, pride, foolishness.

Forgetting the Past

Philippians 3:13

Brothers, I do not consider that I have made it my own. But one thing I do: forgetting what lies behind and straining forward to what lies ahead,

Isaiah 43:18-19

"Remember not the former things, nor consider the things of old. Behold, I am doing a new thing; now it springs forth, do you not perceive it? I will make a way in the wilderness and rivers in the desert.

2 Corinthians 5:17

Therefore, if anyone is in Christ, he is a new creation. The old has passed away; behold, the new has come.

Ephesians 4:31-32

Let all bitterness and wrath and anger and clamor and slander be put away from you, along with all malice. Be kind to one another, tenderhearted, forgiving one another, as God in Christ forgave you.

Isaiah 43:25

"I, I am he who blots out your transgressions for my own sake, and I will not remember your sins.

1 John 1:9

If we confess our sins, he is faithful and just to forgive us our sins and to cleanse us from all unrighteousness.

Forgiveness

Ephesians 4:32

Be kind to one another, tenderhearted, forgiving one another, as God in Christ forgave you.

Mark 11:25

And whenever you stand praying, forgive, if you have anything against anyone, so that your Father also who is in heaven may forgive you your trespasses."

1 John 1:9

If we confess our sins, he is faithful and just to forgive us our sins and to cleanse us from all unrighteousness.

Matthew 18:21-22

Then Peter came up and said to him, "Lord, how often will my brother sin against me, and I forgive him? As many as seven times?" Jesus said to him, "I do not say to you seven times, but seventy times seven.

Matthew 6:14-15

For if you forgive others their trespasses, your heavenly Father will also forgive you, but if you do not forgive others their trespasses, neither will your Father forgive your trespasses.

Luke 6:37

"Judge not, and you will not be judged; condemn not, and you will not be condemned; forgive, and you will be forgiven;

Colossians 3:13

Bearing with one another and, if one has a complaint against another, forgiving each other; as the Lord has forgiven you, so you also must forgive.

James 5:16

Therefore, confess your sins to one another and pray for one another, that you may be healed. The prayer of a righteous person has great power as it is working.

Luke 6:27

"But I say to you who hear, Love your enemies, do good to those who hate you,

Psalm 103:10-14

He does not deal with us according to our sins, nor repay us according to our iniquities. For as high as the heavens are above the earth, so great is his steadfast love toward those who fear him; as far as the east is from the west, so far does he remove our transgressions from us. As a father shows compassion to his children, so the Lord shows compassion to those who fear him. For he knows our frame; he remembers that we are dust.

Fortune-Telling

Leviticus 19:31

"Do not turn to mediums or necromancers; do not seek them out, and so make yourselves unclean by them: I am the Lord your God.

Leviticus 20:6
"If a person turns to mediums and necromancers, whoring after them, I will set my face against that person and will cut him off from among his people.

Leviticus 20:27

"A man or a woman who is a medium or a necromancer shall surely be put to death. They shall be stoned with stones; their blood shall be upon them."

2 Kings 21:6

And he burned his son as an offering and used fortune-telling and omens and dealt with mediums and with necromancers. He did much evil in the sight of the Lord, provoking him to anger.

Isaiah 8:19

And when they say to you, "Inquire of the mediums and the necromancers who chirp and mutter," should not a people inquire of their God? Should they inquire of the dead on behalf of the living?

Free Will

Proverbs 16:9

The heart of man plans his way, but the Lord establishes his steps.

Joshua 24:15

And if it is evil in your eyes to serve the Lord, choose this day whom you will serve, whether the gods your fathers served in the region beyond the River, or the gods of the Amorites in whose land you dwell. But as for me and my house, we will serve the Lord."

John 7:17

If anyone's will is to do God's will, he will know whether the teaching is from God or whether I am speaking on my own authority.

John 1:12-13

But to all who did receive him, who believed in his name, he gave the right to become children of God, who were born, not of blood nor of the will of the flesh nor of the will of man, but of God.

Revelation 3:20

Behold, I stand at the door and knock. If anyone hears my voice and opens the door, I will come in to him and eat with him, and he with me.

1 Corinthians 10:13

No temptation has overtaken you that is not common to man. God is faithful, and he will not let you be tempted beyond your ability, but with the temptation he will also provide the way of escape, that you may be able to endure it.

Deuteronomy 30:19-20

I call heaven and earth to witness against you today, that I have set before you life and death, blessing and curse. Therefore, choose life, that you and your offspring may live, loving the Lord your God, obeying his voice and holding fast to him, for he is your life and length of days, that you may dwell in the land that the Lord swore to your fathers, to Abraham, to Isaac, and to Jacob, to give them."

Freedom

Galatians 5:1
For freedom Christ has set us free; stand firm therefore, and do not submit again to a yoke of slavery.

Galatians 5:13
For you were called to freedom, brothers. Only do not use your freedom as an opportunity for the flesh, but through love serve one another.

2 Corinthians 3:17
Now the Lord is the Spirit, and where the Spirit of the Lord is, there is freedom.

1 Peter 2:16
Live as people who are free, not using your freedom as a cover-up for evil, but living as servants of God.

John 8:32
And you will know the truth, and the truth will set you free."

John 8:36
So if the Son sets you free, you will be free indeed.

Isaiah 61:1
The Spirit of the Lord God is upon me, because the Lord has anointed me to bring good news to the poor; he has sent me to bind up the brokenhearted, to proclaim liberty to the captives, and the opening of the prison to those who are bound;

Romans 6:22
But now that you have been set free from sin and have become slaves of God, the fruit you get leads to sanctification and its end, eternal life.

James 1:25
But the one who looks into the perfect law, the law of liberty, and perseveres, being no hearer who forgets but a doer who acts, he will be blessed in his doing.

2 Timothy 1:7
For God gave us a spirit not of fear but of power and love and self-control.

Psalm 119:45
And I shall walk in a wide place, for I have sought your precepts.

Friendship

Proverbs 18:24
A man of many companions may come to ruin, but there is a friend who sticks closer than a brother.

Ecclesiastes 4:9-12

Two are better than one, because they have a good reward for their toil. For if they fall, one will lift up his fellow. But woe to him who is alone when he falls and has not another to lift him up! Again, if two lie together, they keep warm, but how can one keep warm alone? And though a man might prevail against one who is alone, two will withstand him—a threefold cord is not quickly broken.

John 15:13

Greater love has no one than this, that someone lay down his life for his friends.

Proverbs 27:17

Iron sharpens iron, and one man sharpens another.

Proverbs 17:17

A friend loves at all times, and a brother is born for adversity.

1 Corinthians 15:33

Do not be deceived: "Bad company ruins good morals."

1 Thessalonians 5:11

Therefore encourage one another and build one another up, just as you are doing.

Proverbs 27:9

Oil and perfume make the heart glad, and the sweetness of a friend comes from his earnest counsel.

Proverbs 27:6

Faithful are the wounds of a friend; profuse are the kisses of an enemy.

Job 6:14

"He who withholds kindness from a friend forsakes the fear of the Almighty.

Hebrews 10:24-25

And let us consider how to stir up one another to love and good works, not neglecting to meet together, as is the habit of some, but encouraging one another, and all the more as you see the Day drawing near.

1 Peter 4:8-10

Above all, keep loving one another earnestly, since love covers a multitude of sins. Show hospitality to one another without grumbling. As each has received a gift, use it to serve one another, as good stewards of God's varied grace:

Fruits of the Spirit

Galatians 5:22-23

But the fruit of the Spirit is love, joy, peace, patience, kindness, goodness, faithfulness, gentleness, self-control; against such things there is no law.

Romans 8:6

For to set the mind on the flesh is death, but to set the mind on the Spirit is life and peace.

Frustration

John 16:33

I have said these things to you, that in me you may have peace. In the world you will have tribulation. But take heart; I have overcome the world."

Isaiah 41:10

Fear not, for I am with you; be not dismayed, for I am your God; I will strengthen you, I will help you, I will uphold you with my righteous right hand.

Galatians 6:9

And let us not grow weary of doing good, for in due season we will reap, if we do not give up.

Psalm 34:18

The Lord is near to the brokenhearted and saves the crushed in spirit.

1 Peter 5:7

Casting all your anxieties on him, because he cares for you.

Philippians 4:7

And the peace of God, which surpasses all understanding, will guard your hearts and your minds in Christ Jesus.

Matthew 11:28-29

Come to me, all who labor and are heavy laden, and I will give you rest. Take my yoke upon you, and learn from me, for I am gentle and lowly in heart, and you will find rest for your souls.

Romans 8:28

And we know that for those who love God all things work together for good, for those who are called according to his purpose.

Psalm 4:4-5

Be angry, and do not sin; ponder in your own hearts on your beds, and be silent. Selah Offer right sacrifices, and put your trust in the Lord.

Gambling

Proverbs 13:11

Wealth gained hastily will dwindle, but whoever gathers little by little will increase it.

1 Timothy 6:10

For the love of money is a root of all kinds of evils. It is through this craving that some have wandered away from the faith and pierced themselves with many pangs.

Hebrews 13:5

Keep your life free from love of money, and be content with what you have, for he has said, "I will never leave you nor forsake you."

1 Timothy 6:9-10

But those who desire to be rich fall into temptation, into a snare, into many senseless and harmful desires that plunge people into ruin and destruction. For the love of money is a root of all kinds of evils. It is through this craving that some have wandered away from the faith and pierced themselves with many pangs.

Matthew 6:24

"No one can serve two masters, for either he will hate the one and love the other, or he will be devoted to the one and despise the other. You cannot serve God and money.

Ecclesiastes 5:10

He who loves money will not be satisfied with money, nor he who loves wealth with his income; this also is vanity.

Gathering Together

Hebrews 10:24-25

And let us consider how to stir up one another to love and good works, not neglecting to meet together, as is the habit of some, but encouraging one another, and all the more as you see the Day drawing near.

Matthew 18:20

For where two or three are gathered in my name, there am I among them."

Colossians 3:16

Let the word of Christ dwell in you richly, teaching and admonishing one another in all wisdom, singing psalms and hymns and spiritual songs, with thankfulness in your hearts to God.

1 Corinthians 14:26

What then, brothers? When you come together, each one has a hymn, a lesson, a revelation, a tongue, or an interpretation. Let all things be done for building up.

Matthew 12:30

Whoever is not with me is against me, and whoever does not gather with me scatters.

1 Thessalonians 5:11

Therefore encourage one another and build one another up, just as you are doing.

1 Peter 2:9

But you are a chosen race, a royal priesthood, a holy nation, a people for his own possession, that you may proclaim the excellencies of him who called you out of darkness into his marvelous light.

Acts 2:1

When the day of Pentecost arrived, they were all together in one place.

Generational Curses

Numbers 14:18

'The Lord is slow to anger and abounding in steadfast love, forgiving iniquity and transgression, but he will by no means clear the guilty, visiting the iniquity of the fathers on the children, to the third and the fourth generation.'

Exodus 20:5

You shall not bow down to them or serve them, for I the Lord your God am a jealous God, visiting the iniquity of the fathers on the children to the third and the fourth generation of those who hate me,

Deuteronomy 24:16

"Fathers shall not be put to death because of their children, nor shall children be put to death because of their fathers. Each one shall be put to death for his own sin.

Galatians 3:13

Christ redeemed us from the curse of the law by becoming a curse for us—for it is written, "Cursed is everyone who is hanged on a tree"—

John 9:1-3

As he passed by, he saw a man blind from birth. And his disciples asked him, "Rabbi, who sinned, this man or his parents, that he was born blind?" Jesus answered, "It was not that this man sinned, or his parents, but that the works of God might be displayed in him.

John 8:36

So if the Son sets you free, you will be free indeed.

Ezekiel 18:19-20

"Yet you say, 'Why should not the son suffer for the iniquity of the father?' When the son has done what is just and right, and has been careful to observe all my statutes, he shall surely live. The soul who sins shall die. The son shall not suffer for the iniquity of the father, nor the father suffer for the iniquity of the son. The righteousness of the righteous shall be upon himself, and the wickedness of the wicked shall be upon himself.

Generosity

Acts 20:35
In all things I have shown you that by working hard in this way we must help the weak and remember the words of the Lord Jesus, how he himself said, 'It is more blessed to give than to receive.'"

Luke 6:38
Give, and it will be given to you. Good measure, pressed down, shaken together, running over, will be put into your lap. For with the measure you use it will be measured back to you."

Proverbs 11:24-25
One gives freely, yet grows all the richer; another withholds what he should give, and only suffers want. Whoever brings blessing will be enriched, and one who waters will himself be watered.

Luke 21:1-4
Jesus looked up and saw the rich putting their gifts into the offering box, and he saw a poor widow put in two small copper coins. And he said, "Truly, I tell you, this poor widow has put in more than all of them. For they all contributed out of their abundance, but she out of her poverty put in all she had to live on."

Proverbs 19:17
Whoever is generous to the poor lends to the Lord, and he will repay him for his deed.

Matthew 6:21
For where your treasure is, there your heart will be also.

1 Timothy 6:17-19
As for the rich in this present age, charge them not to be haughty, nor to set their hopes on the uncertainty of riches, but on God, who richly provides us with everything to enjoy. They are to do good, to be rich in good works, to be generous and ready to share, thus storing up treasure for themselves as a good foundation for the future, so that they may take hold of that which is truly life.

2 Corinthians 9:6
The point is this: whoever sows sparingly will also reap sparingly, and whoever sows bountifully will also reap bountifully.

Matthew 10:42
And whoever gives one of these little ones even a cup of cold water because he is a disciple, truly, I say to you, he will by no means lose his reward."

2 Corinthians 9:7
Each one must give as he has decided in his heart, not reluctantly or under compulsion, for God loves a cheerful giver.

Gentleness

Titus 3:2
To speak evil of no one, to avoid quarreling, to be gentle, and to show perfect courtesy toward all people.

1 Peter 3:15

But in your hearts honor Christ the Lord as holy, always being prepared to make a defense to anyone who asks you for a reason for the hope that is in you; yet do it with gentleness and respect,

Proverbs 15:1

A soft answer turns away wrath, but a harsh word stirs up anger.

Psalm 18:35

You have given me the shield of your salvation, and your right hand supported me, and your gentleness made me great.

2 Timothy 2:24-26

And the Lord's servant must not be quarrelsome but kind to everyone, able to teach, patiently enduring evil, correcting his opponents with gentleness. God may perhaps grant them repentance leading to a knowledge of the truth, and they may come to their senses and escape from the snare of the devil, after being captured by him to do his will.

James 3:17

But the wisdom from above is first pure, then peaceable, gentle, open to reason, full of mercy and good fruits, impartial and sincere.

Galatians 5:22-23

But the fruit of the Spirit is love, joy, peace, patience, kindness, goodness, faithfulness, gentleness, self-control; against such things there is no law.

Galatians 6:1

Brothers, if anyone is caught in any transgression, you who are spiritual should restore him in a spirit of gentleness. Keep watch on yourself, lest you too be tempted.

Matthew 11:29

Take my yoke upon you, and learn from me, for I am gentle and lowly in heart, and you will find rest for your souls.

Ephesians 4:2

With all humility and gentleness, with patience, bearing with one another in love,

Philippians 4:5

Let your reasonableness be known to everyone. The Lord is at hand;

Gift

James 1:17

Every good gift and every perfect gift is from above, coming down from the Father of lights with whom there is no variation or shadow due to change.

2 Corinthians 9:15

Thanks be to God for his inexpressible gift!

Romans 6:23

For the wages of sin is death, but the free gift of God is eternal life in Christ Jesus our Lord.

Ephesians 2:8-9

For by grace you have been saved through faith. And this is not your own doing; it is the gift of God, not a result of works, so that no one may boast.

John 3:16

"For God so loved the world, that he gave his only Son, that whoever believes in him should not perish but have eternal life.

1 Peter 4:10

As each has received a gift, use it to serve one another, as good stewards of God's varied grace:

Romans 11:29

For the gifts and the calling of God are irrevocable.

1 Timothy 4:14-16

Do not neglect the gift you have, which was given you by prophecy when the council of elders laid their hands on you. Practice these things, immerse yourself in them, so that all may see your progress. Keep a close watch on yourself and on the teaching. Persist in this, for by so doing you will save both yourself and your hearers.

Gifts of the Spirit

1 Peter 4:10

As each has received a gift, use it to serve one another, as good stewards of God's varied grace:

Romans 12:6-8

Having gifts that differ according to the grace given to us, let us use them: if prophecy, in proportion to our faith; if service, in our serving; the one who teaches, in his teaching; the one who exhorts, in his exhortation; the one who contributes, in generosity; the one who leads, with zeal; the one who does acts of mercy, with cheerfulness.

Romans 12:6

Having gifts that differ according to the grace given to us, let us use them: if prophecy, in proportion to our faith;

1 Corinthians 12:7-11

To each is given the manifestation of the Spirit for the common good. For to one is given through the Spirit the utterance of wisdom, and to another the utterance of knowledge according to the same Spirit, to another faith by the same Spirit, to another gifts of healing by the one Spirit, to another the working of miracles, to another prophecy, to another the ability to distinguish between spirits, to another various kinds of tongues, to another the interpretation of tongues. All these are empowered by one and the same Spirit, who apportions to each one individually as he wills.

Ephesians 4:11

And he gave the apostles, the prophets, the evangelists, the shepherds and teachers,

Giving

2 Corinthians 9:7

Each one must give as he has decided in his heart, not reluctantly or under compulsion, for God loves a cheerful giver.

Acts 20:35

In all things I have shown you that by working hard in this way we must help the weak and remember the words of the Lord Jesus, how he himself said, 'It is more blessed to give than to receive.'"

Luke 6:38

Give, and it will be given to you. Good measure, pressed down, shaken together, running over, will be put into your lap. For with the measure you use it will be measured back to you."

2 Corinthians 9:6

The point is this: whoever sows sparingly will also reap sparingly, and whoever sows bountifully will also reap bountifully.

Malachi 3:10

Bring the full tithe into the storehouse, that there may be food in my house. And thereby put me to the test, says the Lord of hosts, if I will not open the windows of heaven for you and pour down for you a blessing until there is no more need.

Matthew 6:1-4

"Beware of practicing your righteousness before other people in order to be seen by them, for then you will have no reward from your Father who is in heaven. "Thus, when you give to the needy, sound no trumpet before you, as the hypocrites do in the synagogues and in the streets, that they may be praised by others. Truly, I say to you, they have received their reward. But when you give to the needy, do not let your left hand know what your right hand is doing, so that your giving may be in secret. And your Father who sees in secret will reward you.

1 Timothy 6:17-19

As for the rich in this present age, charge them not to be haughty, nor to set their hopes on the uncertainty of riches, but on God, who richly provides us with everything to enjoy. They are to do good, to be rich in good works, to be generous and ready to share, thus storing up treasure for themselves as a good foundation for the future, so that they may take hold of that which is truly life.

Giving up

Galatians 6:9

And let us not grow weary of doing good, for in due season we will reap, if we do not give up.

Joshua 1:9

Have I not commanded you? Be strong and courageous. Do not be frightened, and do not be dismayed, for the Lord your God is with you wherever you go."

2 Chronicles 15:7

But you, take courage! Do not let your hands be weak, for your work shall be rewarded."

Romans 12:11-12

Do not be slothful in zeal, be fervent in spirit, serve the Lord. Rejoice in hope, be patient in tribulation, be constant in prayer.

2 Timothy 4:7

I have fought the good fight, I have finished the race, I have kept the faith.

1 Corinthians 16:13

Be watchful, stand firm in the faith, act like men, be strong.

Mark 10:27

Jesus looked at them and said, "With man it is impossible, but not with God. For all things are possible with God."

Matthew 11:28

Come to me, all who labor and are heavy laden, and I will give you rest.

Glory of God

1 Corinthians 10:31

So, whether you eat or drink, or whatever you do, do all to the glory of God.

Hebrews 1:3

He is the radiance of the glory of God and the exact imprint of his nature, and he upholds the universe by the word of his power. After making purification for sins, he sat down at the right hand of the Majesty on high,

Philippians 2:9-11

Therefore, God has highly exalted him and bestowed on him the name that is above every name, so that at the name of Jesus every knee should bow, in heaven and on earth and under the earth, and every tongue confess that Jesus Christ is Lord, to the glory of God the Father.

John 11:40

Jesus said to her, "Did I not tell you that if you believed you would see the glory of God?"

Isaiah 60:1

Arise, shine, for your light has come, and the glory of the Lord has risen upon you.

Isaiah 42:8

I am the Lord; that is my name; my glory I give to no other, nor my praise to carved idols.

Gluttony

Philippians 3:19
Their end is destruction, their god is their belly, and they glory in their shame, with minds set on earthly things.

Proverbs 23:20-21
Be not among drunkards or among gluttonous eaters of meat, for the drunkard and the glutton will come to poverty, and slumber will clothe them with rags.

God

Isaiah 40:28
Have you not known? Have you not heard? The Lord is the everlasting God, the Creator of the ends of the earth. He does not faint or grow weary; his understanding is unsearchable.

Revelation 1:8
"I am the Alpha and the Omega," says the Lord God, "who is and who was and who is to come, the Almighty."

Jeremiah 10:10
But the Lord is the true God; he is the living God and the everlasting King. At his wrath the earth quakes, and the nations cannot endure his indignation.

Jeremiah 51:15
"It is he who made the earth by his power, who established the world by his wisdom, and by his understanding stretched out the heavens.

Psalm 18:30
This God—his way is perfect; the word of the Lord proves true; he is a shield for all those who take refuge in him.

Isaiah 44:6
Thus says the Lord, the King of Israel and his Redeemer, the Lord of hosts: "I am the first and I am the last; besides me there is no god.

Revelation 4:11
"Worthy are you, our Lord and God, to receive glory and honor and power, for you created all things, and by your will they existed and were created."

Jeremiah 10:12
It is he who made the earth by his power, who established the world by his wisdom, and by his understanding stretched out the heavens.

God Answering Prayers

1 John 5:14-15
And this is the confidence that we have toward him, that if we ask anything according to his will he hears us. And if we know that he hears us in whatever we ask, we know that we have the requests that we have asked of him.

James 4:3
You ask and do not receive, because you ask wrongly, to spend it on your passions.

John 15:7
If you abide in me, and my words abide in you, ask whatever you wish, and it will be done for you.

Isaiah 65:24
Before they call I will answer; while they are yet speaking I will hear.

Hebrews 11:6
And without faith it is impossible to please him, for whoever would draw near to God must believe that he exists and that he rewards those who seek him.

John 15:16
You did not choose me, but I chose you and appointed you that you should go and bear fruit and that your fruit should abide, so that whatever you ask the Father in my name, he may give it to you.

1 Thessalonians 5:17
Pray without ceasing,

Godliness

1 Timothy 4:8
For while bodily training is of some value, godliness is of value in every way, as it holds promise for the present life and also for the life to come.

2 Peter 3:11
Since all these things are thus to be dissolved, what sort of people ought you to be in lives of holiness and godliness,

2 Timothy 3:12
Indeed, all who desire to live a godly life in Christ Jesus will be persecuted,

2 Peter 1:5-8
For this very reason, make every effort to supplement your faith with virtue, and virtue with knowledge, and knowledge with self-control, and self-control with steadfastness, and steadfastness with godliness, and godliness with brotherly affection, and brotherly affection with love. For if these qualities are yours and are increasing, they keep you from being ineffective or unfruitful in the knowledge of our Lord Jesus Christ.

1 Timothy 6:6
Now there is great gain in godliness with contentment,

Psalm 1:1-3
Blessed is the man who walks not in the counsel of the wicked, nor stands in the way of sinners, nor sits in the seat of scoffers; but his delight is in the law of the Lord, and on his law he meditates day and night. He is like a tree planted by streams of water that yields its fruit in its season, and its leaf does not wither. In all that he does, he prospers.

Golden Rule

Matthew 7:12
"So whatever you wish that others would do to you, do also to them, for this is the Law and the Prophets.

Luke 6:31
And as you wish that others would do to you, do so to them.

Galatians 5:14
For the whole law is fulfilled in one word: "You shall love your neighbor as yourself."

Gospel

Romans 1:16
For I am not ashamed of the gospel, for it is the power of God for salvation to everyone who believes, to the Jew first and also to the Greek.

Romans 10:9-13
Because, if you confess with your mouth that Jesus is Lord and believe in your heart that God raised him from the dead, you will be saved. For with the heart one believes and is justified, and with the mouth one confesses and is saved. For the Scripture says, "Everyone who believes in him will not be put to shame." For there is no distinction between Jew and Greek; for the same Lord is Lord of all, bestowing his riches on all who call on him. For "everyone who calls on the name of the Lord will be saved."

Mark 16:15
And he said to them, "Go into all the world and proclaim the gospel to the whole creation.

Gossip

Proverbs 20:19
Whoever goes about slandering reveals secrets; therefore do not associate with a simple babbler.

Proverbs 16:28
A dishonest man spreads strife, and a whisperer separates close friends.

Proverbs 11:13
Whoever goes about slandering reveals secrets, but he who is trustworthy in spirit keeps a thing covered.

Ephesians 4:29
Let no corrupting talk come out of your mouths, but only such as is good for building up, as fits the occasion, that it may give grace to those who hear.

Proverbs 26:20
For lack of wood the fire goes out, and where there is no whisperer, quarreling ceases.

Leviticus 19:16
You shall not go around as a slanderer among your people, and you shall not stand up against the life of your neighbor: I am the Lord.

Proverbs 18:8
The words of a whisperer are like delicious morsels; they go down into the inner parts of the body.

2 Corinthians 12:20
For I fear that perhaps when I come I may find you not as I wish, and that you may find me not as you wish—that perhaps there may be quarreling, jealousy, anger, hostility, slander, gossip, conceit, and disorder.

1 Timothy 5:13
Besides that, they learn to be idlers, going about from house to house, and not only idlers, but also gossips and busybodies, saying what they should not.

James 1:26
If anyone thinks he is religious and does not bridle his tongue but deceives his heart, this person's religion is worthless.

Exodus 23:1
"You shall not spread a false report. You shall not join hands with a wicked man to be a malicious witness.

Government

Romans 13:1
Let every person be subject to the governing authorities. For there is no authority except from God, and those that exist have been instituted by God.

Acts 5:29
But Peter and the apostles answered, "We must obey God rather than men.

1 Peter 2:13-17
Be subject for the Lord's sake to every human institution, whether it be to the emperor as supreme, or to governors as sent by him to punish those who do evil and to praise those who do good. For this is the will of God, that by doing good you should put to silence the ignorance of foolish people. Live as people who are free, not using your freedom as a cover-up for evil, but living as servants of God. Honor everyone. Love the brotherhood. Fear God. Honor the emperor.

1 Timothy 2:1-2

First of all, then, I urge that supplications, prayers, intercessions, and thanksgivings be made for all people, for kings and all who are in high positions, that we may lead a peaceful and quiet life, godly and dignified in every way.

Grace

2 Corinthians 12:9

But he said to me, "My grace is sufficient for you, for my power is made perfect in weakness." Therefore I will boast all the more gladly of my weaknesses, so that the power of Christ may rest upon me.

Ephesians 2:8-9

For by grace you have been saved through faith. And this is not your own doing; it is the gift of God, not a result of works, so that no one may boast.

Romans 6:14

For sin will have no dominion over you, since you are not under law but under grace.

Romans 11:6

But if it is by grace, it is no longer on the basis of works; otherwise grace would no longer be grace.

James 4:6

But he gives more grace. Therefore it says, "God opposes the proud, but gives grace to the humble."

1 Corinthians 15:10

But by the grace of God I am what I am, and his grace toward me was not in vain. On the contrary, I worked harder than any of them, though it was not I, but the grace of God that is with me.

Hebrews 4:16

Let us then with confidence draw near to the throne of grace, that we may receive mercy and find grace to help in time of need.

John 1:16

And from his fullness we have all received, grace upon grace.

Gratitude

1 Thessalonians 5:18

Give thanks in all circumstances; for this is the will of God in Christ Jesus for you.

Psalm 118:24

This is the day that the Lord has made; let us rejoice and be glad in it.

Colossians 3:17

And whatever you do, in word or deed, do everything in the name of the Lord Jesus, giving thanks to God the Father through him.

Psalm 136:1

Give thanks to the Lord, for he is good, for his steadfast love endures forever.

James 1:17

Every good gift and every perfect gift is from above, coming down from the Father of lights with whom there is no variation or shadow due to change.

Ephesians 1:16

I do not cease to give thanks for you, remembering you in my prayers,

Colossians 3:15

And let the peace of Christ rule in your hearts, to which indeed you were called in one body. And be thankful.

Hebrews 12:28

Therefore, let us be grateful for receiving a kingdom that cannot be shaken, and thus let us offer to God acceptable worship, with reverence and awe,

Greed

1 Timothy 6:9-10

But those who desire to be rich fall into temptation, into a snare, into many senseless and harmful desires that plunge people into ruin and destruction. For the love of money is a root of all kinds of evils. It is through this craving that some have wandered away from the faith and pierced themselves with many pangs.

Proverbs 28:25

A greedy man stirs up strife, but the one who trusts in the Lord will be enriched.

Hebrews 13:5

Keep your life free from love of money, and be content with what you have, for he has said, "I will never leave you nor forsake you."

Luke 12:15

And he said to them, "Take care, and be on your guard against all covetousness, for one's life does not consist in the abundance of his possessions."

Proverbs 15:27

Whoever is greedy for unjust gain troubles his own household, but he who hates bribes will live.

Matthew 6:24

"No one can serve two masters, for either he will hate the one and love the other, or he will be devoted to the one and despise the other. You cannot serve God and money.

Proverbs 11:24

One gives freely, yet grows all the richer; another withholds what he should give, and only suffers want.

1 Corinthians 6:9-11

Or do you not know that the unrighteous will not inherit the kingdom of God? Do not be deceived: neither the sexually immoral, nor idolaters, nor adulterers, nor men who practice homosexuality, nor thieves, nor the greedy, nor drunkards, nor revilers, nor swindlers will inherit the kingdom of God. And such were some of you. But you were washed, you were sanctified, you were justified in the name of the Lord Jesus Christ and by the Spirit of our God.

1 John 2:16

For all that is in the world—the desires of the flesh and the desires of the eyes and pride in possessions—is not from the Father but is from the world.

Ecclesiastes 5:10

He who loves money will not be satisfied with money, nor he who loves wealth with his income; this also is vanity.

Grief

Psalm 34:18

The Lord is near to the brokenhearted and saves the crushed in spirit.

Revelation 21:4

He will wipe away every tear from their eyes, and death shall be no more, neither shall there be mourning, nor crying, nor pain anymore, for the former things have passed away."

2 Corinthians 1:3-4

Blessed be the God and Father of our Lord Jesus Christ, the Father of mercies and God of all comfort, who comforts us in all our affliction, so that we may be able to comfort those who are in any affliction, with the comfort with which we ourselves are comforted by God.

Psalm 147:3

He heals the brokenhearted and binds up their wounds.

1 Peter 5:7

Casting all your anxieties on him, because he cares for you.

Matthew 5:4

"Blessed are those who mourn, for they shall be comforted.

Psalm 73:26

My flesh and my heart may fail, but God is the strength of my heart and my portion forever.

Grumbling

Philippians 2:14

Do all things without grumbling or questioning,

Philippians 2:14-16
Do all things without grumbling or questioning, that you may be blameless and innocent, children of God without blemish in the midst of a crooked and twisted generation, among whom you shine as lights in the world, holding fast to the word of life, so that in the day of Christ I may be proud that I did not run in vain or labor in vain.

Exodus 16:7-8
And in the morning you shall see the glory of the Lord, because he has heard your grumbling against the Lord. For what are we, that you grumble against us?" And Moses said, "When the Lord gives you in the evening meat to eat and in the morning bread to the full, because the Lord has heard your grumbling that you grumble against him—what are we? Your grumbling is not against us but against the Lord."

James 5:9
Do not grumble against one another, brothers, so that you may not be judged; behold, the Judge is standing at the door.

Numbers 14:27
"How long shall this wicked congregation grumble against me? I have heard the grumblings of the people of Israel, which they grumble against me.

1 Corinthians 10:8-11
We must not indulge in sexual immorality as some of them did, and twenty-three thousand fell in a single day. We must not put Christ to the test, as some of them did and were destroyed by serpents, nor grumble, as some of them did and were destroyed by the Destroyer. Now these things happened to them as an example, but they were written down for our instruction, on whom the end of the ages has come.

Guidance

Proverbs 3:5-6
Trust in the Lord with all your heart, and do not lean on your own understanding. In all your ways acknowledge him, and he will make straight your paths.

Psalm 32:8
I will instruct you and teach you in the way you should go; I will counsel you with my eye upon you.

John 16:13
When the Spirit of truth comes, he will guide you into all the truth, for he will not speak on his own authority, but whatever he hears he will speak, and he will declare to you the things that are to come.

Isaiah 30:21
And your ears shall hear a word behind you, saying, "This is the way, walk in it," when you turn to the right or when you turn to the left.

Matthew 7:7-11
"Ask, and it will be given to you; seek, and you will find; knock, and it will be opened to you. For everyone who asks receives, and the one who seeks finds, and to the one who knocks it will be opened. Or which one of you, if his son asks him for bread, will give him a stone? Or if he asks for a fish, will give him a

serpent? If you then, who are evil, know how to give good gifts to your children, how much more will your Father who is in heaven give good things to those who ask him!

Psalm 119:105

Your word is a lamp to my feet and a light to my path.

James 1:5-6

If any of you lacks wisdom, let him ask God, who gives generously to all without reproach, and it will be given him. But let him ask in faith, with no doubting, for the one who doubts is like a wave of the sea that is driven and tossed by the wind.

Psalm 25:4-5

Make me to know your ways, O Lord; teach me your paths. Lead me in your truth and teach me, for you are the God of my salvation; for you I wait all the day long.

John 14:26

But the Helper, the Holy Spirit, whom the Father will send in my name, he will teach you all things and bring to your remembrance all that I have said to you.

Psalm 37:23-24

The steps of a man are established by the Lord, when he delights in his way; though he fall, he shall not be cast headlong, for the Lord upholds his hand.

Proverbs 16:9

The heart of man plans his way, but the Lord establishes his steps.

Guilt

1 John 1:9

If we confess our sins, he is faithful and just to forgive us our sins and to cleanse us from all unrighteousness.

Romans 8:1

There is therefore now no condemnation for those who are in Christ Jesus.

Romans 5:1

Therefore, since we have been justified by faith, we have peace with God through our Lord Jesus Christ.

Romans 3:23

For all have sinned and fall short of the glory of God,

Habits

Romans 12:2

Do not be conformed to this world, but be transformed by the renewal of your mind, that by testing you may discern what is the will of God, what is good and acceptable and perfect.

1 Corinthians 10:13

No temptation has overtaken you that is not common to man. God is faithful, and he will not let you be tempted beyond your ability, but with the temptation he will also provide the way of escape, that you may be able to endure it.

1 Corinthians 6:12

"All things are lawful for me," but not all things are helpful. "All things are lawful for me," but I will not be enslaved by anything.

Mark 7:20-23

And he said, "What comes out of a person is what defiles him. For from within, out of the heart of man, come evil thoughts, sexual immorality, theft, murder, adultery, coveting, wickedness, deceit, sensuality, envy, slander, pride, foolishness. All these evil things come from within, and they defile a person."

Hands of God

1 Peter 5:6

Humble yourselves, therefore, under the mighty hand of God so that at the proper time he may exalt you,

John 10:29

My Father, who has given them to me, is greater than all, and no one is able to snatch them out of the Father's hand.

Psalm 110:1

A Psalm of David. The Lord says to my Lord: "Sit at my right hand, until I make your enemies your footstool."

Ezra 8:21-23

Then I proclaimed a fast there, at the river Ahava, that we might humble ourselves before our God, to seek from him a safe journey for ourselves, our children, and all our goods. For I was ashamed to ask the king for a band of soldiers and horsemen to protect us against the enemy on our way, since we had told the king, "The hand of our God is for good on all who seek him, and the power of his wrath is against all who forsake him." So we fasted and implored our God for this, and he listened to our entreaty.

Isaiah 49:14-16

But Zion said, "The Lord has forsaken me; my Lord has forgotten me." "Can a woman forget her nursing child, that she should have no compassion on the son of her womb? Even these may forget, yet I will not forget you. Behold, I have engraved you on the palms of my hands; your walls are continually before me.

Isaiah 41:13-14

For I, the Lord your God, hold your right hand; it is I who say to you, "Fear not, I am the one who helps you." Fear not, you worm Jacob, you men of Israel! I am the one who helps you, declares the Lord; your Redeemer is the Holy One of Israel.

Ezekiel 1:3

The word of the Lord came to Ezekiel the priest, the son of Buzi, in the land of the Chaldeans by the Chebar canal, and the hand of the Lord was upon him there.

Isaiah 41:10

Fear not, for I am with you; be not dismayed, for I am your God; I will strengthen you, I will help you, I will uphold you with my righteous right hand.

Isaiah 49:16

Behold, I have engraved you on the palms of my hands; your walls are continually before me.

Isaiah 48:13

My hand laid the foundation of the earth, and my right hand spread out the heavens; when I call to them, they stand forth together.

Happiness

Psalm 37:4

Delight yourself in the Lord, and he will give you the desires of your heart.

Ecclesiastes 3:12

I perceived that there is nothing better for them than to be joyful and to do good as long as they live;

Philippians 4:4

Rejoice in the Lord always; again I will say, Rejoice.

Isaiah 12:2

"Behold, God is my salvation; I will trust, and will not be afraid; for the Lord God is my strength and my song, and he has become my salvation."

Proverbs 14:13

Even in laughter the heart may ache, and the end of joy may be grief.

Isaiah 12:3

With joy you will draw water from the wells of salvation.

Philippians 4:7

And the peace of God, which surpasses all understanding, will guard your hearts and your minds in Christ Jesus.

1 Peter 3:14

But even if you should suffer for righteousness' sake, you will be blessed. Have no fear of them, nor be troubled,

Ecclesiastes 3:13

Also that everyone should eat and drink and take pleasure in all his toil—this is God's gift to man.

Hard Times

James 1:12

Blessed is the man who remains steadfast under trial, for when he has stood the test he will receive the crown of life, which God has promised to those who love him.

Isaiah 41:10

Fear not, for I am with you; be not dismayed, for I am your God; I will strengthen you, I will help you, I will uphold you with my righteous right hand.

Philippians 4:6-8

Do not be anxious about anything, but in everything by prayer and supplication with thanksgiving let your requests be made known to God. And the peace of God, which surpasses all understanding, will guard your hearts and your minds in Christ Jesus. Finally, brothers, whatever is true, whatever is honorable, whatever is just, whatever is pure, whatever is lovely, whatever is commendable, if there is any excellence, if there is anything worthy of praise, think about these things.

Romans 8:31

What then shall we say to these things? If God is for us, who can be against us?

Romans 8:18

For I consider that the sufferings of this present time are not worth comparing with the glory that is to be revealed to us.

Romans 8:28

And we know that for those who love God all things work together for good, for those who are called according to his purpose.

Joshua 1:9

Have I not commanded you? Be strong and courageous. Do not be frightened, and do not be dismayed, for the Lord your God is with you wherever you go."

Psalm 50:15

And call upon me in the day of trouble; I will deliver you, and you shall glorify me."

2 Corinthians 1:3-4

Blessed be the God and Father of our Lord Jesus Christ, the Father of mercies and God of all comfort, who comforts us in all our affliction, so that we may be able to comfort those who are in any affliction, with the comfort with which we ourselves are comforted by God.

John 16:33

I have said these things to you, that in me you may have peace. In the world you will have tribulation. But take heart; I have overcome the world."

Hard Work

Colossians 3:23

Whatever you do, work heartily, as for the Lord and not for men,

Proverbs 13:4

The soul of the sluggard craves and gets nothing, while the soul of the diligent is richly supplied.

Proverbs 14:23

In all toil there is profit, but mere talk tends only to poverty.

Philippians 4:13

I can do all things through him who strengthens me.

2 Thessalonians 3:10-12

For even when we were with you, we would give you this command: If anyone is not willing to work, let him not eat. For we hear that some among you walk in idleness, not busy at work, but busybodies. Now such persons we command and encourage in the Lord Jesus Christ to do their work quietly and to earn their own living.

Proverbs 16:3

Commit your work to the Lord, and your plans will be established.

Philippians 2:14-15

Do all things without grumbling or questioning, that you may be blameless and innocent, children of God without blemish in the midst of a crooked and twisted generation, among whom you shine as lights in the world,

1 Corinthians 10:31

So, whether you eat or drink, or whatever you do, do all to the glory of God.

Proverbs 12:24

The hand of the diligent will rule, while the slothful will be put to forced labor.

1 Thessalonians 4:11-12

And to aspire to live quietly, and to mind your own affairs, and to work with your hands, as we instructed you, so that you may walk properly before outsiders and be dependent on no one.

Luke 1:37

For nothing will be impossible with God."

Colossians 3:17

And whatever you do, in word or deed, do everything in the name of the Lord Jesus, giving thanks to God the Father through him.

Hardship

James 1:12

Blessed is the man who remains steadfast under trial, for when he has stood the test he will receive the crown of life, which God has promised to those who love him.

Romans 5:3-5

More than that, we rejoice in our sufferings, knowing that suffering produces endurance, and endurance produces character, and character produces hope, and hope does not put us to shame, because God's love has been poured into our hearts through the Holy Spirit who has been given to us.

Philippians 4:13

I can do all things through him who strengthens me.

Romans 8:35-39

Who shall separate us from the love of Christ? Shall tribulation, or distress, or persecution, or famine, or nakedness, or danger, or sword? As it is written, "For your sake we are being killed all the day long; we are regarded as sheep to be slaughtered." No, in all these things we are more than conquerors through him who loved us. For I am sure that neither death nor life, nor angels nor rulers, nor things present nor things to come, nor powers, nor height nor depth, nor anything else in all creation, will be able to separate us from the love of God in Christ Jesus our Lord.

2 Corinthians 12:9-10

But he said to me, "My grace is sufficient for you, for my power is made perfect in weakness." Therefore, I will boast all the more gladly of my weaknesses, so that the power of Christ may rest upon me. For the sake of Christ, then, I am content with weaknesses, insults, hardships, persecutions, and calamities. For when I am weak, then I am strong.

James 1:2-4

Count it all joy, my brothers, when you meet trials of various kinds, for you know that the testing of your faith produces steadfastness. And let steadfastness have its full effect, that you may be perfect and complete, lacking in nothing.

Matthew 11:28

Come to me, all who labor and are heavy laden, and I will give you rest.

Joshua 1:9

Have I not commanded you? Be strong and courageous. Do not be frightened, and do not be dismayed, for the Lord your God is with you wherever you go.

Harmony

Romans 12:16-18
Live in harmony with one another. Do not be haughty, but associate with the lowly. Never be wise in your own sight. Repay no one evil for evil, but give thought to do what is honorable in the sight of all. If possible, so far as it depends on you, live peaceably with all.

1 Peter 3:8
Finally, all of you, have unity of mind, sympathy, brotherly love, a tender heart, and a humble mind.

Romans 14:19
So then let us pursue what makes for peace and for mutual upbuilding.

Harvest Time

Luke 10:2
And he said to them, "The harvest is plentiful, but the laborers are few. Therefore, pray earnestly to the Lord of the harvest to send out laborers into his harvest.

John 4:35
Do you not say, 'There are yet four months, then comes the harvest'? Look, I tell you, lift up your eyes, and see that the fields are white for harvest.

Matthew 13:30
Let both grow together until the harvest, and at harvest time I will tell the reapers, Gather the weeds first and bind them in bundles to be burned, but gather the wheat into my barn.'"

Hate

1 John 4:20
If anyone says, "I love God," and hates his brother, he is a liar; for he who does not love his brother whom he has seen cannot love God whom he has not seen.

Proverbs 10:12
Hatred stirs up strife, but love covers all offenses.

1 John 3:15
Everyone who hates his brother is a murderer, and you know that no murderer has eternal life abiding in him.

Proverbs 6:16-19
There are six things that the Lord hates, seven that are an abomination to him: haughty eyes, a lying tongue, and hands that shed innocent blood, a heart that devises wicked plans, feet that make haste to run to evil, a false witness who breathes out lies, and one who sows discord among brothers.

Leviticus 19:17

"You shall not hate your brother in your heart, but you shall reason frankly with your neighbor, lest you incur sin because of him.

1 John 2:9

Whoever says he is in the light and hates his brother is still in darkness.

1 Corinthians 13:4-7

Love is patient and kind; love does not envy or boast; it is not arrogant or rude. It does not insist on its own way; it is not irritable or resentful; it does not rejoice at wrongdoing, but rejoices with the truth. Love bears all things, believes all things, hopes all things, endures all things.

Ephesians 4:29

Let no corrupting talk come out of your mouths, but only such as is good for building up, as fits the occasion, that it may give grace to those who hear.

Proverbs 15:1

A soft answer turns away wrath, but a harsh word stirs up anger.

1 John 2:11

But whoever hates his brother is in the darkness and walks in the darkness, and does not know where he is going, because the darkness has blinded his eyes.

Proverbs 8:13

The fear of the Lord is hatred of evil. Pride and arrogance and the way of evil and perverted speech I hate.

John 15:18

"If the world hates you, know that it has hated me before it hated you.

Hatred

1 John 4:20

If anyone says, "I love God," and hates his brother, he is a liar; for he who does not love his brother whom he has seen cannot love God whom he has not seen.

1 John 2:9

Whoever says he is in the light and hates his brother is still in darkness.

Proverbs 10:12

Hatred stirs up strife, but love covers all offenses.

Matthew 6:15

But if you do not forgive others their trespasses, neither will your Father forgive your trespasses.

Matthew 5:44

But I say to you, Love your enemies and pray for those who persecute you,

John 15:18

"If the world hates you, know that it has hated me before it hated you.

Proverbs 26:24-26

Whoever hates disguises himself with his lips and harbors deceit in his heart; when he speaks graciously, believe him not, for there are seven abominations in his heart; though his hatred be covered with deception, his wickedness will be exposed in the assembly.

1 John 2:11

But whoever hates his brother is in the darkness and walks in the darkness, and does not know where he is going, because the darkness has blinded his eyes.

Having a Baby

Psalm 127:3-5

Behold, children are a heritage from the Lord, the fruit of the womb a reward. Like arrows in the hand of a warrior are the children of one's youth. Blessed is the man who fills his quiver with them! He shall not be put to shame when he speaks with his enemies in the gate.

Genesis 1:28

And God blessed them. And God said to them, "Be fruitful and multiply and fill the earth and subdue it and have dominion over the fish of the sea and over the birds of the heavens and over every living thing that moves on the earth."

Jeremiah 1:5

"Before I formed you in the womb I knew you, and before you were born I consecrated you; I appointed you a prophet to the nations."

Proverbs 22:6

Train up a child in the way he should go; even when he is old he will not depart from it.

Healing

Jeremiah 17:14

Heal me, O Lord, and I shall be healed; save me, and I shall be saved, for you are my praise.

Isaiah 41:10

Fear not, for I am with you; be not dismayed, for I am your God; I will strengthen you, I will help you, I will uphold you with my righteous right hand.

1 Peter 2:24

He himself bore our sins in his body on the tree, that we might die to sin and live to righteousness. By his wounds you have been healed.

Jeremiah 33:6

Behold, I will bring to it health and healing, and I will heal them and reveal to them abundance of prosperity and security.

Isaiah 53:5

But he was wounded for our transgressions; he was crushed for our iniquities; upon him was the chastisement that brought us peace, and with his stripes we are healed.

Psalm 103:2-4

Bless the Lord, O my soul, and forget not all his benefits, who forgives all your iniquity, who heals all your diseases, who redeems your life from the pit, who crowns you with steadfast love and mercy,

James 5:15

And the prayer of faith will save the one who is sick, and the Lord will raise him up. And if he has committed sins, he will be forgiven.

Psalm 147:3

He heals the brokenhearted and binds up their wounds.

Psalm 41:3

The Lord sustains him on his sickbed; in his illness you restore him to full health.

3 John 1:2

Beloved, I pray that all may go well with you and that you may be in good health, as it goes well with your soul.

James 5:16

Therefore, confess your sins to one another and pray for one another, that you may be healed. The prayer of a righteous person has great power as it is working.

Proverbs 17:22

A joyful heart is good medicine, but a crushed spirit dries up the bones.

Health

3 John 1:2

Beloved, I pray that all may go well with you and that you may be in good health, as it goes well with your soul.

1 Corinthians 6:19-20

Or do you not know that your body is a temple of the Holy Spirit within you, whom you have from God? You are not your own, for you were bought with a price. So glorify God in your body.

Proverbs 17:22

A joyful heart is good medicine, but a crushed spirit dries up the bones.

Exodus 15:26

Saying, "If you will diligently listen to the voice of the Lord your God, and do that which is right in his eyes, and give ear to his commandments and keep all his statutes, I will put none of the diseases on you that I put on the Egyptians, for I am the Lord, your healer."

Proverbs 3:7-8

Be not wise in your own eyes; fear the Lord, and turn away from evil. It will be healing to your flesh and refreshment to your bones.

Proverbs 16:24

Gracious words are like a honeycomb, sweetness to the soul and health to the body.

Exodus 23:25

You shall serve the Lord your God, and he will bless your bread and your water, and I will take sickness away from among you.

1 Corinthians 10:31

So, whether you eat or drink, or whatever you do, do all to the glory of God.

Psalm 147:3

He heals the brokenhearted and binds up their wounds.

1 Timothy 4:8

For while bodily training is of some value, godliness is of value in every way, as it holds promise for the present life and also for the life to come.

Jeremiah 33:6

Behold, I will bring to it health and healing, and I will heal them and reveal to them abundance of prosperity and security.

Proverbs 4:20-22

My son, be attentive to my words; incline your ear to my sayings. Let them not escape from your sight; keep them within your heart. For they are life to those who find them, and healing to all their flesh.

Hearing God

John 10:27

My sheep hear my voice, and I know them, and they follow me.

Romans 10:17

So faith comes from hearing, and hearing through the word of Christ.

Jeremiah 33:3

Call to me and I will answer you, and will tell you great and hidden things that you have not known.

John 8:47

Whoever is of God hears the words of God. The reason why you do not hear them is that you are not of God."

Isaiah 30:21

And your ears shall hear a word behind you, saying, "This is the way, walk in it," when you turn to the right or when you turn to the left.

John 16:13

When the Spirit of truth comes, he will guide you into all the truth, for he will not speak on his own authority, but whatever he hears he will speak, and he will declare to you the things that are to come.

Luke 11:28

But he said, "Blessed rather are those who hear the word of God and keep it!"

Hebrews 4:12

For the word of God is living and active, sharper than any two-edged sword, piercing to the division of soul and of spirit, of joints and of marrow, and discerning the thoughts and intentions of the heart.

John 6:63

It is the Spirit who gives life; the flesh is no help at all. The words that I have spoken to you are spirit and life.

Psalm 32:8-9

I will instruct you and teach you in the way you should go; I will counsel you with my eye upon you. Be not like a horse or a mule, without understanding, which must be curbed with bit and bridle, or it will not stay near you.

John 14:16-17

And I will ask the Father, and he will give you another Helper, to be with you forever, even the Spirit of truth, whom the world cannot receive, because it neither sees him nor knows him. You know him, for he dwells with you and will be in you.

Heart

Psalm 51:10

Create in me a clean heart, O God, and renew a right spirit within me.

Ezekiel 36:26

And I will give you a new heart, and a new spirit I will put within you. And I will remove the heart of stone from your flesh and give you a heart of flesh.

Jeremiah 17:9

The heart is deceitful above all things, and desperately sick; who can understand it?

Proverbs 4:23

Keep your heart with all vigilance, for from it flow the springs of life.

Matthew 5:8

"Blessed are the pure in heart, for they shall see God.

Jeremiah 17:10

"I the Lord search the heart and test the mind, to give every man according to his ways, according to the fruit of his deeds."

Hebrews 4:12

For the word of God is living and active, sharper than any two-edged sword, piercing to the division of soul and of spirit, of joints and of marrow, and discerning the thoughts and intentions of the heart.

Psalm 34:18

The Lord is near to the brokenhearted and saves the crushed in spirit.

Proverbs 3:5-6

Trust in the Lord with all your heart, and do not lean on your own understanding. In all your ways acknowledge him, and he will make straight your paths.

Proverbs 21:2

Every way of a man is right in his own eyes, but the Lord weighs the heart.

Ezekiel 11:19

And I will give them one heart, and a new spirit I will put within them. I will remove the heart of stone from their flesh and give them a heart of flesh,

Matthew 15:18-20

But what comes out of the mouth proceeds from the heart, and this defiles a person. For out of the heart come evil thoughts, murder, adultery, sexual immorality, theft, false witness, slander. These are what defile a person. But to eat with unwashed hands does not defile anyone."

1 Samuel 16:7

But the Lord said to Samuel, "Do not look on his appearance or on the height of his stature, because I have rejected him. For the Lord sees not as man sees: man looks on the outward appearance, but the Lord looks on the heart."

James 4:8

Draw near to God, and he will draw near to you. Cleanse your hands, you sinners, and purify your hearts, you double-minded.

Luke 12:33-34

Sell your possessions, and give to the needy. Provide yourselves with moneybags that do not grow old, with a treasure in the heavens that does not fail, where no thief approaches and no moth destroys. For where your treasure is, there will your heart be also.

1 Timothy 1:5

The aim of our charge is love that issues from a pure heart and a good conscience and a sincere faith.

Heartache

Psalm 34:17-20
When the righteous cry for help, the Lord hears and delivers them out of all their troubles. The Lord is near to the brokenhearted and saves the crushed in spirit. Many are the afflictions of the righteous, but the Lord delivers him out of them all. He keeps all his bones; not one of them is broken.

1 Peter 5:7
Casting all your anxieties on him, because he cares for you.

Revelation 21:4
He will wipe away every tear from their eyes, and death shall be no more, neither shall there be mourning, nor crying, nor pain anymore, for the former things have passed away."

Romans 8:28
And we know that for those who love God all things work together for good, for those who are called according to his purpose.

Psalm 147:3
He heals the brokenhearted and binds up their wounds.

Proverbs 3:4-5
So you will find favor and good success in the sight of God and man. Trust in the Lord with all your heart, and do not lean on your own understanding.

Nahum 1:7
The Lord is good, a stronghold in the day of trouble; he knows those who take refuge in him.

Philippians 4:13
I can do all things through him who strengthens me.

John 15:13
Greater love has no one than this, that someone lay down his life for his friends.

Proverbs 15:13-14
A glad heart makes a cheerful face, but by sorrow of heart the spirit is crushed. The heart of him who has understanding seeks knowledge, but the mouths of fools feed on folly.

Heartbreak

Psalm 147:3
He heals the brokenhearted and binds up their wounds.

Psalm 34:18-20
The Lord is near to the brokenhearted and saves the crushed in spirit. Many are the afflictions of the righteous, but the Lord delivers him out of them all. He keeps all his bones; not one of them is broken.

Proverbs 14:13-14

Even in laughter the heart may ache, and the end of joy may be grief. The backslider in heart will be filled with the fruit of his ways, and a good man will be filled with the fruit of his ways.

2 Corinthians 4:9

Persecuted, but not forsaken; struck down, but not destroyed;

John 13:7

Jesus answered him, "What I am doing you do not understand now, but afterward you will understand."

Psalm 39:12

"Hear my prayer, O Lord, and give ear to my cry; hold not your peace at my tears! For I am a sojourner with you, a guest, like all my fathers.

Psalm 55:22

Cast your burden on the Lord, and he will sustain you; he will never permit the righteous to be moved.

Proverbs 12:25

Anxiety in a man's heart weighs him down, but a good word makes him glad.

Proverbs 3:5

Trust in the Lord with all your heart, and do not lean on your own understanding.

John 8:32

And you will know the truth, and the truth will set you free."

Heaven

Revelation 21:4

He will wipe away every tear from their eyes, and death shall be no more, neither shall there be mourning, nor crying, nor pain anymore, for the former things have passed away."

John 14:2

In my Father's house are many rooms. If it were not so, would I have told you that I go to prepare a place for you?

1 Corinthians 2:9

But, as it is written, "What no eye has seen, nor ear heard, nor the heart of man imagined, what God has prepared for those who love him"—

John 3:16

"For God so loved the world, that he gave his only Son, that whoever believes in him should not perish but have eternal life.

Revelation 22:1-5

Then the angel showed me the river of the water of life, bright as crystal, flowing from the throne of God and of the Lamb through the middle of the street of the city; also, on either side of the river, the tree of life with its twelve kinds of fruit, yielding its fruit each month. The leaves of the tree were for the healing of the nations. No longer will there be anything accursed, but the throne of God and of the Lamb will be in it, and his servants will worship him. They will see his face, and his name will be on their foreheads. And night will be no more. They will need no light of lamp or sun, for the Lord God will be their light, and they will reign forever and ever.

Romans 10:9-13

Because, if you confess with your mouth that Jesus is Lord and believe in your heart that God raised him from the dead, you will be saved. For with the heart one believes and is justified, and with the mouth one confesses and is saved. For the Scripture says, "Everyone who believes in him will not be put to shame." For there is no distinction between Jew and Greek; for the same Lord is Lord of all, bestowing his riches on all who call on him. For "everyone who calls on the name of the Lord will be saved."

Luke 23:43

And he said to him, "Truly, I say to you, today you will be with me in Paradise."

Matthew 6:19-21

"Do not lay up for yourselves treasures on earth, where moth and rust destroy and where thieves break in and steal, but lay up for yourselves treasures in heaven, where neither moth nor rust destroys and where thieves do not break in and steal. For where your treasure is, there your heart will be also.

Hebrews 11:16

But as it is, they desire a better country, that is, a heavenly one. Therefore, God is not ashamed to be called their God, for he has prepared for them a city.

Hell

Revelation 21:8

But as for the cowardly, the faithless, the detestable, as for murderers, the sexually immoral, sorcerers, idolaters, and all liars, their portion will be in the lake that burns with fire and sulfur, which is the second death."

Matthew 10:28

And do not fear those who kill the body but cannot kill the soul. Rather fear him who can destroy both soul and body in hell.

Matthew 25:46

And these will go away into eternal punishment, but the righteous into eternal life."

Revelation 20:10

And the devil who had deceived them was thrown into the lake of fire and sulfur where the beast and the false prophet were, and they will be tormented day and night forever and ever.

Romans 6:23

For the wages of sin is death, but the free gift of God is eternal life in Christ Jesus our Lord.

Revelation 20:15

And if anyone's name was not found written in the book of life, he was thrown into the lake of fire.

Matthew 25:41

"Then he will say to those on his left, 'Depart from me, you cursed, into the eternal fire prepared for the devil and his angels.

Matthew 5:22

But I say to you that everyone who is angry with his brother will be liable to judgment; whoever insults his brother will be liable to the council; and whoever says, 'You fool!' will be liable to the hell of fire.

Revelation 14:11

And the smoke of their torment goes up forever and ever, and they have no rest, day or night, these worshipers of the beast and its image, and whoever receives the mark of its name."

2 Thessalonians 1:9

They will suffer the punishment of eternal destruction, away from the presence of the Lord and from the glory of his might,

Matthew 13:50

And throw them into the fiery furnace. In that place there will be weeping and gnashing of teeth.

2 Peter 2:4

For if God did not spare angels when they sinned, but cast them into hell and committed them to chains of gloomy darkness to be kept until the judgment;

Jude 1:7

Just as Sodom and Gomorrah and the surrounding cities, which likewise indulged in sexual immorality and pursued unnatural desire, serve as an example by undergoing a punishment of eternal fire.

Holiness

Hebrews 12:14

Strive for peace with everyone, and for the holiness without which no one will see the Lord.

2 Corinthians 7:1

Since we have these promises, beloved, let us cleanse ourselves from every defilement of body and spirit, bringing holiness to completion in the fear of God.

1 Peter 1:14-16

As obedient children, do not be conformed to the passions of your former ignorance, but as he who called you is holy, you also be holy in all your conduct, since it is written, "You shall be holy, for I am holy."

1 Peter 2:9

But you are a chosen race, a royal priesthood, a holy nation, a people for his own possession, that you may proclaim the excellencies of him who called you out of darkness into his marvelous light.

1 Peter 1:15-16

But as he who called you is holy, you also be holy in all your conduct, since it is written, "You shall be holy, for I am holy."

1 Thessalonians 4:7

For God has not called us for impurity, but in holiness.

1 Samuel 2:2

"There is none holy like the Lord; there is none besides you; there is no rock like our God.

Holiness of God

1 Samuel 2:2

"There is none holy like the Lord; there is none besides you; there is no rock like our God.

1 Peter 1:15-16

But as he who called you is holy, you also be holy in all your conduct, since it is written, "You shall be holy, for I am holy."

Isaiah 57:15

For thus says the One who is high and lifted up, who inhabits eternity, whose name is Holy: "I dwell in the high and holy place, and also with him who is of a contrite and lowly spirit, to revive the spirit of the lowly, and to revive the heart of the contrite.

Isaiah 6:3

And one called to another and said: "Holy, holy, holy is the Lord of hosts; the whole earth is full of his glory!"

1 Peter 1:16

Since it is written, "You shall be holy, for I am holy."

Psalm 96:9

Worship the Lord in the splendor of holiness; tremble before him, all the earth!

Leviticus 19:2

"Speak to all the congregation of the people of Israel and say to them, You shall be holy, for I the Lord your God am holy.

Ephesians 1:4

Even as he chose us in him before the foundation of the world, that we should be holy and blameless before him. In love

Hebrews 12:14

Strive for peace with everyone, and for the holiness without which no one will see the Lord.

Revelation 4:8

And the four living creatures, each of them with six wings, are full of eyes all around and within, and day and night they never cease to say, "Holy, holy, holy, is the Lord God Almighty, who was and is and is to come!"

Exodus 15:11

"Who is like you, O Lord, among the gods? Who is like you, majestic in holiness, awesome in glorious deeds, doing wonders?

Holy Communion

1 Corinthians 11:24-27

And when he had given thanks, he broke it, and said, "This is my body which is for you. Do this in remembrance of me." In the same way also he took the cup, after supper, saying, "This cup is the new covenant in my blood. Do this, as often as you drink it, in remembrance of me." For as often as you eat this bread and drink the cup, you proclaim the Lord's death until he comes. Whoever, therefore, eats the bread or drinks the cup of the Lord in an unworthy manner will be guilty concerning the body and blood of the Lord.

Luke 22:19-20

And he took bread, and when he had given thanks, he broke it and gave it to them, saying, "This is my body, which is given for you. Do this in remembrance of me." And likewise the cup after they had eaten, saying, "This cup that is poured out for you is the new covenant in my blood.

1 Corinthians 11:28

Let a person examine himself, then, and so eat of the bread and drink of the cup.

Matthew 26:26-28

Now as they were eating, Jesus took bread, and after blessing it broke it and gave it to the disciples, and said, "Take, eat; this is my body." And he took a cup, and when he had given thanks he gave it to them, saying, "Drink of it, all of you, for this is my blood of the covenant, which is poured out for many for the forgiveness of sins.

John 6:53

So Jesus said to them, "Truly, truly, I say to you, unless you eat the flesh of the Son of Man and drink his blood, you have no life in you.

Acts 2:42

And they devoted themselves to the apostles' teaching and the fellowship, to the breaking of bread and the prayers.

Holy Spirit

John 14:26

But the Helper, the Holy Spirit, whom the Father will send in my name, he will teach you all things and bring to your remembrance all that I have said to you.

Romans 8:26

Likewise the Spirit helps us in our weakness. For we do not know what to pray for as we ought, but the Spirit himself intercedes for us with groanings too deep for words.

Galatians 5:22-23

But the fruit of the Spirit is love, joy, peace, patience, kindness, goodness, faithfulness, gentleness, self-control; against such things there is no law.

Acts 2:38

And Peter said to them, "Repent and be baptized every one of you in the name of Jesus Christ for the forgiveness of your sins, and you will receive the gift of the Holy Spirit.

1 Corinthians 6:19

Or do you not know that your body is a temple of the Holy Spirit within you, whom you have from God? You are not your own,

Isaiah 11:2

And the Spirit of the Lord shall rest upon him, the Spirit of wisdom and understanding, the Spirit of counsel and might, the Spirit of knowledge and the fear of the Lord.

John 14:15-17

"If you love me, you will keep my commandments. And I will ask the Father, and he will give you another Helper, to be with you forever, even the Spirit of truth, whom the world cannot receive, because it neither sees him nor knows him. You know him, for he dwells with you and will be in you.

Acts 1:8

But you will receive power when the Holy Spirit has come upon you, and you will be my witnesses in Jerusalem and in all Judea and Samaria, and to the end of the earth."

Luke 11:13

If you then, who are evil, know how to give good gifts to your children, how much more will the heavenly Father give the Holy Spirit to those who ask him!"

John 16:12-15

"I still have many things to say to you, but you cannot bear them now. When the Spirit of truth comes, he will guide you into all the truth, for he will not speak on his own authority, but whatever he hears he will speak, and he will declare to you the things that are to come. He will glorify me, for he will take what is mine and declare it to you. All that the Father has is mine; therefore I said that he will take what is mine and declare it to you.

2 Corinthians 3:17

Now the Lord is the Spirit, and where the Spirit of the Lord is, there is freedom.

Romans 15:13

May the God of hope fill you with all joy and peace in believing, so that by the power of the Holy Spirit you may abound in hope.

Homosexuality

Leviticus 18:22
You shall not lie with a male as with a woman; it is an abomination.

Leviticus 20:13
If a man lies with a male as with a woman, both of them have committed an abomination; they shall surely be put to death; their blood is upon them.

1 Corinthians 6:9-11
Or do you not know that the unrighteous will not inherit the kingdom of God? Do not be deceived: neither the sexually immoral, nor idolaters, nor adulterers, nor men who practice homosexuality, nor thieves, nor the greedy, nor drunkards, nor revilers, nor swindlers will inherit the kingdom of God. And such were some of you. But you were washed, you were sanctified, you were justified in the name of the Lord Jesus Christ and by the Spirit of our God.

Romans 1:26-27
For this reason God gave them up to dishonorable passions. For their women exchanged natural relations for those that are contrary to nature; and the men likewise gave up natural relations with women and were consumed with passion for one another, men committing shameless acts with men and receiving in themselves the due penalty for their error.

Jude 1:7
Just as Sodom and Gomorrah and the surrounding cities, which likewise indulged in sexual immorality and pursued unnatural desire, serve as an example by undergoing a punishment of eternal fire.

Honesty

Proverbs 12:22
Lying lips are an abomination to the Lord, but those who act faithfully are his delight.

Proverbs 19:1
Better is a poor person who walks in his integrity than one who is crooked in speech and is a fool.

John 8:32
And you will know the truth, and the truth will set you free."

2 Corinthians 8:21
For we aim at what is honorable not only in the Lord's sight but also in the sight of man.

Proverbs 6:16-20
There are six things that the Lord hates, seven that are an abomination to him: haughty eyes, a lying tongue, and hands that shed innocent blood, a heart that devises wicked plans, feet that make haste to run to evil, a false witness who breathes out lies, and one who sows discord among brothers. My son, keep your father's commandment, and forsake not your mother's teaching.

1 Peter 3:10-12

For "Whoever desires to love life and see good days, let him keep his tongue from evil and his lips from speaking deceit; let him turn away from evil and do good; let him seek peace and pursue it. For the eyes of the Lord are on the righteous, and his ears are open to their prayer. But the face of the Lord is against those who do evil."

Proverbs 11:3

The integrity of the upright guides them, but the crookedness of the treacherous destroys them.

Colossians 3:9

Do not lie to one another, seeing that you have put off the old self with its practices

Philippians 4:8-9

Finally, brothers, whatever is true, whatever is honorable, whatever is just, whatever is pure, whatever is lovely, whatever is commendable, if there is any excellence, if there is anything worthy of praise, think about these things. What you have learned and received and heard and seen in me—practice these things, and the God of peace will be with you.

Matthew 5:37

Let what you say be simply 'Yes' or 'No'; anything more than this comes from evil.

Honor

1 Samuel 2:30

Therefore the Lord, the God of Israel, declares: 'I promised that your house and the house of your father should go in and out before me forever,' but now the Lord declares: 'Far be it from me, for those who honor me I will honor, and those who despise me shall be lightly esteemed.

1 Timothy 1:17

To the King of ages, immortal, invisible, the only God, be honor and glory forever and ever. Amen.

Hebrews 13:4

Let marriage be held in honor among all, and let the marriage bed be undefiled, for God will judge the sexually immoral and adulterous.

Deuteronomy 5:16

"'Honor your father and your mother, as the Lord your God commanded you, that your days may be long, and that it may go well with you in the land that the Lord your God is giving you.

Romans 12:9-13

Let love be genuine. Abhor what is evil; hold fast to what is good. Love one another with brotherly affection. Outdo one another in showing honor. Do not be slothful in zeal, be fervent in spirit, serve the Lord. Rejoice in hope, be patient in tribulation, be constant in prayer. Contribute to the needs of the saints and seek to show hospitality.

Hope

Jeremiah 29:11

For I know the plans I have for you, declares the Lord, plans for welfare and not for evil, to give you a future and a hope.

Romans 15:13

May the God of hope fill you with all joy and peace in believing, so that by the power of the Holy Spirit you may abound in hope.

Romans 12:12

Rejoice in hope, be patient in tribulation, be constant in prayer.

Isaiah 40:31

But they who wait for the Lord shall renew their strength; they shall mount up with wings like eagles; they shall run and not be weary; they shall walk and not faint.

Hebrews 11:1

Now faith is the assurance of things hoped for, the conviction of things not seen.

1 Peter 1:3

Blessed be the God and Father of our Lord Jesus Christ! According to his great mercy, he has caused us to be born again to a living hope through the resurrection of Jesus Christ from the dead,

Romans 15:4

For whatever was written in former days was written for our instruction, that through endurance and through the encouragement of the Scriptures we might have hope.

Romans 8:24-25

For in this hope we were saved. Now hope that is seen is not hope. For who hopes for what he sees? But if we hope for what we do not see, we wait for it with patience.

Psalm 39:7

"And now, O Lord, for what do I wait? My hope is in you.

Romans 5:2-5

Through him we have also obtained access by faith into this grace in which we stand, and we rejoice in hope of the glory of God. More than that, we rejoice in our sufferings, knowing that suffering produces endurance, and endurance produces character, and character produces hope, and hope does not put us to shame, because God's love has been poured into our hearts through the Holy Spirit who has been given to us.

Deuteronomy 31:6

Be strong and courageous. Do not fear or be in dread of them, for it is the Lord your God who goes with you. He will not leave you or forsake you."

1 Corinthians 13:13

So now faith, hope, and love abide, these three; but the greatest of these is love.

Hopelessness

Psalm 34:17-20

When the righteous cry for help, the Lord hears and delivers them out of all their troubles. The Lord is near to the brokenhearted and saves the crushed in spirit. Many are the afflictions of the righteous, but the Lord delivers him out of them all. He keeps all his bones; not one of them is broken.

Jeremiah 29:11

For I know the plans I have for you, declares the Lord, plans for welfare and not for evil, to give you a future and a hope.

Philippians 4:6-7

Do not be anxious about anything, but in everything by prayer and supplication with thanksgiving let your requests be made known to God. And the peace of God, which surpasses all understanding, will guard your hearts and your minds in Christ Jesus.

Philippians 4:13

I can do all things through him who strengthens me.

1 Corinthians 10:13

No temptation has overtaken you that is not common to man. God is faithful, and he will not let you be tempted beyond your ability, but with the temptation he will also provide the way of escape, that you may be able to endure it.

Matthew 11:28-30

Come to me, all who labor and are heavy laden, and I will give you rest. Take my yoke upon you, and learn from me, for I am gentle and lowly in heart, and you will find rest for your souls. For my yoke is easy, and my burden is light."

Isaiah 40:31

But they who wait for the Lord shall renew their strength; they shall mount up with wings like eagles; they shall run and not be weary; they shall walk and not faint.

Luke 1:37

For nothing will be impossible with God."

Revelation 21:4

He will wipe away every tear from their eyes, and death shall be no more, neither shall there be mourning, nor crying, nor pain anymore, for the former things have passed away."

Romans 15:13

May the God of hope fill you with all joy and peace in believing, so that by the power of the Holy Spirit you may abound in hope.

James 5:13

Is anyone among you suffering? Let him pray. Is anyone cheerful? Let him sing praise.

Hospitality

Hebrews 13:2

Do not neglect to show hospitality to strangers, for thereby some have entertained angels unawares.

1 Peter 4:9

Show hospitality to one another without grumbling.

Romans 12:13

Contribute to the needs of the saints and seek to show hospitality.

Leviticus 19:34

You shall treat the stranger who sojourns with you as the native among you, and you shall love him as yourself, for you were strangers in the land of Egypt: I am the Lord your God.

Titus 1:8

But hospitable, a lover of good, self-controlled, upright, holy, and disciplined.

Human Nature

Romans 2:14-16

For when Gentiles, who do not have the law, by nature do what the law requires, they are a law to themselves, even though they do not have the law. They show that the work of the law is written on their hearts, while their conscience also bears witness, and their conflicting thoughts accuse or even excuse them on that day when, according to my gospel, God judges the secrets of men by Christ Jesus.

Matthew 15:19

For out of the heart come evil thoughts, murder, adultery, sexual immorality, theft, false witness, slander.

Jeremiah 17:9

The heart is deceitful above all things, and desperately sick; who can understand it?

1 Corinthians 2:14

The natural person does not accept the things of the Spirit of God, for they are folly to him, and he is not able to understand them because they are spiritually discerned.

Mark 7:21-23

For from within, out of the heart of man, come evil thoughts, sexual immorality, theft, murder, adultery, coveting, wickedness, deceit, sensuality, envy, slander, pride, foolishness. All these evil things come from within, and they defile a person."

Isaiah 55:8

For my thoughts are not your thoughts, neither are your ways my ways, declares the Lord.

2 Timothy 1:7

For God gave us a spirit not of fear but of power and love and self-control.

1 John 1:8-10

If we say we have no sin, we deceive ourselves, and the truth is not in us. If we confess our sins, he is faithful and just to forgive us our sins and to cleanse us from all unrighteousness. If we say we have not sinned, we make him a liar, and his word is not in us.

Proverbs 19:3

When a man's folly brings his way to ruin, his heart rages against the Lord.

Humility

Proverbs 22:4

The reward for humility and fear of the Lord is riches and honor and life.

1 Peter 5:5

Likewise, you who are younger, be subject to the elders. Clothe yourselves, all of you, with humility toward one another, for "God opposes the proud but gives grace to the humble."

Colossians 3:12

Put on then, as God's chosen ones, holy and beloved, compassionate hearts, kindness, humility, meekness, and patience,

James 4:6

But he gives more grace. Therefore, it says, "God opposes the proud, but gives grace to the humble."

Proverbs 11:2

When pride comes, then comes disgrace, but with the humble is wisdom.

Ephesians 4:2

With all humility and gentleness, with patience, bearing with one another in love,

Proverbs 15:33

The fear of the Lord is instruction in wisdom, and humility comes before honor.

Proverbs 18:12

Before destruction a man's heart is haughty, but humility comes before honor.

James 4:10

Humble yourselves before the Lord, and he will exalt you.

Micah 6:8

He has told you, O man, what is good; and what does the Lord require of you but to do justice, and to love kindness, and to walk humbly with your God?

Luke 14:11

For everyone who exalts himself will be humbled, and he who humbles himself will be exalted."

1 Peter 5:6

Humble yourselves, therefore, under the mighty hand of God so that at the proper time he may exalt you,

Philippians 2:3

Do nothing from rivalry or conceit, but in humility count others more significant than yourselves.

2 Chronicles 7:14

If my people who are called by my name humble themselves, and pray and seek my face and turn from their wicked ways, then I will hear from heaven and will forgive their sin and heal their land.

Romans 12:3

For by the grace given to me I say to everyone among you not to think of himself more highly than he ought to think, but to think with sober judgment, each according to the measure of faith that God has assigned.

Hunger

Matthew 5:6

"Blessed are those who hunger and thirst for righteousness, for they shall be satisfied.

Proverbs 22:9

Whoever has a bountiful eye will be blessed, for he shares his bread with the poor.

Revelation 7:16

They shall hunger no more, neither thirst anymore; the sun shall not strike them, nor any scorching heat.

Matthew 4:4

But he answered, "It is written, "'Man shall not live by bread alone, but by every word that comes from the mouth of God.'"

James 2:15-17

If a brother or sister is poorly clothed and lacking in daily food, and one of you says to them, "Go in peace, be warmed and filled," without giving them the things needed for the body, what good is that? So also faith by itself, if it does not have works, is dead.

Psalm 42:1-2

To the choirmaster. A Maskil of the Sons of Korah. As a deer pants for flowing streams, so pants my soul for you, O God. My soul thirsts for God, for the living God. When shall I come and appear before God?

Luke 6:21

"Blessed are you who are hungry now, for you shall be satisfied. "Blessed are you who weep now, for you shall laugh.

Psalm 63:1

A Psalm of David, when he was in the wilderness of Judah. O God, you are my God; earnestly I seek you; my soul thirsts for you; my flesh faints for you, as in a dry and weary land where there is no water.

Deuteronomy 8:3

And he humbled you and let you hunger and fed you with manna, which you did not know, nor did your fathers know, that he might make you know that man does not live by bread alone, but man lives by every word that comes from the mouth of the Lord.

John 6:35

Jesus said to them, "I am the bread of life; whoever comes to me shall not hunger, and whoever believes in me shall never thirst.

Hurting Others

Ephesians 4:31-32

Let all bitterness and wrath and anger and clamor and slander be put away from you, along with all malice. Be kind to one another, tenderhearted, forgiving one another, as God in Christ forgave you.

Romans 12:18-20

If possible, so far as it depends on you, live peaceably with all. Beloved, never avenge yourselves, but leave it to the wrath of God, for it is written, "Vengeance is mine, I will repay, says the Lord." To the contrary, "if your enemy is hungry, feed him; if he is thirsty, give him something to drink; for by so doing you will heap burning coals on his head."

Genesis 50:20

As for you, you meant evil against me, but God meant it for good, to bring it about that many people should be kept alive, as they are today.

Colossians 3:25

For the wrongdoer will be paid back for the wrong he has done, and there is no partiality.

Identity

Genesis 1:27

So God created man in his own image, in the image of God he created him; male and female he created them.

2 Corinthians 5:17

Therefore, if anyone is in Christ, he is a new creation. The old has passed away; behold, the new has come.

Jeremiah 1:5

"Before I formed you in the womb I knew you, and before you were born I consecrated you; I appointed you a prophet to the nations."

1 Peter 2:9

But you are a chosen race, a royal priesthood, a holy nation, a people for his own possession, that you may proclaim the excellencies of him who called you out of darkness into his marvelous light.

Jeremiah 29:11

For I know the plans I have for you, declares the Lord, plans for welfare and not for evil, to give you a future and a hope.

Galatians 2:20

I have been crucified with Christ. It is no longer I who live, but Christ who lives in me. And the life I now live in the flesh I live by faith in the Son of God, who loved me and gave himself for me.

1 Corinthians 12:27

Now you are the body of Christ and individually members of it.

1 John 3:1-3

See what kind of love the Father has given to us, that we should be called children of God; and so we are. The reason why the world does not know us is that it did not know him. Beloved, we are God's children now, and what we will be has not yet appeared; but we know that when he appears we shall be like him, because we shall see him as he is. And everyone who thus hopes in him purifies himself as he is pure.

Ephesians 2:10

For we are his workmanship, created in Christ Jesus for good works, which God prepared beforehand, that we should walk in them.

John 15:15

No longer do I call you servants, for the servant does not know what his master is doing; but I have called you friends, for all that I have heard from my Father I have made known to you.

Idleness

1 Timothy 5:13
Besides that, they learn to be idlers, going about from house to house, and not only idlers, but also gossips and busybodies, saying what they should not.

Ecclesiastes 10:18
Through sloth the roof sinks in, and through indolence the house leaks.

Proverbs 19:15
Slothfulness casts into a deep sleep, and an idle person will suffer hunger.

Proverbs 13:4
The soul of the sluggard craves and gets nothing, while the soul of the diligent is richly supplied.

2 Thessalonians 3:10
For even when we were with you, we would give you this command: If anyone is not willing to work, let him not eat. For we hear that some among you walk in idleness, not busy at work, but busybodies.

Proverbs 31:27
She looks well to the ways of her household and does not eat the bread of idleness.

Proverbs 12:24
The hand of the diligent will rule, while the slothful will be put to forced labor.

Proverbs 24:30-34
I passed by the field of a sluggard, by the vineyard of a man lacking sense, and behold, it was all overgrown with thorns; the ground was covered with nettles, and its stone wall was broken down. Then I saw and considered it; I looked and received instruction. A little sleep, a little slumber, a little folding of the hands to rest, and poverty will come upon you like a robber, and want like an armed man.

Idolatry

Exodus 20:3-6
"You shall have no other gods before me. "You shall not make for yourself a carved image, or any likeness of anything that is in heaven above, or that is in the earth beneath, or that is in the water under the earth. You shall not bow down to them or serve them, for I the Lord your God am a jealous God, visiting the iniquity of the fathers on the children to the third and the fourth generation of those who hate me, but showing steadfast love to thousands of those who love me and keep my commandments.

Colossians 3:5
Put to death therefore what is earthly in you: sexual immorality, impurity, passion, evil desire, and covetousness, which is idolatry.

Jonah 2:8
Those who pay regard to vain idols forsake their hope of steadfast love.

1 John 5:21

Little children, keep yourselves from idols.

Leviticus 19:4

Do not turn to idols or make for yourselves any gods of cast metal: I am the Lord your God.

1 Corinthians 10:14

Therefore, my beloved, flee from idolatry.

Ignorance

Ephesians 4:18

They are darkened in their understanding, alienated from the life of God because of the ignorance that is in them, due to their hardness of heart.

Hosea 4:6

My people are destroyed for lack of knowledge; because you have rejected knowledge, I reject you from being a priest to me. And since you have forgotten the law of your God, I also will forget your children.

Acts 17:30

The times of ignorance God overlooked, but now he commands all people everywhere to repent,

Proverbs 22:3

The prudent sees danger and hides himself, but the simple go on and suffer for it.

Proverbs 19:2

Desire without knowledge is not good, and whoever makes haste with his feet misses his way.

Proverbs 8:5

O simple ones, learn prudence; O fools, learn sense.

James 1:5

If any of you lacks wisdom, let him ask God, who gives generously to all without reproach, and it will be given him.

1 John 4:1

Beloved, do not believe every spirit, but test the spirits to see whether they are from God, for many false prophets have gone out into the world.

Luke 23:34

And Jesus said, "Father, forgive them, for they know not what they do." And they cast lots to divide his garments.

Ezekiel 33:6

But if the watchman sees the sword coming and does not blow the trumpet, so that the people are not warned, and the sword comes and takes any one of them, that person is taken away in his iniquity, but his blood I will require at the watchman's hand.

Illness

Psalm 34:17-20
When the righteous cry for help, the Lord hears and delivers them out of all their troubles. The Lord is near to the brokenhearted and saves the crushed in spirit. Many are the afflictions of the righteous, but the Lord delivers him out of them all. He keeps all his bones; not one of them is broken.

2 Corinthians 12:9
But he said to me, "My grace is sufficient for you, for my power is made perfect in weakness." Therefore I will boast all the more gladly of my weaknesses, so that the power of Christ may rest upon me.

Psalm 41:2-4
The Lord protects him and keeps him alive; he is called blessed in the land; you do not give him up to the will of his enemies. The Lord sustains him on his sickbed; in his illness you restore him to full health. As for me, I said, "O Lord, be gracious to me; heal me, for I have sinned against you!"

John 16:33
I have said these things to you, that in me you may have peace. In the world you will have tribulation. But take heart; I have overcome the world."

Matthew 21:22
And whatever you ask in prayer, you will receive, if you have faith."

Philippians 4:19
And my God will supply every need of yours according to his riches in glory in Christ Jesus.

Psalm 29:11
May the Lord give strength to his people! May the Lord bless his people with peace!

1 Corinthians 6:19-20
Or do you not know that your body is a temple of the Holy Spirit within you, whom you have from God? You are not your own, for you were bought with a price. So glorify God in your body.

Image

2 Corinthians 3:18
And we all, with unveiled face, beholding the glory of the Lord, are being transformed into the same image from one degree of glory to another. For this comes from the Lord who is the Spirit.

Colossians 3:10
And have put on the new self, which is being renewed in knowledge after the image of its creator.

Genesis 1:26-27
Then God said, "Let us make man in our image, after our likeness. And let them have dominion over the fish of the sea and over the birds of the heavens and over the livestock and over all the earth and over every creeping thing that creeps on the earth." So God created man in his own image, in the image of God he created him; male and female he created them.

Psalm 17:15

As for me, I shall behold your face in righteousness; when I awake, I shall be satisfied with your likeness.

Immorality

Galatians 5:19-21

Now the works of the flesh are evident: sexual immorality, impurity, sensuality, idolatry, sorcery, enmity, strife, jealousy, fits of anger, rivalries, dissensions, divisions, envy, drunkenness, orgies, and things like these. I warn you, as I warned you before, that those who do such things will not inherit the kingdom of God.

Hebrews 13:4

Let marriage be held in honor among all, and let the marriage bed be undefiled, for God will judge the sexually immoral and adulterous.

1 Corinthians 6:18

Flee from sexual immorality. Every other sin a person commits is outside the body, but the sexually immoral person sins against his own body.

Mark 7:20-23

And he said, "What comes out of a person is what defiles him. For from within, out of the heart of man, come evil thoughts, sexual immorality, theft, murder, adultery, coveting, wickedness, deceit, sensuality, envy, slander, pride, foolishness. All these evil things come from within, and they defile a person."

Matthew 5:28

But I say to you that everyone who looks at a woman with lustful intent has already committed adultery with her in his heart.

Ephesians 5:3

But sexual immorality and all impurity or covetousness must not even be named among you, as is proper among saints.

Matthew 5:32

But I say to you that everyone who divorces his wife, except on the ground of sexual immorality, makes her commit adultery, and whoever marries a divorced woman commits adultery.

Revelation 21:8

But as for the cowardly, the faithless, the detestable, as for murderers, the sexually immoral, sorcerers, idolaters, and all liars, their portion will be in the lake that burns with fire and sulfur, which is the second death."

Impatience

James 5:7-8

Be patient, therefore, brothers, until the coming of the Lord. See how the farmer waits for the precious fruit of the earth, being patient about it, until it receives the early and the late rains. You also, be patient. Establish your hearts, for the coming of the Lord is at hand.

Galatians 5:22

But the fruit of the Spirit is love, joy, peace, patience, kindness, goodness, faithfulness,

Colossians 1:11

May you be strengthened with all power, according to his glorious might, for all endurance and patience with joy,

Isaiah 40:31

But they who wait for the Lord shall renew their strength; they shall mount up with wings like eagles; they shall run and not be weary; they shall walk and not faint.

Psalm 27:14

Wait for the Lord; be strong, and let your heart take courage; wait for the Lord!

Romans 5:3

More than that, we rejoice in our sufferings, knowing that suffering produces endurance,

Ephesians 4:2-3

With all humility and gentleness, with patience, bearing with one another in love, eager to maintain the unity of the Spirit in the bond of peace.

2 Timothy 3:10

You, however, have followed my teaching, my conduct, my aim in life, my faith, my patience, my love, my steadfastness,

Exodus 34:6

The Lord passed before him and proclaimed, "The Lord, the Lord, a God merciful and gracious, slow to anger, and abounding in steadfast love and faithfulness,

Romans 8:28

And we know that for those who love God all things work together for good, for those who are called according to his purpose.

Impossible

Matthew 19:26

But Jesus looked at them and said, "With man this is impossible, but with God all things are possible."

Luke 1:37

For nothing will be impossible with God."

Jeremiah 32:17

'Ah, Lord God! It is you who have made the heavens and the earth by your great power and by your outstretched arm! Nothing is too hard for you.

Genesis 18:14

Is anything too hard for the Lord? At the appointed time I will return to you, about this time next year, and Sarah shall have a son."

Ephesians 3:20

Now to him who is able to do far more abundantly than all that we ask or think, according to the power at work within us,

Mark 9:23

And Jesus said to him, "'If you can'! All things are possible for one who believes."

Matthew 6:33

But seek first the kingdom of God and his righteousness, and all these things will be added to you.

Philippians 4:13

I can do all things through him who strengthens me.

Isaiah 43:18-19

"Remember not the former things, nor consider the things of old. Behold, I am doing a new thing; now it springs forth, do you not perceive it? I will make a way in the wilderness and rivers in the desert.

Hebrews 11:6

And without faith it is impossible to please him, for whoever would draw near to God must believe that he exists and that he rewards those who seek him.

Matthew 17:20

He said to them, "Because of your little faith. For truly, I say to you, if you have faith like a grain of mustard seed, you will say to this mountain, 'Move from here to there,' and it will move, and nothing will be impossible for you."

Incest

Deuteronomy 27:22

"'Cursed be anyone who lies with his sister, whether the daughter of his father or the daughter of his mother.' And all the people shall say, 'Amen.'

Leviticus 18:6

"None of you shall approach any one of his close relatives to uncover nakedness. I am the Lord.

Leviticus 18:7

You shall not uncover the nakedness of your father, which is the nakedness of your mother; she is your mother, you shall not uncover her nakedness.

Leviticus 20:17

"If a man takes his sister, a daughter of his father or a daughter of his mother, and sees her nakedness, and she sees his nakedness, it is a disgrace, and they shall be cut off in the sight of the children of their people. He has uncovered his sister's nakedness, and he shall bear his iniquity.

Individuality

Psalm 139:13-16

For you formed my inward parts; you knitted me together in my mother's womb. I praise you, for I am fearfully and wonderfully made. Wonderful are your works; my soul knows it very well. My frame was not hidden from you, when I was being made in secret, intricately woven in the depths of the earth. Your eyes saw my unformed substance; in your book were written, every one of them, the days that were formed for me, when as yet there was none of them.

Galatians 6:4

But let each one test his own work, and then his reason to boast will be in himself alone and not in his neighbor.

Jeremiah 1:5

"Before I formed you in the womb I knew you, and before you were born I consecrated you; I appointed you a prophet to the nations."

Infatuation

1 Corinthians 13:4-7

Love is patient and kind; love does not envy or boast; it is not arrogant or rude. It does not insist on its own way; it is not irritable or resentful; it does not rejoice at wrongdoing, but rejoices with the truth. Love bears all things, believes all things, hopes all things, endures all things.

1 Peter 5:8

Be sober-minded; be watchful. Your adversary the devil prowls around like a roaring lion, seeking someone to devour.

1 John 4:8

Anyone who does not love does not know God, because God is love.

Infertility

Psalm 113:9

He gives the barren woman a home, making her the joyous mother of children. Praise the Lord!

Mark 11:24

Therefore I tell you, whatever you ask in prayer, believe that you have received it, and it will be yours.

John 16:33

I have said these things to you, that in me you may have peace. In the world you will have tribulation. But take heart; I have overcome the world."

Romans 5:3-5

More than that, we rejoice in our sufferings, knowing that suffering produces endurance, and endurance produces character, and character produces hope, and hope does not put us to shame, because God's love has been poured into our hearts through the Holy Spirit who has been given to us.

Influence

1 Corinthians 15:33

Do not be deceived: "Bad company ruins good morals."

Matthew 5:13-16

"You are the salt of the earth, but if salt has lost its taste, how shall its saltiness be restored? It is no longer good for anything except to be thrown out and trampled under people's feet. "You are the light of the world. A city set on a hill cannot be hidden. Nor do people light a lamp and put it under a basket, but on a stand, and it gives light to all in the house. In the same way, let your light shine before others, so that they may see your good works and give glory to your Father who is in heaven.

Proverbs 27:17

Iron sharpens iron, and one man sharpens another.

Proverbs 13:20

Whoever walks with the wise becomes wise, but the companion of fools will suffer harm.

1 Peter 3:16

Having a good conscience, so that, when you are slandered, those who revile your good behavior in Christ may be put to shame.

Galatians 5:7-9

You were running well. Who hindered you from obeying the truth? This persuasion is not from him who calls you. A little leaven leavens the whole lump.

1 Peter 2:12

Keep your conduct among the Gentiles honorable, so that when they speak against you as evildoers, they may see your good deeds and glorify God on the day of visitation.

1 Peter 3:15

But in your hearts honor Christ the Lord as holy, always being prepared to make a defense to anyone who asks you for a reason for the hope that is in you; yet do it with gentleness and respect,

Matthew 5:13

"You are the salt of the earth, but if salt has lost its taste, how shall its saltiness be restored? It is no longer good for anything except to be thrown out and trampled under people's feet.

Proverbs 9:9

Give instruction to a wise man, and he will be still wiser; teach a righteous man, and he will increase in learning.

Injustice

Proverbs 17:15

He who justifies the wicked and he who condemns the righteous are both alike an abomination to the Lord.

Jeremiah 22:3-5

Thus says the Lord: Do justice and righteousness, and deliver from the hand of the oppressor him who has been robbed. And do no wrong or violence to the resident alien, the fatherless, and the widow, nor shed innocent blood in this place. For if you will indeed obey this word, then there shall enter the gates of this house kings who sit on the throne of David, riding in chariots and on horses, they and their servants and their people. But if you will not obey these words, I swear by myself, declares the Lord, that this house shall become a desolation.

Micah 6:8

He has told you, O man, what is good; and what does the Lord require of you but to do justice, and to love kindness, and to walk humbly with your God?

Psalm 43:1

Vindicate me, O God, and defend my cause against an ungodly people, from the deceitful and unjust man deliver me!

Ecclesiastes 5:8

If you see in a province the oppression of the poor and the violation of justice and righteousness, do not be amazed at the matter, for the high official is watched by a higher, and there are yet higher ones over them.

Leviticus 19:15

"You shall do no injustice in court. You shall not be partial to the poor or defer to the great, but in righteousness shall you judge your neighbor.

Proverbs 29:27

An unjust man is an abomination to the righteous, but one whose way is straight is an abomination to the wicked.

Innocence

Mark 10:14
But when Jesus saw it, he was indignant and said to them, "Let the children come to me; do not hinder them, for to such belongs the kingdom of God.

Matthew 19:14
But Jesus said, "Let the little children come to me and do not hinder them, for to such belongs the kingdom of heaven."

Philippians 4:8
Finally, brothers, whatever is true, whatever is honorable, whatever is just, whatever is pure, whatever is lovely, whatever is commendable, if there is any excellence, if there is anything worthy of praise, think about these things.

Luke 18:16
But Jesus called them to him, saying, "Let the children come to me, and do not hinder them, for to such belongs the kingdom of God.

Insecurities

1 Samuel 16:7
But the Lord said to Samuel, "Do not look on his appearance or on the height of his stature, because I have rejected him. For the Lord sees not as man sees: man looks on the outward appearance, but the Lord looks on the heart."

Romans 2:1
Therefore you have no excuse, O man, every one of you who judges. For in passing judgment on another you condemn yourself, because you, the judge, practice the very same things.

Colossians 3:9-10
Do not lie to one another, seeing that you have put off the old self with its practices and have put on the new self, which is being renewed in knowledge after the image of its creator.

James 5:16
Therefore, confess your sins to one another and pray for one another, that you may be healed. The prayer of a righteous person has great power as it is working.

2 Corinthians 3:18
And we all, with unveiled face, beholding the glory of the Lord, are being transformed into the same image from one degree of glory to another. For this comes from the Lord who is the Spirit.

James 1:20
For the anger of man does not produce the righteousness of God.

Insomnia

Mark 11:24
Therefore I tell you, whatever you ask in prayer, believe that you have received it, and it will be yours.

Philippians 4:6-7
Do not be anxious about anything, but in everything by prayer and supplication with thanksgiving let your requests be made known to God. And the peace of God, which surpasses all understanding, will guard your hearts and your minds in Christ Jesus.

James 1:5-7
If any of you lacks wisdom, let him ask God, who gives generously to all without reproach, and it will be given him. But let him ask in faith, with no doubting, for the one who doubts is like a wave of the sea that is driven and tossed by the wind. For that person must not suppose that he will receive anything from the Lord;

Philippians 4:12-13
I know how to be brought low, and I know how to abound. In any and every circumstance, I have learned the secret of facing plenty and hunger, abundance and need. I can do all things through him who strengthens me.

Instruction

Proverbs 19:20
Listen to advice and accept instruction, that you may gain wisdom in the future.

Psalm 32:8
I will instruct you and teach you in the way you should go; I will counsel you with my eye upon you.

Proverbs 4:13
Keep hold of instruction; do not let go; guard her, for she is your life.

2 Timothy 3:16-17
All Scripture is breathed out by God and profitable for teaching, for reproof, for correction, and for training in righteousness, that the man of God may be competent, equipped for every good work.

John 14:26
But the Helper, the Holy Spirit, whom the Father will send in my name, he will teach you all things and bring to your remembrance all that I have said to you.

Hebrews 4:12
For the word of God is living and active, sharper than any two-edged sword, piercing to the division of soul and of spirit, of joints and of marrow, and discerning the thoughts and intentions of the heart.

Proverbs 10:17
Whoever heeds instruction is on the path to life, but he who rejects reproof leads others astray.

Proverbs 12:1
Whoever loves discipline loves knowledge, but he who hates reproof is stupid.

Insults

James 1:26
If anyone thinks he is religious and does not bridle his tongue but deceives his heart, this person's religion is worthless.

James 4:11-12
Do not speak evil against one another, brothers. The one who speaks against a brother or judges his brother, speaks evil against the law and judges the law. But if you judge the law, you are not a doer of the law but a judge. There is only one lawgiver and judge, he who is able to save and to destroy. But who are you to judge your neighbor?

Proverbs 12:16
The vexation of a fool is known at once, but the prudent ignores an insult.

Proverbs 12:18
There is one whose rash words are like sword thrusts, but the tongue of the wise brings healing.

Ephesians 4:31-32
Let all bitterness and wrath and anger and clamor and slander be put away from you, along with all malice. Be kind to one another, tenderhearted, forgiving one another, as God in Christ forgave you.

Proverbs 11:12
Whoever belittles his neighbor lacks sense, but a man of understanding remains silent.

Proverbs 20:22
Do not say, "I will repay evil"; wait for the Lord, and he will deliver you.

Ephesians 4:26
Be angry and do not sin; do not let the sun go down on your anger,

Integrity

Proverbs 10:9
Whoever walks in integrity walks securely, but he who makes his ways crooked will be found out.

Proverbs 28:6
Better is a poor man who walks in his integrity than a rich man who is crooked in his ways.

Proverbs 11:3
The integrity of the upright guides them, but the crookedness of the treacherous destroys them.

1 John 4:7-10

Beloved, let us love one another, for love is from God, and whoever loves has been born of God and knows God. Anyone who does not love does not know God, because God is love. In this the love of God was made manifest among us, that God sent his only Son into the world, so that we might live through him. In this is love, not that we have loved God but that he loved us and sent his Son to be the propitiation for our sins.

Proverbs 19:1

Better is a poor person who walks in his integrity than one who is crooked in speech and is a fool.

Proverbs 20:7

The righteous who walks in his integrity— blessed are his children after him!

1 Peter 3:16

Having a good conscience, so that, when you are slandered, those who revile your good behavior in Christ may be put to shame.

Proverbs 12:22

Lying lips are an abomination to the Lord, but those who act faithfully are his delight.

Luke 16:10

"One who is faithful in a very little is also faithful in much, and one who is dishonest in a very little is also dishonest in much.

Colossians 3:23

Whatever you do, work heartily, as for the Lord and not for men,

Proverbs 21:3

To do righteousness and justice is more acceptable to the Lord than sacrifice.

2 Corinthians 8:21

For we aim at what is honorable not only in the Lord's sight but also in the sight of man.

Proverbs 4:25-27

Let your eyes look directly forward, and your gaze be straight before you. Ponder the path of your feet; then all your ways will be sure. Do not swerve to the right or to the left; turn your foot away from evil.

Philippians 4:8

Finally, brothers, whatever is true, whatever is honorable, whatever is just, whatever is pure, whatever is lovely, whatever is commendable, if there is any excellence, if there is anything worthy of praise, think about these things.

Luke 6:31

And as you wish that others would do to you, do so to them.

Psalm 41:11-12

By this I know that you delight in me: my enemy will not shout in triumph over me. But you have upheld me because of my integrity, and set me in your presence forever.

Psalm 25:21
May integrity and uprightness preserve me, for I wait for you.

Intelligence

2 Peter 1:5
For this very reason, make every effort to supplement your faith with virtue, and virtue with knowledge,

Proverbs 1:7
The fear of the Lord is the beginning of knowledge; fools despise wisdom and instruction.

Proverbs 2:6
For the Lord gives wisdom; from his mouth come knowledge and understanding;

Daniel 5:14
I have heard of you that the spirit of the gods is in you, and that light and understanding and excellent wisdom are found in you.

Philippians 1:9-11
And it is my prayer that your love may abound more and more, with knowledge and all discernment, so that you may approve what is excellent, and so be pure and blameless for the day of Christ, filled with the fruit of righteousness that comes through Jesus Christ, to the glory and praise of God.

Daniel 1:17
As for these four youths, God gave them learning and skill in all literature and wisdom, and Daniel had understanding in all visions and dreams.

Job 12:3
But I have understanding as well as you; I am not inferior to you. Who does not know such things as these?

Proverbs 10:19
When words are many, transgression is not lacking, but whoever restrains his lips is prudent.

Isaiah 29:12
And when they give the book to one who cannot read, saying, "Read this," he says, "I cannot read."

Intimacy

Hebrews 13:4
Let marriage be held in honor among all, and let the marriage bed be undefiled, for God will judge the sexually immoral and adulterous.

Genesis 2:24

Therefore a man shall leave his father and his mother and hold fast to his wife, and they shall become one flesh.

1 Corinthians 6:18

Flee from sexual immorality. Every other sin a person commits is outside the body, but the sexually immoral person sins against his own body.

1 John 1:9

If we confess our sins, he is faithful and just to forgive us our sins and to cleanse us from all unrighteousness.

Colossians 3:19

Husbands, love your wives, and do not be harsh with them.

Ephesians 5:3

But sexual immorality and all impurity or covetousness must not even be named among you, as is proper among saints.

1 Thessalonians 4:3-5

For this is the will of God, your sanctification: that you abstain from sexual immorality; that each one of you know how to control his own body in holiness and honor, not in the passion of lust like the Gentiles who do not know God;

John 17:3

And this is eternal life, that they know you the only true God, and Jesus Christ whom you have sent.

Malachi 2:15

Did he not make them one, with a portion of the Spirit in their union? And what was the one God seeking? Godly offspring. So guard yourselves in your spirit, and let none of you be faithless to the wife of your youth.

Colossians 3:5

Put to death therefore what is earthly in you: sexual immorality, impurity, passion, evil desire, and covetousness, which is idolatry.

1 Corinthians 7:2

But because of the temptation to sexual immorality, each man should have his own wife and each woman her own husband.

Proverbs 5:18-19

Let your fountain be blessed, and rejoice in the wife of your youth, a lovely deer, a graceful doe. Let her breasts fill you at all times with delight; be intoxicated always in her love.

Intoxication

Proverbs 20:1
Wine is a mocker, strong drink a brawler, and whoever is led astray by it is not wise.

Ephesians 5:18
And do not get drunk with wine, for that is debauchery, but be filled with the Spirit,

Galatians 5:21
Envy, drunkenness, orgies, and things like these. I warn you, as I warned you before, that those who do such things will not inherit the kingdom of God.

Romans 13:13
Let us walk properly as in the daytime, not in orgies and drunkenness, not in sexual immorality and sensuality, not in quarreling and jealousy.

1 Timothy 5:23
(No longer drink only water, but use a little wine for the sake of your stomach and your frequent ailments.)

Proverbs 23:21
For the drunkard and the glutton will come to poverty, and slumber will clothe them with rags.

Galatians 5:19-21
Now the works of the flesh are evident: sexual immorality, impurity, sensuality, idolatry, sorcery, enmity, strife, jealousy, fits of anger, rivalries, dissensions, divisions, envy, drunkenness, orgies, and things like these. I warn you, as I warned you before, that those who do such things will not inherit the kingdom of God.

Isaiah 5:22
Woe to those who are heroes at drinking wine, and valiant men in mixing strong drink,

Isolation

Proverbs 18:1
Whoever isolates himself seeks his own desire; he breaks out against all sound judgment.

Hebrews 10:25
Not neglecting to meet together, as is the habit of some, but encouraging one another, and all the more as you see the Day drawing near.

1 Corinthians 12:14
For the body does not consist of one member but of many

Jealousy

James 3:16

For where jealousy and selfish ambition exist, there will be disorder and every vile practice.

Proverbs 27:4

Wrath is cruel, anger is overwhelming, but who can stand before jealousy?

1 Corinthians 13:4-5

Love is patient and kind; love does not envy or boast; it is not arrogant or rude. It does not insist on its own way; it is not irritable or resentful;

1 Corinthians 3:3

For you are still of the flesh. For while there is jealousy and strife among you, are you not of the flesh and behaving only in a human way?

Galatians 5:19-21

Now the works of the flesh are evident: sexual immorality, impurity, sensuality, idolatry, sorcery, enmity, strife, jealousy, fits of anger, rivalries, dissensions, divisions, envy, drunkenness, orgies, and things like these. I warn you, as I warned you before, that those who do such things will not inherit the kingdom of God.

Exodus 20:17

"You shall not covet your neighbor's house; you shall not covet your neighbor's wife, or his male servant, or his female servant, or his ox, or his donkey, or anything that is your neighbor's."

Jesus Christ

John 14:6

Jesus said to him, "I am the way, and the truth, and the life. No one comes to the Father except through me.

1 Timothy 2:5

For there is one God, and there is one mediator between God and men, the man Christ Jesus,

Proverbs 8:35-36

For whoever finds me finds life and obtains favor from the Lord, but he who fails to find me injures himself; all who hate me love death."

Acts 4:11-12

This Jesus is the stone that was rejected by you, the builders, which has become the cornerstone. And there is salvation in no one else, for there is no other name under heaven given among men by which we must be saved."

John 3:16
"For God so loved the world, that he gave his only Son, that whoever believes in him should not perish but have eternal life.

John 1:1
In the beginning was the Word, and the Word was with God, and the Word was God.

John 1:14
And the Word became flesh and dwelt among us, and we have seen his glory, glory as of the only Son from the Father, full of grace and truth.

Hebrews 13:8
Jesus Christ is the same yesterday and today and forever

Jesus As A Friend

John 15:12-15
"This is my commandment, that you love one another as I have loved you. Greater love has no one than this, that someone lay down his life for his friends. You are my friends if you do what I command you. No longer do I call you servants, for the servant does not know what his master is doing; but I have called you friends, for all that I have heard from my Father I have made known to you.

Jesus Coming Back

Matthew 24:36
"But concerning that day and hour no one knows, not even the angels of heaven, nor the Son, but the Father only.

Revelation 1:7
Behold, he is coming with the clouds, and every eye will see him, even those who pierced him, and all tribes of the earth will wail on account of him. Even so. Amen.

1 Thessalonians 4:16-17
For the Lord himself will descend from heaven with a cry of command, with the voice of an archangel, and with the sound of the trumpet of God. And the dead in Christ will rise first. Then we who are alive, who are left, will be caught up together with them in the clouds to meet the Lord in the air, and so we will always be with the Lord.

Revelation 22:12-13
"Behold, I am coming soon, bringing my recompense with me, to repay everyone for what he has done. I am the Alpha and the Omega, the first and the last, the beginning and the end."

John 14:3
And if I go and prepare a place for you, I will come again and will take you to myself, that where I am you may be also.

Matthew 24:31-33

And he will send out his angels with a loud trumpet call, and they will gather his elect from the four winds, from one end of heaven to the other. "From the fig tree learn its lesson: as soon as its branch becomes tender and puts out its leaves, you know that summer is near. So also, when you see all these things, you know that he is near, at the very gates.

Revelation 1:8

"I am the Alpha and the Omega," says the Lord God, "who is and who was and who is to come, the Almighty."

1 Corinthians 15:52

In a moment, in the twinkling of an eye, at the last trumpet. For the trumpet will sound, and the dead will be raised imperishable, and we shall be changed.

Jewish fulfillment

Zechariah 12:10

"And I will pour out on the house of David and the inhabitants of Jerusalem a spirit of grace and pleas for mercy, so that, when they look on me, on him whom they have pierced, they shall mourn for him, as one mourns for an only child, and weep bitterly over him, as one weeps over a firstborn.

Isaiah 7:14

Therefore, the Lord himself will give you a sign. Behold, the virgin shall conceive and bear a son, and shall call his name Immanuel.

Micah 5:2

But you, O Bethlehem Ephrathah, who are too little to be among the clans of Judah, from you shall come forth for me one who is to be ruler in Israel, whose coming forth is from of old, from ancient days.

Daniel 2:44

And in the days of those kings the God of heaven will set up a kingdom that shall never be destroyed, nor shall the kingdom be left to another people. It shall break in pieces all these kingdoms and bring them to an end, and it shall stand forever,

Psalm 34:20

He keeps all his bones; not one of them is broken.

Zechariah 11:12-13

Then I said to them, "If it seems good to you, give me my wages; but if not, keep them." And they weighed out as my wages thirty pieces of silver. Then the Lord said to me, "Throw it to the potter"—the lordly price at which I was priced by them. So I took the thirty pieces of silver and threw them into the house of the Lord, to the potter.

Zechariah 9:9

Rejoice greatly, O daughter of Zion! Shout aloud, O daughter of Jerusalem! Behold, your king is coming to you; righteous and having salvation is he, humble and mounted on a donkey, on a colt, the foal of a donkey.

Isaiah 11:10

In that day the root of Jesse, who shall stand as a signal for the peoples—of him shall the nations inquire, and his resting place shall be glorious.

Job Loss

Jeremiah 29:11

For I know the plans I have for you, declares the Lord, plans for welfare and not for evil, to give you a future and a hope.

John 16:33

I have said these things to you, that in me you may have peace. In the world you will have tribulation. But take heart; I have overcome the world."

Romans 8:28

And we know that for those who love God all things work together for good, for those who are called according to his purpose.

Isaiah 43:18-19

"Remember not the former things, nor consider the things of old. Behold, I am doing a new thing; now it springs forth, do you not perceive it? I will make a way in the wilderness and rivers in the desert.

Matthew 6:33

But seek first the kingdom of God and his righteousness, and all these things will be added to you.

Journaling

Habakkuk 2:2

And the Lord answered me: "Write the vision; make it plain on tablets, so he may run who reads it.

Jeremiah 30:2

"Thus says the Lord, the God of Israel: Write in a book all the words that I have spoken to you.

Deuteronomy 31:19

"Now therefore write this song and teach it to the people of Israel. Put it in their mouths, that this song may be a witness for me against the people of Israel.

Psalm 119:27

Make me understand the way of your precepts, and I will meditate on your wondrous works.

Psalm 102:18

Let this be recorded for a generation to come, so that a people yet to be created may praise the Lord:

Journey

Jeremiah 29:11

For I know the plans I have for you, declares the Lord, plans for welfare and not for evil, to give you a future and a hope.

Psalm 119:105

Your word is a lamp to my feet and a light to my path.

Proverbs 3:5-6

Trust in the Lord with all your heart, and do not lean on your own understanding. In all your ways acknowledge him, and he will make straight your paths.

Romans 8:38-39

For I am sure that neither death nor life, nor angels nor rulers, nor things present nor things to come, nor powers, nor height nor depth, nor anything else in all creation, will be able to separate us from the love of God in Christ Jesus our Lord.

Joy

Romans 15:13

May the God of hope fill you with all joy and peace in believing, so that by the power of the Holy Spirit you may abound in hope.

Romans 12:12

Rejoice in hope, be patient in tribulation, be constant in prayer.

Philippians 4:4

Rejoice in the Lord always; again I will say, Rejoice.

Galatians 5:22

But the fruit of the Spirit is love, joy, peace, patience, kindness, goodness, faithfulness,

John 16:24

Until now you have asked nothing in my name. Ask, and you will receive, that your joy may be full.

Proverbs 17:22

A joyful heart is good medicine, but a crushed spirit dries up the bones.

John 16:22

So also you have sorrow now, but I will see you again, and your hearts will rejoice, and no one will take your joy from you.

1 Peter 1:8

Though you have not seen him, you love him. Though you do not now see him, you believe in him and rejoice with joy that is inexpressible and filled with glory,

Psalm 16:11

You make known to me the path of life; in your presence there is fullness of joy; at your right hand are pleasures forevermore.

Romans 14:17

For the kingdom of God is not a matter of eating and drinking but of righteousness and peace and joy in the Holy Spirit.

Psalm 118:24

This is the day that the Lord has made; let us rejoice and be glad in it.

James 1:2-4

Count it all joy, my brothers, when you meet trials of various kinds, for you know that the testing of your faith produces steadfastness. And let steadfastness have its full effect, that you may be perfect and complete, lacking in nothing.

Joy in Sufferings

James 1:2-4

Count it all joy, my brothers, when you meet trials of various kinds, for you know that the testing of your faith produces steadfastness. And let steadfastness have its full effect, that you may be perfect and complete, lacking in nothing.

Romans 5:3-5

More than that, we rejoice in our sufferings, knowing that suffering produces endurance, and endurance produces character, and character produces hope, and hope does not put us to shame, because God's love has been poured into our hearts through the Holy Spirit who has been given to us.

1 Peter 4:13

But rejoice insofar as you share Christ's sufferings, that you may also rejoice and be glad when his glory is revealed.

2 Corinthians 12:10

For the sake of Christ, then, I am content with weaknesses, insults, hardships, persecutions, and calamities. For when I am weak, then I am strong.

Romans 12:12

Rejoice in hope, be patient in tribulation, be constant in prayer.

Romans 5:3

More than that, we rejoice in our sufferings, knowing that suffering produces endurance,

John 14:27

Peace I leave with you; my peace I give to you. Not as the world gives do I give to you. Let not your hearts be troubled, neither let them be afraid.

Romans 8:18-21

For I consider that the sufferings of this present time are not worth comparing with the glory that is to be revealed to us. For the creation waits with eager longing for the revealing of the sons of God. For the creation was subjected to futility, not willingly, but because of him who subjected it, in hope that the creation itself will be set free from its bondage to corruption and obtain the freedom of the glory of the children of God.

Psalm 94:19

When the cares of my heart are many, your consolations cheer my soul.

2 Corinthians 12:9

But he said to me, "My grace is sufficient for you, for my power is made perfect in weakness." Therefore, I will boast all the more gladly of my weaknesses, so that the power of Christ may rest upon me.

<u>Judging</u>

John 7:24

Do not judge by appearances, but judge with right judgment."

Luke 6:37

"Judge not, and you will not be judged; condemn not, and you will not be condemned; forgive, and you will be forgiven;

Matthew 7:1-5

"Judge not, that you be not judged. For with the judgment you pronounce you will be judged, and with the measure you use it will be measured to you. Why do you see the speck that is in your brother's eye, but do not notice the log that is in your own eye? Or how can you say to your brother, 'Let me take the speck out of your eye,' when there is the log in your own eye? You hypocrite, first take the log out of your own eye, and then you will see clearly to take the speck out of your brother's eye.

James 4:11-12

Do not speak evil against one another, brothers. The one who speaks against a brother or judges his brother, speaks evil against the law and judges the law. But if you judge the law, you are not a doer of the law but a judge. There is only one lawgiver and judge, he who is able to save and to destroy. But who are you to judge your neighbor?

Romans 2:3

Do you suppose, O man—you who judge those who practice such things and yet do them yourself—that you will escape the judgment of God?

1 Corinthians 5:12

For what have I to do with judging outsiders? Is it not those inside the church whom you are to judge?

Judgement

James 2:13
For judgment is without mercy to one who has shown no mercy. Mercy triumphs over judgment.

2 Corinthians 5:10
For we must all appear before the judgment seat of Christ, so that each one may receive what is due for what he has done in the body, whether good or evil.

Romans 14:12-13
So then each of us will give an account of himself to God. Therefore, let us not pass judgment on one another any longer, but rather decide never to put a stumbling block or hindrance in the way of a brother.

Matthew 12:36
I tell you, on the day of judgment people will give account for every careless word they speak,

Romans 14:10-12
Why do you pass judgment on your brother? Or you, why do you despise your brother? For we will all stand before the judgment seat of God; for it is written, "As I live, says the Lord, every knee shall bow to me, and every tongue shall confess to God." So then each of us will give an account of himself to God.

Matthew 12:37
For by your words you will be justified, and by your words you will be condemned."

Judgement Day

Matthew 12:36
I tell you, on the day of judgment people will give account for every careless word they speak,

Revelation 20:11-15
Then I saw a great white throne and him who was seated on it. From his presence earth and sky fled away, and no place was found for them. And I saw the dead, great and small, standing before the throne, and books were opened. Then another book was opened, which is the book of life. And the dead were judged by what was written in the books, according to what they had done. And the sea gave up the dead who were in it, Death and Hades gave up the dead who were in them, and they were judged, each one of them, according to what they had done. Then Death and Hades were thrown into the lake of fire. This is the second death, the lake of fire. And if anyone's name was not found written in the book of life, he was thrown into the lake of fire.

Hebrews 9:27
And just as it is appointed for man to die once, and after that comes judgment,

1 Corinthians 4:5
Therefore do not pronounce judgment before the time, before the Lord comes, who will bring to light the things now hidden in darkness and will disclose the purposes of the heart. Then each one will receive his commendation from God.

Romans 14:10

Why do you pass judgment on your brother? Or you, why do you despise your brother? For we will all stand before the judgment seat of God;

John 12:48

The one who rejects me and does not receive my words has a judge; the word that I have spoken will judge him on the last day.

Justice

Proverbs 21:15

When justice is done, it is a joy to the righteous but terror to evildoers.

Amos 5:24

But let justice roll down like waters, and righteousness like an ever-flowing stream.

Romans 12:19

Beloved, never avenge yourselves, but leave it to the wrath of God, for it is written, "Vengeance is mine, I will repay, says the Lord."

Isaiah 1:17

Learn to do good; seek justice, correct oppression; bring justice to the fatherless, plead the widow's cause.

Isaiah 30:18

Therefore, the Lord waits to be gracious to you, and therefore he exalts himself to show mercy to you. For the Lord is a God of justice; blessed are all those who wait for him.

Micah 6:8

He has told you, O man, what is good; and what does the Lord require of you but to do justice, and to love kindness, and to walk humbly with your God?

Isaiah 61:8

For I the Lord love justice; I hate robbery and wrong; I will faithfully give them their recompense, and I will make an everlasting covenant with them.

Psalm 37:27-29

Turn away from evil and do good; so shall you dwell forever. For the Lord loves justice; he will not forsake his saints. They are preserved forever, but the children of the wicked shall be cut off. The righteous shall inherit the land and dwell upon it forever.

Psalm 106:3

Blessed are they who observe justice, who do righteousness at all times!

Justification

Romans 5:1
Therefore, since we have been justified by faith, we have peace with God through our Lord Jesus Christ.

Titus 3:7
So that being justified by his grace we might become heirs according to the hope of eternal life.

Galatians 3:24
So then, the law was our guardian until Christ came, in order that we might be justified by faith.

Galatians 2:16-17
Yet we know that a person is not justified by works of the law but through faith in Jesus Christ, so we also have believed in Christ Jesus, in order to be justified by faith in Christ and not by works of the law, because by works of the law no one will be justified. But if, in our endeavor to be justified in Christ, we too were found to be sinners, is Christ then a servant of sin? Certainly not!

Romans 3:28
For we hold that one is justified by faith apart from works of the law.

1 Corinthians 6:11
And such were some of you. But you were washed, you were sanctified, you were justified in the name of the Lord Jesus Christ and by the Spirit of our God.

Philippians 3:9
And be found in him, not having a righteousness of my own that comes from the law, but that which comes through faith in Christ, the righteousness from God that depends on faith—

Romans 8:30
And those whom he predestined he also called, and those whom he called he also justified, and those whom he justified he also glorified.

Romans 5:9
Since, therefore, we have now been justified by his blood, much more shall we be saved by him from the wrath of God.

Romans 4:25
Who was delivered up for our trespasses and raised for our justification.

Karma

Galatians 6:7
Do not be deceived: God is not mocked, for whatever one sows, that will he also reap.

Job 4:8
As I have seen, those who plow iniquity and sow trouble reap the same.

2 Corinthians 5:10
For we must all appear before the judgment seat of Christ, so that each one may receive what is due for what he has done in the body, whether good or evil.

Proverbs 26:27
Whoever digs a pit will fall into it, and a stone will come back on him who starts it rolling.

Luke 6:27
"But I say to you who hear, Love your enemies, do good to those who hate you,

Galatians 6:8-9
For the one who sows to his own flesh will from the flesh reap corruption, but the one who sows to the Spirit will from the Spirit reap eternal life. And let us not grow weary of doing good, for in due season we will reap, if we do not give up.

Matthew 7:12
"So whatever you wish that others would do to you, do also to them, for this is the Law and the Prophets.

Keeping Promises

Numbers 30:2
If a man vows a vow to the Lord, or swears an oath to bind himself by a pledge, he shall not break his word. He shall do according to all that proceeds out of his mouth.

Psalm 89:34
I will not violate my covenant or alter the word that went forth from my lips.

Ecclesiastes 5:4-5
When you vow a vow to God, do not delay paying it, for he has no pleasure in fools. Pay what you vow. It is better that you should not vow than that you should vow and not pay.

Matthew 5:37
Let what you say be simply 'Yes' or 'No'; anything more than this comes from evil.

2 Peter 3:9
The Lord is not slow to fulfill his promise as some count slowness, but is patient toward you, not wishing that any should perish, but that all should reach repentance.

Numbers 23:19

God is not man, that he should lie, or a son of man, that he should change his mind. Has he said, and will he not do it? Or has he spoken, and will he not fulfill it?

Matthew 5:33

"Again you have heard that it was said to those of old, 'You shall not swear falsely, but shall perform to the Lord what you have sworn.'

Joshua 23:14

"And now I am about to go the way of all the earth, and you know in your hearts and souls, all of you, that not one word has failed of all the good things that the Lord your God promised concerning you. All have come to pass for you; not one of them has failed.

Numbers 30:1-2

Moses spoke to the heads of the tribes of the people of Israel, saying, "This is what the Lord has commanded. If a man vows a vow to the Lord, or swears an oath to bind himself by a pledge, he shall not break his word. He shall do according to all that proceeds out of his mouth.

James 5:12

But above all, my brothers, do not swear, either by heaven or by earth or by any other oath, but let your "yes" be yes and your "no" be no, so that you may not fall under condemnation.

Keeping Your Word

Matthew 5:33-37

"Again you have heard that it was said to those of old, 'You shall not swear falsely, but shall perform to the Lord what you have sworn.' But I say to you, Do not take an oath at all, either by heaven, for it is the throne of God, or by the earth, for it is his footstool, or by Jerusalem, for it is the city of the great King. And do not take an oath by your head, for you cannot make one hair white or black. Let what you say be simply 'Yes' or 'No'; anything more than this comes from evil.

Numbers 30:1-2

Moses spoke to the heads of the tribes of the people of Israel, saying, "This is what the Lord has commanded. If a man vows a vow to the Lord, or swears an oath to bind himself by a pledge, he shall not break his word. He shall do according to all that proceeds out of his mouth.

1 John 2:5

But whoever keeps his word, in him truly the love of God is perfected. By this we may know that we are in him:

Ecclesiastes 5:4-7

When you vow a vow to God, do not delay paying it, for he has no pleasure in fools. Pay what you vow. It is better that you should not vow than that you should vow and not pay. Let not your mouth lead you into sin, and do not say before the messenger that it was a mistake. Why should God be angry at your voice and destroy the work of your hands? For when dreams increase and words grow many, there is vanity; but God is the one you must fear.

Keys

Matthew 16:19

I will give you the keys of the kingdom of heaven, and whatever you bind on earth shall be bound in heaven, and whatever you loose on earth shall be loosed in heaven."

Revelation 3:7

"And to the angel of the church in Philadelphia write: 'The words of the holy one, the true one, who has the key of David, who opens and no one will shut, who shuts and no one opens.

Revelation 1:18

And the living one. I died, and behold I am alive forevermore, and I have the keys of Death and Hades.

Isaiah 22:22

And I will place on his shoulder the key of the house of David. He shall open, and none shall shut; and he shall shut, and none shall open.

Luke 11:52

Woe to you lawyers! For you have taken away the key of knowledge. You did not enter yourselves, and you hindered those who were entering."

Revelation 20:1

Then I saw an angel coming down from heaven, holding in his hand the key to the bottomless pit and a great chain.

Revelation 9:1

And the fifth angel blew his trumpet, and I saw a star fallen from heaven to earth, and he was given the key to the shaft of the bottomless pit.

Judges 3:25

And they waited till they were embarrassed. But when he still did not open the doors of the roof chamber, they took the key and opened them, and there lay their lord dead on the floor.

Killing

Exodus 20:13

"You shall not murder.

Matthew 5:21

"You have heard that it was said to those of old, 'You shall not murder; and whoever murders will be liable to judgment.'

Exodus 23:7

Keep far from a false charge, and do not kill the innocent and righteous, for I will not acquit the wicked.

Romans 13:4

For he is God's servant for your good. But if you do wrong, be afraid, for he does not bear the sword in vain. For he is the servant of God, an avenger who carries out God's wrath on the wrongdoer.

Genesis 9:5-6

And for your lifeblood I will require a reckoning: from every beast I will require it and from man. From his fellow man I will require a reckoning for the life of man. "Whoever sheds the blood of man, by man shall his blood be shed, for God made man in his own image.

Ezekiel 33:8

If I say to the wicked, O wicked one, you shall surely die, and you do not speak to warn the wicked to turn from his way, that wicked person shall die in his iniquity, but his blood I will require at your hand.

Romans 13:8-10

Owe no one anything, except to love each other, for the one who loves another has fulfilled the law. For the commandments, "You shall not commit adultery, You shall not murder, You shall not steal, You shall not covet," and any other commandment, are summed up in this word: "You shall love your neighbor as yourself." Love does no wrong to a neighbor; therefore, love is the fulfilling of the law.

Killing Yourself

1 Corinthians 6:19-20

Or do you not know that your body is a temple of the Holy Spirit within you, whom you have from God? You are not your own, for you were bought with a price. So, glorify God in your body.

Exodus 20:13

"You shall not murder.

Romans 10:13

For "everyone who calls on the name of the Lord will be saved."

Romans 12:19

Beloved, never avenge yourselves, but leave it to the wrath of God, for it is written, "Vengeance is mine, I will repay, says the Lord."

Kind Word

Proverbs 16:24

Gracious words are like a honeycomb, sweetness to the soul and health to the body.

Proverbs 15:1

A soft answer turns away wrath, but a harsh word stirs up anger.

Ephesians 4:29

Let no corrupting talk come out of your mouths, but only such as is good for building up, as fits the occasion, that it may give grace to those who hear.

1 Thessalonians 5:11

Therefore encourage one another and build one another up, just as you are doing.

Colossians 4:6

Let your speech always be gracious, seasoned with salt, so that you may know how you ought to answer each person.

Job 4:4

Your words have upheld him who was stumbling, and you have made firm the feeble knees.

Proverbs 25:11

A word fitly spoken is like apples of gold in a setting of silver.

Proverbs 15:23

To make an apt answer is a joy to a man, and a word in season, how good it is!

Psalm 19:14

Let the words of my mouth and the meditation of my heart be acceptable in your sight, O Lord, my rock and my redeemer.

Kindness

Ephesians 4:32

Be kind to one another, tenderhearted, forgiving one another, as God in Christ forgave you.

Luke 6:35

But love your enemies, and do good, and lend, expecting nothing in return, and your reward will be great, and you will be sons of the Most High, for he is kind to the ungrateful and the evil.

Proverbs 11:17

A man who is kind benefits himself, but a cruel man hurts himself.

Colossians 3:12

Put on then, as God's chosen ones, holy and beloved, compassionate hearts, kindness, humility, meekness, and patience,

Proverbs 31:26

She opens her mouth with wisdom, and the teaching of kindness is on her tongue.

1 Corinthians 13:4-7

Love is patient and kind; love does not envy or boast; it is not arrogant or rude. It does not insist on its own way; it is not irritable or resentful; it does not rejoice at wrongdoing, but rejoices with the truth. Love bears all things, believes all things, hopes all things, endures all things.

Proverbs 19:17

Whoever is generous to the poor lends to the Lord, and he will repay him for his deed.

Galatians 6:10
So then, as we have opportunity, let us do good to everyone, and especially to those who are of the household of faith.

Kingdom of God

Matthew 6:33
But seek first the kingdom of God and his righteousness, and all these things will be added to you.

John 18:36
Jesus answered, "My kingdom is not of this world. If my kingdom were of this world, my servants would have been fighting, that I might not be delivered over to the Jews. But my kingdom is not from the world."

Luke 17:20-21
Being asked by the Pharisees when the kingdom of God would come, he answered them, "The kingdom of God is not coming with signs to be observed, nor will they say, 'Look, here it is!' or 'There!' for behold, the kingdom of God is in the midst of you."

Mark 1:15
And saying, "The time is fulfilled, and the kingdom of God is at hand; repent and believe in the gospel."

Romans 14:17
For the kingdom of God is not a matter of eating and drinking but of righteousness and peace and joy in the Holy Spirit.

Daniel 2:44
And in the days of those kings the God of heaven will set up a kingdom that shall never be destroyed, nor shall the kingdom be left to another people. It shall break in pieces all these kingdoms and bring them to an end, and it shall stand forever,

Matthew 4:17
From that time Jesus began to preach, saying, "Repent, for the kingdom of heaven is at hand."

Revelation 11:15
Then the seventh angel blew his trumpet, and there were loud voices in heaven, saying, "The kingdom of the world has become the kingdom of our Lord and of his Christ, and he shall reign forever and ever."

1 Corinthians 6:9
Or do you not know that the unrighteous will not inherit the kingdom of God? Do not be deceived: neither the sexually immoral, nor idolaters, nor adulterers, nor men who practice homosexuality,

Matthew 16:19
I will give you the keys of the kingdom of heaven, and whatever you bind on earth shall be bound in heaven, and whatever you loose on earth shall be loosed in heaven."

Acts 28:31
Proclaiming the kingdom of God and teaching about the Lord Jesus Christ with all boldness and without hindrance.

Matthew 12:28
But if it is by the Spirit of God that I cast out demons, then the kingdom of God has come upon you.

Knowledge

Proverbs 18:15
An intelligent heart acquires knowledge, and the ear of the wise seeks knowledge.

Proverbs 1:7
The fear of the Lord is the beginning of knowledge; fools despise wisdom and instruction.

Proverbs 2:10
For wisdom will come into your heart, and knowledge will be pleasant to your soul;

Hosea 4:6-7
My people are destroyed for lack of knowledge; because you have rejected knowledge, I reject you from being a priest to me. And since you have forgotten the law of your God, I also will forget your children. The more they increased, the more they sinned against me; I will change their glory into shame.

Proverbs 24:5
A wise man is full of strength, and a man of knowledge enhances his might,

Proverbs 15:14
The heart of him who has understanding seeks knowledge, but the mouths of fools feed on folly.

Proverbs 8:10
Take my instruction instead of silver, and knowledge rather than choice gold,

Proverbs 12:1
Whoever loves discipline loves knowledge, but he who hates reproof is stupid.

Psalm 119:66
Teach me good judgment and knowledge, for I believe in your commandments.

Laughter

Proverbs 17:22
A joyful heart is good medicine, but a crushed spirit dries up the bones.

Job 8:21
He will yet fill your mouth with laughter, and your lips with shouting.

Psalm 126:2
Then our mouth was filled with laughter, and our tongue with shouts of joy; then they said among the nations, "The Lord has done great things for them."

Ecclesiastes 3:4
A time to weep, and a time to laugh; a time to mourn, and a time to dance;

Luke 6:21
"Blessed are you who are hungry now, for you shall be satisfied. "Blessed are you who weep now, for you shall laugh.

James 5:13
Is anyone among you suffering? Let him pray. Is anyone cheerful? Let him sing praise.

Proverbs 15:15
All the days of the afflicted are evil, but the cheerful of heart has a continual feast.

Psalm 2:4
He who sits in the heavens laughs; the Lord holds them in derision.

Proverbs 14:13
Even in laughter the heart may ache, and the end of joy may be grief.

Genesis 21:6
And Sarah said, "God has made laughter for me; everyone who hears will laugh over me."

Psalm 37:13
But the Lord laughs at the wicked, for he sees that his day is coming.

Psalm 59:8
But you, O Lord, laugh at them; you hold all the nations in derision.

Ecclesiastes 10:19
Bread is made for laughter, and wine gladdens life, and money answers everything.

Law

Romans 7:12

So the law is holy, and the commandment is holy and righteous and good.

Romans 7:7

What then shall we say? That the law is sin? By no means! Yet if it had not been for the law, I would not have known sin. For I would not have known what it is to covet if the law had not said, "You shall not covet."

1 John 3:4

Everyone who makes a practice of sinning also practices lawlessness; sin is lawlessness.

Luke 16:17

But it is easier for heaven and earth to pass away than for one dot of the Law to become void.

Acts 5:29

But Peter and the apostles answered, "We must obey God rather than men.

John 1:17

For the law was given through Moses; grace and truth came through Jesus Christ.

1 Timothy 1:8-10

Now we know that the law is good, if one uses it lawfully, understanding this, that the law is not laid down for the just but for the lawless and disobedient, for the ungodly and sinners, for the unholy and profane, for those who strike their fathers and mothers, for murderers, the sexually immoral, men who practice homosexuality, enslavers, liars, perjurers, and whatever else is contrary to sound doctrine,

James 2:10

For whoever keeps the whole law but fails in one point has become accountable for all of it.

Romans 13:1

Let every person be subject to the governing authorities. For there is no authority except from God, and those that exist have been instituted by God.

Laziness

Proverbs 13:4

The soul of the sluggard craves and gets nothing, while the soul of the diligent is richly supplied.

Colossians 3:23

Whatever you do, work heartily, as for the Lord and not for men,

2 Thessalonians 3:10

For even when we were with you, we would give you this command: If anyone is not willing to work, let him not eat.

Proverbs 10:4

A slack hand causes poverty, but the hand of the diligent makes rich.

Proverbs 18:9

Whoever is slack in his work is a brother to him who destroys.

1 Timothy 5:8

But if anyone does not provide for his relatives, and especially for members of his household, he has denied the faith and is worse than an unbeliever.

Proverbs 21:25

The desire of the sluggard kills him, for his hands refuse to labor.

Proverbs 24:30-34

I passed by the field of a sluggard, by the vineyard of a man lacking sense, and behold, it was all overgrown with thorns; the ground was covered with nettles, and its stone wall was broken down. Then I saw and considered it; I looked and received instruction. A little sleep, a little slumber, a little folding of the hands to rest, and poverty will come upon you like a robber, and want like an armed man.

Proverbs 20:4

The sluggard does not plow in the autumn; he will seek at harvest and have nothing.

Proverbs 20:13

Love not sleep, lest you come to poverty; open your eyes, and you will have plenty of bread.

Proverbs 19:15

Slothfulness casts into a deep sleep, and an idle person will suffer hunger.

Proverbs 12:24

The hand of the diligent will rule, while the slothful will be put to forced labor.

Leadership

1 Timothy 4:12

Let no one despise you for your youth, but set the believers an example in speech, in conduct, in love, in faith, in purity.

Philippians 2:3

Do nothing from rivalry or conceit, but in humility count others more significant than yourselves.

Matthew 20:25-28

But Jesus called them to him and said, "You know that the rulers of the Gentiles lord it over them, and their great ones exercise authority over them. It shall not be so among you. But whoever would be great among you must be your servant, and whoever would be first among you must be your slave, even as the Son of Man came not to be served but to serve, and to give his life as a ransom for many."

Exodus 18:21

Moreover, look for able men from all the people, men who fear God, who are trustworthy and hate a bribe, and place such men over the people as chiefs of thousands, of hundreds, of fifties, and of tens.

Romans 12:9-13

Let love be genuine. Abhor what is evil; hold fast to what is good. Love one another with brotherly affection. Outdo one another in showing honor. Do not be slothful in zeal, be fervent in spirit, serve the Lord. Rejoice in hope, be patient in tribulation, be constant in prayer. Contribute to the needs of the saints and seek to show hospitality.

Jeremiah 23:1

"Woe to the shepherds who destroy and scatter the sheep of my pasture!" declares the Lord.

Galatians 6:9

And let us not grow weary of doing good, for in due season we will reap, if we do not give up.

Learning

Proverbs 1:5

Let the wise hear and increase in learning, and the one who understands obtain guidance,

Proverbs 18:15

An intelligent heart acquires knowledge, and the ear of the wise seeks knowledge.

Proverbs 1:7

The fear of the Lord is the beginning of knowledge; fools despise wisdom and instruction.

Proverbs 9:9

Give instruction to a wise man, and he will be still wiser; teach a righteous man, and he will increase in learning.

2 Timothy 2:15

Do your best to present yourself to God as one approved, a worker who has no need to be ashamed, rightly handling the word of truth.

Philippians 4:9

What you have learned and received and heard and seen in me—practice these things, and the God of peace will be with you.

Titus 2:1

But as for you, teach what accords with sound doctrine.

Proverbs 22:6

Train up a child in the way he should go; even when he is old he will not depart from it.

2 Timothy 3:7

Always learning and never able to arrive at a knowledge of the truth.

2 Timothy 3:16-17

All Scripture is breathed out by God and profitable for teaching, for reproof, for correction, and for training in righteousness, that the man of God may be competent, equipped for every good work.

Romans 15:4

For whatever was written in former days was written for our instruction, that through endurance and through the encouragement of the Scriptures we might have hope.

2 John 1:9

Everyone who goes on ahead and does not abide in the teaching of Christ, does not have God. Whoever abides in the teaching has both the Father and the Son.

Legalism

Ephesians 2:8-9

For by grace you have been saved through faith. And this is not your own doing; it is the gift of God, not a result of works, so that no one may boast.

John 6:28-29

Then they said to him, "What must we do, to be doing the works of God?" Jesus answered them, "This is the work of God, that you believe in him whom he has sent."

Romans 3:28

For we hold that one is justified by faith apart from works of the law.

Galatians 2:21

I do not nullify the grace of God, for if righteousness were through the law, then Christ died for no purpose.

Galatians 2:16

Yet we know that a person is not justified by works of the law but through faith in Jesus Christ, so we also have believed in Christ Jesus, in order to be justified by faith in Christ and not by works of the law, because by works of the law no one will be justified.

Lent

Matthew 6:16-18

"And when you fast, do not look gloomy like the hypocrites, for they disfigure their faces that their fasting may be seen by others. Truly, I say to you, they have received their reward. But when you fast, anoint your head and wash your face, that your fasting may not be seen by others but by your Father who is in secret. And your Father who sees in secret will reward you.

Joel 2:12-13

"Yet even now," declares the Lord, "return to me with all your heart, with fasting, with weeping, and with mourning; and rend your hearts and not your garments." Return to the Lord your God, for he is gracious and merciful, slow to anger, and abounding in steadfast love; and he relents over disaster.

Liberty

Galatians 5:13
For you were called to freedom, brothers. Only do not use your freedom as an opportunity for the flesh, but through love serve one another.

John 8:36
So if the Son sets you free, you will be free indeed.

Galatians 5:1
For freedom Christ has set us free; stand firm therefore, and do not submit again to a yoke of slavery.

2 Corinthians 3:17
Now the Lord is the Spirit, and where the Spirit of the Lord is, there is freedom.

John 8:32
And you will know the truth, and the truth will set you free."

James 1:25
But the one who looks into the perfect law, the law of liberty, and perseveres, being no hearer who forgets but a doer who acts, he will be blessed in his doing.

Isaiah 61:1
The Spirit of the Lord God is upon me, because the Lord has anointed me to bring good news to the poor; he has sent me to bind up the brokenhearted, to proclaim liberty to the captives, and the opening of the prison to those who are bound;

1 Corinthians 6:12
"All things are lawful for me," but not all things are helpful. "All things are lawful for me," but I will not be enslaved by anything.

2 Peter 2:19
They promise them freedom, but they themselves are slaves of corruption. For whatever overcomes a person, to that he is enslaved.

Romans 8:1-2
There is therefore now no condemnation for those who are in Christ Jesus. For the law of the Spirit of life has set you free in Christ Jesus from the law of sin and death.

1 Peter 2:16
Live as people who are free, not using your freedom as a cover-up for evil, but living as servants of God.

Jeremiah 34:8
The word that came to Jeremiah from the Lord, after King Zedekiah had made a covenant with all the people in Jerusalem to make a proclamation of liberty to them,

Leviticus 25:10

And you shall consecrate the fiftieth year, and proclaim liberty throughout the land to all its inhabitants. It shall be a jubilee for you, when each of you shall return to his property and each of you shall return to his clan.

Life

John 3:16

"For God so loved the world, that he gave his only Son, that whoever believes in him should not perish but have eternal life.

John 14:6

Jesus said to him, "I am the way, and the truth, and the life. No one comes to the Father except through me.

Romans 6:23

For the wages of sin is death, but the free gift of God is eternal life in Christ Jesus our Lord.

John 10:10

The thief comes only to steal and kill and destroy. I came that they may have life and have it abundantly.

Genesis 2:7

Then the Lord God formed the man of dust from the ground and breathed into his nostrils the breath of life, and the man became a living creature.

Jeremiah 29:11

For I know the plans I have for you, declares the Lord, plans for welfare and not for evil, to give you a future and a hope.

Romans 8:28

And we know that for those who love God all things work together for good, for those who are called according to his purpose.

John 6:35

Jesus said to them, "I am the bread of life; whoever comes to me shall not hunger, and whoever believes in me shall never thirst.

Philippians 4:13

I can do all things through him who strengthens me.

Isaiah 40:31

But they who wait for the Lord shall renew their strength; they shall mount up with wings like eagles; they shall run and not be weary; they shall walk and not faint.

Isaiah 41:10

Fear not, for I am with you; be not dismayed, for I am your God; I will strengthen you, I will help you, I will uphold you with my righteous right hand.

Listen

James 1:19
Know this, my beloved brothers: let every person be quick to hear, slow to speak, slow to anger;

Proverbs 19:20
Listen to advice and accept instruction, that you may gain wisdom in the future.

Proverbs 18:13
If one gives an answer before he hears, it is his folly and shame.

Proverbs 2:2
Making your ear attentive to wisdom and inclining your heart to understanding;

Matthew 11:15
He who has ears to hear, let him hear.

Proverbs 19:27
Cease to hear instruction, my son, and you will stray from the words of knowledge.

Proverbs 25:12
Like a gold ring or an ornament of gold is a wise reprover to a listening ear.

Proverbs 1:33
But whoever listens to me will dwell secure and will be at ease, without dread of disaster."

Revelation 2:7
He who has an ear, let him hear what the Spirit says to the churches. To the one who conquers I will grant to eat of the tree of life, which is in the paradise of God.'

John 8:47
Whoever is of God hears the words of God. The reason why you do not hear them is that you are not of God."

Galatians 4:6-9
And because you are sons, God has sent the Spirit of his Son into our hearts, crying, "Abba! Father!" So you are no longer a slave, but a son, and if a son, then an heir through God. Formerly, when you did not know God, you were enslaved to those that by nature are not gods. But now that you have come to know God, or rather to be known by God, how can you turn back again to the weak and worthless elementary principles of the world, whose slaves you want to be once more?

Proverbs 18:2
A fool takes no pleasure in understanding, but only in expressing his opinion.

Mark 9:7
And a cloud overshadowed them, and a voice came out of the cloud, "This is my beloved Son; listen to him."

Loaning Money

Exodus 22:25
"If you lend money to any of my people with you who is poor, you shall not be like a moneylender to him, and you shall not exact interest from him.

Luke 6:34-35
And if you lend to those from whom you expect to receive, what credit is that to you? Even sinners lend to sinners, to get back the same amount. But love your enemies, and do good, and lend, expecting nothing in return, and your reward will be great, and you will be sons of the Most High, for he is kind to the ungrateful and the evil.

Romans 13:8
Owe no one anything, except to love each other, for the one who loves another has fulfilled the law.

Deuteronomy 23:19-20
"You shall not charge interest on loans to your brother, interest on money, interest on food, interest on anything that is lent for interest. You may charge a foreigner interest, but you may not charge your brother interest, that the Lord your God may bless you in all that you undertake in the land that you are entering to take possession of it.

Proverbs 19:17
Whoever is generous to the poor lends to the Lord, and he will repay him for his deed.

Proverbs 22:7
The rich rules over the poor, and the borrower is the slave of the lender.

1 John 3:17
But if anyone has the world's goods and sees his brother in need, yet closes his heart against him, how does God's love abide in him?

Psalm 37:21
The wicked borrows but does not pay back, but the righteous is generous and gives;

1 Timothy 6:10
For the love of money is a root of all kinds of evils. It is through this craving that some have wandered away from the faith and pierced themselves with many pangs.

Loneliness

Isaiah 41:10
Fear not, for I am with you; be not dismayed, for I am your God; I will strengthen you, I will help you, I will uphold you with my righteous right hand.

Deuteronomy 31:6
Be strong and courageous. Do not fear or be in dread of them, for it is the Lord your God who goes with you. He will not leave you or forsake you."

Matthew 28:20

Teaching them to observe all that I have commanded you. And behold, I am with you always, to the end of the age."

Genesis 2:18

Then the Lord God said, "It is not good that the man should be alone; I will make him a helper fit for him."

Psalm 27:10

For my father and my mother have forsaken me, but the Lord will take me in.

1 Peter 5:7

Casting all your anxieties on him, because he cares for you.

Psalm 23:4

Even though I walk through the valley of the shadow of death, I will fear no evil, for you are with me; your rod and your staff, they comfort me.

Hebrews 13:5

Keep your life free from love of money, and be content with what you have, for he has said, "I will never leave you nor forsake you."

Joshua 1:5

No man shall be able to stand before you all the days of your life. Just as I was with Moses, so I will be with you. I will not leave you or forsake you.

John 14:18

"I will not leave you as orphans; I will come to you.

Philippians 4:6-7

Do not be anxious about anything, but in everything by prayer and supplication with thanksgiving let your requests be made known to God. And the peace of God, which surpasses all understanding, will guard your hearts and your minds in Christ Jesus.

Psalm 38:9

O Lord, all my longing is before you; my sighing is not hidden from you.

Psalm 147:3

He heals the brokenhearted and binds up their wounds.

Psalm 68:5-6

Father of the fatherless and protector of widows is God in his holy habitation. God settles the solitary in a home; he leads out the prisoners to prosperity, but the rebellious dwell in a parched land.

Loss

Psalm 34:17-20

When the righteous cry for help, the Lord hears and delivers them out of all their troubles. The Lord is near to the brokenhearted and saves the crushed in spirit. Many are the afflictions of the righteous, but the Lord delivers him out of them all. He keeps all his bones; not one of them is broken.

Matthew 5:4

"Blessed are those who mourn, for they shall be comforted.

2 Corinthians 12:9

But he said to me, "My grace is sufficient for you, for my power is made perfect in weakness." Therefore I will boast all the more gladly of my weaknesses, so that the power of Christ may rest upon me.

Philippians 4:19

And my God will supply every need of yours according to his riches in glory in Christ Jesus.

2 Corinthians 1:3-5

Blessed be the God and Father of our Lord Jesus Christ, the Father of mercies and God of all comfort, who comforts us in all our affliction, so that we may be able to comfort those who are in any affliction, with the comfort with which we ourselves are comforted by God. For as we share abundantly in Christ's sufferings, so through Christ we share abundantly in comfort too.

2 Peter 2:9

Then the Lord knows how to rescue the godly from trials, and to keep the unrighteous under punishment until the day of judgment,

Lost

Isaiah 41:10

Fear not, for I am with you; be not dismayed, for I am your God; I will strengthen you, I will help you, I will uphold you with my righteous right hand.

Ephesians 2:8-9

For by grace you have been saved through faith. And this is not your own doing; it is the gift of God, not a result of works, so that no one may boast.

Love

1 Corinthians 16:14

Let all that you do be done in love.

John 3:16

"For God so loved the world, that he gave his only Son, that whoever believes in him should not perish but have eternal life.

1 John 4:8
Anyone who does not love does not know God, because God is love.

1 Peter 4:8
Above all, keep loving one another earnestly, since love covers a multitude of sins.

Colossians 3:14
And above all these put on love, which binds everything together in perfect harmony.

John 13:34-35
A new commandment I give to you, that you love one another: just as I have loved you, you also are to love one another. By this all people will know that you are my disciples, if you have love for one another."

John 15:13
Greater love has no one than this, that someone lay down his life for his friends.

1 Corinthians 13:13
So now faith, hope, and love abide, these three; but the greatest of these is love.

Mark 12:29-31
Jesus answered, "The most important is, 'Hear, O Israel: The Lord our God, the Lord is one. And you shall love the Lord your God with all your heart and with all your soul and with all your mind and with all your strength.' The second is this: 'You shall love your neighbor as yourself.' There is no other commandment greater than these."

1 John 4:19
We love because he first loved us.

Matthew 22:36-40
"Teacher, which is the great commandment in the Law?" And he said to him, "You shall love the Lord your God with all your heart and with all your soul and with all your mind. This is the great and first commandment. And a second is like it: You shall love your neighbor as yourself. On these two commandments depend all the Law and the Prophets."

Proverbs 10:12
Hatred stirs up strife, but love covers all offenses.

Love (Brotherly)

Romans 12:10
Love one another with brotherly affection. Outdo one another in showing honor.

Hebrews 13:1
Let brotherly love continue.

1 John 4:20

If anyone says, "I love God," and hates his brother, he is a liar; for he who does not love his brother whom he has seen cannot love God whom he has not seen.

1 Corinthians 13:4-8

Love is patient and kind; love does not envy or boast; it is not arrogant or rude. It does not insist on its own way; it is not irritable or resentful; it does not rejoice at wrongdoing, but rejoices with the truth. Love bears all things, believes all things, hopes all things, endures all things. Love never ends. As for prophecies, they will pass away; as for tongues, they will cease; as for knowledge, it will pass away.

John 15:13

Greater love has no one than this, that someone lay down his life for his friends.

1 John 4:7

Beloved, let us love one another, for love is from God, and whoever loves has been born of God and knows God.

1 John 3:18

Little children, let us not love in word or talk but in deed and in truth.

1 Peter 3:8

Finally, all of you, have unity of mind, sympathy, brotherly love, a tender heart, and a humble mind.

John 13:34-35

A new commandment I give to you, that you love one another: just as I have loved you, you also are to love one another. By this all people will know that you are my disciples, if you have love for one another."

1 Corinthians 16:14

Let all that you do be done in love.

1 Thessalonians 4:9

Now concerning brotherly love you have no need for anyone to write to you, for you yourselves have been taught by God to love one another,

Love (Unconditional)

John 3:16

"For God so loved the world, that he gave his only Son, that whoever believes in him should not perish but have eternal life.

Romans 5:8

But God shows his love for us in that while we were still sinners, Christ died for us.

1 John 4:8

Anyone who does not love does not know God, because God is love.

1 John 4:16

So we have come to know and to believe the love that God has for us. God is love, and whoever abides in love abides in God, and God abides in him.

1 John 4:18

There is no fear in love, but perfect love casts out fear. For fear has to do with punishment, and whoever fears has not been perfected in love.

1 Corinthians 13:4-7

Love is patient and kind; love does not envy or boast; it is not arrogant or rude. It does not insist on its own way; it is not irritable or resentful; it does not rejoice at wrongdoing, but rejoices with the truth. Love bears all things, believes all things, hopes all things, endures all things.

1 Peter 4:8

Above all, keep loving one another earnestly, since love covers a multitude of sins.

1 John 3:16

By this we know love, that he laid down his life for us, and we ought to lay down our lives for the brothers.

John 15:13

Greater love has no one than this, that someone lay down his life for his friends.

Luke 6:27

"But I say to you who hear, Love your enemies, do good to those who hate you,

Romans 8:35

Who shall separate us from the love of Christ? Shall tribulation, or distress, or persecution, or famine, or nakedness, or danger, or sword?

Love Your Enemies

Matthew 5:44

But I say to you, Love your enemies and pray for those who persecute you,

Luke 6:27

"But I say to you who hear, Love your enemies, do good to those who hate you,

Romans 12:20

To the contrary, "if your enemy is hungry, feed him; if he is thirsty, give him something to drink; for by so doing you will heap burning coals on his head."

Romans 12:14

Bless those who persecute you; bless and do not curse them.

Leviticus 19:18

You shall not take vengeance or bear a grudge against the sons of your own people, but you shall love your neighbor as yourself: I am the Lord.

1 John 4:7

Beloved, let us love one another, for love is from God, and whoever loves has been born of God and knows God.

Luke 23:34

And Jesus said, "Father, forgive them, for they know not what they do." And they cast lots to divide his garments.

Luke 6:35

But love your enemies, and do good, and lend, expecting nothing in return, and your reward will be great, and you will be sons of the Most High, for he is kind to the ungrateful and the evil.

Acts 7:60

And falling to his knees he cried out with a loud voice, "Lord, do not hold this sin against them." And when he had said this, he fell asleep.

Exodus 23:5

If you see the donkey of one who hates you lying down under its burden, you shall refrain from leaving him with it; you shall rescue it with him.

Proverbs 25:21-22

If your enemy is hungry, give him bread to eat, and if he is thirsty, give him water to drink, for you will heap burning coals on his head, and the Lord will reward you.

Love Your Neighbor

Mark 12:31

The second is this: 'You shall love your neighbor as yourself.' There is no other commandment greater than these."

1 John 4:7

Beloved, let us love one another, for love is from God, and whoever loves has been born of God and knows God.

Leviticus 19:18

You shall not take vengeance or bear a grudge against the sons of your own people, but you shall love your neighbor as yourself: I am the Lord.

1 Corinthians 16:14

Let all that you do be done in love.

Matthew 22:37-40

And he said to him, "You shall love the Lord your God with all your heart and with all your soul and with all your mind. This is the great and first commandment. And a second is like it: You shall love your neighbor as yourself. On these two commandments depend all the Law and the Prophets."

Romans 13:10

Love does no wrong to a neighbor; therefore love is the fulfilling of the law.

Galatians 5:14

For the whole law is fulfilled in one word: "You shall love your neighbor as yourself."

1 Peter 4:8

Above all, keep loving one another earnestly, since love covers a multitude of sins.

1 John 4:19

We love because he first loved us.

Love Yourself

1 Corinthians 6:19

Or do you not know that your body is a temple of the Holy Spirit within you, whom you have from God? You are not your own,

1 Corinthians 6:20

For you were bought with a price. So glorify God in your body.

1 Corinthians 13:4-7

Love is patient and kind; love does not envy or boast; it is not arrogant or rude. It does not insist on its own way; it is not irritable or resentful; it does not rejoice at wrongdoing, but rejoices with the truth. Love bears all things, believes all things, hopes all things, endures all things.

2 Timothy 3:1-5

But understand this, that in the last days there will come times of difficulty. For people will be lovers of self, lovers of money, proud, arrogant, abusive, disobedient to their parents, ungrateful, unholy, heartless, unappeasable, slanderous, without self-control, brutal, not loving good, treacherous, reckless, swollen with conceit, lovers of pleasure rather than lovers of God, having the appearance of godliness, but denying its power. Avoid such people.

Ezra 10:4

Arise, for it is your task, and we are with you; be strong and do it."

Leviticus 19:18

You shall not take vengeance or bear a grudge against the sons of your own people, but you shall love your neighbor as yourself: I am the Lord.

Matthew 22:37-39

And he said to him, "You shall love the Lord your God with all your heart and with all your soul and with all your mind. This is the great and first commandment. And a second is like it: You shall love your neighbor as yourself.

1 Corinthians 13:13

So now faith, hope, and love abide, these three; but the greatest of these is love.

Romans 13:9

For the commandments, "You shall not commit adultery, You shall not murder, You shall not steal, You shall not covet," and any other commandment, are summed up in this word: "You shall love your neighbor as yourself."

Loving God

Luke 10:27

And he answered, "You shall love the Lord your God with all your heart and with all your soul and with all your strength and with all your mind, and your neighbor as yourself."

Deuteronomy 6:5

You shall love the Lord your God with all your heart and with all your soul and with all your might.

1 John 4:19

We love because he first loved us.

John 3:16

"For God so loved the world, that he gave his only Son, that whoever believes in him should not perish but have eternal life.

John 14:21

Whoever has my commandments and keeps them, he it is who loves me. And he who loves me will be loved by my Father, and I will love him and manifest myself to him."

Deuteronomy 7:9

Know therefore that the Lord your God is God, the faithful God who keeps covenant and steadfast love with those who love him and keep his commandments, to a thousand generations,

John 14:15

"If you love me, you will keep my commandments.

Romans 5:8

But God shows his love for us in that while we were still sinners, Christ died for us.

1 John 3:1

See what kind of love the Father has given to us, that we should be called children of God; and so we are. The reason why the world does not know us is that it did not know him.

Matthew 6:24

"No one can serve two masters, for either he will hate the one and love the other, or he will be devoted to the one and despise the other. You cannot serve God and money.

John 14:23-24

Jesus answered him, "If anyone loves me, he will keep my word, and my Father will love him, and we will come to him and make our home with him. Whoever does not love me does not keep my words. And the word that you hear is not mine but the Father's who sent me.

Galatians 2:20

I have been crucified with Christ. It is no longer I who live, but Christ who lives in me. And the life I now live in the flesh I live by faith in the Son of God, who loved me and gave himself for me.

Mark 12:29-31

Jesus answered, "The most important is, 'Hear, O Israel: The Lord our God, the Lord is one. And you shall love the Lord your God with all your heart and with all your soul and with all your mind and with all your strength.' The second is this: 'You shall love your neighbor as yourself.' There is no other commandment greater than these."

1 John 4:7-8

Beloved, let us love one another, for love is from God, and whoever loves has been born of God and knows God. Anyone who does not love does not know God, because God is love.

1 John 4:16

So we have come to know and to believe the love that God has for us. God is love, and whoever abides in love abides in God, and God abides in him.

1 John 5:3

For this is the love of God, that we keep his commandments. And his commandments are not burdensome.

Low Self-Esteem

Song of Solomon 4:7

You are altogether beautiful, my love; there is no flaw in you.

1 Samuel 16:7

But the Lord said to Samuel, "Do not look on his appearance or on the height of his stature, because I have rejected him. For the Lord sees not as man sees: man looks on the outward appearance, but the Lord looks on the heart."

Psalm 139:14

I praise you, for I am fearfully and wonderfully made. Wonderful are your works; my soul knows it very well.

Philippians 4:13

I can do all things through him who strengthens me.

1 Corinthians 10:13

No temptation has overtaken you that is not common to man. God is faithful, and he will not let you be tempted beyond your ability, but with the temptation he will also provide the way of escape, that you may be able to endure it.

Matthew 11:28-30

Come to me, all who labor and are heavy laden, and I will give you rest. Take my yoke upon you, and learn from me, for I am gentle and lowly in heart, and you will find rest for your souls. For my yoke is easy, and my burden is light."

1 John 3:1

See what kind of love the Father has given to us, that we should be called children of God; and so we are. The reason why the world does not know us is that it did not know him.

Jeremiah 1:6-8

Then I said, "Ah, Lord God! Behold, I do not know how to speak, for I am only a youth." But the Lord said to me, "Do not say, 'I am only a youth'; for to all to whom I send you, you shall go, and whatever I command you, you shall speak. Do not be afraid of them, for I am with you to deliver you, declares the Lord."

Exodus 4:10-12

But Moses said to the Lord, "Oh, my Lord, I am not eloquent, either in the past or since you have spoken to your servant, but I am slow of speech and of tongue." Then the Lord said to him, "Who has made man's mouth? Who makes him mute, or deaf, or seeing, or blind? Is it not I, the Lord? Now therefore go, and I will be with your mouth and teach you what you shall speak."

1 Peter 2:9

But you are a chosen race, a royal priesthood, a holy nation, a people for his own possession, that you may proclaim the excellencies of him who called you out of darkness into his marvelous light.

Loyalty

Proverbs 18:24

A man of many companions may come to ruin, but there is a friend who sticks closer than a brother.

Proverbs 17:17

A friend loves at all times, and a brother is born for adversity.

Ruth 1:16-17

But Ruth said, "Do not urge me to leave you or to return from following you. For where you go I will go, and where you lodge I will lodge. Your people shall be my people, and your God my God. Where you die I will die, and there will I be buried. May the Lord do so to me and more also if anything but death parts me from you."

Matthew 26:35

Peter said to him, "Even if I must die with you, I will not deny you!" And all the disciples said the same.

1 Corinthians 16:13-14

Be watchful, stand firm in the faith, act like men, be strong. Let all that you do be done in love.

Proverbs 21:21

Whoever pursues righteousness and kindness will find life, righteousness, and honor.

Matthew 18:15

"If your brother sins against you, go and tell him his fault, between you and him alone. If he listens to you, you have gained your brother.

Titus 3:1

Remind them to be submissive to rulers and authorities, to be obedient, to be ready for every good work,

Matthew 26:33

Peter answered him, "Though they all fall away because of you, I will never fall away."

Romans 13:1

Let every person be subject to the governing authorities. For there is no authority except from God, and those that exist have been instituted by God.

Proverbs 3:3

Let not steadfast love and faithfulness forsake you; bind them around your neck; write them on the tablet of your heart.

Lust

Matthew 5:28

But I say to you that everyone who looks at a woman with lustful intent has already committed adultery with her in his heart.

1 John 2:16

For all that is in the world—the desires of the flesh and the desires of the eyes and pride in possessions— is not from the Father but is from the world.

Galatians 5:16

But I say, walk by the Spirit, and you will not gratify the desires of the flesh.

2 Timothy 2:22

So flee youthful passions and pursue righteousness, faith, love, and peace, along with those who call on the Lord from a pure heart.

Colossians 3:5

Put to death therefore what is earthly in you: sexual immorality, impurity, passion, evil desire, and covetousness, which is idolatry.

1 Corinthians 6:18

Flee from sexual immorality. Every other sin a person commits is outside the body, but the sexually immoral person sins against his own body.

Proverbs 6:25

Do not desire her beauty in your heart, and do not let her capture you with her eyelashes;

Job 31:1

"I have made a covenant with my eyes; how then could I gaze at a virgin?

1 Peter 2:11

Beloved, I urge you as sojourners and exiles to abstain from the passions of the flesh, which wage war against your soul.

1 Thessalonians 4:3-5

For this is the will of God, your sanctification: that you abstain from sexual immorality; that each one of you know how to control his own body in holiness and honor, not in the passion of lust like the Gentiles who do not know God;

James 1:14-15

But each person is tempted when he is lured and enticed by his own desire. Then desire when it has conceived gives birth to sin, and sin when it is fully grown brings forth death.

Galatians 5:19-21

Now the works of the flesh are evident: sexual immorality, impurity, sensuality, idolatry, sorcery, enmity, strife, jealousy, fits of anger, rivalries, dissensions, divisions, envy, drunkenness, orgies, and things like these. I warn you, as I warned you before, that those who do such things will not inherit the kingdom of God.

Lying

Proverbs 6:16-19

There are six things that the Lord hates, seven that are an abomination to him: haughty eyes, a lying tongue, and hands that shed innocent blood, a heart that devises wicked plans, feet that make haste to run to evil, a false witness who breathes out lies, and one who sows discord among brothers.

Proverbs 12:22

Lying lips are an abomination to the Lord, but those who act faithfully are his delight.

Proverbs 19:9

A false witness will not go unpunished, and he who breathes out lies will perish.

Psalm 101:7

No one who practices deceit shall dwell in my house; no one who utters lies shall continue before my eyes.

Colossians 3:9-10

Do not lie to one another, seeing that you have put off the old self with its practices and have put on the new self, which is being renewed in knowledge after the image of its creator.

Proverbs 12:19

Truthful lips endure forever, but a lying tongue is but for a moment.

Luke 8:17

For nothing is hidden that will not be made manifest, nor is anything secret that will not be known and come to light.

John 8:44

You are of your father the devil, and your will is to do your father's desires. He was a murderer from the beginning, and has nothing to do with the truth, because there is no truth in him. When he lies, he speaks out of his own character, for he is a liar and the father of lies.

Ephesians 4:25

Therefore, having put away falsehood, let each one of you speak the truth with his neighbor, for we are members one of another.

1 John 2:4

Whoever says "I know him" but does not keep his commandments is a liar, and the truth is not in him,

Exodus 20:16

"You shall not bear false witness against your neighbor.

Revelation 21:8

But as for the cowardly, the faithless, the detestable, as for murderers, the sexually immoral, sorcerers, idolaters, and all liars, their portion will be in the lake that burns with fire and sulfur, which is the second death."

Proverbs 19:5

A false witness will not go unpunished, and he who breathes out lies will not escape.

1 John 1:9

If we confess our sins, he is faithful and just to forgive us our sins and to cleanse us from all unrighteousness.

Leviticus 19:11

"You shall not steal; you shall not deal falsely; you shall not lie to one another.

Proverbs 24:28

Be not a witness against your neighbor without cause, and do not deceive with your lips.

Proverbs 21:6

The getting of treasures by a lying tongue is a fleeting vapor and a snare of death.

Matthew 15:18-20

But what comes out of the mouth proceeds from the heart, and this defiles a person. For out of the heart come evil thoughts, murder, adultery, sexual immorality, theft, false witness, slander. These are what defile a person. But to eat with unwashed hands does not defile anyone."

Psalm 58:3

The wicked are estranged from the womb; they go astray from birth, speaking lies.

James 3:14

But if you have bitter jealousy and selfish ambition in your hearts, do not boast and be false to the truth.

Proverbs 14:5

A faithful witness does not lie, but a false witness breathes out lies.

Psalm 109:2

For wicked and deceitful mouths are opened against me, speaking against me with lying tongues.

Magic

Leviticus 19:31
"Do not turn to mediums or necromancers; do not seek them out, and so make yourselves unclean by them: I am the Lord your God.

Revelation 21:8
But as for the cowardly, the faithless, the detestable, as for murderers, the sexually immoral, sorcerers, idolaters, and all liars, their portion will be in the lake that burns with fire and sulfur, which is the second death."

1 John 4:1
Beloved, do not believe every spirit, but test the spirits to see whether they are from God, for many false prophets have gone out into the world.

2 Kings 21:6
And he burned his son as an offering and used fortune-telling and omens and dealt with mediums and with necromancers. He did much evil in the sight of the Lord, provoking him to anger.

Isaiah 8:19
And when they say to you, "Inquire of the mediums and the necromancers who chirp and mutter," should not a people inquire of their God? Should they inquire of the dead on behalf of the living?

Acts 19:19
And a number of those who had practiced magic arts brought their books together and burned them in the sight of all. And they counted the value of them and found it came to fifty thousand pieces of silver.

Colossians 2:8
See to it that no one takes you captive by philosophy and empty deceit, according to human tradition, according to the elemental spirits of the world, and not according to Christ.

Deuteronomy 18:10-12
There shall not be found among you anyone who burns his son or his daughter as an offering, anyone who practices divination or tells fortunes or interprets omens, or a sorcerer or a charmer or a medium or a necromancer or one who inquires of the dead, for whoever does these things is an abomination to the Lord. And because of these abominations the Lord your God is driving them out before you.

Malice

Ephesians 4:31-32
Let all bitterness and wrath and anger and clamor and slander be put away from you, along with all malice. Be kind to one another, tenderhearted, forgiving one another, as God in Christ forgave you.

Proverbs 15:1
A soft answer turns away wrath, but a harsh word stirs up anger.

Proverbs 12:16

The vexation of a fool is known at once, but the prudent ignores an insult.

James 1:19-20

Know this, my beloved brothers: let every person be quick to hear, slow to speak, slow to anger; for the anger of man does not produce the righteousness of God.

Matthew 7:12

"So whatever you wish that others would do to you, do also to them, for this is the Law and the Prophets.

Psalm 37:8-9

Refrain from anger, and forsake wrath! Fret not yourself; it tends only to evil. For the evildoers shall be cut off, but those who wait for the Lord shall inherit the land.

Colossians 3:12-14

Put on then, as God's chosen ones, holy and beloved, compassionate hearts, kindness, humility, meekness, and patience, bearing with one another and, if one has a complaint against another, forgiving each other; as the Lord has forgiven you, so you also must forgive. And above all these put on love, which binds everything together in perfect harmony.

Matthew 6:14-15

For if you forgive others their trespasses, your heavenly Father will also forgive you, but if you do not forgive others their trespasses, neither will your Father forgive your trespasses.

James 4:11-12

Do not speak evil against one another, brothers. The one who speaks against a brother or judges his brother, speaks evil against the law and judges the law. But if you judge the law, you are not a doer of the law but a judge. There is only one lawgiver and judge, he who is able to save and to destroy. But who are you to judge your neighbor?

James 1:26

If anyone thinks he is religious and does not bridle his tongue but deceives his heart, this person's religion is worthless.

Manipulation

Matthew 7:15

"Beware of false prophets, who come to you in sheep's clothing but inwardly are ravenous wolves.

2 Timothy 3:1-5

But understand this, that in the last days there will come times of difficulty. For people will be lovers of self, lovers of money, proud, arrogant, abusive, disobedient to their parents, ungrateful, unholy, heartless, unappeasable, slanderous, without self-control, brutal, not loving good, treacherous, reckless, swollen with conceit, lovers of pleasure rather than lovers of God, having the appearance of godliness, but denying its power. Avoid such people.

Matthew 24:4

And Jesus answered them, "See that no one leads you astray.

Marriage

Hebrews 13:4
Let marriage be held in honor among all, and let the marriage bed be undefiled, for God will judge the sexually immoral and adulterous.

Proverbs 18:22
He who finds a wife finds a good thing and obtains favor from the Lord.

Genesis 2:24
Therefore a man shall leave his father and his mother and hold fast to his wife, and they shall become one flesh.

1 Corinthians 13:4-7
Love is patient and kind; love does not envy or boast; it is not arrogant or rude. It does not insist on its own way; it is not irritable or resentful; it does not rejoice at wrongdoing, but rejoices with the truth. Love bears all things, believes all things, hopes all things, endures all things.

Proverbs 21:9
It is better to live in a corner of the housetop than in a house shared with a quarrelsome wife.

Proverbs 19:14
House and wealth are inherited from fathers, but a prudent wife is from the Lord.

Materialism

Hebrews 13:5
Keep your life free from love of money, and be content with what you have, for he has said, "I will never leave you nor forsake you."

1 John 2:16
For all that is in the world—the desires of the flesh and the desires of the eyes and pride in possessions—is not from the Father but is from the world.

Luke 12:15
And he said to them, "Take care, and be on your guard against all covetousness, for one's life does not consist in the abundance of his possessions."

1 Timothy 6:9-10
But those who desire to be rich fall into temptation, into a snare, into many senseless and harmful desires that plunge people into ruin and destruction. For the love of money is a root of all kinds of evils. It is through this craving that some have wandered away from the faith and pierced themselves with many pangs.

Matthew 6:19-21

"Do not lay up for yourselves treasures on earth, where moth and rust destroy and where thieves break in and steal, but lay up for yourselves treasures in heaven, where neither moth nor rust destroys and where thieves do not break in and steal. For where your treasure is, there your heart will be also.

Ecclesiastes 5:10

He who loves money will not be satisfied with money, nor he who loves wealth with his income; this also is vanity.

Luke 12:33-34

Sell your possessions, and give to the needy. Provide yourselves with moneybags that do not grow old, with a treasure in the heavens that does not fail, where no thief approaches and no moth destroys. For where your treasure is, there will your heart be also.

Matthew 6:33

But seek first the kingdom of God and his righteousness, and all these things will be added to you.

1 Timothy 6:17-19

As for the rich in this present age, charge them not to be haughty, nor to set their hopes on the uncertainty of riches, but on God, who richly provides us with everything to enjoy. They are to do good, to be rich in good works, to be generous and ready to share, thus storing up treasure for themselves as a good foundation for the future, so that they may take hold of that which is truly life.

Maturity

1 Corinthians 14:20

Brothers, do not be children in your thinking. Be infants in evil, but in your thinking be mature.

1 Corinthians 13:11

When I was a child, I spoke like a child, I thought like a child, I reasoned like a child. When I became a man, I gave up childish ways.

Ephesians 4:14-15

So that we may no longer be children, tossed to and fro by the waves and carried about by every wind of doctrine, by human cunning, by craftiness in deceitful schemes. Rather, speaking the truth in love, we are to grow up in every way into him who is the head, into Christ,

Ephesians 4:13

Until we all attain to the unity of the faith and of the knowledge of the Son of God, to mature manhood, to the measure of the stature of the fullness of Christ,

Hebrews 5:12-13

For though by this time you ought to be teachers, you need someone to teach you again the basic principles of the oracles of God. You need milk, not solid food, for everyone who lives on milk is unskilled in the word of righteousness, since he is a child.

2 Peter 3:18

But grow in the grace and knowledge of our Lord and Savior Jesus Christ. To him be the glory both now and to the day of eternity. Amen.

Hebrews 6:1-3

Therefore, let us leave the elementary doctrine of Christ and go on to maturity, not laying again a foundation of repentance from dead works and of faith toward God, and of instruction about washings, the laying on of hands, the resurrection of the dead, and eternal judgment. And this we will do if God permits.

Romans 5:3-4

More than that, we rejoice in our sufferings, knowing that suffering produces endurance, and endurance produces character, and character produces hope,

Hebrews 5:12-14

For though by this time you ought to be teachers, you need someone to teach you again the basic principles of the oracles of God. You need milk, not solid food, for everyone who lives on milk is unskilled in the word of righteousness, since he is a child. But solid food is for the mature, for those who have their powers of discernment trained by constant practice to distinguish good from evil.

1 Peter 2:2

Like newborn infants, long for the pure spiritual milk, that by it you may grow up into salvation—

Medicine

Proverbs 17:22

A joyful heart is good medicine, but a crushed spirit dries up the bones.

Ezekiel 47:12

And on the banks, on both sides of the river, there will grow all kinds of trees for food. Their leaves will not wither, nor their fruit fail, but they will bear fresh fruit every month, because the water for them flows from the sanctuary. Their fruit will be for food, and their leaves for healing."

1 Timothy 5:23

(No longer drink only water, but use a little wine for the sake of your stomach and your frequent ailments.)

Isaiah 38:21

Now Isaiah had said, "Let them take a cake of figs and apply it to the boil, that he may recover."

Matthew 9:12

But when he heard it, he said, "Those who are well have no need of a physician, but those who are sick.

Luke 10:34

He went to him and bound up his wounds, pouring on oil and wine. Then he set him on his own animal and brought him to an inn and took care of him.

Jeremiah 8:22

Is there no balm in Gilead? Is there no physician there? Why then has the health of the daughter of my people not been restored?

Revelation 22:2

Through the middle of the street of the city; also, on either side of the river, the tree of life with its twelve kinds of fruit, yielding its fruit each month. The leaves of the tree were for the healing of the nations.

Psalm 103:3

Who forgives all your iniquity, who heals all your diseases,

James 5:15

And the prayer of faith will save the one who is sick, and the Lord will raise him up. And if he has committed sins, he will be forgiven.

Meditation

Joshua 1:8

This Book of the Law shall not depart from your mouth, but you shall meditate on it day and night, so that you may be careful to do according to all that is written in it. For then you will make your way prosperous, and then you will have good success.

Psalm 19:14

Let the words of my mouth and the meditation of my heart be acceptable in your sight, O Lord, my rock and my redeemer.

Psalm 1:2

But his delight is in the law of the Lord, and on his law he meditates day and night.

Psalm 119:15

I will meditate on your precepts and fix my eyes on your ways.

Psalm 104:34

May my meditation be pleasing to him, for I rejoice in the Lord.

Philippians 4:8

Finally, brothers, whatever is true, whatever is honorable, whatever is just, whatever is pure, whatever is lovely, whatever is commendable, if there is any excellence, if there is anything worthy of praise, think about these things.

Psalm 119:97

Oh how I love your law! It is my meditation all the day.

Psalm 49:3

My mouth shall speak wisdom; the meditation of my heart shall be understanding.

Psalm 63:6

When I remember you upon my bed, and meditate on you in the watches of the night;

Proverbs 4:20-22

My son, be attentive to my words; incline your ear to my sayings. Let them not escape from your sight; keep them within your heart. For they are life to those who find them, and healing to all their flesh.

Isaiah 26:3

You keep him in perfect peace whose mind is stayed on you, because he trusts in you.

Psalm 143:5

I remember the days of old; I meditate on all that you have done; I ponder the work of your hands.

Mediums

Leviticus 19:31

"Do not turn to mediums or necromancers; do not seek them out, and so make yourselves unclean by them: I am the Lord your God.

Leviticus 20:6

"If a person turns to mediums and necromancers, whoring after them, I will set my face against that person and will cut him off from among his people.

Isaiah 8:19

And when they say to you, "Inquire of the mediums and the necromancers who chirp and mutter," should not a people inquire of their God? Should they inquire of the dead on behalf of the living?

Leviticus 20:27

"A man or a woman who is a medium or a necromancer shall surely be put to death. They shall be stoned with stones; their blood shall be upon them."

Deuteronomy 18:9-12

"When you come into the land that the Lord your God is giving you, you shall not learn to follow the abominable practices of those nations. There shall not be found among you anyone who burns his son or his daughter as an offering, anyone who practices divination or tells fortunes or interprets omens, or a sorcerer or a charmer or a medium or a necromancer or one who inquires of the dead, for whoever does these things is an abomination to the Lord. And because of these abominations the Lord your God is driving them out before you.

Meekness

Matthew 5:5

"Blessed are the meek, for they shall inherit the earth.

Titus 3:2

To speak evil of no one, to avoid quarreling, to be gentle, and to show perfect courtesy toward all people.

Psalm 37:11

But the meek shall inherit the land and delight themselves in abundant peace.

Matthew 11:29

Take my yoke upon you, and learn from me, for I am gentle and lowly in heart, and you will find rest for your souls.

Psalm 25:9

He leads the humble in what is right, and teaches the humble his way.

James 3:13

Who is wise and understanding among you? By his good conduct let him show his works in the meekness of wisdom.

1 Peter 3:4

But let your adorning be the hidden person of the heart with the imperishable beauty of a gentle and quiet spirit, which in God's sight is very precious.

1 Peter 3:15

But in your hearts honor Christ the Lord as holy, always being prepared to make a defense to anyone who asks you for a reason for the hope that is in you; yet do it with gentleness and respect,

Numbers 12:3

Now the man Moses was very meek, more than all people who were on the face of the earth.

Mental Illness

Psalm 34:17-20

When the righteous cry for help, the Lord hears and delivers them out of all their troubles. The Lord is near to the brokenhearted and saves the crushed in spirit. Many are the afflictions of the righteous, but the Lord delivers him out of them all. He keeps all his bones; not one of them is broken.

Philippians 4:6-7

Do not be anxious about anything, but in everything by prayer and supplication with thanksgiving let your requests be made known to God. And the peace of God, which surpasses all understanding, will guard your hearts and your minds in Christ Jesus.

2 Timothy 1:7

For God gave us a spirit not of fear but of power and love and self-control.

Isaiah 41:10

Fear not, for I am with you; be not dismayed, for I am your God; I will strengthen you, I will help you, I will uphold you with my righteous right hand.

Matthew 4:24

So his fame spread throughout all Syria, and they brought him all the sick, those afflicted with various diseases and pains, those oppressed by demons, epileptics, and paralytics, and he healed them.

John 16:33

I have said these things to you, that in me you may have peace. In the world you will have tribulation. But take heart; I have overcome the world."

1 Peter 5:7

Casting all your anxieties on him, because he cares for you.

Mentoring

Proverbs 27:17

Iron sharpens iron, and one man sharpens another.

Titus 2:3-5

Older women likewise are to be reverent in behavior, not slanderers or slaves to much wine. They are to teach what is good, and so train the young women to love their husbands and children, to be self-controlled, pure, working at home, kind, and submissive to their own husbands, that the word of God may not be reviled.

1 Peter 5:1-5

So I exhort the elders among you, as a fellow elder and a witness of the sufferings of Christ, as well as a partaker in the glory that is going to be revealed: shepherd the flock of God that is among you, exercising oversight, not under compulsion, but willingly, as God would have you; not for shameful gain, but eagerly; not domineering over those in your charge, but being examples to the flock. And when the chief Shepherd appears, you will receive the unfading crown of glory. Likewise, you who are younger, be subject to the elders. Clothe yourselves, all of you, with humility toward one another, for "God opposes the proud but gives grace to the humble."

Proverbs 22:6

Train up a child in the way he should go; even when he is old he will not depart from it.

Psalm 145:4

One generation shall commend your works to another, and shall declare your mighty acts.

2 Timothy 2:2

And what you have heard from me in the presence of many witnesses entrust to faithful men who will be able to teach others also.

Psalm 71:18

So even to old age and gray hairs, O God, do not forsake me, until I proclaim your might to another generation, your power to all those to come.

Proverbs 9:9

Give instruction to a wise man, and he will be still wiser; teach a righteous man, and he will increase in learning.

1 Corinthians 11:1

Be imitators of me, as I am of Christ.

1 Thessalonians 2:8

So, being affectionately desirous of you, we were ready to share with you not only the gospel of God but also our own selves, because you had become very dear to us.

Proverbs 13:20

Whoever walks with the wise becomes wise, but the companion of fools will suffer harm.

Mercy

Luke 6:36

Be merciful, even as your Father is merciful.

James 2:13

For judgment is without mercy to one who has shown no mercy. Mercy triumphs over judgment.

Matthew 5:7

"Blessed are the merciful, for they shall receive mercy.

Matthew 9:13

Go and learn what this means, 'I desire mercy, and not sacrifice.' For I came not to call the righteous, but sinners."

Hebrews 4:16

Let us then with confidence draw near to the throne of grace, that we may receive mercy and find grace to help in time of need.

1 John 1:9

If we confess our sins, he is faithful and just to forgive us our sins and to cleanse us from all unrighteousness.

1 Peter 1:3

Blessed be the God and Father of our Lord Jesus Christ! According to his great mercy, he has caused us to be born again to a living hope through the resurrection of Jesus Christ from the dead,

Micah 6:8

He has told you, O man, what is good; and what does the Lord require of you but to do justice, and to love kindness, and to walk humbly with your God?

Lamentations 3:22-23

The steadfast love of the Lord never ceases; his mercies never come to an end; they are new every morning; great is your faithfulness.

Messiah

John 4:25-26

The woman said to him, "I know that Messiah is coming (he who is called Christ). When he comes, he will tell us all things." Jesus said to her, "I who speak to you am he."

Isaiah 7:14

Therefore, the Lord himself will give you a sign. Behold, the virgin shall conceive and bear a son, and shall call his name Immanuel.

Micah 5:2

But you, O Bethlehem Ephrathah, who are too little to be among the clans of Judah, from you shall come forth for me one who is to be ruler in Israel, whose coming forth is from of old, from ancient days.

John 1:41

He first found his own brother Simon and said to him, "We have found the Messiah" (which means Christ).

John 14:6

Jesus said to him, "I am the way, and the truth, and the life. No one comes to the Father except through me.

Malachi 3:1

Behold, I send my messenger, and he will prepare the way before me. And the Lord whom you seek will suddenly come to his temple; and the messenger of the covenant in whom you delight, behold, he is coming, says the Lord of hosts.

Zechariah 9:9

Rejoice greatly, O daughter of Zion! Shout aloud, O daughter of Jerusalem! Behold, your king is coming to you; righteous and having salvation is he, humble and mounted on a donkey, on a colt, the foal of a donkey.

Deuteronomy 18:15

"The Lord your God will raise up for you a prophet like me from among you, from your brothers—it is to him you shall listen—

Genesis 49:10

The scepter shall not depart from Judah, nor the ruler's staff from between his feet, until tribute comes to him; and to him shall be the obedience of the peoples.

Isaiah 11:1

There shall come forth a shoot from the stump of Jesse, and a branch from his roots shall bear fruit.

Mind

Romans 8:5-6
For those who live according to the flesh set their minds on the things of the flesh, but those who live according to the Spirit set their minds on the things of the Spirit. For to set the mind on the flesh is death, but to set the mind on the Spirit is life and peace.

Romans 12:1-2
I appeal to you therefore, brothers, by the mercies of God, to present your bodies as a living sacrifice, holy and acceptable to God, which is your spiritual worship. Do not be conformed to this world, but be transformed by the renewal of your mind, that by testing you may discern what is the will of God, what is good and acceptable and perfect.

Colossians 3:2
Set your minds on things that are above, not on things that are on earth.

Isaiah 26:3
You keep him in perfect peace whose mind is stayed on you, because he trusts in you.

Colossians 2:8
See to it that no one takes you captive by philosophy and empty deceit, according to human tradition, according to the elemental spirits of the world, and not according to Christ.

2 Corinthians 10:5
We destroy arguments and every lofty opinion raised against the knowledge of God, and take every thought captive to obey Christ,

2 Timothy 1:7
For God gave us a spirit not of fear but of power and love and self-control.

Philippians 4:6-8
Do not be anxious about anything, but in everything by prayer and supplication with thanksgiving let your requests be made known to God. And the peace of God, which surpasses all understanding, will guard your hearts and your minds in Christ Jesus. Finally, brothers, whatever is true, whatever is honorable, whatever is just, whatever is pure, whatever is lovely, whatever is commendable, if there is any excellence, if there is anything worthy of praise, think about these things.

1 Peter 5:8
Be sober-minded; be watchful. Your adversary the devil prowls around like a roaring lion, seeking someone to devour.

Ministry

Ephesians 4:11-13
And he gave the apostles, the prophets, the evangelists, the shepherds and teachers, to equip the saints for the work of ministry, for building up the body of Christ, until we all attain to the unity of the faith and of

the knowledge of the Son of God, to mature manhood, to the measure of the stature of the fullness of Christ,

2 Timothy 2:15
Do your best to present yourself to God as one approved, a worker who has no need to be ashamed, rightly handling the word of truth.

Romans 10:13-15
For "everyone who calls on the name of the Lord will be saved." How then will they call on him in whom they have not believed? And how are they to believe in him of whom they have never heard? And how are they to hear without someone preaching? And how are they to preach unless they are sent? As it is written, "How beautiful are the feet of those who preach the good news!"

1 Timothy 4:12
Let no one despise you for your youth, but set the believers an example in speech, in conduct, in love, in faith, in purity.

Hebrews 13:7
Remember your leaders, those who spoke to you the word of God. Consider the outcome of their way of life, and imitate their faith.

Acts 20:24
But I do not account my life of any value nor as precious to myself, if only I may finish my course and the ministry that I received from the Lord Jesus, to testify to the gospel of the grace of God.

Miracles

Acts 4:30
While you stretch out your hand to heal, and signs and wonders are performed through the name of your holy servant Jesus."

John 4:48
So Jesus said to him, "Unless you see signs and wonders you will not believe."

Matthew 17:20
He said to them, "Because of your little faith. For truly, I say to you, if you have faith like a grain of mustard seed, you will say to this mountain, 'Move from here to there,' and it will move, and nothing will be impossible for you."

Acts 3:16
And his name—by faith in his name—has made this man strong whom you see and know, and the faith that is through Jesus has given the man this perfect health in the presence of you all.

Mark 16:17
And these signs will accompany those who believe: in my name they will cast out demons; they will speak in new tongues;

John 14:12

"Truly, truly, I say to you, whoever believes in me will also do the works that I do; and greater works than these will he do, because I am going to the Father.

Acts 19:11

And God was doing extraordinary miracles by the hands of Paul,

Psalm 77:14

You are the God who works wonders; you have made known your might among the peoples.

John 11:4

But when Jesus heard it he said, "This illness does not lead to death. It is for the glory of God, so that the Son of God may be glorified through it."

Mocking

Proverbs 17:5

Whoever mocks the poor insults his Maker; he who is glad at calamity will not go unpunished.

Psalm 1:1

Blessed is the man who walks not in the counsel of the wicked, nor stands in the way of sinners, nor sits in the seat of scoffers;

Proverbs 15:12

A scoffer does not like to be reproved; he will not go to the wise.

2 Peter 3:3-7

Knowing this first of all, that scoffers will come in the last days with scoffing, following their own sinful desires. They will say, "Where is the promise of his coming? For ever since the fathers fell asleep, all things are continuing as they were from the beginning of creation." For they deliberately overlook this fact, that the heavens existed long ago, and the earth was formed out of water and through water by the word of God, and that by means of these the world that then existed was deluged with water and perished. But by the same word the heavens and earth that now exist are stored up for fire, being kept until the day of judgment and destruction of the ungodly.

Isaiah 57:4

Whom are you mocking? Against whom do you open your mouth wide and stick out your tongue? Are you not children of transgression, the offspring of deceit,

Proverbs 14:6-9

A scoffer seeks wisdom in vain, but knowledge is easy for a man of understanding. Leave the presence of a fool, for there you do not meet words of knowledge. The wisdom of the prudent is to discern his way, but the folly of fools is deceiving. Fools mock at the guilt offering, but the upright enjoy acceptance.

Molestation

Matthew 18:6

But whoever causes one of these little ones who believe in me to sin, it would be better for him to have a great millstone fastened around his neck and to be drowned in the depth of the sea.

Mark 9:42

"Whoever causes one of these little ones who believe in me to sin, it would be better for him if a great millstone were hung around his neck and he were thrown into the sea.

Deuteronomy 22:25-27

"But if in the open country a man meets a young woman who is betrothed, and the man seizes her and lies with her, then only the man who lay with her shall die. But you shall do nothing to the young woman; she has committed no offense punishable by death. For this case is like that of a man attacking and murdering his neighbor, because he met her in the open country, and though the betrothed young woman cried for help there was no one to rescue her.

Galatians 5:19-21

Now the works of the flesh are evident: sexual immorality, impurity, sensuality, idolatry, sorcery, enmity, strife, jealousy, fits of anger, rivalries, dissensions, divisions, envy, drunkenness, orgies, and things like these. I warn you, as I warned you before, that those who do such things will not inherit the kingdom of God.

Luke 17:2

It would be better for him if a millstone were hung around his neck and he were cast into the sea than that he should cause one of these little ones to sin.

Money

Hebrews 13:5

Keep your life free from love of money, and be content with what you have, for he has said, "I will never leave you nor forsake you."

1 Timothy 6:10

For the love of money is a root of all kinds of evils. It is through this craving that some have wandered away from the faith and pierced themselves with many pangs.

Proverbs 22:7

The rich rules over the poor, and the borrower is the slave of the lender.

Matthew 6:24

"No one can serve two masters, for either he will hate the one and love the other, or he will be devoted to the one and despise the other. You cannot serve God and money.

Proverbs 13:11

Wealth gained hastily will dwindle, but whoever gathers little by little will increase it.

Ecclesiastes 5:10

He who loves money will not be satisfied with money, nor he who loves wealth with his income; this also is vanity.

Luke 12:15

And he said to them, "Take care, and be on your guard against all covetousness, for one's life does not consist in the abundance of his possessions."

Matthew 6:19-21

"Do not lay up for yourselves treasures on earth, where moth and rust destroy and where thieves break in and steal, but lay up for yourselves treasures in heaven, where neither moth nor rust destroys and where thieves do not break in and steal. For where your treasure is, there your heart will be also.

Monogamy

1 Corinthians 7:2

But because of the temptation to sexual immorality, each man should have his own wife and each woman her own husband.

Deuteronomy 17:17

And he shall not acquire many wives for himself, lest his heart turn away, nor shall he acquire for himself excessive silver and gold.

Morality

Romans 13:8-10

Owe no one anything, except to love each other, for the one who loves another has fulfilled the law. For the commandments, "You shall not commit adultery, You shall not murder, You shall not steal, You shall not covet," and any other commandment, are summed up in this word: "You shall love your neighbor as yourself." Love does no wrong to a neighbor; therefore love is the fulfilling of the law.

Matthew 7:12

"So whatever you wish that others would do to you, do also to them, for this is the Law and the Prophets.

Mark 7:20-23

And he said, "What comes out of a person is what defiles him. For from within, out of the heart of man, come evil thoughts, sexual immorality, theft, murder, adultery, coveting, wickedness, deceit, sensuality, envy, slander, pride, foolishness. All these evil things come from within, and they defile a person."

1 Corinthians 6:9-11

Or do you not know that the unrighteous will not inherit the kingdom of God? Do not be deceived: neither the sexually immoral, nor idolaters, nor adulterers, nor men who practice homosexuality, nor thieves, nor the greedy, nor drunkards, nor revilers, nor swindlers will inherit the kingdom of God. And such were some of you. But you were washed, you were sanctified, you were justified in the name of the Lord Jesus Christ and by the Spirit of our God.

1 Corinthians 15:33
Do not be deceived: "Bad company ruins good morals."

Mother

Proverbs 29:15
The rod and reproof give wisdom, but a child left to himself brings shame to his mother.

Psalm 127:3
Behold, children are a heritage from the Lord, the fruit of the womb a reward.

Ephesians 6:2
"Honor your father and mother" (this is the first commandment with a promise),

Proverbs 22:6
Train up a child in the way he should go; even when he is old he will not depart from it.

Exodus 20:12
"Honor your father and your mother, that your days may be long in the land that the Lord your God is giving you.

Proverbs 23:22-25
Listen to your father who gave you life, and do not despise your mother when she is old. Buy truth, and do not sell it; buy wisdom, instruction, and understanding. The father of the righteous will greatly rejoice; he who fathers a wise son will be glad in him. Let your father and mother be glad; let her who bore you rejoice.

Proverbs 31:28-29
Her children rise up and call her blessed; her husband also, and he praises her: "Many women have done excellently, but you surpass them all."

Leviticus 19:3
Every one of you shall revere his mother and his father, and you shall keep my Sabbaths: I am the Lord your God.

Proverbs 20:20
If one curses his father or his mother, his lamp will be put out in utter darkness.

Proverbs 6:20
My son, keep your father's commandment, and forsake not your mother's teaching.

Proverbs 10:1
The proverbs of Solomon. A wise son makes a glad father, but a foolish son is a sorrow to his mother.

Luke 18:20
You know the commandments: 'Do not commit adultery, Do not murder, Do not steal, Do not bear false witness, Honor your father and mother.'"

Motherhood

Proverbs 31:28
Her children rise up and call her blessed; her husband also, and he praises her:

Isaiah 66:13
As one whom his mother comforts, so I will comfort you; you shall be comforted in Jerusalem.

Isaiah 49:15
"Can a woman forget her nursing child, that she should have no compassion on the son of her womb? Even these may forget, yet I will not forget you.

Proverbs 22:6
Train up a child in the way he should go; even when he is old he will not depart from it.

Mourning

Matthew 5:4
"Blessed are those who mourn, for they shall be comforted.

Revelation 21:4
He will wipe away every tear from their eyes, and death shall be no more, neither shall there be mourning, nor crying, nor pain anymore, for the former things have passed away."

1 Thessalonians 4:13
But we do not want you to be uninformed, brothers, about those who are asleep, that you may not grieve as others do who have no hope.

John 11:25-26
Jesus said to her, "I am the resurrection and the life. Whoever believes in me, though he die, yet shall he live, and everyone who lives and believes in me shall never die. Do you believe this?"

Isaiah 61:2-3
To proclaim the year of the Lord's favor, and the day of vengeance of our God; to comfort all who mourn; to grant to those who mourn in Zion— to give them a beautiful headdress instead of ashes, the oil of gladness instead of mourning, the garment of praise instead of a faint spirit; that they may be called oaks of righteousness, the planting of the Lord, that he may be glorified.

Psalm 34:18
The Lord is near to the brokenhearted and saves the crushed in spirit.

Psalm 116:15
Precious in the sight of the Lord is the death of his saints.

Mouth

Ephesians 4:29
Let no corrupting talk come out of your mouths, but only such as is good for building up, as fits the occasion, that it may give grace to those who hear.

Psalm 141:3
Set a guard, O Lord, over my mouth; keep watch over the door of my lips!

Matthew 12:36-37
I tell you, on the day of judgment people will give account for every careless word they speak, for by your words you will be justified, and by your words you will be condemned."

Proverbs 30:32-33
If you have been foolish, exalting yourself, or if you have been devising evil, put your hand on your mouth. For pressing milk produces curds, pressing the nose produces blood, and pressing anger produces strife.

Proverbs 10:19
When words are many, transgression is not lacking, but whoever restrains his lips is prudent.

1 John 1:9
If we confess our sins, he is faithful and just to forgive us our sins and to cleanse us from all unrighteousness.

James 1:19
Know this, my beloved brothers: let every person be quick to hear, slow to speak, slow to anger;

Murder

Leviticus 24:17
"Whoever takes a human life shall surely be put to death.

Exodus 20:13
"You shall not murder.

Romans 12:19
Beloved, never avenge yourselves, but leave it to the wrath of God, for it is written, "Vengeance is mine, I will repay, says the Lord."

1 John 3:12
We should not be like Cain, who was of the evil one and murdered his brother. And why did he murder him? Because his own deeds were evil and his brother's righteous.

1 John 3:15
Everyone who hates his brother is a murderer, and you know that no murderer has eternal life abiding in him.

Revelation 21:8
But as for the cowardly, the faithless, the detestable, as for murderers, the sexually immoral, sorcerers, idolaters, and all liars, their portion will be in the lake that burns with fire and sulfur, which is the second death."

Genesis 9:6
"Whoever sheds the blood of man, by man shall his blood be shed, for God made man in his own image.

Music

Ephesians 5:19
Addressing one another in psalms and hymns and spiritual songs, singing and making melody to the Lord with your heart,

Psalm 105:2
Sing to him, sing praises to him; tell of all his wondrous works!

Psalm 104:33
I will sing to the Lord as long as I live; I will sing praise to my God while I have being.

Psalm 95:1
Oh come, let us sing to the Lord; let us make a joyful noise to the rock of our salvation!

Colossians 3:16
Let the word of Christ dwell in you richly, teaching and admonishing one another in all wisdom, singing psalms and hymns and spiritual songs, with thankfulness in your hearts to God.

James 5:13
Is anyone among you suffering? Let him pray. Is anyone cheerful? Let him sing praise.

Psalm 71:23
My lips will shout for joy, when I sing praises to you; my soul also, which you have redeemed.

Ecclesiastes 7:5
It is better for a man to hear the rebuke of the wise than to hear the song of fools.

Psalm 100:1-5
A Psalm for giving thanks. Make a joyful noise to the Lord, all the earth! Serve the Lord with gladness! Come into his presence with singing! Know that the Lord, he is God! It is he who made us, and we are his; we are his people, and the sheep of his pasture. Enter his gates with thanksgiving, and his courts with praise! Give thanks to him; bless his name! For the Lord is good; his steadfast love endures forever, and his faithfulness to all generations.

Hebrews 2:12

Saying, "I will tell of your name to my brothers; in the midst of the congregation I will sing your praise."

Philippians 4:8

Finally, brothers, whatever is true, whatever is honorable, whatever is just, whatever is pure, whatever is lovely, whatever is commendable, if there is any excellence, if there is anything worthy of praise, think about these things.

Psalm 135:3

Praise the Lord, for the Lord is good; sing to his name, for it is pleasant!

Amos 6:5

Who sing idle songs to the sound of the harp and like David invent for themselves instruments of music,

Job 21:12

They sing to the tambourine and the lyre and rejoice to the sound of the pipe.

2 Chronicles 5:13

And it was the duty of the trumpeters and singers to make themselves heard in unison in praise and thanksgiving to the Lord), and when the song was raised, with trumpets and cymbals and other musical instruments, in praise to the Lord, "For he is good, for his steadfast love endures forever," the house, the house of the Lord, was filled with a cloud,

Psalm 57:7

My heart is steadfast, O God, my heart is steadfast! I will sing and make melody!

1 Corinthians 14:15

What am I to do? I will pray with my spirit, but I will pray with my mind also; I will sing praise with my spirit, but I will sing with my mind also

Nagging

Proverbs 21:9

It is better to live in a corner of the housetop than in a house shared with a quarrelsome wife.

Proverbs 21:19

It is better to live in a desert land than with a quarrelsome and fretful woman.

Ephesians 4:29

Let no corrupting talk come out of your mouths, but only such as is good for building up, as fits the occasion, that it may give grace to those who hear.

1 Peter 5:3

Not domineering over those in your charge, but being examples to the flock.

Colossians 3:21

Fathers, do not provoke your children, lest they become discouraged.

Ephesians 6:4

Fathers, do not provoke your children to anger, but bring them up in the discipline and instruction of the Lord.

Proverbs 27:15-16

A continual dripping on a rainy day and a quarrelsome wife are alike; to restrain her is to restrain the wind or to grasp oil in one's right hand.

Narcissism

2 Timothy 3:1-7

But understand this, that in the last days there will come times of difficulty. For people will be lovers of self, lovers of money, proud, arrogant, abusive, disobedient to their parents, ungrateful, unholy, heartless, unappeasable, slanderous, without self-control, brutal, not loving good, treacherous, reckless, swollen with conceit, lovers of pleasure rather than lovers of God, having the appearance of godliness, but denying its power. Avoid such people. For among them are those who creep into households and capture weak women, burdened with sins and led astray by various passions, always learning and never able to arrive at a knowledge of the truth.

1 Peter 5:5-6

Likewise, you who are younger, be subject to the elders. Clothe yourselves, all of you, with humility toward one another, for "God opposes the proud but gives grace to the humble." Humble yourselves, therefore, under the mighty hand of God so that at the proper time he may exalt you,

Romans 16:17-19

I appeal to you, brothers, to watch out for those who cause divisions and create obstacles contrary to the doctrine that you have been taught; avoid them. For such persons do not serve our Lord Christ, but their own appetites, and by smooth talk and flattery they deceive the hearts of the naive. For your obedience is known to all, so that I rejoice over you, but I want you to be wise as to what is good and innocent as to what is evil.

Proverbs 18:12
Before destruction a man's heart is haughty, but humility comes before honor.

Proverbs 4:16
For they cannot sleep unless they have done wrong; they are robbed of sleep unless they have made someone stumble.

Titus 1:16
They profess to know God, but they deny him by their works. They are detestable, disobedient, unfit for any good work.

Psalm 36:1-3
To the choirmaster. Of David, the servant of the Lord. Transgression speaks to the wicked deep in his heart; there is no fear of God before his eyes. For he flatters himself in his own eyes that his iniquity cannot be found out and hated. The words of his mouth are trouble and deceit; he has ceased to act wisely and do good.

Proverbs 16:18
Pride goes before destruction, and a haughty spirit before a fall.

Natural Disasters

Mark 13:7-9
And when you hear of wars and rumors of wars, do not be alarmed. This must take place, but the end is not yet. For nation will rise against nation, and kingdom against kingdom. There will be earthquakes in various places; there will be famines. These are but the beginning of the birth pains. "But be on your guard. For they will deliver you over to councils, and you will be beaten in synagogues, and you will stand before governors and kings for my sake, to bear witness before them.

Isaiah 45:7
I form light and create darkness, I make well-being and create calamity, I am the Lord, who does all these things.

Matthew 24:7
For nation will rise against nation, and kingdom against kingdom, and there will be famines and earthquakes in various places.

Luke 21:11
There will be great earthquakes, and in various places famines and pestilences. And there will be terrors and great signs from heaven.

Luke 21:25
"And there will be signs in sun and moon and stars, and on the earth distress of nations in perplexity because of the roaring of the sea and the waves,

Nature

Job 12:7-10

"But ask the beasts, and they will teach you; the birds of the heavens, and they will tell you; or the bushes of the earth, and they will teach you; and the fish of the sea will declare to you. Who among all these does not know that the hand of the Lord has done this? In his hand is the life of every living thing and the breath of all mankind.

Psalm 145:5

On the glorious splendor of your majesty, and on your wondrous works, I will meditate.

Psalm 96:11-12

Let the heavens be glad, and let the earth rejoice; let the sea roar, and all that fills it; let the field exult, and everything in it! Then shall all the trees of the forest sing for joy

Ecclesiastes 3:11

He has made everything beautiful in its time. Also, he has put eternity into man's heart, yet so that he cannot find out what God has done from the beginning to the end.

Isaiah 55:12

"For you shall go out in joy and be led forth in peace; the mountains and the hills before you shall break forth into singing, and all the trees of the field shall clap their hands.

Psalm 69:34

Let heaven and earth praise him, the seas and everything that moves in them.
Negative People

Negative Thinking

Philippians 4:8-9

Finally, brothers, whatever is true, whatever is honorable, whatever is just, whatever is pure, whatever is lovely, whatever is commendable, if there is any excellence, if there is anything worthy of praise, think about these things. What you have learned and received and heard and seen in me—practice these things, and the God of peace will be with you.

1 Peter 5:8

Be sober-minded; be watchful. Your adversary the devil prowls around like a roaring lion, seeking someone to devour.

2 Corinthians 10:4-5

For the weapons of our warfare are not of the flesh but have divine power to destroy strongholds. We destroy arguments and every lofty opinion raised against the knowledge of God, and take every thought captive to obey Christ,

Luke 6:37

"Judge not, and you will not be judged; condemn not, and you will not be condemned; forgive, and you will be forgiven;

Proverbs 3:5-6

Trust in the Lord with all your heart, and do not lean on your own understanding. In all your ways acknowledge him, and he will make straight your paths.

Psalm 94:19

When the cares of my heart are many, your consolations cheer my soul.

Isaiah 41:10

Fear not, for I am with you; be not dismayed, for I am your God; I will strengthen you, I will help you, I will uphold you with my righteous right hand.

Isaiah 26:3

You keep him in perfect peace whose mind is stayed on you, because he trusts in you.

Hebrews 4:12

For the word of God is living and active, sharper than any two-edged sword, piercing to the division of soul and of spirit, of joints and of marrow, and discerning the thoughts and intentions of the heart.

James 3:14-15

But if you have bitter jealousy and selfish ambition in your hearts, do not boast and be false to the truth. This is not the wisdom that comes down from above, but is earthly, unspiritual, demonic.

Proverbs 4:23

Keep your heart with all vigilance, for from it flow the springs of life.

Negativity

Titus 3:10

As for a person who stirs up division, after warning him once and then twice, have nothing more to do with him,

Philippians 4:8

Finally, brothers, whatever is true, whatever is honorable, whatever is just, whatever is pure, whatever is lovely, whatever is commendable, if there is any excellence, if there is anything worthy of praise, think about these things.

2 Timothy 3:5

Having the appearance of godliness, but denying its power. Avoid such people.

Galatians 5:25

If we live by the Spirit, let us also walk by the Spirit.

2 Timothy 4:3-4

For the time is coming when people will not endure sound teaching, but having itching ears they will accumulate for themselves teachers to suit their own passions, and will turn away from listening to the truth and wander off into myths.

Proverbs 17:14

The beginning of strife is like letting out water, so quit before the quarrel breaks out.

Ephesians 5:20

Giving thanks always and for everything to God the Father in the name of our Lord Jesus Christ,

1 Corinthians 15:33

Do not be deceived: "Bad company ruins good morals."

Neglect

Hebrews 2:3

How shall we escape if we neglect such a great salvation? It was declared at first by the Lord, and it was attested to us by those who heard,

Matthew 6:24

"No one can serve two masters, for either he will hate the one and love the other, or he will be devoted to the one and despise the other. You cannot serve God and money.

Malachi 3:10

Bring the full tithe into the storehouse, that there may be food in my house. And thereby put me to the test, says the Lord of hosts, if I will not open the windows of heaven for you and pour down for you a blessing until there is no more need.

Nervousness

Philippians 4:6-7

Do not be anxious about anything, but in everything by prayer and supplication with thanksgiving let your requests be made known to God. And the peace of God, which surpasses all understanding, will guard your hearts and your minds in Christ Jesus.

1 Peter 5:7

Casting all your anxieties on him, because he cares for you.

Isaiah 41:10

Fear not, for I am with you; be not dismayed, for I am your God; I will strengthen you, I will help you, I will uphold you with my righteous right hand.

John 14:27

Peace I leave with you; my peace I give to you. Not as the world gives do I give to you. Let not your hearts be troubled, neither let them be afraid.

Matthew 6:34

"Therefore, do not be anxious about tomorrow, for tomorrow will be anxious for itself. Sufficient for the day is its own trouble.

Psalm 55:22

Cast your burden on the Lord, and he will sustain you; he will never permit the righteous to be moved.

Psalm 56:3

When I am afraid, I put my trust in you.

Proverbs 12:25

Anxiety in a man's heart weighs him down, but a good word makes him glad.

2 Timothy 1:7

For God gave us a spirit not of fear but of power and love and self-control.

Psalm 94:19

When the cares of my heart are many, your consolations cheer my soul.

Psalm 34:4

I sought the Lord, and he answered me and delivered me from all my fears.

Proverbs 3:5-6

Trust in the Lord with all your heart, and do not lean on your own understanding. In all your ways acknowledge him, and he will make straight your paths.

New Beginnings

2 Corinthians 5:17

Therefore, if anyone is in Christ, he is a new creation. The old has passed away; behold, the new has come.

Jeremiah 29:11

For I know the plans I have for you, declares the Lord, plans for welfare and not for evil, to give you a future and a hope.

Isaiah 43:18-19

"Remember not the former things, nor consider the things of old. Behold, I am doing a new thing; now it springs forth, do you not perceive it? I will make a way in the wilderness and rivers in the desert.

Isaiah 43:19

Behold, I am doing a new thing; now it springs forth, do you not perceive it? I will make a way in the wilderness and rivers in the desert.

Ephesians 4:22-24

To put off your old self, which belongs to your former manner of life and is corrupt through deceitful desires, and to be renewed in the spirit of your minds, and to put on the new self, created after the likeness of God in true righteousness and holiness.

Lamentations 3:22-24

The steadfast love of the Lord never ceases; his mercies never come to an end; they are new every morning; great is your faithfulness. "The Lord is my portion," says my soul, "therefore I will hope in him."

New Creation in Christ

Galatians 2:20

I have been crucified with Christ. It is no longer I who live, but Christ who lives in me. And the life I now live in the flesh I live by faith in the Son of God, who loved me and gave himself for me.

Isaiah 43:18-19

"Remember not the former things, nor consider the things of old. Behold, I am doing a new thing; now it springs forth, do you not perceive it? I will make a way in the wilderness and rivers in the desert.

2 Corinthians 5:17-21

Therefore, if anyone is in Christ, he is a new creation. The old has passed away; behold, the new has come. All this is from God, who through Christ reconciled us to himself and gave us the ministry of reconciliation; that is, in Christ God was reconciling the world to himself, not counting their trespasses against them, and entrusting to us the message of reconciliation. Therefore, we are ambassadors for Christ, God making his appeal through us. We implore you on behalf of Christ, be reconciled to God. For our sake he made him to be sin who knew no sin, so that in him we might become the righteousness of God.

Colossians 3:9-10

Do not lie to one another, seeing that you have put off the old self with its practices and have put on the new self, which is being renewed in knowledge after the image of its creator.

Ephesians 2:10

For we are his workmanship, created in Christ Jesus for good works, which God prepared beforehand, that we should walk in them.

Ezekiel 11:19-20

And I will give them one heart, and a new spirit I will put within them. I will remove the heart of stone from their flesh and give them a heart of flesh, that they may walk in my statutes and keep my rules and obey them. And they shall be my people, and I will be their God.

Nightmares

Proverbs 3:24

If you lie down, you will not be afraid; when you lie down, your sleep will be sweet.

Psalm 4:8

In peace I will both lie down and sleep; for you alone, O Lord, make me dwell in safety.

Psalm 91:5

You will not fear the terror of the night, nor the arrow that flies by day,

2 Timothy 1:7

For God gave us a spirit not of fear but of power and love and self-control.

James 4:7

Submit yourselves therefore to God. Resist the devil, and he will flee from you.

Psalm 91:1-4

He who dwells in the shelter of the Most High will abide in the shadow of the Almighty. I will say to the Lord, "My refuge and my fortress, my God, in whom I trust." For he will deliver you from the snare of the fowler and from the deadly pestilence. He will cover you with his pinions, and under his wings you will find refuge; his faithfulness is a shield and buckler.

Non-Believers

1 Corinthians 15:33

Do not be deceived: "Bad company ruins good morals."

2 Corinthians 6:14

Do not be unequally yoked with unbelievers. For what partnership has righteousness with lawlessness? Or what fellowship has light with darkness?

John 3:16

"For God so loved the world, that he gave his only Son, that whoever believes in him should not perish but have eternal life.

2 John 1:9-11

Everyone who goes on ahead and does not abide in the teaching of Christ, does not have God. Whoever abides in the teaching has both the Father and the Son. If anyone comes to you and does not bring this teaching, do not receive him into your house or give him any greeting, for whoever greets him takes part in his wicked works.

2 Chronicles 15:12-13

And they entered into a covenant to seek the Lord, the God of their fathers, with all their heart and with all their soul, but that whoever would not seek the Lord, the God of Israel, should be put to death, whether young or old, man or woman.

1 Corinthians 7:13-14

If any woman has a husband who is an unbeliever, and he consents to live with her, she should not divorce him. For the unbelieving husband is made holy because of his wife, and the unbelieving wife is made holy because of her husband. Otherwise your children would be unclean, but as it is, they are holy.

Oaths

Matthew 5:33-37
"Again you have heard that it was said to those of old, 'You shall not swear falsely, but shall perform to the Lord what you have sworn.' But I say to you, Do not take an oath at all, either by heaven, for it is the throne of God, or by the earth, for it is his footstool, or by Jerusalem, for it is the city of the great King. And do not take an oath by your head, for you cannot make one hair white or black. Let what you say be simply 'Yes' or 'No'; anything more than this comes from evil.

James 5:12
But above all, my brothers, do not swear, either by heaven or by earth or by any other oath, but let your "yes" be yes and your "no" be no, so that you may not fall under condemnation.

Numbers 30:2
If a man vows a vow to the Lord, or swears an oath to bind himself by a pledge, he shall not break his word. He shall do according to all that proceeds out of his mouth.

Deuteronomy 23:21-23
"If you make a vow to the Lord your God, you shall not delay fulfilling it, for the Lord your God will surely require it of you, and you will be guilty of sin. But if you refrain from vowing, you will not be guilty of sin. You shall be careful to do what has passed your lips, for you have voluntarily vowed to the Lord your God what you have promised with your mouth.

Hebrews 6:13
For when God made a promise to Abraham, since he had no one greater by whom to swear, he swore by himself,

Hebrews 6:16-17
For people swear by something greater than themselves, and in all their disputes an oath is final for confirmation. So when God desired to show more convincingly to the heirs of the promise the unchangeable character of his purpose, he guaranteed it with an oath,

Psalm 15:4
In whose eyes a vile person is despised, but who honors those who fear the Lord; who swears to his own hurt and does not change;

Leviticus 19:12
You shall not swear by my name falsely, and so profane the name of your God: I am the Lord.

Obedience

John 14:15
"If you love me, you will keep my commandments.

Acts 5:29
But Peter and the apostles answered, "We must obey God rather than men.

1 Peter 1:14

As obedient children, do not be conformed to the passions of your former ignorance,

1 John 5:3

For this is the love of God, that we keep his commandments. And his commandments are not burdensome.

Isaiah 1:19

If you are willing and obedient, you shall eat the good of the land;

Luke 6:46

"Why do you call me 'Lord, Lord,' and not do what I tell you?

Exodus 23:22

"But if you carefully obey his voice and do all that I say, then I will be an enemy to your enemies and an adversary to your adversaries.

Psalm 119:30

I have chosen the way of faithfulness; I set your rules before me.

2 Kings 18:6

For he held fast to the Lord. He did not depart from following him, but kept the commandments that the Lord commanded Moses.

John 14:31

But I do as the Father has commanded me, so that the world may know that I love the Father. Rise, let us go from here.

1 John 3:24

Whoever keeps his commandments abides in God, and God in him. And by this we know that he abides in us, by the Spirit whom he has given us.

John 8:51

Truly, truly, I say to you, if anyone keeps my word, he will never see death."

Luke 11:28

But he said, "Blessed rather are those who hear the word of God and keep it!"

Jeremiah 7:23

But this command I gave them: 'Obey my voice, and I will be your God, and you shall be my people. And walk in all the way that I command you, that it may be well with you.'

Psalm 119:60

I hasten and do not delay to keep your commandments.

Philippians 2:8
And being found in human form, he humbled himself by becoming obedient to the point of death, even death on a cross.

John 14:23
Jesus answered him, "If anyone loves me, he will keep my word, and my Father will love him, and we will come to him and make our home with him.

Obsession

1 John 2:15-17
Do not love the world or the things in the world. If anyone loves the world, the love of the Father is not in him. For all that is in the world—the desires of the flesh and the desires of the eyes and pride in possessions—is not from the Father but is from the world. And the world is passing away along with its desires, but whoever does the will of God abides forever.

Mark 12:29-31
Jesus answered, "The most important is, 'Hear, O Israel: The Lord our God, the Lord is one. And you shall love the Lord your God with all your heart and with all your soul and with all your mind and with all your strength.' The second is this: 'You shall love your neighbor as yourself.' There is no other commandment greater than these."

Mark 7:20-23
And he said, "What comes out of a person is what defiles him. For from within, out of the heart of man, come evil thoughts, sexual immorality, theft, murder, adultery, coveting, wickedness, deceit, sensuality, envy, slander, pride, foolishness. All these evil things come from within, and they defile a person."

Romans 5:3-4
More than that, we rejoice in our sufferings, knowing that suffering produces endurance, and endurance produces character, and character produces hope,

Matthew 6:24
"No one can serve two masters, for either he will hate the one and love the other, or he will be devoted to the one and despise the other. You cannot serve God and money.

2 Corinthians 10:4-5
For the weapons of our warfare are not of the flesh but have divine power to destroy strongholds. We destroy arguments and every lofty opinion raised against the knowledge of God, and take every thought captive to obey Christ,

Obstacles

Romans 8:28
And we know that for those who love God all things work together for good, for those who are called according to his purpose.

James 1:2-4

Count it all joy, my brothers, when you meet trials of various kinds, for you know that the testing of your faith produces steadfastness. And let steadfastness have its full effect, that you may be perfect and complete, lacking in nothing.

2 Corinthians 12:8-10

Three times I pleaded with the Lord about this, that it should leave me. But he said to me, "My grace is sufficient for you, for my power is made perfect in weakness." Therefore I will boast all the more gladly of my weaknesses, so that the power of Christ may rest upon me. For the sake of Christ, then, I am content with weaknesses, insults, hardships, persecutions, and calamities. For when I am weak, then I am strong.

Romans 16:17

I appeal to you, brothers, to watch out for those who cause divisions and create obstacles contrary to the doctrine that you have been taught; avoid them.

Romans 5:3-5

More than that, we rejoice in our sufferings, knowing that suffering produces endurance, and endurance produces character, and character produces hope, and hope does not put us to shame, because God's love has been poured into our hearts through the Holy Spirit who has been given to us.

Isaiah 57:14

And it shall be said, "Build up, build up, prepare the way, remove every obstruction from my people's way."

Matthew 17:20

He said to them, "Because of your little faith. For truly, I say to you, if you have faith like a grain of mustard seed, you will say to this mountain, 'Move from here to there,' and it will move, and nothing will be impossible for you."

Occult

Leviticus 19:31

"Do not turn to mediums or necromancers; do not seek them out, and so make yourselves unclean by them: I am the Lord your God.

Revelation 21:8

But as for the cowardly, the faithless, the detestable, as for murderers, the sexually immoral, sorcerers, idolaters, and all liars, their portion will be in the lake that burns with fire and sulfur, which is the second death."

Leviticus 20:6

"If a person turns to mediums and necromancers, whoring after them, I will set my face against that person and will cut him off from among his people.

Isaiah 8:19

And when they say to you, "Inquire of the mediums and the necromancers who chirp and mutter," should not a people inquire of their God? Should they inquire of the dead on behalf of the living?

Exodus 22:18

"You shall not permit a sorceress to live.

2 Chronicles 33:6

And he burned his sons as an offering in the Valley of the Son of Hinnom, and used fortune-telling and omens and sorcery, and dealt with mediums and with necromancers. He did much evil in the sight of the Lord, provoking him to anger.

Revelation 22:15

Outside are the dogs and sorcerers and the sexually immoral and murderers and idolaters, and everyone who loves and practices falsehood.

2 Kings 21:6

And he burned his son as an offering and used fortune-telling and omens and dealt with mediums and with necromancers. He did much evil in the sight of the Lord, provoking him to anger.

1 Samuel 15:23

For rebellion is as the sin of divination, and presumption is as iniquity and idolatry. Because you have rejected the word of the Lord, he has also rejected you from being king."

Leviticus 20:27

"A man or a woman who is a medium or a necromancer shall surely be put to death. They shall be stoned with stones; their blood shall be upon them."

Offences

Proverbs 19:11

Good sense makes one slow to anger, and it is his glory to overlook an offense.

Ecclesiastes 7:21-22

Do not take to heart all the things that people say, lest you hear your servant cursing you. Your heart knows that many times you yourself have cursed others.

Proverbs 18:19

A brother offended is more unyielding than a strong city, and quarreling is like the bars of a castle.

Matthew 18:15-17

"If your brother sins against you, go and tell him his fault, between you and him alone. If he listens to you, you have gained your brother. But if he does not listen, take one or two others along with you, that every charge may be established by the evidence of two or three witnesses. If he refuses to listen to them, tell it to the church. And if he refuses to listen even to the church, let him be to you as a Gentile and a tax collector.

Luke 17:3-4

Pay attention to yourselves! If your brother sins, rebuke him, and if he repents, forgive him, and if he sins against you seven times in the day, and turns to you seven times, saying, 'I repent,' you must forgive him."

James 3:16
For where jealousy and selfish ambition exist, there will be disorder and every vile practice.

Ephesians 4:2-3
With all humility and gentleness, with patience, bearing with one another in love, eager to maintain the unity of the Spirit in the bond of peace.

Proverbs 6:16-19
There are six things that the Lord hates, seven that are an abomination to him: haughty eyes, a lying tongue, and hands that shed innocent blood, a heart that devises wicked plans, feet that make haste to run to evil, a false witness who breathes out lies, and one who sows discord among brothers.

Leviticus 19:18
You shall not take vengeance or bear a grudge against the sons of your own people, but you shall love your neighbor as yourself: I am the Lord.

Omnipotence

Revelation 19:6
Then I heard what seemed to be the voice of a great multitude, like the roar of many waters and like the sound of mighty peals of thunder, crying out, "Hallelujah! For the Lord our God the Almighty reigns.

Matthew 19:26
But Jesus looked at them and said, "With man this is impossible, but with God all things are possible."

Hebrews 1:3
He is the radiance of the glory of God and the exact imprint of his nature, and he upholds the universe by the word of his power. After making purification for sins, he sat down at the right hand of the Majesty on high,

Luke 1:37
For nothing will be impossible with God."

Job 42:2
"I know that you can do all things, and that no purpose of yours can be thwarted.

Psalm 147:5
Great is our Lord, and abundant in power; his understanding is beyond measure.

Isaiah 40:28
Have you not known? Have you not heard? The Lord is the everlasting God, the Creator of the ends of the earth. He does not faint or grow weary; his understanding is unsearchable.

Romans 1:20
For his invisible attributes, namely, his eternal power and divine nature, have been clearly perceived, ever since the creation of the world, in the things that have been made. So they are without excuse.

Ephesians 3:20
Now to him who is able to do far more abundantly than all that we ask or think, according to the power at work within us,

Psalm 139:7-10
Where shall I go from your Spirit? Or where shall I flee from your presence? If I ascend to heaven, you are there! If I make my bed in Sheol, you are there! If I take the wings of the morning and dwell in the uttermost parts of the sea, even there your hand shall lead me, and your right hand shall hold me.

Jeremiah 32:17
'Ah, Lord God! It is you who have made the heavens and the earth by your great power and by your outstretched arm! Nothing is too hard for you.

Omnipresence

Proverbs 15:3
The eyes of the Lord are in every place, keeping watch on the evil and the good.

Jeremiah 23:24
Can a man hide himself in secret places so that I cannot see him? declares the Lord. Do I not fill heaven and earth? declares the Lord.

Psalm 139:7-10
Where shall I go from your Spirit? Or where shall I flee from your presence? If I ascend to heaven, you are there! If I make my bed in Sheol, you are there! If I take the wings of the morning and dwell in the uttermost parts of the sea, even there your hand shall lead me, and your right hand shall hold me.

Psalm 139:7
Where shall I go from your Spirit? Or where shall I flee from your presence?

Omniscience

Psalm 147:5
Great is our Lord, and abundant in power; his understanding is beyond measure.

1 John 3:20
For whenever our heart condemns us, God is greater than our heart, and he knows everything.

Hebrews 4:13
And no creature is hidden from his sight, but all are naked and exposed to the eyes of him to whom we must give account.

Jeremiah 1:5
"Before I formed you in the womb I knew you, and before you were born I consecrated you; I appointed you a prophet to the nations."

Proverbs 15:3

The eyes of the Lord are in every place, keeping watch on the evil and the good.

Isaiah 40:28

Have you not known? Have you not heard? The Lord is the everlasting God, the Creator of the ends of the earth. He does not faint or grow weary; his understanding is unsearchable.

1 Chronicles 28:9

"And you, Solomon my son, know the God of your father and serve him with a whole heart and with a willing mind, for the Lord searches all hearts and understands every plan and thought. If you seek him, he will be found by you, but if you forsake him, he will cast you off forever.

Acts 1:24

And they prayed and said, "You, Lord, who know the hearts of all, show which one of these two you have chosen

Matthew 10:30

But even the hairs of your head are all numbered.

Jeremiah 23:24

Can a man hide himself in secret places so that I cannot see him? declares the Lord. Do I not fill heaven and earth? declares the Lord.

Psalm 147:4

He determines the number of the stars; he gives to all of them their names.

Oppression

Psalm 9:9

The Lord is a stronghold for the oppressed, a stronghold in times of trouble.

Proverbs 14:31

Whoever oppresses a poor man insults his Maker, but he who is generous to the needy honors him.

Psalm 72:4

May he defend the cause of the poor of the people, give deliverance to the children of the needy, and crush the oppressor!

Isaiah 1:17

Learn to do good; seek justice, correct oppression; bring justice to the fatherless, plead the widow's cause.

Psalm 34:18

The Lord is near to the brokenhearted and saves the crushed in spirit.

Zechariah 7:10

Do not oppress the widow, the fatherless, the sojourner, or the poor, and let none of you devise evil against another in your heart."

Psalm 119:134

Redeem me from man's oppression, that I may keep your precepts.

Luke 4:18-19

"The Spirit of the Lord is upon me, because he has anointed me to proclaim good news to the poor. He has sent me to proclaim liberty to the captives and recovering of sight to the blind, to set at liberty those who are oppressed, to proclaim the year of the Lord's favor."

Psalm 146:7

Who executes justice for the oppressed, who gives food to the hungry. The Lord sets the prisoners free;

Proverbs 22:16

Whoever oppresses the poor to increase his own wealth, or gives to the rich, will only come to poverty.

Malachi 3:5

"Then I will draw near to you for judgment. I will be a swift witness against the sorcerers, against the adulterers, against those who swear falsely, against those who oppress the hired worker in his wages, the widow and the fatherless, against those who thrust aside the sojourner, and do not fear me, says the Lord of hosts.

Optimism

Joshua 1:9

Have I not commanded you? Be strong and courageous. Do not be frightened, and do not be dismayed, for the Lord your God is with you wherever you go."

Romans 8:28

And we know that for those who love God all things work together for good, for those who are called according to his purpose.

Philippians 4:13

I can do all things through him who strengthens me.

Proverbs 4:23

Keep your heart with all vigilance, for from it flow the springs of life.

Ephesians 4:29

Let no corrupting talk come out of your mouths, but only such as is good for building up, as fits the occasion, that it may give grace to those who hear.

John 3:16

"For God so loved the world, that he gave his only Son, that whoever believes in him should not perish but have eternal life.

1 Corinthians 13:7

Love bears all things, believes all things, hopes all things, endures all things.

Ephesians 6:11

Put on the whole armor of God, that you may be able to stand against the schemes of the devil.

Outreach

Mark 16:15

And he said to them, "Go into all the world and proclaim the gospel to the whole creation.

Jeremiah 1:7

But the Lord said to me, "Do not say, 'I am only a youth'; for to all to whom I send you, you shall go, and whatever I command you, you shall speak.

Romans 10:14

How then will they call on him in whom they have not believed? And how are they to believe in him of whom they have never heard? And how are they to hear without someone preaching?

Matthew 28:19

Go therefore and make disciples of all nations, baptizing them in the name of the Father and of the Son and of the Holy Spirit,

Acts 1:8

But you will receive power when the Holy Spirit has come upon you, and you will be my witnesses in Jerusalem and in all Judea and Samaria, and to the end of the earth."

Overcoming

Romans 12:21

Do not be overcome by evil, but overcome evil with good.

John 16:33

I have said these things to you, that in me you may have peace. In the world you will have tribulation. But take heart; I have overcome the world."

1 Peter 5:7

Casting all your anxieties on him, because he cares for you.

James 1:19-20

Know this, my beloved brothers: let every person be quick to hear, slow to speak, slow to anger; for the anger of man does not produce the righteousness of God.

Psalm 103:1-5

Of David. Bless the Lord, O my soul, and all that is within me, bless his holy name! Bless the Lord, O my soul, and forget not all his benefits, who forgives all your iniquity, who heals all your diseases, who redeems your life from the pit, who crowns you with steadfast love and mercy, who satisfies you with good so that your youth is renewed like the eagle's.

1 John 4:18
There is no fear in love, but perfect love casts out fear. For fear has to do with punishment, and whoever fears has not been perfected in love.

Romans 12:1-2
I appeal to you therefore, brothers, by the mercies of God, to present your bodies as a living sacrifice, holy and acceptable to God, which is your spiritual worship. Do not be conformed to this world, but be transformed by the renewal of your mind, that by testing you may discern what is the will of God, what is good and acceptable and perfect.

Overeating

1 Corinthians 10:31
So, whether you eat or drink, or whatever you do, do all to the glory of God.

1 Corinthians 6:19-20
Or do you not know that your body is a temple of the Holy Spirit within you, whom you have from God? You are not your own, for you were bought with a price. So glorify God in your body.

Proverbs 23:2
And put a knife to your throat if you are given to appetite.

Proverbs 23:20-21
Be not among drunkards or among gluttonous eaters of meat, for the drunkard and the glutton will come to poverty, and slumber will clothe them with rags.

Proverbs 25:27
It is not good to eat much honey, nor is it glorious to seek one's own glory.

Philippians 3:19
Their end is destruction, their god is their belly, and they glory in their shame, with minds set on earthly things.

Philippians 4:13
I can do all things through him who strengthens me.

1 Corinthians 3:16
Do you not know that you are God's temple and that God's Spirit dwells in you?

Overwhelmed

Psalm 34:17-20
When the righteous cry for help, the Lord hears and delivers them out of all their troubles. The Lord is near to the brokenhearted and saves the crushed in spirit. Many are the afflictions of the righteous, but the Lord delivers him out of them all. He keeps all his bones; not one of them is broken.

Philippians 4:19
And my God will supply every need of yours according to his riches in glory in Christ Jesus.

2 Corinthians 12:9
But he said to me, "My grace is sufficient for you, for my power is made perfect in weakness." Therefore, I will boast all the more gladly of my weaknesses, so that the power of Christ may rest upon me.

Matthew 11:28
Come to me, all who labor and are heavy laden, and I will give you rest.

Matthew 19:26
But Jesus looked at them and said, "With man this is impossible, but with God all things are possible."

Romans 8:1
There is therefore now no condemnation for those who are in Christ Jesus.

Jeremiah 15:16
Your words were found, and I ate them, and your words became to me a joy and the delight of my heart, for I am called by your name, O Lord, God of hosts.

2 Timothy 2:15
Do your best to present yourself to God as one approved, a worker who has no need to be ashamed, rightly handling the word of truth.

Proverbs 22:6
Train up a child in the way he should go; even when he is old he will not depart from it.

Pain

Revelation 21:4
He will wipe away every tear from their eyes, and death shall be no more, neither shall there be mourning, nor crying, nor pain anymore, for the former things have passed away."

Romans 8:18
For I consider that the sufferings of this present time are not worth comparing with the glory that is to be revealed to us.

Psalm 41:3
The Lord sustains him on his sickbed; in his illness you restore him to full health.

Job 30:17
The night racks my bones, and the pain that gnaws me takes no rest.

Philippians 4:13
I can do all things through him who strengthens me.

1 Peter 4:19
Therefore, let those who suffer according to God's will entrust their souls to a faithful Creator while doing good.

Panic Attacks

Isaiah 41:10
Fear not, for I am with you; be not dismayed, for I am your God; I will strengthen you, I will help you, I will uphold you with my righteous right hand.

Isaiah 43:1-2
But now thus says the Lord, he who created you, O Jacob, he who formed you, O Israel: "Fear not, for I have redeemed you; I have called you by name, you are mine. When you pass through the waters, I will be with you; and through the rivers, they shall not overwhelm you; when you walk through fire you shall not be burned, and the flame shall not consume you.

Hebrews 13:6
So we can confidently say, "The Lord is my helper; I will not fear; what can man do to me?"

Philippians 4:6
Do not be anxious about anything, but in everything by prayer and supplication with thanksgiving let your requests be made known to God.

2 Timothy 1:7
For God gave us a spirit not of fear but of power and love and self-control.

Proverbs 3:5-6

Trust in the Lord with all your heart, and do not lean on your own understanding. In all your ways acknowledge him, and he will make straight your paths.

James 1:2-4

Count it all joy, my brothers, when you meet trials of various kinds, for you know that the testing of your faith produces steadfastness. And let steadfastness have its full effect, that you may be perfect and complete, lacking in nothing.

Isaiah 41:13

For I, the Lord your God, hold your right hand; it is I who say to you, "Fear not, I am the one who helps you."

Psalm 46:10

"Be still, and know that I am God. I will be exalted among the nations, I will be exalted in the earth!"

1 John 4:4

Little children, you are from God and have overcome them, for he who is in you is greater than he who is in the world.

Paranoia

Philippians 4:6-7

Do not be anxious about anything, but in everything by prayer and supplication with thanksgiving let your requests be made known to God. And the peace of God, which surpasses all understanding, will guard your hearts and your minds in Christ Jesus.

Proverbs 3:5

Trust in the Lord with all your heart, and do not lean on your own understanding.

2 Timothy 1:7

For God gave us a spirit not of fear but of power and love and self-control.

Joshua 1:9

Have I not commanded you? Be strong and courageous. Do not be frightened, and do not be dismayed, for the Lord your God is with you wherever you go."

Parenting

Proverbs 22:6

Train up a child in the way he should go; even when he is old he will not depart from it.

Ephesians 6:4

Fathers, do not provoke your children to anger, but bring them up in the discipline and instruction of the Lord.

Colossians 3:21
Fathers, do not provoke your children, lest they become discouraged.

Proverbs 13:24
Whoever spares the rod hates his son, but he who loves him is diligent to discipline him.

Psalm 127:3
Behold, children are a heritage from the Lord, the fruit of the womb a reward.

Proverbs 29:15
The rod and reproof give wisdom, but a child left to himself brings shame to his mother.

Titus 2:7
Show yourself in all respects to be a model of good works, and in your teaching show integrity, dignity,

Proverbs 29:17
Discipline your son, and he will give you rest; he will give delight to your heart.

Passover

Leviticus 23:4-8
"These are the appointed feasts of the Lord, the holy convocations, which you shall proclaim at the time appointed for them. In the first month, on the fourteenth day of the month at twilight, is the Lord's Passover. And on the fifteenth day of the same month is the Feast of Unleavened Bread to the Lord; for seven days you shall eat unleavened bread. On the first day you shall have a holy convocation; you shall not do any ordinary work. But you shall present a food offering to the Lord for seven days. On the seventh day is a holy convocation; you shall not do any ordinary work."

1 Corinthians 5:7
Cleanse out the old leaven that you may be a new lump, as you really are unleavened. For Christ, our Passover lamb, has been sacrificed.

Matthew 26:26-28
Now as they were eating, Jesus took bread, and after blessing it broke it and gave it to the disciples, and said, "Take, eat; this is my body." And he took a cup, and when he had given thanks he gave it to them, saying, "Drink of it, all of you, for this is my blood of the covenant, which is poured out for many for the forgiveness of sins.

Exodus 23:15
You shall keep the Feast of Unleavened Bread. As I commanded you, you shall eat unleavened bread for seven days at the appointed time in the month of Abib, for in it you came out of Egypt. None shall appear before me empty-handed.

Numbers 9:14
And if a stranger sojourns among you and would keep the Passover to the Lord, according to the statute of the Passover and according to its rule, so shall he do. You shall have one statute, both for the sojourner and for the native."

1 Corinthians 5:8

Let us therefore celebrate the festival, not with the old leaven, the leaven of malice and evil, but with the unleavened bread of sincerity and truth.

Patience

Romans 12:12

Rejoice in hope, be patient in tribulation, be constant in prayer.

Galatians 6:9

And let us not grow weary of doing good, for in due season we will reap, if we do not give up.

Romans 8:25

But if we hope for what we do not see, we wait for it with patience.

Psalm 37:7-9

Be still before the Lord and wait patiently for him; fret not yourself over the one who prospers in his way, over the man who carries out evil devices! Refrain from anger, and forsake wrath! Fret not yourself; it tends only to evil. For the evildoers shall be cut off, but those who wait for the Lord shall inherit the land.

Ephesians 4:2

With all humility and gentleness, with patience, bearing with one another in love,

Philippians 4:6

Do not be anxious about anything, but in everything by prayer and supplication with thanksgiving let your requests be made known to God.

1 Corinthians 13:4

Love is patient and kind; love does not envy or boast; it is not arrogant

Jeremiah 29:11

For I know the plans I have for you, declares the Lord, plans for welfare and not for evil, to give you a future and a hope.

Isaiah 40:31

But they who wait for the Lord shall renew their strength; they shall mount up with wings like eagles; they shall run and not be weary; they shall walk and not faint.

Proverbs 15:18

A hot-tempered man stirs up strife, but he who is slow to anger quiets contention.

Colossians 3:12

Put on then, as God's chosen ones, holy and beloved, compassionate hearts, kindness, humility, meekness, and patience,

Ecclesiastes 7:9

Be not quick in your spirit to become angry, for anger lodges in the bosom of fools.

Peace

John 16:33
I have said these things to you, that in me you may have peace. In the world you will have tribulation. But take heart; I have overcome the world."

2 Thessalonians 3:16
Now may the Lord of peace himself give you peace at all times in every way. The Lord be with you all.

Isaiah 26:3
You keep him in perfect peace whose mind is stayed on you, because he trusts in you.

Matthew 5:9
"Blessed are the peacemakers, for they shall be called sons of God.

Philippians 4:6
Do not be anxious about anything, but in everything by prayer and supplication with thanksgiving let your requests be made known to God.

Romans 12:18
If possible, so far as it depends on you, live peaceably with all.

Colossians 3:15
And let the peace of Christ rule in your hearts, to which indeed you were called in one body. And be thankful.

1 Peter 5:7
Casting all your anxieties on him, because he cares for you.

Hebrews 12:14
Strive for peace with everyone, and for the holiness without which no one will see the Lord.

Romans 15:13
May the God of hope fill you with all joy and peace in believing, so that by the power of the Holy Spirit you may abound in hope.

John 14:27
Peace I leave with you; my peace I give to you. Not as the world gives do I give to you. Let not your hearts be troubled, neither let them be afraid.

1 Peter 3:11
Let him turn away from evil and do good; let him seek peace and pursue it.

Peacemakers

Matthew 5:9
"Blessed are the peacemakers, for they shall be called sons of God.

Romans 12:18
If possible, so far as it depends on you, live peaceably with all.

Matthew 7:12
"So whatever you wish that others would do to you, do also to them, for this is the Law and the Prophets.

Pedophile

Mark 9:42
"Whoever causes one of these little ones who believe in me to sin, it would be better for him if a great millstone were hung around his neck and he were thrown into the sea.

Revelation 21:8
But as for the cowardly, the faithless, the detestable, as for murderers, the sexually immoral, sorcerers, idolaters, and all liars, their portion will be in the lake that burns with fire and sulfur, which is the second death."

Peer Pressure

Proverbs 13:20
Whoever walks with the wise becomes wise, but the companion of fools will suffer harm.

Romans 12:2
Do not be conformed to this world, but be transformed by the renewal of your mind, that by testing you may discern what is the will of God, what is good and acceptable and perfect.

Galatians 1:10
For am I now seeking the approval of man, or of God? Or am I trying to please man? If I were still trying to please man, I would not be a servant of Christ.

1 Corinthians 10:13
No temptation has overtaken you that is not common to man. God is faithful, and he will not let you be tempted beyond your ability, but with the temptation he will also provide the way of escape, that you may be able to endure it.

1 Corinthians 15:33-34
Do not be deceived: "Bad company ruins good morals." Wake up from your drunken stupor, as is right, and do not go on sinning. For some have no knowledge of God. I say this to your shame.

Proverbs 1:10
My son, if sinners entice you, do not consent.

Acts 5:29

But Peter and the apostles answered, "We must obey God rather than men.

Perfectionism

2 Corinthians 12:9-10

But he said to me, "My grace is sufficient for you, for my power is made perfect in weakness." Therefore I will boast all the more gladly of my weaknesses, so that the power of Christ may rest upon me. For the sake of Christ, then, I am content with weaknesses, insults, hardships, persecutions, and calamities. For when I am weak, then I am strong.

1 John 1:8

If we say we have no sin, we deceive ourselves, and the truth is not in us.

Persecution

2 Timothy 3:12

Indeed, all who desire to live a godly life in Christ Jesus will be persecuted,

John 15:18

"If the world hates you, know that it has hated me before it hated you.

1 Peter 4:12-14

Beloved, do not be surprised at the fiery trial when it comes upon you to test you, as though something strange were happening to you. But rejoice insofar as you share Christ's sufferings, that you may also rejoice and be glad when his glory is revealed. If you are insulted for the name of Christ, you are blessed, because the Spirit of glory and of God rests upon you.

Matthew 5:44

But I say to you, Love your enemies and pray for those who persecute you,

2 Corinthians 12:10

For the sake of Christ, then, I am content with weaknesses, insults, hardships, persecutions, and calamities. For when I am weak, then I am strong.

Luke 6:22

"Blessed are you when people hate you and when they exclude you and revile you and spurn your name as evil, on account of the Son of Man!

Matthew 5:10-12

"Blessed are those who are persecuted for righteousness' sake, for theirs is the kingdom of heaven. "Blessed are you when others revile you and persecute you and utter all kinds of evil against you falsely on my account. Rejoice and be glad, for your reward is great in heaven, for so they persecuted the prophets who were before you.

1 Peter 3:17
For it is better to suffer for doing good, if that should be God's will, than for doing evil.

Perseverance

Galatians 6:9
And let us not grow weary of doing good, for in due season we will reap, if we do not give up.

Hebrews 12:1-2
Therefore, since we are surrounded by so great a cloud of witnesses, let us also lay aside every weight, and sin which clings so closely, and let us run with endurance the race that is set before us, looking to Jesus, the founder and perfecter of our faith, who for the joy that was set before him endured the cross, despising the shame, and is seated at the right hand of the throne of God.

Romans 5:3
More than that, we rejoice in our sufferings, knowing that suffering produces endurance,

1 Corinthians 9:24-27
Do you not know that in a race all the runners run, but only one receives the prize? So run that you may obtain it. Every athlete exercises self-control in all things. They do it to receive a perishable wreath, but we an imperishable. So I do not run aimlessly; I do not box as one beating the air. But I discipline my body and keep it under control, lest after preaching to others I myself should be disqualified.

2 Thessalonians 3:13
As for you, brothers, do not grow weary in doing good.

Persistence

Galatians 6:9
And let us not grow weary of doing good, for in due season we will reap, if we do not give up.

Luke 11:9-10
And I tell you, ask, and it will be given to you; seek, and you will find; knock, and it will be opened to you. For everyone who asks receives, and the one who seeks finds, and to the one who knocks it will be opened.

Proverbs 24:16
For the righteous falls seven times and rises again, but the wicked stumble in times of calamity.

Personality

1 Samuel 16:7
But the Lord said to Samuel, "Do not look on his appearance or on the height of his stature, because I have rejected him. For the Lord sees not as man sees: man looks on the outward appearance, but the Lord looks on the heart."

Romans 12:4-6

For as in one body we have many members, and the members do not all have the same function, so we, though many, are one body in Christ, and individually members one of another. Having gifts that differ according to the grace given to us, let us use them: if prophecy, in proportion to our faith;

1 Corinthians 12:14-18

For the body does not consist of one member but of many. If the foot should say, "Because I am not a hand, I do not belong to the body," that would not make it any less a part of the body. And if the ear should say, "Because I am not an eye, I do not belong to the body," that would not make it any less a part of the body. If the whole body were an eye, where would be the sense of hearing? If the whole body were an ear, where would be the sense of smell? But as it is, God arranged the members in the body, each one of them, as he chose.

Romans 7:15-17

For I do not understand my own actions. For I do not do what I want, but I do the very thing I hate. Now if I do what I do not want, I agree with the law, that it is good. So now it is no longer I who do it, but sin that dwells within me.

Psalm 139:14

I praise you, for I am fearfully and wonderfully made. Wonderful are your works; my soul knows it very well.

Proverbs 27:19

As in water face reflects face, so the heart of man reflects the man.

Phobias

2 Timothy 1:7

For God gave us a spirit not of fear but of power and love and self-control.

1 John 4:18

There is no fear in love, but perfect love casts out fear. For fear has to do with punishment, and whoever fears has not been perfected in love.

2 Corinthians 10:5

We destroy arguments and every lofty opinion raised against the knowledge of God, and take every thought captive to obey Christ,

Polygamy

Exodus 21:10

If he takes another wife to himself, he shall not diminish her food, her clothing, or her marital rights.

Deuteronomy 21:15-17

"If a man has two wives, the one loved and the other unloved, and both the loved and the unloved have borne him children, and if the firstborn son belongs to the unloved, then on the day when he assigns his possessions as an inheritance to his sons, he may not treat the son of the loved as the firstborn in preference to the son of the unloved, who is the firstborn, but he shall acknowledge the firstborn, the son of the unloved, by giving him a double portion of all that he has, for he is the firstfruits of his strength. The right of the firstborn is his.

Poor

Proverbs 19:17
Whoever is generous to the poor lends to the Lord, and he will repay him for his deed.

Proverbs 28:27
Whoever gives to the poor will not want, but he who hides his eyes will get many a curse.

Luke 12:33-34
Sell your possessions, and give to the needy. Provide yourselves with moneybags that do not grow old, with a treasure in the heavens that does not fail, where no thief approaches and no moth destroys. For where your treasure is, there will your heart be also.

Proverbs 14:31
Whoever oppresses a poor man insults his Maker, but he who is generous to the needy honors him.

Acts 20:35
In all things I have shown you that by working hard in this way we must help the weak and remember the words of the Lord Jesus, how he himself said, 'It is more blessed to give than to receive.'"

Hebrews 13:16
Do not neglect to do good and to share what you have, for such sacrifices are pleasing to God.

Proverbs 22:9
Whoever has a bountiful eye will be blessed, for he shares his bread with the poor.

James 1:27
Religion that is pure and undefiled before God, the Father, is this: to visit orphans and widows in their affliction, and to keep oneself unstained from the world.

Matthew 5:42
Give to the one who begs from you, and do not refuse the one who would borrow from you.

Proverbs 29:7
A righteous man knows the rights of the poor; a wicked man does not understand such knowledge.

Luke 21:1-4
Jesus looked up and saw the rich putting their gifts into the offering box, and he saw a poor widow put in two small copper coins. And he said, "Truly, I tell you, this poor widow has put in more than all of them. For they all contributed out of their abundance, but she out of her poverty put in all she had to live on."

Popularity

Luke 9:25
For what does it profit a man if he gains the whole world and loses or forfeits himself?

Proverbs 13:20
Whoever walks with the wise becomes wise, but the companion of fools will suffer harm.

Pornography

Matthew 5:28
But I say to you that everyone who looks at a woman with lustful intent has already committed adultery with her in his heart.

1 Corinthians 6:18-20
Flee from sexual immorality. Every other sin a person commits is outside the body, but the sexually immoral person sins against his own body. Or do you not know that your body is a temple of the Holy Spirit within you, whom you have from God? You are not your own, for you were bought with a price. So glorify God in your body.

1 Corinthians 10:13
No temptation has overtaken you that is not common to man. God is faithful, and he will not let you be tempted beyond your ability, but with the temptation he will also provide the way of escape, that you may be able to endure it.

Hebrews 13:4
Let marriage be held in honor among all, and let the marriage bed be undefiled, for God will judge the sexually immoral and adulterous.

1 John 2:16
For all that is in the world—the desires of the flesh and the desires of the eyes and pride in possessions—is not from the Father but is from the world.

Psalm 119:37
Turn my eyes from looking at worthless things; and give me life in your ways.

Philippians 4:8
Finally, brothers, whatever is true, whatever is honorable, whatever is just, whatever is pure, whatever is lovely, whatever is commendable, if there is any excellence, if there is anything worthy of praise, think about these things.

Poverty

Leviticus 25:35
"If your brother becomes poor and cannot maintain himself with you, you shall support him as though he were a stranger and a sojourner, and he shall live with you.

2 Corinthians 8:9

For you know the grace of our Lord Jesus Christ, that though he was rich, yet for your sake he became poor, so that you by his poverty might become rich.

Proverbs 22:2

The rich and the poor meet together; the Lord is the maker of them all.

Proverbs 20:13

Love not sleep, lest you come to poverty; open your eyes, and you will have plenty of bread.

Proverbs 31:8-9

Open your mouth for the mute, for the rights of all who are destitute. Open your mouth, judge righteously, defend the rights of the poor and needy.

Proverbs 28:6

Better is a poor man who walks in his integrity than a rich man who is crooked in his ways.

Ecclesiastes 9:16

But I say that wisdom is better than might, though the poor man's wisdom is despised and his words are not heard.

Luke 6:20-21

And he lifted up his eyes on his disciples, and said: "Blessed are you who are poor, for yours is the kingdom of God. "Blessed are you who are hungry now, for you shall be satisfied. "Blessed are you who weep now, for you shall laugh.

Proverbs 17:5

Whoever mocks the poor insults his Maker; he who is glad at calamity will not go unpunished.

Proverbs 29:7

A righteous man knows the rights of the poor; a wicked man does not understand such knowledge.

Proverbs 22:7

The rich rules over the poor, and the borrower is the slave of the lender.

Proverbs 28:11

A rich man is wise in his own eyes, but a poor man who has understanding will find him out.

Power

2 Timothy 1:7

For God gave us a spirit not of fear but of power and love and self-control.

Acts 1:8

But you will receive power when the Holy Spirit has come upon you, and you will be my witnesses in Jerusalem and in all Judea and Samaria, and to the end of the earth."

Philippians 4:13

I can do all things through him who strengthens me.

Luke 10:19

Behold, I have given you authority to tread on serpents and scorpions, and over all the power of the enemy, and nothing shall hurt you.

Ephesians 6:10

Finally, be strong in the Lord and in the strength of his might.

1 Corinthians 4:20

For the kingdom of God does not consist in talk but in power.

Ephesians 3:20

Now to him who is able to do far more abundantly than all that we ask or think, according to the power at work within us,

1 Corinthians 6:14

And God raised the Lord and will also raise us up by his power.

2 Corinthians 12:9

But he said to me, "My grace is sufficient for you, for my power is made perfect in weakness." Therefore I will boast all the more gladly of my weaknesses, so that the power of Christ may rest upon me.

Isaiah 40:29-31

He gives power to the faint, and to him who has no might he increases strength. Even youths shall faint and be weary, and young men shall fall exhausted; but they who wait for the Lord shall renew their strength; they shall mount up with wings like eagles; they shall run and not be weary; they shall walk and not faint.

Praise

Hebrews 13:15

Through him then let us continually offer up a sacrifice of praise to God, that is, the fruit of lips that acknowledge his name.

Psalm 100:1-5

A Psalm for giving thanks. Make a joyful noise to the Lord, all the earth! Serve the Lord with gladness! Come into his presence with singing! Know that the Lord, he is God! It is he who made us, and we are his; we are his people, and the sheep of his pasture. Enter his gates with thanksgiving, and his courts with praise! Give thanks to him; bless his name! For the Lord is good; his steadfast love endures forever, and his faithfulness to all generations.

Psalm 99:3

Let them praise your great and awesome name! Holy is he!

Psalm 109:30

With my mouth I will give great thanks to the Lord; I will praise him in the midst of the throng.

Psalm 106:1

Praise the Lord! Oh give thanks to the Lord, for he is good, for his steadfast love endures forever!

Prayer

Philippians 4:6

Do not be anxious about anything, but in everything by prayer and supplication with thanksgiving let your requests be made known to God.

Mark 11:24

Therefore I tell you, whatever you ask in prayer, believe that you have received it, and it will be yours.

John 15:7

If you abide in me, and my words abide in you, ask whatever you wish, and it will be done for you.

1 Thessalonians 5:17

Pray without ceasing,

Romans 8:26

Likewise the Spirit helps us in our weakness. For we do not know what to pray for as we ought, but the Spirit himself intercedes for us with groanings too deep for words.

Luke 11:9

And I tell you, ask, and it will be given to you; seek, and you will find; knock, and it will be opened to you.

James 5:16

Therefore, confess your sins to one another and pray for one another, that you may be healed. The prayer of a righteous person has great power as it is working.

Jeremiah 33:3

Call to me and I will answer you, and will tell you great and hidden things that you have not known.

Matthew 26:41

Watch and pray that you may not enter into temptation. The spirit indeed is willing, but the flesh is weak."

Ephesians 6:18

Praying at all times in the Spirit, with all prayer and supplication. To that end keep alert with all perseverance, making supplication for all the saints,

1 Timothy 2:1-4

First of all, then, I urge that supplications, prayers, intercessions, and thanksgivings be made for all people, for kings and all who are in high positions, that we may lead a peaceful and quiet life, godly and dignified in every way. This is good, and it is pleasing in the sight of God our Savior, who desires all people to be saved and to come to the knowledge of the truth.

Matthew 6:5-8

"And when you pray, you must not be like the hypocrites. For they love to stand and pray in the synagogues and at the street corners, that they may be seen by others. Truly, I say to you, they have received their reward. But when you pray, go into your room and shut the door and pray to your Father who is in secret. And your Father who sees in secret will reward you. "And when you pray, do not heap up empty phrases as the Gentiles do, for they think that they will be heard for their many words. Do not be like them, for your Father knows what you need before you ask him.

Predestined

Romans 8:29

For those whom he foreknew he also predestined to be conformed to the image of his Son, in order that he might be the firstborn among many brothers.

Ephesians 1:11

In him we have obtained an inheritance, having been predestined according to the purpose of him who works all things according to the counsel of his will,

Ephesians 1:5

He predestined us for adoption as sons through Jesus Christ, according to the purpose of his will,

Romans 8:29-30

For those whom he foreknew he also predestined to be conformed to the image of his Son, in order that he might be the firstborn among many brothers. And those whom he predestined he also called, and those whom he called he also justified, and those whom he justified he also glorified.

Pregnancy

Psalm 127:3

Behold, children are a heritage from the Lord, the fruit of the womb a reward.

Jeremiah 1:4-5

Now the word of the Lord came to me, saying, "Before I formed you in the womb I knew you, and before you were born I consecrated you; I appointed you a prophet to the nations."

Jeremiah 1:5

"Before I formed you in the womb I knew you, and before you were born I consecrated you; I appointed you a prophet to the nations."

John 16:21

When a woman is giving birth, she has sorrow because her hour has come, but when she has delivered the baby, she no longer remembers the anguish, for joy that a human being has been born into the world.

Psalm 139:13

For you formed my inward parts; you knitted me together in my mother's womb.

Ecclesiastes 11:5

As you do not know the way the spirit comes to the bones in the womb of a woman with child, so you do not know the work of God who makes everything.

Job 31:15

Did not he who made me in the womb make him? And did not one fashion us in the womb?

Luke 1:44-45

For behold, when the sound of your greeting came to my ears, the baby in my womb leaped for joy. And blessed is she who believed that there would be a fulfillment of what was spoken to her from the Lord."

Isaiah 49:15

"Can a woman forget her nursing child, that she should have no compassion on the son of her womb? Even these may forget, yet I will not forget you.

Pride

Proverbs 11:2

When pride comes, then comes disgrace, but with the humble is wisdom.

Proverbs 16:18

Pride goes before destruction, and a haughty spirit before a fall.

Proverbs 29:23

One's pride will bring him low, but he who is lowly in spirit will obtain honor.

Proverbs 8:13

The fear of the Lord is hatred of evil. Pride and arrogance and the way of evil and perverted speech I hate.

James 4:6

But he gives more grace. Therefore it says, "God opposes the proud, but gives grace to the humble."

Proverbs 16:5

Everyone who is arrogant in heart is an abomination to the Lord; be assured, he will not go unpunished.

Psalm 10:4

In the pride of his face the wicked does not seek him; all his thoughts are, "There is no God."

Proverbs 18:12

Before destruction a man's heart is haughty, but humility comes before honor.

1 John 2:16

For all that is in the world—the desires of the flesh and the desires of the eyes and pride in possessions—is not from the Father but is from the world.

Romans 12:16

Live in harmony with one another. Do not be haughty, but associate with the lowly. Never be wise in your own sight.

Proverbs 13:10

By insolence comes nothing but strife, but with those who take advice is wisdom.

Galatians 6:3

For if anyone thinks he is something, when he is nothing, he deceives himself.

Priorities

Matthew 6:33

But seek first the kingdom of God and his righteousness, and all these things will be added to you.

Romans 12:2

Do not be conformed to this world, but be transformed by the renewal of your mind, that by testing you may discern what is the will of God, what is good and acceptable and perfect.

Luke 12:34

For where your treasure is, there will your heart be also.

Exodus 20:3

"You shall have no other gods before me.

1 Timothy 3:5

For if someone does not know how to manage his own household, how will he care for God's church?

Prison

Matthew 25:36

I was naked and you clothed me, I was sick and you visited me, I was in prison and you came to me.'

Isaiah 61:1

The Spirit of the Lord God is upon me, because the Lord has anointed me to bring good news to the poor; he has sent me to bind up the brokenhearted, to proclaim liberty to the captives, and the opening of the prison to those who are bound;

Hebrews 13:3

Remember those who are in prison, as though in prison with them, and those who are mistreated, since you also are in the body.

Ezra 7:26

Whoever will not obey the law of your God and the law of the king, let judgment be strictly executed on him, whether for death or for banishment or for confiscation of his goods or for imprisonment."

Psalm 69:33

For the Lord hears the needy and does not despise his own people who are prisoners.

2 Timothy 2:9

For which I am suffering, bound with chains as a criminal. But the word of God is not bound!

Acts 12:5

So Peter was kept in prison, but earnest prayer for him was made to God by the church.

Philippians 1:27

Only let your manner of life be worthy of the gospel of Christ, so that whether I come and see you or am absent, I may hear of you that you are standing firm in one spirit, with one mind striving side by side for the faith of the gospel,

Privacy

Luke 12:2-3

Nothing is covered up that will not be revealed, or hidden that will not be known. Therefore whatever you have said in the dark shall be heard in the light, and what you have whispered in private rooms shall be proclaimed on the housetops.

1 Thessalonians 4:11

And to aspire to live quietly, and to mind your own affairs, and to work with your hands, as we instructed you,

Hebrews 4:12-13

For the word of God is living and active, sharper than any two-edged sword, piercing to the division of soul and of spirit, of joints and of marrow, and discerning the thoughts and intentions of the heart. And no creature is hidden from his sight, but all are naked and exposed to the eyes of him to whom we must give account.

Problem Solving

Philippians 4:6

Do not be anxious about anything, but in everything by prayer and supplication with thanksgiving let your requests be made known to God.

Proverbs 3:5

Trust in the Lord with all your heart, and do not lean on your own understanding.

Matthew 18:15-18

"If your brother sins against you, go and tell him his fault, between you and him alone. If he listens to you, you have gained your brother. But if he does not listen, take one or two others along with you, that every charge may be established by the evidence of two or three witnesses. If he refuses to listen to them, tell it to the church. And if he refuses to listen even to the church, let him be to you as a Gentile and a tax collector. Truly, I say to you, whatever you bind on earth shall be bound in heaven, and whatever you loose on earth shall be loosed in heaven.

Philippians 4:13

I can do all things through him who strengthens me.

Proverbs 3:6

In all your ways acknowledge him, and he will make straight your paths.

Matthew 7:7

"Ask, and it will be given to you; seek, and you will find; knock, and it will be opened to you.

Psalm 50:15

And call upon me in the day of trouble; I will deliver you, and you shall glorify me."

Mark 11:22-25

And Jesus answered them, "Have faith in God. Truly, I say to you, whoever says to this mountain, 'Be taken up and thrown into the sea,' and does not doubt in his heart, but believes that what he says will come to pass, it will be done for him. Therefore I tell you, whatever you ask in prayer, believe that you have received it, and it will be yours. And whenever you stand praying, forgive, if you have anything against anyone, so that your Father also who is in heaven may forgive you your trespasses."

1 John 1:9

If we confess our sins, he is faithful and just to forgive us our sins and to cleanse us from all unrighteousness.

Procrastination

Proverbs 13:4

The soul of the sluggard craves and gets nothing, while the soul of the diligent is richly supplied.

Ephesians 5:15-17

Look carefully then how you walk, not as unwise but as wise, making the best use of the time, because the days are evil. Therefore do not be foolish, but understand what the will of the Lord is.

Proverbs 12:24

The hand of the diligent will rule, while the slothful will be put to forced labor.

Proverbs 20:4

The sluggard does not plow in the autumn; he will seek at harvest and have nothing.

Proverbs 27:1

Do not boast about tomorrow, for you do not know what a day may bring.

Profanity

Exodus 20:7
"You shall not take the name of the Lord your God in vain, for the Lord will not hold him guiltless who takes his name in vain.

Matthew 12:36
I tell you, on the day of judgment people will give account for every careless word they speak,

James 3:10
From the same mouth come blessing and cursing. My brothers, these things ought not to be so.

2 Timothy 2:16
But avoid irreverent babble, for it will lead people into more and more ungodliness,

Proverbs 18:21
Death and life are in the power of the tongue, and those who love it will eat its fruits.

Psalm 34:13
Keep your tongue from evil and your lips from speaking deceit.

Matthew 15:11
It is not what goes into the mouth that defiles a person, but what comes out of the mouth; this defiles a person."

Promises of God

Philippians 4:19
And my God will supply every need of yours according to his riches in glory in Christ Jesus.

Jeremiah 29:11
For I know the plans I have for you, declares the Lord, plans for welfare and not for evil, to give you a future and a hope.

2 Peter 1:4
By which he has granted to us his precious and very great promises, so that through them you may become partakers of the divine nature, having escaped from the corruption that is in the world because of sinful desire.

1 John 1:9
If we confess our sins, he is faithful and just to forgive us our sins and to cleanse us from all unrighteousness.

Isaiah 41:10
Fear not, for I am with you; be not dismayed, for I am your God; I will strengthen you, I will help you, I will uphold you with my righteous right hand.

2 Corinthians 1:20
For all the promises of God find their Yes in him. That is why it is through him that we utter our Amen to God for his glory.

John 14:27
Peace I leave with you; my peace I give to you. Not as the world gives do I give to you. Let not your hearts be troubled, neither let them be afraid.

John 3:16
"For God so loved the world, that he gave his only Son, that whoever believes in him should not perish but have eternal life.

Isaiah 40:29-31
He gives power to the faint, and to him who has no might he increases strength. Even youths shall faint and be weary, and young men shall fall exhausted; but they who wait for the Lord shall renew their strength; they shall mount up with wings like eagles; they shall run and not be weary; they shall walk and not faint.

Psalm 84:11
For the Lord God is a sun and shield; the Lord bestows favor and honor. No good thing does he withhold from those who walk uprightly.

Matthew 11:28-29
Come to me, all who labor and are heavy laden, and I will give you rest. Take my yoke upon you, and learn from me, for I am gentle and lowly in heart, and you will find rest for your souls.

Joshua 23:14
"And now I am about to go the way of all the earth, and you know in your hearts and souls, all of you, that not one word has failed of all the good things that the Lord your God promised concerning you. All have come to pass for you; not one of them has failed.

Prophecy

2 Peter 1:21
For no prophecy was ever produced by the will of man, but men spoke from God as they were carried along by the Holy Spirit.

1 John 4:1
Beloved, do not believe every spirit, but test the spirits to see whether they are from God, for many false prophets have gone out into the world.

1 Thessalonians 5:20
Do not despise prophecies,

Matthew 7:21-23

"Not everyone who says to me, 'Lord, Lord,' will enter the kingdom of heaven, but the one who does the will of my Father who is in heaven. On that day many will say to me, 'Lord, Lord, did we not prophesy in your name, and cast out demons in your name, and do many mighty works in your name?' And then will I declare to them, 'I never knew you; depart from me, you workers of lawlessness.'

Joel 2:28

"And it shall come to pass afterward, that I will pour out my Spirit on all flesh; your sons and your daughters shall prophesy, your old men shall dream dreams, and your young men shall see visions.

Prosperity

Deuteronomy 8:18

You shall remember the Lord your God, for it is he who gives you power to get wealth, that he may confirm his covenant that he swore to your fathers, as it is this day.

Jeremiah 29:11

For I know the plans I have for you, declares the Lord, plans for welfare and not for evil, to give you a future and a hope.

Philippians 4:19

And my God will supply every need of yours according to his riches in glory in Christ Jesus.

Malachi 3:10

Bring the full tithe into the storehouse, that there may be food in my house. And thereby put me to the test, says the Lord of hosts, if I will not open the windows of heaven for you and pour down for you a blessing until there is no more need.

3 John 1:2

Beloved, I pray that all may go well with you and that you may be in good health, as it goes well with your soul.

Joshua 1:8

This Book of the Law shall not depart from your mouth, but you shall meditate on it day and night, so that you may be careful to do according to all that is written in it. For then you will make your way prosperous, and then you will have good success.

Psalm 128:2

You shall eat the fruit of the labor of your hands; you shall be blessed, and it shall be well with you.

2 Corinthians 9:8

And God is able to make all grace abound to you, so that having all sufficiency in all things at all times, you may abound in every good work.

Psalm 1:3

He is like a tree planted by streams of water that yields its fruit in its season, and its leaf does not wither. In all that he does, he prospers.

Joshua 1:9

Have I not commanded you? Be strong and courageous. Do not be frightened, and do not be dismayed, for the Lord your God is with you wherever you go."

2 Corinthians 8:9

For you know the grace of our Lord Jesus Christ, that though he was rich, yet for your sake he became poor, so that you by his poverty might become rich.

Proverbs 28:25

A greedy man stirs up strife, but the one who trusts in the Lord will be enriched.

Protection

Psalm 34:7

The angel of the Lord encamps around those who fear him, and delivers them.

2 Thessalonians 3:3

But the Lord is faithful. He will establish you and guard you against the evil one.

Isaiah 54:17

No weapon that is fashioned against you shall succeed, and you shall confute every tongue that rises against you in judgment. This is the heritage of the servants of the Lord and their vindication from me, declares the Lord."

Isaiah 41:10

Fear not, for I am with you; be not dismayed, for I am your God; I will strengthen you, I will help you, I will uphold you with my righteous right hand.

Romans 12:19

Beloved, never avenge yourselves, but leave it to the wrath of God, for it is written, "Vengeance is mine, I will repay, says the Lord."

Psalm 46:1

To the choirmaster. Of the Sons of Korah. According to Alamoth. A Song. God is our refuge and strength, a very present help in trouble.

Psalm 17:8

Keep me as the apple of your eye; hide me in the shadow of your wings,

Psalm 138:7

Though I walk in the midst of trouble, you preserve my life; you stretch out your hand against the wrath of my enemies, and your right hand delivers me.

Deuteronomy 31:6

Be strong and courageous. Do not fear or be in dread of them, for it is the Lord your God who goes with you. He will not leave you or forsake you."

Prudence

Proverbs 8:12

"I, wisdom, dwell with prudence, and I find knowledge and discretion.

Proverbs 27:12

The prudent sees danger and hides himself, but the simple go on and suffer for it.

Proverbs 13:16

In everything the prudent acts with knowledge, but a fool flaunts his folly.

Psychic

Leviticus 19:31

"Do not turn to mediums or necromancers; do not seek them out, and so make yourselves unclean by them: I am the Lord your God.

Leviticus 20:6

"If a person turns to mediums and necromancers, whoring after them, I will set my face against that person and will cut him off from among his people.

1 John 4:1

Beloved, do not believe every spirit, but test the spirits to see whether they are from God, for many false prophets have gone out into the world.

Leviticus 20:27

"A man or a woman who is a medium or a necromancer shall surely be put to death. They shall be stoned with stones; their blood shall be upon them."

Deuteronomy 18:9-12

"When you come into the land that the Lord your God is giving you, you shall not learn to follow the abominable practices of those nations. There shall not be found among you anyone who burns his son or his daughter as an offering, anyone who practices divination or tells fortunes or interprets omens, or a sorcerer or a charmer or a medium or a necromancer or one who inquires of the dead, for whoever does these things is an abomination to the Lord. And because of these abominations the Lord your God is driving them out before you.

Galatians 5:19-21

Now the works of the flesh are evident: sexual immorality, impurity, sensuality, idolatry, sorcery, enmity, strife, jealousy, fits of anger, rivalries, dissensions, divisions, envy, drunkenness, orgies, and things like these. I warn you, as I warned you before, that those who do such things will not inherit the kingdom of God.

Matthew 7:15

"Beware of false prophets, who come to you in sheep's clothing but inwardly are ravenous wolves.

Revelation 21:8

But as for the cowardly, the faithless, the detestable, as for murderers, the sexually immoral, sorcerers, idolaters, and all liars, their portion will be in the lake that burns with fire and sulfur, which is the second death."

2 Chronicles 33:6

And he burned his sons as an offering in the Valley of the Son of Hinnom, and used fortune-telling and omens and sorcery, and dealt with mediums and with necromancers. He did much evil in the sight of the Lord, provoking him to anger.

Purity

Matthew 5:8

"Blessed are the pure in heart, for they shall see God.

Psalm 119:9

How can a young man keep his way pure? By guarding it according to your word.

1 Timothy 4:12

Let no one despise you for your youth, but set the believers an example in speech, in conduct, in love, in faith, in purity.

Psalm 51:10

Create in me a clean heart, O God, and renew a right spirit within me.

1 John 1:9

If we confess our sins, he is faithful and just to forgive us our sins and to cleanse us from all unrighteousness.

Purpose

Jeremiah 29:11

For I know the plans I have for you, declares the Lord, plans for welfare and not for evil, to give you a future and a hope.

Matthew 28:18-20

And Jesus came and said to them, "All authority in heaven and on earth has been given to me. Go therefore and make disciples of all nations, baptizing them in the name of the Father and of the Son and of the Holy Spirit, teaching them to observe all that I have commanded you. And behold, I am with you always, to the end of the age."

Romans 8:28

And we know that for those who love God all things work together for good, for those who are called according to his purpose.

Ecclesiastes 12:13-14

The end of the matter; all has been heard. Fear God and keep his commandments, for this is the whole duty of man. For God will bring every deed into judgment, with every secret thing, whether good or evil.

Proverbs 16:4

The Lord has made everything for its purpose, even the wicked for the day of trouble.

Purpose in Life

Matthew 28:19-20

Go therefore and make disciples of all nations, baptizing them in the name of the Father and of the Son and of the Holy Spirit, teaching them to observe all that I have commanded you. And behold, I am with you always, to the end of the age."

Romans 8:28

And we know that for those who love God all things work together for good, for those who are called according to his purpose.

Ecclesiastes 12:13-14

The end of the matter; all has been heard. Fear God and keep his commandments, for this is the whole duty of man. For God will bring every deed into judgment, with every secret thing, whether good or evil.

Romans 12:2

Do not be conformed to this world, but be transformed by the renewal of your mind, that by testing you may discern what is the will of God, what is good and acceptable and perfect.

Psalm 138:8

The Lord will fulfill his purpose for me; your steadfast love, O Lord, endures forever. Do not forsake the work of your hands.

1 Corinthians 10:31

So, whether you eat or drink, or whatever you do, do all to the glory of God.

Purpose of Man

Ecclesiastes 12:13

The end of the matter; all has been heard. Fear God and keep his commandments, for this is the whole duty of man.

1 Corinthians 10:31

So, whether you eat or drink, or whatever you do, do all to the glory of God.

Genesis 1:26

Then God said, "Let us make man in our image, after our likeness. And let them have dominion over the fish of the sea and over the birds of the heavens and over the livestock and over all the earth and over every creeping thing that creeps on the earth."

Romans 12:1

I appeal to you therefore, brothers, by the mercies of God, to present your bodies as a living sacrifice, holy and acceptable to God, which is your spiritual worship.

Proverbs 19:21

Many are the plans in the mind of a man, but it is the purpose of the Lord that will stand.

Isaiah 43:21

The people whom I formed for myself that they might declare my praise

.

Qualifications of Elders

1 Timothy 3:1-2
The saying is trustworthy: If anyone aspires to the office of overseer, he desires a noble task. Therefore, an overseer must be above reproach, the husband of one wife, sober-minded, self-controlled, respectable, hospitable, able to teach,

Titus 1:5-9
This is why I left you in Crete, so that you might put what remained into order, and appoint elders in every town as I directed you— if anyone is above reproach, the husband of one wife, and his children are believers and not open to the charge of debauchery or insubordination. For an overseer, as God's steward, must be above reproach. He must not be arrogant or quick-tempered or a drunkard or violent or greedy for gain, but hospitable, a lover of good, self-controlled, upright, holy, and disciplined. He must hold firm to the trustworthy word as taught, so that he may be able to give instruction in sound doctrine and also to rebuke those who contradict it.

Acts 20:28
Pay careful attention to yourselves and to all the flock, in which the Holy Spirit has made you overseers, to care for the church of God, which he obtained with his own blood.

1 Timothy 5:17
Let the elders who rule well be considered worthy of double honor, especially those who labor in preaching and teaching.

1 Timothy 3:6
He must not be a recent convert, or he may become puffed up with conceit and fall into the condemnation of the devil.

Qualities of a Good Leader

1 Timothy 4:12
Let no one despise you for your youth, but set the believers an example in speech, in conduct, in love, in faith, in purity.

Galatians 6:9
And let us not grow weary of doing good, for in due season we will reap, if we do not give up.

1 Timothy 3:2-7
Therefore, an overseer must be above reproach, the husband of one wife, sober-minded, self-controlled, respectable, hospitable, able to teach, not a drunkard, not violent but gentle, not quarrelsome, not a lover of money. He must manage his own household well, with all dignity keeping his children submissive, for if someone does not know how to manage his own household, how will he care for God's church? He must not be a recent convert, or he may become puffed up with conceit and fall into the condemnation of the devil. Moreover, he must be well thought of by outsiders, so that he may not fall into disgrace, into a snare of the devil.

Philippians 2:3
Do nothing from rivalry or conceit, but in humility count others more significant than yourselves.

Matthew 20:26
It shall not be so among you. But whoever would be great among you must be your servant,

Proverbs 4:23
Keep your heart with all vigilance, for from it flow the springs of life.

Exodus 18:21
Moreover, look for able men from all the people, men who fear God, who are trustworthy and hate a bribe, and place such men over the people as chiefs of thousands, of hundreds, of fifties, and of tens.

Colossians 3:12-13
Put on then, as God's chosen ones, holy and beloved, compassionate hearts, kindness, humility, meekness, and patience, bearing with one another and, if one has a complaint against another, forgiving each other; as the Lord has forgiven you, so you also must forgive

Quarreling

Titus 3:9-11
But avoid foolish controversies, genealogies, dissensions, and quarrels about the law, for they are unprofitable and worthless. As for a person who stirs up division, after warning him once and then twice, have nothing more to do with him, knowing that such a person is warped and sinful; he is self-condemned.

Proverbs 20:3
It is an honor for a man to keep aloof from strife, but every fool will be quarreling.

2 Timothy 2:23
Have nothing to do with foolish, ignorant controversies; you know that they breed quarrels.

James 4:1
What causes quarrels and what causes fights among you? Is it not this, that your passions are at war within you?

Proverbs 26:17
Whoever meddles in a quarrel not his own is like one who takes a passing dog by the ears.

Proverbs 21:19
It is better to live in a desert land than with a quarrelsome and fretful woman.

Proverbs 17:14
The beginning of strife is like letting out water, so quit before the quarrel breaks out.

Questioning God

Isaiah 55:8-9
For my thoughts are not your thoughts, neither are your ways my ways, declares the Lord. For as the heavens are higher than the earth, so are my ways higher than your ways and my thoughts than your thoughts.

James 1:5-6
If any of you lacks wisdom, let him ask God, who gives generously to all without reproach, and it will be given him. But let him ask in faith, with no doubting, for the one who doubts is like a wave of the sea that is driven and tossed by the wind.

Habakkuk 1:2
O Lord, how long shall I cry for help, and you will not hear? Or cry to you "Violence!" and you will not save?

Isaiah 45:9-12
"Woe to him who strives with him who formed him, a pot among earthen pots! Does the clay say to him who forms it, 'What are you making?' or 'Your work has no handles'? Woe to him who says to a father, 'What are you begetting?' or to a woman, 'With what are you in labor?'" Thus says the Lord, the Holy One of Israel, and the one who formed him: "Ask me of things to come; will you command me concerning my children and the work of my hands? I made the earth and created man on it; it was my hands that stretched out the heavens, and I commanded all their host.

Romans 9:20
But who are you, O man, to answer back to God? Will what is molded say to its molder, "Why have you made me like this?"

Questioning Your Faith

1 Corinthians 3:11-15
For no one can lay a foundation other than that which is laid, which is Jesus Christ. Now if anyone builds on the foundation with gold, silver, precious stones, wood, hay, straw— each one's work will become manifest, for the Day will disclose it, because it will be revealed by fire, and the fire will test what sort of work each one has done. If the work that anyone has built on the foundation survives, he will receive a reward. If anyone's work is burned up, he will suffer loss, though he himself will be saved, but only as through fire.

Jude 1:22
And have mercy on those who doubt;

Ephesians 2:8
For by grace you have been saved through faith. And this is not your own doing; it is the gift of God,

Mark 11:24
Therefore, I tell you, whatever you ask in prayer, believe that you have received it, and it will be yours.

Quick Temper

Proverbs 14:17
A man of quick temper acts foolishly, and a man of evil devices is hated.

Proverbs 15:1
A soft answer turns away wrath, but a harsh word stirs up anger.

James 1:20
For the anger of man does not produce the righteousness of God.

Proverbs 29:11
A fool gives full vent to his spirit, but a wise man quietly holds it back.

Proverbs 14:29
Whoever is slow to anger has great understanding, but he who has a hasty temper exalts folly.

Proverbs 16:32
Whoever is slow to anger is better than the mighty, and he who rules his spirit than he who takes a city.

James 1:19
Know this, my beloved brothers: let every person be quick to hear, slow to speak, slow to anger;

Ephesians 4:26-27
Be angry and do not sin; do not let the sun go down on your anger, and give no opportunity to the devil.

Colossians 3:8
But now you must put them all away: anger, wrath, malice, slander, and obscene talk from your mouth.

Proverbs 15:18
A hot-tempered man stirs up strife, but he who is slow to anger quiets contention.

Proverbs 19:11
Good sense makes one slow to anger, and it is his glory to overlook an offense.

Quiet Time

Matthew 6:6
But when you pray, go into your room and shut the door and pray to your Father who is in secret. And your Father who sees in secret will reward you.

Psalm 1:2
But his delight is in the law of the Lord, and on his law he meditates day and night.

Quitting

Philippians 4:13
I can do all things through him who strengthens me.

Galatians 6:9
And let us not grow weary of doing good, for in due season we will reap, if we do not give up.

Hebrews 12:1
Therefore, since we are surrounded by so great a cloud of witnesses, let us also lay aside every weight, and sin which clings so closely, and let us run with endurance the race that is set before us,

2 Corinthians 12:9
But he said to me, "My grace is sufficient for you, for my power is made perfect in weakness." Therefore, I will boast all the more gladly of my weaknesses, so that the power of Christ may rest upon me.

Matthew 19:26
But Jesus looked at them and said, "With man this is impossible, but with God all things are possible.

Racism

Galatians 3:28
There is neither Jew nor Greek, there is neither slave nor free, there is no male and female, for you are all one in Christ Jesus.

John 7:24
Do not judge by appearances, but judge with right judgment."

Acts 10:34-35
So Peter opened his mouth and said: "Truly I understand that God shows no partiality, but in every nation anyone who fears him and does what is right is acceptable to him.

Acts 17:26
And he made from one man every nation of mankind to live on all the face of the earth, having determined allotted periods and the boundaries of their dwelling place,

Romans 2:11
For God shows no partiality.

John 13:34
A new commandment I give to you, that you love one another: just as I have loved you, you also are to love one another.

Acts 10:34
So Peter opened his mouth and said: "Truly I understand that God shows no partiality,

Romans 10:12
For there is no distinction between Jew and Greek; for the same Lord is Lord of all, bestowing his riches on all who call on him.

James 2:9
But if you show partiality, you are committing sin and are convicted by the law as transgressors.

Revelation 7:9
After this I looked, and behold, a great multitude that no one could number, from every nation, from all tribes and peoples and languages, standing before the throne and before the Lamb, clothed in white robes, with palm branches in their hands,

Rage

Psalm 37:8
Refrain from anger, and forsake wrath! Fret not yourself; it tends only to evil.

James 1:19-20

Know this, my beloved brothers: let every person be quick to hear, slow to speak, slow to anger; for the anger of man does not produce the righteousness of God.

Proverbs 15:1

A soft answer turns away wrath, but a harsh word stirs up anger.

Colossians 3:8

But now you must put them all away: anger, wrath, malice, slander, and obscene talk from your mouth.

Ephesians 4:31

Let all bitterness and wrath and anger and clamor and slander be put away from you, along with all malice.

Ephesians 4:26

Be angry and do not sin; do not let the sun go down on your anger,

Proverbs 14:29

Whoever is slow to anger has great understanding, but he who has a hasty temper exalts folly.

Proverbs 15:18

A hot-tempered man stirs up strife, but he who is slow to anger quiets contention.

Proverbs 16:32

Whoever is slow to anger is better than the mighty, and he who rules his spirit than he who takes a city.

Ecclesiastes 7:9

Be not quick in your spirit to become angry, for anger lodges in the bosom of fools.

Rape

Deuteronomy 22:28-29

"If a man meets a virgin who is not betrothed, and seizes her and lies with her, and they are found, then the man who lay with her shall give to the father of the young woman fifty shekels of silver, and she shall be his wife, because he has violated her. He may not divorce her all his days.

Deuteronomy 22:23-24

"If there is a betrothed virgin, and a man meets her in the city and lies with her, then you shall bring them both out to the gate of that city, and you shall stone them to death with stones, the young woman because she did not cry for help though she was in the city, and the man because he violated his neighbor's wife. So you shall purge the evil from your midst.

Deuteronomy 22:25-27

"But if in the open country a man meets a young woman who is betrothed, and the man seizes her and lies with her, then only the man who lay with her shall die. But you shall do nothing to the young woman; she has committed no offense punishable by death. For this case is like that of a man attacking and murdering his neighbor, because he met her in the open country, and though the betrothed young woman cried for help there was no one to rescue her.

Exodus 22:16-17

"If a man seduces a virgin who is not betrothed and lies with her, he shall give the bride-price for her and make her his wife. If her father utterly refuses to give her to him, he shall pay money equal to the bride-price for virgins.

Psalm 9:9

The Lord is a stronghold for the oppressed, a stronghold in times of trouble.

Rebellion

1 Samuel 15:23

For rebellion is as the sin of divination, and presumption is as iniquity and idolatry. Because you have rejected the word of the Lord, he has also rejected you from being king."

Proverbs 17:11

An evil man seeks only rebellion, and a cruel messenger will be sent against him.

Psalm 68:6

God settles the solitary in a home; he leads out the prisoners to prosperity, but the rebellious dwell in a parched land.

Deuteronomy 28:47-48

Because you did not serve the Lord your God with joyfulness and gladness of heart, because of the abundance of all things, therefore you shall serve your enemies whom the Lord will send against you, in hunger and thirst, in nakedness, and lacking everything. And he will put a yoke of iron on your neck until he has destroyed you.

Rebuking

Proverbs 27:5

Better is open rebuke than hidden love.

Matthew 18:15-17

"If your brother sins against you, go and tell him his fault, between you and him alone. If he listens to you, you have gained your brother. But if he does not listen, take one or two others along with you, that every charge may be established by the evidence of two or three witnesses. If he refuses to listen to them, tell it to the church. And if he refuses to listen even to the church, let him be to you as a Gentile and a tax collector.

1 Timothy 5:20

As for those who persist in sin, rebuke them in the presence of all, so that the rest may stand in fear.

Galatians 6:1

Brothers, if anyone is caught in any transgression, you who are spiritual should restore him in a spirit of gentleness. Keep watch on yourself, lest you too be tempted.

Titus 2:15

Declare these things; exhort and rebuke with all authority. Let no one disregard you.

2 Timothy 4:2

Preach the word; be ready in season and out of season; reprove, rebuke, and exhort, with complete patience and teaching.

2 Timothy 3:16-17

All Scripture is breathed out by God and profitable for teaching, for reproof, for correction, and for training in righteousness, that the man of God may be competent, equipped for every good work.

James 5:20

Let him know that whoever brings back a sinner from his wandering will save his soul from death and will cover a multitude of sins.

Reconciliation

Ephesians 4:32

Be kind to one another, tenderhearted, forgiving one another, as God in Christ forgave you.

2 Corinthians 5:18

All this is from God, who through Christ reconciled us to himself and gave us the ministry of reconciliation;

Romans 5:10

For if while we were enemies we were reconciled to God by the death of his Son, much more, now that we are reconciled, shall we be saved by his life.

Matthew 18:15-17

"If your brother sins against you, go and tell him his fault, between you and him alone. If he listens to you, you have gained your brother. But if he does not listen, take one or two others along with you, that every charge may be established by the evidence of two or three witnesses. If he refuses to listen to them, tell it to the church. And if he refuses to listen even to the church, let him be to you as a Gentile and a tax collector.

2 Corinthians 5:18-21

All this is from God, who through Christ reconciled us to himself and gave us the ministry of reconciliation; that is, in Christ God was reconciling the world to himself, not counting their trespasses against them, and entrusting to us the message of reconciliation. Therefore, we are ambassadors for Christ, God making his appeal through us. We implore you on behalf of Christ, be reconciled to God. For our sake he made him to be sin who knew no sin, so that in him we might become the righteousness of God.

Matthew 5:23-26

So if you are offering your gift at the altar and there remember that your brother has something against you, leave your gift there before the altar and go. First be reconciled to your brother, and then come and offer your gift. Come to terms quickly with your accuser while you are going with him to court, lest your accuser hand you over to the judge, and the judge to the guard, and you be put in prison. Truly, I say to you, you will never get out until you have paid the last penny.

Colossians 1:20

And through him to reconcile to himself all things, whether on earth or in heaven, making peace by the blood of his cross.

Hebrews 12:14

Strive for peace with everyone, and for the holiness without which no one will see the Lord.

Luke 17:3

Pay attention to yourselves! If your brother sins, rebuke him, and if he repents, forgive him,

Redeem

Ephesians 1:7

In him we have redemption through his blood, the forgiveness of our trespasses, according to the riches of his grace,

Colossians 1:14

In whom we have redemption, the forgiveness of sins.

Galatians 2:20

I have been crucified with Christ. It is no longer I who live, but Christ who lives in me. And the life I now live in the flesh I live by faith in the Son of God, who loved me and gave himself for me.

Titus 2:14

Who gave himself for us to redeem us from all lawlessness and to purify for himself a people for his own possession who are zealous for good works.

Colossians 1:20-22

And through him to reconcile to himself all things, whether on earth or in heaven, making peace by the blood of his cross. And you, who once were alienated and hostile in mind, doing evil deeds, he has now reconciled in his body of flesh by his death, in order to present you holy and blameless and above reproach before him,

Psalm 111:9

He sent redemption to his people; he has commanded his covenant forever. Holy and awesome is his name!

1 Corinthians 1:30

And because of him you are in Christ Jesus, who became to us wisdom from God, righteousness and sanctification and redemption,

Psalm 130:7

O Israel, hope in the Lord! For with the Lord there is steadfast love, and with him is plentiful redemption.

1 Peter 1:18-19
Knowing that you were ransomed from the futile ways inherited from your forefathers, not with perishable things such as silver or gold, but with the precious blood of Christ, like that of a lamb without blemish or spot.

1 John 3:16
By this we know love, that he laid down his life for us, and we ought to lay down our lives for the brothers.

1 Corinthians 6:20
For you were bought with a price. So glorify God in your body.

Regret

Philippians 3:13
Brothers, I do not consider that I have made it my own. But one thing I do: forgetting what lies behind and straining forward to what lies ahead,

2 Corinthians 7:10
For godly grief produces a repentance that leads to salvation without regret, whereas worldly grief produces death.

1 John 1:9
If we confess our sins, he is faithful and just to forgive us our sins and to cleanse us from all unrighteousness.

Philippians 3:13-15
Brothers, I do not consider that I have made it my own. But one thing I do: forgetting what lies behind and straining forward to what lies ahead, I press on toward the goal for the prize of the upward call of God in Christ Jesus. Let those of us who are mature think this way, and if in anything you think otherwise, God will reveal that also to you.

Isaiah 43:18-19
"Remember not the former things, nor consider the things of old. Behold, I am doing a new thing; now it springs forth, do you not perceive it? I will make a way in the wilderness and rivers in the desert.

Mark 11:24
Therefore, I tell you, whatever you ask in prayer, believe that you have received it, and it will be yours.

Reincarnation

Hebrews 9:27
And just as it is appointed for man to die once, and after that comes judgment,

Job 14:10-12
But a man dies and is laid low; man breathes his last, and where is he? As waters fail from a lake and a river wastes away and dries up, so a man lies down and rises not again; till the heavens are no more he will not awake or be roused out of his sleep.

Ecclesiastes 12:7

And the dust returns to the earth as it was, and the spirit returns to God who gave it.

Rejection

Psalm 34:17-20

When the righteous cry for help, the Lord hears and delivers them out of all their troubles. The Lord is near to the brokenhearted and saves the crushed in spirit. Many are the afflictions of the righteous, but the Lord delivers him out of them all. He keeps all his bones; not one of them is broken.

John 15:18

"If the world hates you, know that it has hated me before it hated you.

1 Peter 2:4

As you come to him, a living stone rejected by men but in the sight of God chosen and precious,

Psalm 27:10

For my father and my mother have forsaken me, but the Lord will take me in.

2 Corinthians 12:9

But he said to me, "My grace is sufficient for you, for my power is made perfect in weakness." Therefore I will boast all the more gladly of my weaknesses, so that the power of Christ may rest upon me.

Psalm 94:14

For the Lord will not forsake his people; he will not abandon his heritage;

Isaiah 53:3

He was despised and rejected by men; a man of sorrows, and acquainted with grief; and as one from whom men hide their faces he was despised, and we esteemed him not.

John 1:11

He came to his own, and his own people did not receive him.

1 Peter 5:7

Casting all your anxieties on him, because he cares for you.

Luke 10:16

"The one who hears you hears me, and the one who rejects you rejects me, and the one who rejects me rejects him who sent me."

Psalm 118:22

The stone that the builders rejected has become the cornerstone.

Rejoice

Psalm 118:24
This is the day that the Lord has made; let us rejoice and be glad in it.

Psalm 5:11
But let all who take refuge in you rejoice; let them ever sing for joy, and spread your protection over them, that those who love your name may exult in you.

1 Thessalonians 5:16
Rejoice always,

Romans 5:3-4
More than that, we rejoice in our sufferings, knowing that suffering produces endurance, and endurance produces character, and character produces hope,

Philippians 4:4-7
Rejoice in the Lord always; again I will say, Rejoice. Let your reasonableness be known to everyone. The Lord is at hand; do not be anxious about anything, but in everything by prayer and supplication with thanksgiving let your requests be made known to God. And the peace of God, which surpasses all understanding, will guard your hearts and your minds in Christ Jesus.

Romans 15:13
May the God of hope fill you with all joy and peace in believing, so that by the power of the Holy Spirit you may abound in hope.

Galatians 5:22
But the fruit of the Spirit is love, joy, peace, patience, kindness, goodness, faithfulness,

Relationships

1 Corinthians 13:4-7
Love is patient and kind; love does not envy or boast; it is not arrogant or rude. It does not insist on its own way; it is not irritable or resentful; it does not rejoice at wrongdoing, but rejoices with the truth. Love bears all things, believes all things, hopes all things, endures all things.

Genesis 2:24
Therefore a man shall leave his father and his mother and hold fast to his wife, and they shall become one flesh.

Genesis 2:18
Then the Lord God said, "It is not good that the man should be alone; I will make him a helper fit for him."

1 Corinthians 6:18
Flee from sexual immorality. Every other sin a person commits is outside the body, but the sexually immoral person sins against his own body.

2 Corinthians 6:14

Do not be unequally yoked with unbelievers. For what partnership has righteousness with lawlessness? Or what fellowship has light with darkness?

Romans 12:1-2

I appeal to you therefore, brothers, by the mercies of God, to present your bodies as a living sacrifice, holy and acceptable to God, which is your spiritual worship. Do not be conformed to this world, but be transformed by the renewal of your mind, that by testing you may discern what is the will of God, what is good and acceptable and perfect.

Removing Sin

1 John 1:9

If we confess our sins, he is faithful and just to forgive us our sins and to cleanse us from all unrighteousness.

1 Corinthians 10:13

No temptation has overtaken you that is not common to man. God is faithful, and he will not let you be tempted beyond your ability, but with the temptation he will also provide the way of escape, that you may be able to endure it.

Romans 3:23

For all have sinned and fall short of the glory of God,

2 Corinthians 5:21

For our sake he made him to be sin who knew no sin, so that in him we might become the righteousness of God.

Romans 6:23

For the wages of sin is death, but the free gift of God is eternal life in Christ Jesus our Lord.

Romans 5:8

But God shows his love for us in that while we were still sinners, Christ died for us.

Galatians 5:16

But I say, walk by the Spirit, and you will not gratify the desires of the flesh.

Matthew 18:15

"If your brother sins against you, go and tell him his fault, between you and him alone. If he listens to you, you have gained your brother.

Proverbs 28:13

Whoever conceals his transgressions will not prosper, but he who confesses and forsakes them will obtain mercy.

Galatians 5:19-21

Now the works of the flesh are evident: sexual immorality, impurity, sensuality, idolatry, sorcery, enmity, strife, jealousy, fits of anger, rivalries, dissensions, divisions, envy, drunkenness, orgies, and things like these. I warn you, as I warned you before, that those who do such things will not inherit the kingdom of God.

James 4:17

So whoever knows the right thing to do and fails to do it, for him it is sin.

Repentance

Acts 3:19

Repent therefore, and turn again, that your sins may be blotted out,

2 Peter 3:9

The Lord is not slow to fulfill his promise as some count slowness, but is patient toward you, not wishing that any should perish, but that all should reach repentance.

Matthew 4:17

From that time Jesus began to preach, saying, "Repent, for the kingdom of heaven is at hand."

Acts 2:38

And Peter said to them, "Repent and be baptized every one of you in the name of Jesus Christ for the forgiveness of your sins, and you will receive the gift of the Holy Spirit.

Acts 17:30

The times of ignorance God overlooked, but now he commands all people everywhere to repent,

Matthew 3:8

Bear fruit in keeping with repentance.

Romans 2:4

Or do you presume on the riches of his kindness and forbearance and patience, not knowing that God's kindness is meant to lead you to repentance?

1 John 1:9

If we confess our sins, he is faithful and just to forgive us our sins and to cleanse us from all unrighteousness.

2 Chronicles 7:14

If my people who are called by my name humble themselves, and pray and seek my face and turn from their wicked ways, then I will hear from heaven and will forgive their sin and heal their land.

Acts 11:18

When they heard these things they fell silent. And they glorified God, saying, "Then to the Gentiles also God has granted repentance that leads to life."

Luke 13:3

No, I tell you; but unless you repent, you will all likewise perish.

Luke 5:32

I have not come to call the righteous but sinners to repentance."

Revelation 2:5

Remember therefore from where you have fallen; repent, and do the works you did at first. If not, I will come to you and remove your lampstand from its place, unless you repent.

Proverbs 28:13

Whoever conceals his transgressions will not prosper, but he who confesses and forsakes them will obtain mercy.

2 Timothy 2:25

Correcting his opponents with gentleness. God may perhaps grant them repentance leading to a knowledge of the truth,

Acts 5:31

God exalted him at his right hand as Leader and Savior, to give repentance to Israel and forgiveness of sins.

Mark 1:15

And saying, "The time is fulfilled, and the kingdom of God is at hand; repent and believe in the gospel."

Revelation 3:19

Those whom I love, I reprove and discipline, so be zealous and repent.

Matthew 3:2

"Repent, for the kingdom of heaven is at hand."

Luke 15:7

Just so, I tell you, there will be more joy in heaven over one sinner who repents than over ninety-nine righteous persons who need no repentance.

2 Corinthians 7:10

For godly grief produces a repentance that leads to salvation without regret, whereas worldly grief produces death.

Reputation

Proverbs 22:1

A good name is to be chosen rather than great riches, and favor is better than silver or gold.

Ecclesiastes 7:1

A good name is better than precious ointment, and the day of death than the day of birth.

Philippians 2:7

But made himself nothing, taking the form of a servant, being born in the likeness of men.

1 Peter 2:12

Keep your conduct among the Gentiles honorable, so that when they speak against you as evildoers, they may see your good deeds and glorify God on the day of visitation.

Ecclesiastes 10:1

Dead flies make the perfumer's ointment give off a stench; so a little folly outweighs wisdom and honor.

Matthew 5:16

In the same way, let your light shine before others, so that they may see your good works and give glory to your Father who is in heaven.

1 Timothy 3:7

Moreover, he must be well thought of by outsiders, so that he may not fall into disgrace, into a snare of the devil.

Proverbs 10:7

The memory of the righteous is a blessing, but the name of the wicked will rot.

Resentment

Mark 11:25
And whenever you stand praying, forgive, if you have anything against anyone, so that your Father also who is in heaven may forgive you your trespasses."

1 Peter 5:10
And after you have suffered a little while, the God of all grace, who has called you to his eternal glory in Christ, will himself restore, confirm, strengthen, and establish you.

Responsibility

Ephesians 4:31-32

Let all bitterness and wrath and anger and clamor and slander be put away from you, along with all malice. Be kind to one another, tenderhearted, forgiving one another, as God in Christ forgave you.

Proverbs 15:1

A soft answer turns away wrath, but a harsh word stirs up anger.

Matthew 18:15

"If your brother sins against you, go and tell him his fault, between you and him alone. If he listens to you, you have gained your brother.

Colossians 3:13

Bearing with one another and, if one has a complaint against another, forgiving each other; as the Lord has forgiven you, so you also must forgive.

Matthew 5:9

"Blessed are the peacemakers, for they shall be called sons of God.

Ephesians 4:26

Be angry and do not sin; do not let the sun go down on your anger,

Responsibility

Galatians 6:5

For each will have to bear his own load.

1 Timothy 5:8

But if anyone does not provide for his relatives, and especially for members of his household, he has denied the faith and is worse than an unbeliever.

1 Corinthians 3:8

He who plants and he who waters are one, and each will receive his wages according to his labor.

Romans 12:6-8

Having gifts that differ according to the grace given to us, let us use them: if prophecy, in proportion to our faith; if service, in our serving; the one who teaches, in his teaching; the one who exhorts, in his exhortation; the one who contributes, in generosity; the one who leads, with zeal; the one who does acts of mercy, with cheerfulness.

Proverbs 22:6

Train up a child in the way he should go; even when he is old he will not depart from it.

Ezekiel 18:20

The soul who sins shall die. The son shall not suffer for the iniquity of the father, nor the father suffer for the iniquity of the son. The righteousness of the righteous shall be upon himself, and the wickedness of the wicked shall be upon himself.

Luke 12:47-48

And that servant who knew his master's will but did not get ready or act according to his will, will receive a severe beating. But the one who did not know, and did what deserved a beating, will receive a light beating. Everyone to whom much was given, of him much will be required, and from him to whom they entrusted much, they will demand the more.

Matthew 12:37

For by your words you will be justified, and by your words you will be condemned."

Luke 16:10

"One who is faithful in a very little is also faithful in much, and one who is dishonest in a very little is also dishonest in much.

Rest

Matthew 11:28-30

Come to me, all who labor and are heavy laden, and I will give you rest. Take my yoke upon you, and learn from me, for I am gentle and lowly in heart, and you will find rest for your souls. For my yoke is easy, and my burden is light."

Exodus 33:14

And he said, "My presence will go with you, and I will give you rest."

Mark 6:31

And he said to them, "Come away by yourselves to a desolate place and rest a while." For many were coming and going, and they had no leisure even to eat.

Psalm 127:2

It is in vain that you rise up early and go late to rest, eating the bread of anxious toil; for he gives to his beloved sleep.

Psalm 4:8

In peace I will both lie down and sleep; for you alone, O Lord, make me dwell in safety.

Psalm 37:7

Be still before the Lord and wait patiently for him; fret not yourself over the one who prospers in his way, over the man who carries out evil devices!

Psalm 46:10

"Be still, and know that I am God. I will be exalted among the nations, I will be exalted in the earth!"

Philippians 4:6-7

Do not be anxious about anything, but in everything by prayer and supplication with thanksgiving let your requests be made known to God. And the peace of God, which surpasses all understanding, will guard your hearts and your minds in Christ Jesus.

Genesis 2:2-3

And on the seventh day God finished his work that he had done, and he rested on the seventh day from all his work that he had done. So God blessed the seventh day and made it holy, because on it God rested from all his work that he had done in creation.

Isaiah 30:15

For thus said the Lord God, the Holy One of Israel, "In returning and rest you shall be saved; in quietness and in trust shall be your strength." But you were unwilling,

Hebrews 4:9-10

So then, there remains a Sabbath rest for the people of God, for whoever has entered God's rest has also rested from his works as God did from his.

Jeremiah 6:16

Thus says the Lord: "Stand by the roads, and look, and ask for the ancient paths, where the good way is; and walk in it, and find rest for your souls. But they said, 'We will not walk in it.'

Restoration

Joel 2:25-26

I will restore to you the years that the swarming locust has eaten, the hopper, the destroyer, and the cutter, my great army, which I sent among you. "You shall eat in plenty and be satisfied, and praise the name of the Lord your God, who has dealt wondrously with you. And my people shall never again be put to shame.

Jeremiah 30:17

For I will restore health to you, and your wounds I will heal, declares the Lord, because they have called you an outcast: 'It is Zion, for whom no one cares!'

Psalm 51:12

Restore to me the joy of your salvation, and uphold me with a willing spirit.

Isaiah 61:7

Instead of your shame there shall be a double portion; instead of dishonor they shall rejoice in their lot; therefore in their land they shall possess a double portion; they shall have everlasting joy.

Job 42:10

And the Lord restored the fortunes of Job, when he had prayed for his friends. And the Lord gave Job twice as much as he had before.

Acts 3:19-21

Repent therefore, and turn again, that your sins may be blotted out, that times of refreshing may come from the presence of the Lord, and that he may send the Christ appointed for you, Jesus, whom heaven must receive until the time for restoring all the things about which God spoke by the mouth of his holy prophets long ago.

1 Peter 5:10

And after you have suffered a little while, the God of all grace, who has called you to his eternal glory in Christ, will himself restore, confirm, strengthen, and establish you.

1 John 5:4

For everyone who has been born of God overcomes the world. And this is the victory that has overcome the world—our faith.

Mark 11:24

Therefore I tell you, whatever you ask in prayer, believe that you have received it, and it will be yours.

Resurrection

John 11:25
Jesus said to her, "I am the resurrection and the life. Whoever believes in me, though he die, yet shall he live,

1 Peter 1:3
Blessed be the God and Father of our Lord Jesus Christ! According to his great mercy, he has caused us to be born again to a living hope through the resurrection of Jesus Christ from the dead,

1 Thessalonians 4:14
For since we believe that Jesus died and rose again, even so, through Jesus, God will bring with him those who have fallen asleep.

Romans 8:11
If the Spirit of him who raised Jesus from the dead dwells in you, he who raised Christ Jesus from the dead will also give life to your mortal bodies through his Spirit who dwells in you.

John 6:40
For this is the will of my Father, that everyone who looks on the Son and believes in him should have eternal life, and I will raise him up on the last day."

John 11:25-26
Jesus said to her, "I am the resurrection and the life. Whoever believes in me, though he die, yet shall he live, and everyone who lives and believes in me shall never die. Do you believe this?"

1 Corinthians 6:14
And God raised the Lord and will also raise us up by his power.

Romans 6:4
We were buried therefore with him by baptism into death, in order that, just as Christ was raised from the dead by the glory of the Father, we too might walk in newness of life.

Luke 14:14
And you will be blessed, because they cannot repay you. For you will be repaid at the resurrection of the just."

Isaiah 26:19
Your dead shall live; their bodies shall rise. You who dwell in the dust, awake and sing for joy! For your dew is a dew of light, and the earth will give birth to the dead.

1 Thessalonians 4:16
For the Lord himself will descend from heaven with a cry of command, with the voice of an archangel, and with the sound of the trumpet of God. And the dead in Christ will rise first.

Daniel 12:2

And many of those who sleep in the dust of the earth shall awake, some to everlasting life, and some to shame and everlasting contempt.

Acts 3:15

And you killed the Author of life, whom God raised from the dead. To this we are witnesses.

John 14:19

Yet a little while and the world will see me no more, but you will see me. Because I live, you also will live.

Revenge

Romans 12:17-21

Repay no one evil for evil, but give thought to do what is honorable in the sight of all. If possible, so far as it depends on you, live peaceably with all. Beloved, never avenge yourselves, but leave it to the wrath of God, for it is written, "Vengeance is mine, I will repay, says the Lord." To the contrary, "if your enemy is hungry, feed him; if he is thirsty, give him something to drink; for by so doing you will heap burning coals on his head." Do not be overcome by evil, but overcome evil with good.

1 Peter 3:9

Do not repay evil for evil or reviling for reviling, but on the contrary, bless, for to this you were called, that you may obtain a blessing.

Matthew 5:38-39

"You have heard that it was said, 'An eye for an eye and a tooth for a tooth.' But I say to you, Do not resist the one who is evil. But if anyone slaps you on the right cheek, turn to him the other also.

Proverbs 24:29

Do not say, "I will do to him as he has done to me; I will pay the man back for what he has done."

Leviticus 19:18

You shall not take vengeance or bear a grudge against the sons of your own people, but you shall love your neighbor as yourself: I am the Lord.

1 Thessalonians 5:15

See that no one repays anyone evil for evil, but always seek to do good to one another and to everyone.

Romans 12:17

Repay no one evil for evil, but give thought to do what is honorable in the sight of all.

Mark 11:25

And whenever you stand praying, forgive, if you have anything against anyone, so that your Father also who is in heaven may forgive you your trespasses."

Reward

James 1:12
Blessed is the man who remains steadfast under trial, for when he has stood the test he will receive the crown of life, which God has promised to those who love him.

Colossians 3:23-24
Whatever you do, work heartily, as for the Lord and not for men, knowing that from the Lord you will receive the inheritance as your reward. You are serving the Lord Christ.

Matthew 16:27
For the Son of Man is going to come with his angels in the glory of his Father, and then he will repay each person according to what he has done.

Righteousness

1 John 3:7
Little children, let no one deceive you. Whoever practices righteousness is righteous, as he is righteous.

1 John 2:29
If you know that he is righteous, you may be sure that everyone who practices righteousness has been born of him.

Romans 5:1-5
Therefore, since we have been justified by faith, we have peace with God through our Lord Jesus Christ. Through him we have also obtained access by faith into this grace in which we stand, and we rejoice in hope of the glory of God. More than that, we rejoice in our sufferings, knowing that suffering produces endurance, and endurance produces character, and character produces hope, and hope does not put us to shame, because God's love has been poured into our hearts through the Holy Spirit who has been given to us.

Psalm 106:3
Blessed are they who observe justice, who do righteousness at all times!

Isaiah 33:15-17
He who walks righteously and speaks uprightly, who despises the gain of oppressions, who shakes his hands, lest they hold a bribe, who stops his ears from hearing of bloodshed and shuts his eyes from looking on evil, he will dwell on the heights; his place of defense will be the fortresses of rocks; his bread will be given him; his water will be sure. Your eyes will behold the king in his beauty; they will see a land that stretches afar.

Matthew 5:20
For I tell you, unless your righteousness exceeds that of the scribes and Pharisees, you will never enter the kingdom of heaven.

1 Peter 3:14

But even if you should suffer for righteousness' sake, you will be blessed. Have no fear of them, nor be troubled,

2 Corinthians 5:21

For our sake he made him to be sin who knew no sin, so that in him we might become the righteousness of God.

1 Peter 5:10

And after you have suffered a little while, the God of all grace, who has called you to his eternal glory in Christ, will himself restore, confirm, strengthen, and establish you.

Romans 10:4

For Christ is the end of the law for righteousness to everyone who believes.

2 Timothy 2:22

So flee youthful passions and pursue righteousness, faith, love, and peace, along with those who call on the Lord from a pure heart.

1 John 5:18

We know that everyone who has been born of God does not keep on sinning, but he who was born of God protects him, and the evil one does not touch him.

Ezekiel 18:5-9

"If a man is righteous and does what is just and right— if he does not eat upon the mountains or lift up his eyes to the idols of the house of Israel, does not defile his neighbor's wife or approach a woman in her time of menstrual impurity, does not oppress anyone, but restores to the debtor his pledge, commits no robbery, gives his bread to the hungry and covers the naked with a garment, does not lend at interest or take any profit, withholds his hand from injustice, executes true justice between man and man, walks in my statutes, and keeps my rules by acting faithfully—he is righteous; he shall surely live, declares the Lord God.

Romans 8:4-6

In order that the righteous requirement of the law might be fulfilled in us, who walk not according to the flesh but according to the Spirit. For those who live according to the flesh set their minds on the things of the flesh, but those who live according to the Spirit set their minds on the things of the Spirit. For to set the mind on the flesh is death, but to set the mind on the Spirit is life and peace.

Philippians 3:9

And be found in him, not having a righteousness of my own that comes from the law, but that which comes through faith in Christ, the righteousness from God that depends on faith—

Matthew 6:33

But seek first the kingdom of God and his righteousness, and all these things will be added to you
.

Sabbath

Exodus 20:8-11

"Remember the Sabbath day, to keep it holy. Six days you shall labor, and do all your work, but the seventh day is a Sabbath to the Lord your God. On it you shall not do any work, you, or your son, or your daughter, your male servant, or your female servant, or your livestock, or the sojourner who is within your gates. For in six days the Lord made heaven and earth, the sea, and all that is in them, and rested on the seventh day. Therefore the Lord blessed the Sabbath day and made it holy.

Mark 2:27

And he said to them, "The Sabbath was made for man, not man for the Sabbath.

Exodus 31:13

"You are to speak to the people of Israel and say, 'Above all you shall keep my Sabbaths, for this is a sign between me and you throughout your generations, that you may know that I, the Lord, sanctify you.

Genesis 2:3

So God blessed the seventh day and made it holy, because on it God rested from all his work that he had done in creation.

Luke 23:56

Then they returned and prepared spices and ointments. On the Sabbath they rested according to the commandment.

Isaiah 58:13

"If you turn back your foot from the Sabbath, from doing your pleasure on my holy day, and call the Sabbath a delight and the holy day of the Lord honorable; if you honor it, not going your own ways, or seeking your own pleasure, or talking idly;

Sacrifice

Hebrews 13:16 Do not neglect to do good and to share what you have, for such sacrifices are pleasing to God.

Romans 12:1-2

I appeal to you therefore, brothers, by the mercies of God, to present your bodies as a living sacrifice, holy and acceptable to God, which is your spiritual worship. Do not be conformed to this world, but be transformed by the renewal of your mind, that by testing you may discern what is the will of God, what is good and acceptable and perfect.

Romans 5:8

But God shows his love for us in that while we were still sinners, Christ died for us.

John 3:16

"For God so loved the world, that he gave his only Son, that whoever believes in him should not perish but have eternal life.

Hosea 6:6
For I desire steadfast love and not sacrifice, the knowledge of God rather than burnt offerings.

Proverbs 21:3
To do righteousness and justice is more acceptable to the Lord than sacrifice.

John 15:12-14
"This is my commandment, that you love one another as I have loved you. Greater love has no one than this, that someone lay down his life for his friends. You are my friends if you do what I command you.

Hebrews 13:15 ESV / 109 helpful votes
Through him then let us continually offer up a sacrifice of praise to God, that is, the fruit of lips that acknowledge his name.

Sadness

Psalm 34:18
The Lord is near to the brokenhearted and saves the crushed in spirit.

John 14:1
"Let not your hearts be troubled. Believe in God; believe also in me.

Psalm 55:22
Cast your burden on the Lord, and he will sustain you; he will never permit the righteous to be moved.

Jeremiah 29:11
For I know the plans I have for you, declares the Lord, plans for welfare and not for evil, to give you a future and a hope.

Psalm 18:2
The Lord is my rock and my fortress and my deliverer, my God, my rock, in whom I take refuge, my shield, and the horn of my salvation, my stronghold.

1 Peter 5:7
Casting all your anxieties on him, because he cares for you.

James 5:13
Is anyone among you suffering? Let him pray. Is anyone cheerful? Let him sing praise.

Safety

Psalm 4:8
In peace I will both lie down and sleep; for you alone, O Lord, make me dwell in safety.

Joshua 1:9
Have I not commanded you? Be strong and courageous. Do not be frightened, and do not be dismayed, for the Lord your God is with you wherever you go."

Ephesians 6:11

Put on the whole armor of God, that you may be able to stand against the schemes of the devil.

Proverbs 11:14

Where there is no guidance, a people falls, but in an abundance of counselors there is safety.

Psalm 28:7

The Lord is my strength and my shield; in him my heart trusts, and I am helped; my heart exults, and with my song I give thanks to him.

Salvation

Ephesians 2:8-9

For by grace you have been saved through faith. And this is not your own doing; it is the gift of God, not a result of works, so that no one may boast.

Titus 3:5

He saved us, not because of works done by us in righteousness, but according to his own mercy, by the washing of regeneration and renewal of the Holy Spirit,

Romans 10:9

Because, if you confess with your mouth that Jesus is Lord and believe in your heart that God raised him from the dead, you will be saved.

Acts 4:12

And there is salvation in no one else, for there is no other name under heaven given among men by which we must be saved."

Ephesians 2:8

For by grace you have been saved through faith. And this is not your own doing; it is the gift of God,

John 14:6

Jesus said to him, "I am the way, and the truth, and the life. No one comes to the Father except through me.

Matthew 7:21

"Not everyone who says to me, 'Lord, Lord,' will enter the kingdom of heaven, but the one who does the will of my Father who is in heaven.

John 6:44

No one can come to me unless the Father who sent me draws him. And I will raise him up on the last day.

Acts 16:30-33

Then he brought them out and said, "Sirs, what must I do to be saved?" And they said, "Believe in the Lord Jesus, and you will be saved, you and your household." And they spoke the word of the Lord to him and to all who were in his house. And he took them the same hour of the night and washed their wounds; and he was baptized at once, he and all his family.

Same-Sex Marriage

Leviticus 18:22
You shall not lie with a male as with a woman; it is an abomination.

Leviticus 20:13
If a man lies with a male as with a woman, both of them have committed an abomination; they shall surely be put to death; their blood is upon them.

Romans 1:26-27
For this reason God gave them up to dishonorable passions. For their women exchanged natural relations for those that are contrary to nature; and the men likewise gave up natural relations with women and were consumed with passion for one another, men committing shameless acts with men and receiving in themselves the due penalty for their error.

Mark 10:6-9
But from the beginning of creation, 'God made them male and female.' 'Therefore a man shall leave his father and mother and hold fast to his wife, and the two shall become one flesh.' So they are no longer two but one flesh. What therefore God has joined together, let not man separate."

1 Corinthians 6:9-11
Or do you not know that the unrighteous will not inherit the kingdom of God? Do not be deceived: neither the sexually immoral, nor idolaters, nor adulterers, nor men who practice homosexuality, nor thieves, nor the greedy, nor drunkards, nor revilers, nor swindlers will inherit the kingdom of God. And such were some of you. But you were washed, you were sanctified, you were justified in the name of the Lord Jesus Christ and by the Spirit of our God.

Genesis 2:24
Therefore a man shall leave his father and his mother and hold fast to his wife, and they shall become one flesh.

1 Timothy 1:9-10
Understanding this, that the law is not laid down for the just but for the lawless and disobedient, for the ungodly and sinners, for the unholy and profane, for those who strike their fathers and mothers, for murderers, the sexually immoral, men who practice homosexuality, enslavers, liars, perjurers, and whatever else is contrary to sound doctrine,

Matthew 19:4-6
He answered, "Have you not read that he who created them from the beginning made them male and female, and said, 'Therefore a man shall leave his father and his mother and hold fast to his wife, and the two shall become one flesh'? So they are no longer two but one flesh. What therefore God has joined together, let not man separate."

1 Corinthians 6:9-10

Or do you not know that the unrighteous will not inherit the kingdom of God? Do not be deceived: neither the sexually immoral, nor idolaters, nor adulterers, nor men who practice homosexuality, nor thieves, nor the greedy, nor drunkards, nor revilers, nor swindlers will inherit the kingdom of God.

Sanctification

2 Timothy 2:21

Therefore, if anyone cleanses himself from what is dishonorable, he will be a vessel for honorable use, set apart as holy, useful to the master of the house, ready for every good work.

1 Thessalonians 5:23

Now may the God of peace himself sanctify you completely, and may your whole spirit and soul and body be kept blameless at the coming of our Lord Jesus Christ.

John 17:17

Sanctify them in the truth; your word is truth.

Galatians 2:20

I have been crucified with Christ. It is no longer I who live, but Christ who lives in me. And the life I now live in the flesh I live by faith in the Son of God, who loved me and gave himself for me.

2 Thessalonians 2:13

But we ought always to give thanks to God for you, brothers beloved by the Lord, because God chose you as the firstfruits to be saved, through sanctification by the Spirit and belief in the truth.

2 Corinthians 5:17

Therefore, if anyone is in Christ, he is a new creation. The old has passed away; behold, the new has come.

1 Thessalonians 4:3

For this is the will of God, your sanctification: that you abstain from sexual immorality;

1 Corinthians 6:11

And such were some of you. But you were washed, you were sanctified, you were justified in the name of the Lord Jesus Christ and by the Spirit of our God.

Romans 6:6

We know that our old self was crucified with him in order that the body of sin might be brought to nothing, so that we would no longer be enslaved to sin.

Hebrews 13:12

So Jesus also suffered outside the gate in order to sanctify the people through his own blood.

Hebrews 10:14 ESV / 101 helpful votes

For by a single offering he has perfected for all time those who are being sanctified.

Satan.

1 Peter 5:8
Be sober-minded; be watchful. Your adversary the devil prowls around like a roaring lion, seeking someone to devour.

1 John 3:8
Whoever makes a practice of sinning is of the devil, for the devil has been sinning from the beginning. The reason the Son of God appeared was to destroy the works of the devil.

John 8:44
You are of your father the devil, and your will is to do your father's desires. He was a murderer from the beginning, and has nothing to do with the truth, because there is no truth in him. When he lies, he speaks out of his own character, for he is a liar and the father of lies.

2 Corinthians 11:14
And no wonder, for even Satan disguises himself as an angel of light.

James 4:7
Submit yourselves therefore to God. Resist the devil, and he will flee from you.

Revelation 12:9
And the great dragon was thrown down, that ancient serpent, who is called the devil and Satan, the deceiver of the whole world—he was thrown down to the earth, and his angels were thrown down with him.

2 Corinthians 11:3
But I am afraid that as the serpent deceived Eve by his cunning, your thoughts will be led astray from a sincere and pure devotion to Christ.

Romans 16:20
The God of peace will soon crush Satan under your feet. The grace of our Lord Jesus Christ be with you.

2 Corinthians 4:4
In their case the god of this world has blinded the minds of the unbelievers, to keep them from seeing the light of the gospel of the glory of Christ, who is the image of God.

John 10:10
The thief comes only to steal and kill and destroy. I came that they may have life and have it abundantly.

Ephesians 6:11
Put on the whole armor of God, that you may be able to stand against the schemes of the devil.

Luke 10:18
And he said to them, "I saw Satan fall like lightning from heaven.

Ephesians 4:27
And give no opportunity to the devil.

Matthew 16:23
But he turned and said to Peter, "Get behind me, Satan! You are a hindrance to me. For you are not setting your mind on the things of God, but on the things of man."

Seasons

Daniel 2:21
He changes times and seasons; he removes kings and sets up kings; he gives wisdom to the wise and knowledge to those who have understanding;

Genesis 8:22
While the earth remains, seedtime and harvest, cold and heat, summer and winter, day and night, shall not cease."

Galatians 6:9
And let us not grow weary of doing good, for in due season we will reap, if we do not give up.

Acts 1:7
He said to them, "It is not for you to know times or seasons that the Father has fixed by his own authority.

Psalm 104:19
He made the moon to mark the seasons; the sun knows its time for setting.

Psalm 1:3 ES
He is like a tree planted by streams of water that yields its fruit in its season, and its leaf does not wither. In all that he does, he prospers.

Genesis 1:14
And God said, "Let there be lights in the expanse of the heavens to separate the day from the night. And let them be for signs and for seasons, and for days and years,

1 Thessalonians 5:1
Now concerning the times and the seasons, brothers, you have no need to have anything written to you.

Isaiah 55:10-11
"For as the rain and the snow come down from heaven and do not return there but water the earth, making it bring forth and sprout, giving seed to the sower and bread to the eater, so shall my word be that goes out from my mouth; it shall not return to me empty, but it shall accomplish that which I purpose, and shall succeed in the thing for which I sent it.

Matthew 24:32
"From the fig tree learn its lesson: as soon as its branch becomes tender and puts out its leaves, you know that summer is near.

1 Peter 1:6
In this you rejoice, though now for a little while, if necessary, you have been grieved by various trials,

Song of Solomon 2:11-13
For behold, the winter is past; the rain is over and gone. The flowers appear on the earth, the time of singing has come, and the voice of the turtledove is heard in our land. The fig tree ripens its figs, and the vines are in blossom; they give forth fragrance. Arise, my love, my beautiful one, and come away.

Exodus 12:2
"This month shall be for you the beginning of months. It shall be the first month of the year for you.

Ecclesiastes 3:1
For everything there is a season, and a time for every matter under heaven:

Self-Care

1 Corinthians 6:19-20
Or do you not know that your body is a temple of the Holy Spirit within you, whom you have from God? You are not your own, for you were bought with a price. So glorify God in your body.

3 John 1:2
Beloved, I pray that all may go well with you and that you may be in good health, as it goes well with your soul.

1 Corinthians 3:16-17
Do you not know that you are God's temple and that God's Spirit dwells in you? If anyone destroys God's temple, God will destroy him. For God's temple is holy, and you are that temple.

Hebrews 4:9-11
So then, there remains a Sabbath rest for the people of God, for whoever has entered God's rest has also rested from his works as God did from his. Let us therefore strive to enter that rest, so that no one may fall by the same sort of disobedience.

Philippians 4:13
I can do all things through him who strengthens me.

Self-Confidence

Philippians 4:13
I can do all things through him who strengthens me.

2 Timothy 1:7
For God gave us a spirit not of fear but of power and love and self-control.

Hebrews 10:35-36

Therefore do not throw away your confidence, which has a great reward. For you have need of endurance, so that when you have done the will of God you may receive what is promised.

Hebrews 13:6

So we can confidently say, "The Lord is my helper; I will not fear; what can man do to me?"

Joshua 1:9

Have I not commanded you? Be strong and courageous. Do not be frightened, and do not be dismayed, for the Lord your God is with you wherever you go."

Psalm 139:13-14

For you formed my inward parts; you knitted me together in my mother's womb. I praise you, for I am fearfully and wonderfully made. Wonderful are your works; my soul knows it very well.

Psalm 27:3

Though an army encamp against me, my heart shall not fear; though war arise against me, yet I will be confident.

Ephesians 4:29

Let no corrupting talk come out of your mouths, but only such as is good for building up, as fits the occasion, that it may give grace to those who hear.

Proverbs 3:6

In all your ways acknowledge him, and he will make straight your paths.

1 John 4:18

There is no fear in love, but perfect love casts out fear. For fear has to do with punishment, and whoever fears has not been perfected in love.

Psalm 138:8

The Lord will fulfill his purpose for me; your steadfast love, O Lord, endures forever. Do not forsake the work of your hands.

Self-Control

Proverbs 25:28

A man without self-control is like a city broken into and left without walls.

Titus 1:8

But hospitable, a lover of good, self-controlled, upright, holy, and disciplined.

2 Timothy 1:7

For God gave us a spirit not of fear but of power and love and self-control.

1 Peter 4:7

The end of all things is at hand; therefore, be self-controlled and sober-minded for the sake of your prayers.

Galatians 5:22-23

But the fruit of the Spirit is love, joy, peace, patience, kindness, goodness, faithfulness, gentleness, self-control; against such things there is no law.

Proverbs 16:32

Whoever is slow to anger is better than the mighty, and he who rules his spirit than he who takes a city.

2 Peter 1:5-6

For this very reason, make every effort to supplement your faith with virtue, and virtue with knowledge, and knowledge with self-control, and self-control with steadfastness, and steadfastness with godliness,

Titus 2:6

Likewise, urge the younger men to be self-controlled.

Self-Defense

Luke 11:21

When a strong man, fully armed, guards his own palace, his goods are safe;

Exodus 22:2-3

If a thief is found breaking in and is struck so that he dies, there shall be no bloodguilt for him, but if the sun has risen on him, there shall be bloodguilt for him. He shall surely pay. If he has nothing, then he shall be sold for his theft.

Self-Denial

Luke 9:23-24

And he said to all, "If anyone would come after me, let him deny himself and take up his cross daily and follow me. For whoever would save his life will lose it, but whoever loses his life for my sake will save it.

Titus 2:11-12

For the grace of God has appeared, bringing salvation for all people, training us to renounce ungodliness and worldly passions, and to live self-controlled, upright, and godly lives in the present age,

Galatians 2:20

I have been crucified with Christ. It is no longer I who live, but Christ who lives in me. And the life I now live in the flesh I live by faith in the Son of God, who loved me and gave himself for me.

Luke 9:23

And he said to all, "If anyone would come after me, let him deny himself and take up his cross daily and follow me.

Self-Destruction

Proverbs 16:18
Pride goes before destruction, and a haughty spirit before a fall.

Proverbs 18:12
Before destruction a man's heart is haughty, but humility comes before honor.

Self-discipline

Hebrews 12:11
For the moment all discipline seems painful rather than pleasant, but later it yields the peaceful fruit of righteousness to those who have been trained by it.

Proverbs 25:28
A man without self-control is like a city broken into and left without walls.

1 Corinthians 9:24-27
Do you not know that in a race all the runners run, but only one receives the prize? So run that you may obtain it. Every athlete exercises self-control in all things. They do it to receive a perishable wreath, but we an imperishable. So I do not run aimlessly; I do not box as one beating the air. But I discipline my body and keep it under control, lest after preaching to others I myself should be disqualified.

2 Timothy 1:7
For God gave us a spirit not of fear but of power and love and self-control.

Galatians 5:22-23
But the fruit of the Spirit is love, joy, peace, patience, kindness, goodness, faithfulness, gentleness, self-control; against such things there is no law.

Proverbs 13:4
The soul of the sluggard craves and gets nothing, while the soul of the diligent is richly supplied.

Titus 2:11-14
For the grace of God has appeared, bringing salvation for all people, training us to renounce ungodliness and worldly passions, and to live self-controlled, upright, and godly lives in the present age, waiting for our blessed hope, the appearing of the glory of our great God and Savior Jesus Christ, who gave himself for us to redeem us from all lawlessness and to purify for himself a people for his own possession who are zealous for good works.

Self-Doubt

Jeremiah 29:11
For I know the plans I have for you, declares the Lord, plans for welfare and not for evil, to give you a future and a hope.

2 Timothy 1:7
For God gave us a spirit not of fear but of power and love and self-control.

Ephesians 6:10
Finally, be strong in the Lord and in the strength of his might.

Psalm 118:24
This is the day that the Lord has made; let us rejoice and be glad in it.

John 3:16
"For God so loved the world, that he gave his only Son, that whoever believes in him should not perish but have eternal life.

Ruth 3:11
And now, my daughter, do not fear. I will do for you all that you ask, for all my fellow townsmen know that you are a worthy woman.

Philippians 2:13
For it is God who works in you, both to will and to work for his good pleasure.

Self-Love

Ephesians 5:29
For no one ever hated his own flesh, but nourishes and cherishes it, just as Christ does the church,

2 Timothy 3:1-5
But understand this, that in the last days there will come times of difficulty. For people will be lovers of self, lovers of money, proud, arrogant, abusive, disobedient to their parents, ungrateful, unholy, heartless, unappeasable, slanderous, without self-control, brutal, not loving good, treacherous, reckless, swollen with conceit, lovers of pleasure rather than lovers of God, having the appearance of godliness, but denying its power. Avoid such people.

Matthew 22:37-39
And he said to him, "You shall love the Lord your God with all your heart and with all your soul and with all your mind. This is the great and first commandment. And a second is like it: You shall love your neighbor as yourself.

1 Corinthians 13:4-7
Love is patient and kind; love does not envy or boast; it is not arrogant or rude. It does not insist on its own way; it is not irritable or resentful; it does not rejoice at wrongdoing, but rejoices with the truth. Love bears all things, believes all things, hopes all things, endures all things.

Mark 12:31
The second is this: 'You shall love your neighbor as yourself.' There is no other commandment greater than these."

Psalm 139:14

I praise you, for I am fearfully and wonderfully made. Wonderful are your works; my soul knows it very well.

1 John 4:16

So we have come to know and to believe the love that God has for us. God is love, and whoever abides in love abides in God, and God abides in him.

Philippians 2:3

Do nothing from rivalry or conceit, but in humility count others more significant than yourselves.

Self-Pity

1 Thessalonians 5:18

Give thanks in all circumstances; for this is the will of God in Christ Jesus for you.

Romans 12:2

Do not be conformed to this world, but be transformed by the renewal of your mind, that by testing you may discern what is the will of God, what is good and acceptable and perfect.

Matthew 11:28-30

Come to me, all who labor and are heavy laden, and I will give you rest. Take my yoke upon you, and learn from me, for I am gentle and lowly in heart, and you will find rest for your souls. For my yoke is easy, and my burden is light."

James 5:13

Is anyone among you suffering? Let him pray. Is anyone cheerful? Let him sing praise.

Self-Respect

1 Corinthians 6:20

For you were bought with a price. So glorify God in your body.

2 Corinthians 5:17

Therefore, if anyone is in Christ, he is a new creation. The old has passed away; behold, the new has come.

Romans 12:2-3

Do not be conformed to this world, but be transformed by the renewal of your mind, that by testing you may discern what is the will of God, what is good and acceptable and perfect. For by the grace given to me I say to everyone among you not to think of himself more highly than he ought to think, but to think with sober judgment, each according to the measure of faith that God has assigned.

Psalm 139:14

I praise you, for I am fearfully and wonderfully made. Wonderful are your works; my soul knows it very well.

Galatians 2:20

I have been crucified with Christ. It is no longer I who live, but Christ who lives in me. And the life I now live in the flesh I live by faith in the Son of God, who loved me and gave himself for me.

Psalm 139:13-14

For you formed my inward parts; you knitted me together in my mother's womb. I praise you, for I am fearfully and wonderfully made. Wonderful are your works; my soul knows it very well.

Self-Righteousness

Ephesians 2:8-9

For by grace you have been saved through faith. And this is not your own doing; it is the gift of God, not a result of works, so that no one may boast.

Romans 3:10

As it is written: "None is righteous, no, not one;

Isaiah 64:6

We have all become like one who is unclean, and all our righteous deeds are like a polluted garment. We all fade like a leaf, and our iniquities, like the wind, take us away.

Romans 10:3

For, being ignorant of the righteousness of God, and seeking to establish their own, they did not submit to God's righteousness.

Matthew 7:1-5

"Judge not, that you be not judged. For with the judgment you pronounce you will be judged, and with the measure you use it will be measured to you. Why do you see the speck that is in your brother's eye, but do not notice the log that is in your own eye? Or how can you say to your brother, 'Let me take the speck out of your eye,' when there is the log in your own eye? You hypocrite, first take the log out of your own eye, and then you will see clearly to take the speck out of your brother's eye.

Luke 18:9

He also told this parable to some who trusted in themselves that they were righteous, and treated others with contempt:

Romans 14:1

As for the one who is weak in faith, welcome him, but not to quarrel over opinions.

1 John 4:19-21

We love because he first loved us. If anyone says, "I love God," and hates his brother, he is a liar; for he who does not love his brother whom he has seen cannot love God whom he has not seen. And this commandment we have from him: whoever loves God must also love his brother.

Titus 3:5

He saved us, not because of works done by us in righteousness, but according to his own mercy, by the washing of regeneration and renewal of the Holy Spirit,

Self-Worth

Psalm 139:13-15

For you formed my inward parts; you knitted me together in my mother's womb. I praise you, for I am fearfully and wonderfully made. Wonderful are your works; my soul knows it very well. My frame was not hidden from you, when I was being made in secret, intricately woven in the depths of the earth.

Jeremiah 29:11

For I know the plans I have for you, declares the Lord, plans for welfare and not for evil, to give you a future and a hope.

Luke 12:6-7

Are not five sparrows sold for two pennies? And not one of them is forgotten before God. Why, even the hairs of your head are all numbered. Fear not; you are of more value than many sparrows.

1 Corinthians 10:13

No temptation has overtaken you that is not common to man. God is faithful, and he will not let you be tempted beyond your ability, but with the temptation he will also provide the way of escape, that you may be able to endure it.

Romans 12:2

Do not be conformed to this world, but be transformed by the renewal of your mind, that by testing you may discern what is the will of God, what is good and acceptable and perfect.

Hebrews 13:5

Keep your life free from love of money, and be content with what you have, for he has said, "I will never leave you nor forsake you."

Colossians 3:12-14

Put on then, as God's chosen ones, holy and beloved, compassionate hearts, kindness, humility, meekness, and patience, bearing with one another and, if one has a complaint against another, forgiving each other; as the Lord has forgiven you, so you also must forgive. And above all these put on love, which binds everything together in perfect harmony.

Selfishness

2 Timothy 3:2-4

For people will be lovers of self, lovers of money, proud, arrogant, abusive, disobedient to their parents, ungrateful, unholy, heartless, unappeasable, slanderous, without self-control, brutal, not loving good, treacherous, reckless, swollen with conceit, lovers of pleasure rather than lovers of God,

1 John 3:17

But if anyone has the world's goods and sees his brother in need, yet closes his heart against him, how does God's love abide in him?

1 Corinthians 10:24

Let no one seek his own good, but the good of his neighbor.

Philippians 2:3-4

Do nothing from rivalry or conceit, but in humility count others more significant than yourselves. Let each of you look not only to his own interests, but also to the interests of others.

1 Corinthians 13:4-6

Love is patient and kind; love does not envy or boast; it is not arrogant or rude. It does not insist on its own way; it is not irritable or resentful; it does not rejoice at wrongdoing, but rejoices with the truth.

Philippians 2:21

For they all seek their own interests, not those of Jesus Christ.

Galatians 6:2

Bear one another's burdens, and so fulfill the law of Christ.

James 3:16

For where jealousy and selfish ambition exist, there will be disorder and every vile practice.

Separation from God

Isaiah 59:1-2

Behold, the Lord's hand is not shortened, that it cannot save, or his ear dull, that it cannot hear; but your iniquities have made a separation between you and your God, and your sins have hidden his face from you so that he does not hear.

2 Thessalonians 1:9

They will suffer the punishment of eternal destruction, away from the presence of the Lord and from the glory of his might,

Romans 3:23

For all have sinned and fall short of the glory of God,

Isaiah 53:6

All we like sheep have gone astray; we have turned—every one—to his own way; and the Lord has laid on him the iniquity of us all.

John 3:3

Jesus answered him, "Truly, truly, I say to you, unless one is born again he cannot see the kingdom of God."

Servant Leaders

Mark 10:42-45

And Jesus called them to him and said to them, "You know that those who are considered rulers of the Gentiles lord it over them, and their great ones exercise authority over them. But it shall not be so among you. But whoever would be great among you must be your servant, and whoever would be first among you must be slave of all. For even the Son of Man came not to be served but to serve, and to give his life as a ransom for many."

1 Peter 5:3
Not domineering over those in your charge, but being examples to the flock.

John 13:12-15
When he had washed their feet and put on his outer garments and resumed his place, he said to them, "Do you understand what I have done to you? You call me Teacher and Lord, and you are right, for so I am. If I then, your Lord and Teacher, have washed your feet, you also ought to wash one another's feet. For I have given you an example, that you also should do just as I have done to you.

Luke 22:26
But not so with you. Rather, let the greatest among you become as the youngest, and the leader as one who serves.

Acts 20:35
In all things I have shown you that by working hard in this way we must help the weak and remember the words of the Lord Jesus, how he himself said, 'It is more blessed to give than to receive.'"

Hebrews 13:7
Remember your leaders, those who spoke to you the word of God. Consider the outcome of their way of life, and imitate their faith.

Servanthood

Luke 22:27
For who is the greater, one who reclines at table or one who serves? Is it not the one who reclines at table? But I am among you as the one who serves.

Philippians 2:7
But made himself nothing, taking the form of a servant, being born in the likeness of men.

John 12:26
If anyone serves me, he must follow me; and where I am, there will my servant be also. If anyone serves me, the Father will honor him.

Colossians 3:17
And whatever you do, in word or deed, do everything in the name of the Lord Jesus, giving thanks to God the Father through him.

Ephesians 5:21
Submitting to one another out of reverence for Christ.

Sex

Hebrews 13:4

Let marriage be held in honor among all, and let the marriage bed be undefiled, for God will judge the sexually immoral and adulterous.

1 Corinthians 7:3-5

The husband should give to his wife her conjugal rights, and likewise the wife to her husband. For the wife does not have authority over her own body, but the husband does. Likewise the husband does not have authority over his own body, but the wife does. Do not deprive one another, except perhaps by agreement for a limited time, that you may devote yourselves to prayer; but then come together again, so that Satan may not tempt you because of your lack of self-control.

1 Corinthians 6:18

Flee from sexual immorality. Every other sin a person commits is outside the body, but the sexually immoral person sins against his own body.

Genesis 2:24

Therefore a man shall leave his father and his mother and hold fast to his wife, and they shall become one flesh.

1 Corinthians 7:2

But because of the temptation to sexual immorality, each man should have his own wife and each woman her own husband.

Proverbs 5:18-19

Let your fountain be blessed, and rejoice in the wife of your youth, a lovely deer, a graceful doe. Let her breasts fill you at all times with delight; be intoxicated always in her love.

1 Thessalonians 4:3-5

For this is the will of God, your sanctification: that you abstain from sexual immorality; that each one of you know how to control his own body in holiness and honor, not in the passion of lust like the Gentiles who do not know God;

Matthew 5:28

But I say to you that everyone who looks at a woman with lustful intent has already committed adultery with her in his heart.

1 Corinthians 6:18-20

Flee from sexual immorality. Every other sin a person commits is outside the body, but the sexually immoral person sins against his own body. Or do you not know that your body is a temple of the Holy Spirit within you, whom you have from God? You are not your own, for you were bought with a price. So glorify God in your body.

Shame

Isaiah 61:7

Instead of your shame there shall be a double portion; instead of dishonor they shall rejoice in their lot; therefore in their land they shall possess a double portion; they shall have everlasting joy.

Isaiah 50:7

But the Lord God helps me; therefore I have not been disgraced; therefore I have set my face like a flint, and I know that I shall not be put to shame.

1 John 1:9

If we confess our sins, he is faithful and just to forgive us our sins and to cleanse us from all unrighteousness.

Hebrews 12:2

Looking to Jesus, the founder and perfecter of our faith, who for the joy that was set before him endured the cross, despising the shame, and is seated at the right hand of the throne of God.

Psalm 34:4-5

I sought the Lord, and he answered me and delivered me from all my fears. Those who look to him are radiant, and their faces shall never be ashamed.

Romans 10:11

For the Scripture says, "Everyone who believes in him will not be put to shame."

Psalm 31:17

O Lord, let me not be put to shame, for I call upon you; let the wicked be put to shame; let them go silently to Sheol.

Mark 8:38

For whoever is ashamed of me and of my words in this adulterous and sinful generation, of him will the Son of Man also be ashamed when he comes in the glory of his Father with the holy angels."

1 Corinthians 10:13

No temptation has overtaken you that is not common to man. God is faithful, and he will not let you be tempted beyond your ability, but with the temptation he will also provide the way of escape, that you may be able to endure it.

Romans 8:1

There is therefore now no condemnation for those who are in Christ Jesus.

Sickness

3 John 1:2

Beloved, I pray that all may go well with you and that you may be in good health, as it goes well with your soul.

Romans 5:3-4

More than that, we rejoice in our sufferings, knowing that suffering produces endurance, and endurance produces character, and character produces hope,

James 5:14-15

Is anyone among you sick? Let him call for the elders of the church, and let them pray over him, anointing him with oil in the name of the Lord. And the prayer of faith will save the one who is sick, and the Lord will raise him up. And if he has committed sins, he will be forgiven.

1 Peter 2:24

He himself bore our sins in his body on the tree, that we might die to sin and live to righteousness. By his wounds you have been healed.

Revelation 21:4

He will wipe away every tear from their eyes, and death shall be no more, neither shall there be mourning, nor crying, nor pain anymore, for the former things have passed away."

Sorrow

Revelation 21:4

He will wipe away every tear from their eyes, and death shall be no more, neither shall there be mourning, nor crying, nor pain anymore, for the former things have passed away."

John 16:33

I have said these things to you, that in me you may have peace. In the world you will have tribulation. But take heart; I have overcome the world."

Psalm 30:5

For his anger is but for a moment, and his favor is for a lifetime. Weeping may tarry for the night, but joy comes with the morning.

Romans 8:18

For I consider that the sufferings of this present time are not worth comparing with the glory that is to be revealed to us.

2 Corinthians 7:10

For godly grief produces a repentance that leads to salvation without regret, whereas worldly grief produces death.

Matthew 5:4

"Blessed are those who mourn, for they shall be comforted.

Isaiah 35:10

And the ransomed of the Lord shall return and come to Zion with singing; everlasting joy shall be upon their heads; they shall obtain gladness and joy, and sorrow and sighing shall flee away.

1 Thessalonians 4:13

But we do not want you to be uninformed, brothers, about those who are asleep, that you may not grieve as others do who have no hope.

1 Peter 5:7

Casting all your anxieties on him, because he cares for you.

Proverbs 10:22

The blessing of the Lord makes rich, and he adds no sorrow with it.

Sovereignty

Psalm 115:3

Our God is in the heavens; he does all that he pleases.

1 Chronicles 29:11-12

Yours, O Lord, is the greatness and the power and the glory and the victory and the majesty, for all that is in the heavens and in the earth is yours. Yours is the kingdom, O Lord, and you are exalted as head above all. Both riches and honor come from you, and you rule over all. In your hand are power and might, and in your hand it is to make great and to give strength to all.

Proverbs 16:9

The heart of man plans his way, but the Lord establishes his steps.

Job 42:2

"I know that you can do all things, and that no purpose of yours can be thwarted.

Isaiah 46:9-10

Remember the former things of old; for I am God, and there is no other; I am God, and there is none like me, declaring the end from the beginning and from ancient times things not yet done, saying, 'My counsel shall stand, and I will accomplish all my purpose,'

Proverbs 19:21

Many are the plans in the mind of a man, but it is the purpose of the Lord that will stand.

Psalm 103:19

The Lord has established his throne in the heavens, and his kingdom rules over all.

Spanking Children

Proverbs 13:24

Whoever spares the rod hates his son, but he who loves him is diligent to discipline him.

Proverbs 23:13-14

Do not withhold discipline from a child; if you strike him with a rod, he will not die. If you strike him with the rod, you will save his soul from Sheol.

Hebrews 12:11

For the moment all discipline seems painful rather than pleasant, but later it yields the peaceful fruit of righteousness to those who have been trained by it.

Stealing

Ephesians 4:28

Let the thief no longer steal, but rather let him labor, doing honest work with his own hands, so that he may have something to share with anyone in need.

Exodus 20:15

"You shall not steal.

Leviticus 19:11

"You shall not steal; you shall not deal falsely; you shall not lie to one another.

Proverbs 10:2

Treasures gained by wickedness do not profit, but righteousness delivers from death.

Exodus 22:7

"If a man gives to his neighbor money or goods to keep safe, and it is stolen from the man's house, then, if the thief is found, he shall pay double.

Romans 13:9

For the commandments, "You shall not commit adultery, You shall not murder, You shall not steal, You shall not covet," and any other commandment, are summed up in this word: "You shall love your neighbor as yourself."

Stewardship

1 Peter 4:10

As each has received a gift, use it to serve one another, as good stewards of God's varied grace:

Genesis 1:28

And God blessed them. And God said to them, "Be fruitful and multiply and fill the earth and subdue it and have dominion over the fish of the sea and over the birds of the heavens and over every living thing that moves on the earth."

Genesis 2:15

The Lord God took the man and put him in the garden of Eden to work it and keep it.

2 Corinthians 9:6-7

The point is this: whoever sows sparingly will also reap sparingly, and whoever sows bountifully will also reap bountifully. Each one must give as he has decided in his heart, not reluctantly or under compulsion, for God loves a cheerful giver.

Stranger

Hebrews 13:1-2
Let brotherly love continue. Do not neglect to show hospitality to strangers, for thereby some have entertained angels unawares.

Matthew 25:35
For I was hungry and you gave me food, I was thirsty and you gave me drink, I was a stranger and you welcomed me,

Leviticus 19:34
You shall treat the stranger who sojourns with you as the native among you, and you shall love him as yourself, for you were strangers in the land of Egypt: I am the Lord your God.

Galatians 3:28
There is neither Jew nor Greek, there is neither slave nor free, there is no male and female, for you are all one in Christ Jesus.

Stress

Philippians 4:6
Do not be anxious about anything, but in everything by prayer and supplication with thanksgiving let your requests be made known to God.

John 14:27
Peace I leave with you; my peace I give to you. Not as the world gives do I give to you. Let not your hearts be troubled, neither let them be afraid.

Psalm 55:22
Cast your burden on the Lord, and he will sustain you; he will never permit the righteous to be moved.

Psalm 118:5-6
Out of my distress I called on the Lord; the Lord answered me and set me free. The Lord is on my side; I will not fear. What can man do to me?

Proverbs 12:25
Anxiety in a man's heart weighs him down, but a good word makes him glad.

Matthew 11:28-30
Come to me, all who labor and are heavy laden, and I will give you rest. Take my yoke upon you, and learn from me, for I am gentle and lowly in heart, and you will find rest for your souls. For my yoke is easy, and my burden is light."

Romans 8:31
What then shall we say to these things? If God is for us, who can be against us?

Strife

2 Timothy 2:23-25

Have nothing to do with foolish, ignorant controversies; you know that they breed quarrels. And the Lord's servant must not be quarrelsome but kind to everyone, able to teach, patiently enduring evil, correcting his opponents with gentleness. God may perhaps grant them repentance leading to a knowledge of the truth,

Proverbs 10:12

Hatred stirs up strife, but love covers all offenses.

Proverbs 16:28

A dishonest man spreads strife, and a whisperer separates close friends.

Proverbs 20:3

It is an honor for a man to keep aloof from strife, but every fool will be quarreling.

James 3:14-16

But if you have bitter jealousy and selfish ambition in your hearts, do not boast and be false to the truth. This is not the wisdom that comes down from above, but is earthly, unspiritual, demonic. For where jealousy and selfish ambition exist, there will be disorder and every vile practice.

Proverbs 29:22

A man of wrath stirs up strife, and one given to anger causes much transgression.

Stronghold

2 Corinthians 10:3-5

For though we walk in the flesh, we are not waging war according to the flesh. For the weapons of our warfare are not of the flesh but have divine power to destroy strongholds. We destroy arguments and every lofty opinion raised against the knowledge of God, and take every thought captive to obey Christ,

1 Corinthians 10:13

No temptation has overtaken you that is not common to man. God is faithful, and he will not let you be tempted beyond your ability, but with the temptation he will also provide the way of escape, that you may be able to endure it.

Romans 12:2

Do not be conformed to this world, but be transformed by the renewal of your mind, that by testing you may discern what is the will of God, what is good and acceptable and perfect.

Ephesians 6:12

For we do not wrestle against flesh and blood, but against the rulers, against the authorities, against the cosmic powers over this present darkness, against the spiritual forces of evil in the heavenly places.

Success

Proverbs 16:3

Commit your work to the Lord, and your plans will be established.

Philippians 4:13

I can do all things through him who strengthens me.

Psalm 37:4

Delight yourself in the Lord, and he will give you the desires of your heart.

Proverbs 3:1-4

My son, do not forget my teaching, but let your heart keep my commandments, for length of days and years of life and peace they will add to you. Let not steadfast love and faithfulness forsake you; bind them around your neck; write them on the tablet of your heart. So you will find favor and good success in the sight of God and man.

James 4:10

Humble yourselves before the Lord, and he will exalt you.

Suffering

1 Peter 5:10

And after you have suffered a little while, the God of all grace, who has called you to his eternal glory in Christ, will himself restore, confirm, strengthen, and establish you.

Romans 8:18

For I consider that the sufferings of this present time are not worth comparing with the glory that is to be revealed to us.

Romans 5:3-5

More than that, we rejoice in our sufferings, knowing that suffering produces endurance, and endurance produces character, and character produces hope, and hope does not put us to shame, because God's love has been poured into our hearts through the Holy Spirit who has been given to us.

Romans 8:28

And we know that for those who love God all things work together for good, for those who are called according to his purpose.

James 1:2-4

Count it all joy, my brothers, when you meet trials of various kinds, for you know that the testing of your faith produces steadfastness. And let steadfastness have its full effect, that you may be perfect and complete, lacking in nothing.

John 16:33

I have said these things to you, that in me you may have peace. In the world you will have tribulation. But take heart; I have overcome the world."

Revelation 21:4
He will wipe away every tear from their eyes, and death shall be no more, neither shall there be mourning, nor crying, nor pain anymore, for the former things have passed away."

Psalm 34:19
Many are the afflictions of the righteous, but the Lord delivers him out of them all.

2 Timothy 3:12
Indeed, all who desire to live a godly life in Christ Jesus will be persecuted,

Romans 5:3-4
More than that, we rejoice in our sufferings, knowing that suffering produces endurance, and endurance produces character, and character produces hope,

2 Corinthians 4:17
For this light momentary affliction is preparing for us an eternal weight of glory beyond all comparison,

Suicide

1 Corinthians 3:16-17
Do you not know that you are God's temple and that God's Spirit dwells in you? If anyone destroys God's temple, God will destroy him. For God's temple is holy, and you are that temple.

Ecclesiastes 7:17
Be not overly wicked, neither be a fool. Why should you die before your time?

Psalm 34:17-20
When the righteous cry for help, the Lord hears and delivers them out of all their troubles. The Lord is near to the brokenhearted and saves the crushed in spirit. Many are the afflictions of the righteous, but the Lord delivers him out of them all. He keeps all his bones; not one of them is broken.

1 Corinthians 6:19-20
Or do you not know that your body is a temple of the Holy Spirit within you, whom you have from God? You are not your own, for you were bought with a price. So glorify God in your body

Taxes

Matthew 22:17-21
Tell us, then, what you think. Is it lawful to pay taxes to Caesar, or not?" But Jesus, aware of their malice, said, "Why put me to the test, you hypocrites? Show me the coin for the tax." And they brought him a denarius. And Jesus said to them, "Whose likeness and inscription is this?" They said, "Caesar's." Then he said to them, "Therefore render to Caesar the things that are Caesar's, and to God the things that are God's."

Romans 13:6-7
For because of this you also pay taxes, for the authorities are ministers of God, attending to this very thing. Pay to all what is owed to them: taxes to whom taxes are owed, revenue to whom revenue is owed, respect to whom respect is owed, honor to whom honor is owed.

Teamwork

Ecclesiastes 4:9-12
Two are better than one, because they have a good reward for their toil. For if they fall, one will lift up his fellow. But woe to him who is alone when he falls and has not another to lift him up! Again, if two lie together, they keep warm, but how can one keep warm alone? And though a man might prevail against one who is alone, two will withstand him—a threefold cord is not quickly broken.

Proverbs 27:17
Iron sharpens iron, and one man sharpens another.

Ephesians 4:16
From whom the whole body, joined and held together by every joint with which it is equipped, when each part is working properly, makes the body grow so that it builds itself up in love.

1 Corinthians 1:10
I appeal to you, brothers, by the name of our Lord Jesus Christ, that all of you agree, and that there be no divisions among you, but that you be united in the same mind and the same judgment.

Romans 15:5-6
May the God of endurance and encouragement grant you to live in such harmony with one another, in accord with Christ Jesus, that together you may with one voice glorify the God and Father of our Lord Jesus Christ.

1 Peter 4:10
As each has received a gift, use it to serve one another, as good stewards of God's varied grace:

Tears

Psalm 56:8
You have kept count of my tossings; put my tears in your bottle. Are they not in your book?

Revelation 21:4

He will wipe away every tear from their eyes, and death shall be no more, neither shall there be mourning, nor crying, nor pain anymore, for the former things have passed away."

Psalm 126:5

Those who sow in tears shall reap with shouts of joy!

Revelation 7:17

For the Lamb in the midst of the throne will be their shepherd, and he will guide them to springs of living water, and God will wipe away every tear from their eyes."

Psalm 42:3

My tears have been my food day and night, while they say to me all the day long, "Where is your God?"

John 11:35

Jesus wept.

Isaiah 25:8

He will swallow up death forever; and the Lord God will wipe away tears from all faces, and the reproach of his people he will take away from all the earth, for the Lord has spoken.

Psalm 80:5

You have fed them with the bread of tears and given them tears to drink in full measure.

Psalm 39:12

"Hear my prayer, O Lord, and give ear to my cry; hold not your peace at my tears! For I am a sojourner with you, a guest, like all my fathers.

Job 16:20

My friends scorn me; my eye pours out tears to God,

Isaiah 38:5

"Go and say to Hezekiah, Thus says the Lord, the God of David your father: I have heard your prayer; I have seen your tears. Behold, I will add fifteen years to your life.

Psalm 6:6

I am weary with my moaning; every night I flood my bed with tears; I drench my couch with my weeping.

2 Kings 20:5

"Turn back, and say to Hezekiah the leader of my people, Thus says the Lord, the God of David your father: I have heard your prayer; I have seen your tears. Behold, I will heal you. On the third day you shall go up to the house of the Lord,

Teenagers

1 Timothy 4:12
Let no one despise you for your youth, but set the believers an example in speech, in conduct, in love, in faith, in purity.

2 Timothy 2:22-26
So flee youthful passions and pursue righteousness, faith, love, and peace, along with those who call on the Lord from a pure heart. Have nothing to do with foolish, ignorant controversies; you know that they breed quarrels. And the Lord's servant must not be quarrelsome but kind to everyone, able to teach, patiently enduring evil, correcting his opponents with gentleness. God may perhaps grant them repentance leading to a knowledge of the truth, and they may come to their senses and escape from the snare of the devil, after being captured by him to do his will.

1 Corinthians 10:13
No temptation has overtaken you that is not common to man. God is faithful, and he will not let you be tempted beyond your ability, but with the temptation he will also provide the way of escape, that you may be able to endure it.

Isaiah 40:30-31
Even youths shall faint and be weary, and young men shall fall exhausted; but they who wait for the Lord shall renew their strength; they shall mount up with wings like eagles; they shall run and not be weary; they shall walk and not faint.

2 Kings 15:2
He was sixteen years old when he began to reign, and he reigned fifty-two years in Jerusalem. His mother's name was Jecoliah of Jerusalem.

2 Timothy 1:7
For God gave us a spirit not of fear but of power and love and self-control.

1 Peter 5:7
Casting all your anxieties on him, because he cares for you.

Ecclesiastes 11:9
Rejoice, O young man, in your youth, and let your heart cheer you in the days of your youth. Walk in the ways of your heart and the sight of your eyes. But know that for all these things God will bring you into judgment.

Temptation

1 Corinthians 10:13
No temptation has overtaken you that is not common to man. God is faithful, and he will not let you be tempted beyond your ability, but with the temptation he will also provide the way of escape, that you may be able to endure it.

Matthew 26:41

Watch and pray that you may not enter into temptation. The spirit indeed is willing, but the flesh is weak."

James 1:12-16

Blessed is the man who remains steadfast under trial, for when he has stood the test he will receive the crown of life, which God has promised to those who love him. Let no one say when he is tempted, "I am being tempted by God," for God cannot be tempted with evil, and he himself tempts no one. But each person is tempted when he is lured and enticed by his own desire. Then desire when it has conceived gives birth to sin, and sin when it is fully grown brings forth death. Do not be deceived, my beloved brothers.

James 4:7

Submit yourselves therefore to God. Resist the devil, and he will flee from you.

Hebrews 2:18

For because he himself has suffered when tempted, he is able to help those who are being tempted.

Ephesians 6:11

Put on the whole armor of God, that you may be able to stand against the schemes of the devil.

Mark 14:38

Watch and pray that you may not enter into temptation. The spirit indeed is willing, but the flesh is weak."

Terminal Illness

2 Corinthians 1:3-4

Blessed be the God and Father of our Lord Jesus Christ, the Father of mercies and God of all comfort, who comforts us in all our affliction, so that we may be able to comfort those who are in any affliction, with the comfort with which we ourselves are comforted by God.

Deuteronomy 31:6

Be strong and courageous. Do not fear or be in dread of them, for it is the Lord your God who goes with you. He will not leave you or forsake you."

Romans 12:12

Rejoice in hope, be patient in tribulation, be constant in prayer.

Isaiah 41:10

Fear not, for I am with you; be not dismayed, for I am your God; I will strengthen you, I will help you, I will uphold you with my righteous right hand.

Philippians 4:13

I can do all things through him who strengthens me.

Revelation 21:4

He will wipe away every tear from their eyes, and death shall be no more, neither shall there be mourning, nor crying, nor pain anymore, for the former things have passed away."

John 5:24

Truly, truly, I say to you, whoever hears my word and believes him who sent me has eternal life. He does not come into judgment, but has passed from death to life.

Terrorism

Proverbs 6:16-19

There are six things that the Lord hates, seven that are an abomination to him: haughty eyes, a lying tongue, and hands that shed innocent blood, a heart that devises wicked plans, feet that make haste to run to evil, a false witness who breathes out lies, and one who sows discord among brothers.

Romans 12:19-21

Beloved, never avenge yourselves, but leave it to the wrath of God, for it is written, "Vengeance is mine, I will repay, says the Lord." To the contrary, "if your enemy is hungry, feed him; if he is thirsty, give him something to drink; for by so doing you will heap burning coals on his head." Do not be overcome by evil, but overcome evil with good.

Psalm 34:14

Turn away from evil and do good; seek peace and pursue it.

Matthew 24:9-14

"Then they will deliver you up to tribulation and put you to death, and you will be hated by all nations for my name's sake. And then many will fall away and betray one another and hate one another. And many false prophets will arise and lead many astray. And because lawlessness will be increased, the love of many will grow cold. But the one who endures to the end will be saved. And this gospel of the kingdom will be proclaimed throughout the whole world as a testimony to all nations, and then the end will come.

Matthew 24:6-8

And you will hear of wars and rumors of wars. See that you are not alarmed, for this must take place, but the end is not yet. For nation will rise against nation, and kingdom against kingdom, and there will be famines and earthquakes in various places. All these are but the beginning of the birth pains.

Matthew 5:44-48

But I say to you, Love your enemies and pray for those who persecute you, so that you may be sons of your Father who is in heaven. For he makes his sun rise on the evil and on the good, and sends rain on the just and on the unjust. For if you love those who love you, what reward do you have? Do not even the tax collectors do the same? And if you greet only your brothers, what more are you doing than others? Do not even the Gentiles do the same? You therefore must be perfect, as your heavenly Father is perfect.

Psalm 10:17-18

O Lord, you hear the desire of the afflicted; you will strengthen their heart; you will incline your ear to do justice to the fatherless and the oppressed, so that man who is of the earth may strike terror no more.

Isaiah 2:4

He shall judge between the nations, and shall decide disputes for many peoples; and they shall beat their swords into plowshares, and their spears into pruning hooks; nation shall not lift up sword against nation, neither shall they learn war anymore.

Matthew 5:38-39

"You have heard that it was said, 'An eye for an eye and a tooth for a tooth.' But I say to you, Do not resist the one who is evil. But if anyone slaps you on the right cheek, turn to him the other also.

Luke 12:4

"I tell you, my friends, do not fear those who kill the body, and after that have nothing more that they can do.

Thankfulness

1 Thessalonians 5:18

Give thanks in all circumstances; for this is the will of God in Christ Jesus for you.

Ephesians 5:20

Giving thanks always and for everything to God the Father in the name of our Lord Jesus Christ,

Psalm 106:1

Praise the Lord! Oh give thanks to the Lord, for he is good, for his steadfast love endures forever!

Psalm 100:4

Enter his gates with thanksgiving, and his courts with praise! Give thanks to him; bless his name!

Philippians 4:6

Do not be anxious about anything, but in everything by prayer and supplication with thanksgiving let your requests be made known to God.

Psalm 107:1

Oh give thanks to the Lord, for he is good, for his steadfast love endures forever!

Colossians 4:2

Continue steadfastly in prayer, being watchful in it with thanksgiving.

Colossians 3:15-17

And let the peace of Christ rule in your hearts, to which indeed you were called in one body. And be thankful. Let the word of Christ dwell in you richly, teaching and admonishing one another in all wisdom, singing psalms and hymns and spiritual songs, with thankfulness in your hearts to God. And whatever you do, in word or deed, do everything in the name of the Lord Jesus, giving thanks to God the Father through him.

Psalm 28:7

The Lord is my strength and my shield; in him my heart trusts, and I am helped; my heart exults, and with my song I give thanks to him.

Time

2 Peter 3:8
But do not overlook this one fact, beloved, that with the Lord one day is as a thousand years, and a thousand years as one day.

Psalm 90:12
So teach us to number our days that we may get a heart of wisdom.

Ephesians 5:16
Making the best use of the time, because the days are evil.

Proverbs 16:9
The heart of man plans his way, but the Lord establishes his steps.

James 4:13-15
Come now, you who say, "Today or tomorrow we will go into such and such a town and spend a year there and trade and make a profit"— yet you do not know what tomorrow will bring. What is your life? For you are a mist that appears for a little time and then vanishes. Instead you ought to say, "If the Lord wills, we will live and do this or that."

James 4:14
Yet you do not know what tomorrow will bring. What is your life? For you are a mist that appears for a little time and then vanishes.

Jeremiah 29:11
For I know the plans I have for you, declares the Lord, plans for welfare and not for evil, to give you a future and a hope.

Psalm 31:15
My times are in your hand; rescue me from the hand of my enemies and from my persecutors!

Ephesians 1:10
As a plan for the fullness of time, to unite all things in him, things in heaven and things on earth.

Time Management

Ephesians 5:15-17
Look carefully then how you walk, not as unwise but as wise, making the best use of the time, because the days are evil. Therefore do not be foolish, but understand what the will of the Lord is.

Psalm 90:12
So teach us to number our days that we may get a heart of wisdom.

Colossians 4:5
Walk in wisdom toward outsiders, making the best use of the time.

Matthew 6:33

But seek first the kingdom of God and his righteousness, and all these things will be added to you.

Ecclesiastes 3:8

A time to love, and a time to hate; a time for war, and a time for peace.

Luke 14:28

For which of you, desiring to build a tower, does not first sit down and count the cost, whether he has enough to complete it?

Proverbs 16:9

The heart of man plans his way, but the Lord establishes his steps.

Tithing

Malachi 3:8-10

Will man rob God? Yet you are robbing me. But you say, 'How have we robbed you?' In your tithes and contributions. You are cursed with a curse, for you are robbing me, the whole nation of you. Bring the full tithe into the storehouse, that there may be food in my house. And thereby put me to the test, says the Lord of hosts, if I will not open the windows of heaven for you and pour down for you a blessing until there is no more need.

2 Corinthians 9:6-8

The point is this: whoever sows sparingly will also reap sparingly, and whoever sows bountifully will also reap bountifully. Each one must give as he has decided in his heart, not reluctantly or under compulsion, for God loves a cheerful giver. And God is able to make all grace abound to you, so that having all sufficiency in all things at all times, you may abound in every good work.

Luke 6:38

Give, and it will be given to you. Good measure, pressed down, shaken together, running over, will be put into your lap. For with the measure you use it will be measured back to you."

Proverbs 3:9

Honor the Lord with your wealth and with the first fruits of all your produce;

Mark 12:41-44

And he sat down opposite the treasury and watched the people putting money into the offering box. Many rich people put in large sums. And a poor widow came and put in two small copper coins, which make a penny. And he called his disciples to him and said to them, "Truly, I say to you, this poor widow has put in more than all those who are contributing to the offering box. For they all contributed out of their abundance, but she out of her poverty has put in everything she had, all she had to live on."

Matthew 23:23

"Woe to you, scribes and Pharisees, hypocrites! For you tithe mint and dill and cumin, and have neglected the weightier matters of the law: justice and mercy and faithfulness. These you ought to have done, without neglecting the others.

Leviticus 27:30

"Every tithe of the land, whether of the seed of the land or of the fruit of the trees, is the Lord's; it is holy to the Lord.

Togetherness

1 Peter 4:8

Above all, keep loving one another earnestly, since love covers a multitude of sins.

Philippians 2:2

Complete my joy by being of the same mind, having the same love, being in full accord and of one mind.

Matthew 18:20

For where two or three are gathered in my name, there am I among them."

Tongues

1 Corinthians 14:39

So, my brothers, earnestly desire to prophesy, and do not forbid speaking in tongues.

1 Corinthians 14:2

For one who speaks in a tongue speaks not to men but to God; for no one understands him, but he utters mysteries in the Spirit.

1 Corinthians 14:27

If any speak in a tongue, let there be only two or at most three, and each in turn, and let someone interpret.

1 Corinthians 13:8

Love never ends. As for prophecies, they will pass away; as for tongues, they will cease; as for knowledge, it will pass away.

1 Corinthians 12:10

To another the working of miracles, to another prophecy, to another the ability to distinguish between spirits, to another various kinds of tongues, to another the interpretation of tongues.

Mark 16:17

And these signs will accompany those who believe: in my name they will cast out demons; they will speak in new tongues;

Acts 10:46

For they were hearing them speaking in tongues and extolling God. Then Peter declared,

James 1:26

If anyone thinks he is religious and does not bridle his tongue but deceives his heart, this person's religion is worthless.

Traditions

2 Thessalonians 2:15
So then, brothers, stand firm and hold to the traditions that you were taught by us, either by our spoken word or by our letter.

Colossians 2:8
See to it that no one takes you captive by philosophy and empty deceit, according to human tradition, according to the elemental spirits of the world, and not according to Christ.

Matthew 15:3
He answered them, "And why do you break the commandment of God for the sake of your tradition?

1 Corinthians 11:2
Now I commend you because you remember me in everything and maintain the traditions even as I delivered them to you.

Matthew 15:6
He need not honor his father.' So for the sake of your tradition you have made void the word of God.

Tragedy

John 16:33
I have said these things to you, that in me you may have peace. In the world you will have tribulation. But take heart; I have overcome the world."

Psalm 34:18
The Lord is near to the brokenhearted and saves the crushed in spirit.

Romans 12:19
Beloved, never avenge yourselves, but leave it to the wrath of God, for it is written, "Vengeance is mine, I will repay, says the Lord."

Isaiah 61:1-3
The Spirit of the Lord God is upon me, because the Lord has anointed me to bring good news to the poor; he has sent me to bind up the brokenhearted, to proclaim liberty to the captives, and the opening of the prison to those who are bound; to proclaim the year of the Lord's favor, and the day of vengeance of our God; to comfort all who mourn; to grant to those who mourn in Zion— to give them a beautiful headdress instead of ashes, the oil of gladness instead of mourning, the garment of praise instead of a faint spirit; that they may be called oaks of righteousness, the planting of the Lord, that he may be glorified.

Lamentations 3:31-33
For the Lord will not cast off forever, but, though he cause grief, he will have compassion according to the abundance of his steadfast love; for he does not willingly afflict or grieve the children of men.

Training UP A Child

Proverbs 22:6
Train up a child in the way he should go; even when he is old he will not depart from it.

Ephesians 6:4
Fathers, do not provoke your children to anger, but bring them up in the discipline and instruction of the Lord.

Proverbs 23:13-14
Do not withhold discipline from a child; if you strike him with a rod, he will not die. If you strike him with the rod, you will save his soul from Sheol.

Proverbs 29:15
The rod and reproof give wisdom, but a child left to himself brings shame to his mother.

Proverbs 29:17
Discipline your son, and he will give you rest; he will give delight to your heart.

Proverbs 22:15
Folly is bound up in the heart of a child, but the rod of discipline drives it far from him.

Psalm 127:3
Behold, children are a heritage from the Lord, the fruit of the womb a reward.

Proverbs 13:24
Whoever spares the rod hates his son, but he who loves him is diligent to discipline him.

Trials

Romans 5:3-5
More than that, we rejoice in our sufferings, knowing that suffering produces endurance, and endurance produces character, and character produces hope, and hope does not put us to shame, because God's love has been poured into our hearts through the Holy Spirit who has been given to us.

James 1:2-4
Count it all joy, my brothers, when you meet trials of various kinds, for you know that the testing of your faith produces steadfastness. And let steadfastness have its full effect, that you may be perfect and complete, lacking in nothing.

1 Peter 4:12-13
Beloved, do not be surprised at the fiery trial when it comes upon you to test you, as though something strange were happening to you. But rejoice insofar as you share Christ's sufferings, that you may also rejoice and be glad when his glory is revealed.

James 1:12
Blessed is the man who remains steadfast under trial, for when he has stood the test he will receive the crown of life, which God has promised to those who love him.

2 Corinthians 6:4-8
But as servants of God we commend ourselves in every way: by great endurance, in afflictions, hardships, calamities, beatings, imprisonments, riots, labors, sleepless nights, hunger; by purity, knowledge, patience, kindness, the Holy Spirit, genuine love; by truthful speech, and the power of God; with the weapons of righteousness for the right hand and for the left; through honor and dishonor, through slander and praise. We are treated as impostors, and yet are true;

Trinity

Matthew 28:19
Go therefore and make disciples of all nations, baptizing them in the name of the Father and of the Son and of the Holy Spirit,

1 Corinthians 8:6
Yet for us there is one God, the Father, from whom are all things and for whom we exist, and one Lord, Jesus Christ, through whom are all things and through whom we exist.

John 14:26
But the Helper, the Holy Spirit, whom the Father will send in my name, he will teach you all things and bring to your remembrance all that I have said to you.

John 15:26
"But when the Helper comes, whom I will send to you from the Father, the Spirit of truth, who proceeds from the Father, he will bear witness about me.

2 Corinthians 13:14
The grace of the Lord Jesus Christ and the love of God and the fellowship of the Holy Spirit be with you all.

Matthew 3:16-17
And when Jesus was baptized, immediately he went up from the water, and behold, the heavens were opened to him, and he saw the Spirit of God descending like a dove and coming to rest on him; and behold, a voice from heaven said, "This is my beloved Son, with whom I am well pleased."

Genesis 1:26
Then God said, "Let us make man in our image, after our likeness. And let them have dominion over the fish of the sea and over the birds of the heavens and over the livestock and over all the earth and over every creeping thing that creeps on the earth."

Trust

Proverbs 3:5
Trust in the Lord with all your heart, and do not lean on your own understanding.

Psalm 56:3-4

When I am afraid, I put my trust in you. In God, whose word I praise, in God I trust; I shall not be afraid. What can flesh do to me?

Jeremiah 29:11

For I know the plans I have for you, declares the Lord, plans for welfare and not for evil, to give you a future and a hope.

1 John 4:18

There is no fear in love, but perfect love casts out fear. For fear has to do with punishment, and whoever fears has not been perfected in love.

Psalm 37:5

Commit your way to the Lord; trust in him, and he will act.

Unanswered Prayer

James 4:3
You ask and do not receive, because you ask wrongly, to spend it on your passions.

Matthew 21:22
And whatever you ask in prayer, you will receive, if you have faith."

James 1:6
But let him ask in faith, with no doubting, for the one who doubts is like a wave of the sea that is driven and tossed by the wind.

1 John 5:14
And this is the confidence that we have toward him, that if we ask anything according to his will he hears us.

Mark 11:24
Therefore, I tell you, whatever you ask in prayer, believe that you have received it, and it will be yours.

Matthew 7:7
"Ask, and it will be given to you; seek, and you will find; knock, and it will be opened to you.

Psalm 66:18
If I had cherished iniquity in my heart, the Lord would not have listened.

Isaiah 59:2
But your iniquities have made a separation between you and your God, and your sins have hidden his face from you so that he does not hear.

Unbelievers

2 Corinthians 6:14-18
Do not be unequally yoked with unbelievers. For what partnership has righteousness with lawlessness? Or what fellowship has light with darkness? What accord has Christ with Belial? Or what portion does a believer share with an unbeliever? What agreement has the temple of God with idols? For we are the temple of the living God; as God said, "I will make my dwelling among them and walk among them, and I will be their God, and they shall be my people. Therefore, go out from their midst, and be separate from them, says the Lord, and touch no unclean thing; then I will welcome you, and I will be a father to you, and you shall be sons and daughters to me, says the Lord Almighty."

Ephesians 4:18
They are darkened in their understanding, alienated from the life of God because of the ignorance that is in them, due to their hardness of heart.

1 Corinthians 5:9-13

I wrote to you in my letter not to associate with sexually immoral people— not at all meaning the sexually immoral of this world, or the greedy and swindlers, or idolaters, since then you would need to go out of the world. But now I am writing to you not to associate with anyone who bears the name of brother if he is guilty of sexual immorality or greed, or is an idolater, reviler, drunkard, or swindler—not even to eat with such a one. For what have I to do with judging outsiders? Is it not those inside the church whom you are to judge? God judges those outside. "Purge the evil person from among you."

2 Corinthians 4:4

In their case the god of this world has blinded the minds of the unbelievers, to keep them from seeing the light of the gospel of the glory of Christ, who is the image of God.

1 Timothy 5:8

But if anyone does not provide for his relatives, and especially for members of his household, he has denied the faith and is worse than an unbeliever.

Proverbs 24:20

For the evil man has no future; the lamp of the wicked will be put out.

Romans 6:23

For the wages of sin is death, but the free gift of God is eternal life in Christ Jesus our Lord.

1 Corinthians 15:33

Do not be deceived: "Bad company ruins good morals."

Uncertainty

Philippians 4:6-7

Do not be anxious about anything, but in everything by prayer and supplication with thanksgiving let your requests be made known to God. And the peace of God, which surpasses all understanding, will guard your hearts and your minds in Christ Jesus.

1 Peter 5:7

Casting all your anxieties on him, because he cares for you.

Jeremiah 29:11

For I know the plans I have for you, declares the Lord, plans for welfare and not for evil, to give you a future and a hope.

Proverbs 3:5-6

Trust in the Lord with all your heart, and do not lean on your own understanding. In all your ways acknowledge him, and he will make straight your paths.

Psalm 55:22

Cast your burden on the Lord, and he will sustain you; he will never permit the righteous to be moved.

Hebrews 10:35

Therefore, do not throw away your confidence, which has a great reward.

Hebrews 11:6

And without faith it is impossible to please him, for whoever would draw near to God must believe that he exists and that he rewards those who seek him.

John 14:26

But the Helper, the Holy Spirit, whom the Father will send in my name, he will teach you all things and bring to your remembrance all that I have said to you.

Understanding

Proverbs 18:2

A fool takes no pleasure in understanding, but only in expressing his opinion.

Psalm 119:130

The unfolding of your words gives light; it imparts understanding to the simple.

Proverbs 14:29

Whoever is slow to anger has great understanding, but he who has a hasty temper exalts folly.

Proverbs 2:2-5

Making your ear attentive to wisdom and inclining your heart to understanding; yes, if you call out for insight and raise your voice for understanding, if you seek it like silver and search for it as for hidden treasures, then you will understand the fear of the Lord and find the knowledge of God.

Proverbs 17:27

Whoever restrains his words has knowledge, and he who has a cool spirit is a man of understanding.

Colossians 4:6

Let your speech always be gracious, seasoned with salt, so that you may know how you ought to answer each person.

Proverbs 3:5

Trust in the Lord with all your heart, and do not lean on your own understanding.

Proverbs 4:7

The beginning of wisdom is this: Get wisdom, and whatever you get, get insight.

Unemployment

Jeremiah 29:11-14

For I know the plans I have for you, declares the Lord, plans for welfare and not for evil, to give you a future and a hope. Then you will call upon me and come and pray to me, and I will hear you. You will seek me and find me, when you seek me with all your heart. I will be found by you, declares the Lord, and I will restore your fortunes and gather you from all the nations and all the places where I have driven you, declares the Lord, and I will bring you back to the place from which I sent you into exile.

Philippians 4:6
Do not be anxious about anything, but in everything by prayer and supplication with thanksgiving let your requests be made known to God.

Deuteronomy 15:7-8
"If among you, one of your brothers should become poor, in any of your towns within your land that the Lord your God is giving you, you shall not harden your heart or shut your hand against your poor brother, but you shall open your hand to him and lend him sufficient for his need, whatever it may be.

Matthew 6:28
And why are you anxious about clothing? Consider the lilies of the field, how they grow: they neither toil nor spin,

Romans 8:28
And we know that for those who love God all things work together for good, for those who are called according to his purpose.

Hebrews 11:6
And without faith it is impossible to please him, for whoever would draw near to God must believe that he exists and that he rewards those who seek him.

Matthew 11:28-30
Come to me, all who labor and are heavy laden, and I will give you rest. Take my yoke upon you, and learn from me, for I am gentle and lowly in heart, and you will find rest for your souls. For my yoke is easy, and my burden is light."

Unequally Yoked

2 Corinthians 6:14
Do not be unequally yoked with unbelievers. For what partnership has righteousness with lawlessness? Or what fellowship has light with darkness?

1 Corinthians 7:15
But if the unbelieving partner separates, let it be so. In such cases the brother or sister is not enslaved. God has called you to peace.

Unforgiveness

Mark 11:25
And whenever you stand praying, forgive, if you have anything against anyone, so that your Father also who is in heaven may forgive you your trespasses."

Matthew 6:14-15

For if you forgive others their trespasses, your heavenly Father will also forgive you, but if you do not forgive others their trespasses, neither will your Father forgive your trespasses.

Ephesians 4:32

Be kind to one another, tenderhearted, forgiving one another, as God in Christ forgave you.

Ephesians 4:26-27

Be angry and do not sin; do not let the sun go down on your anger, and give no opportunity to the devil.

1 John 1:9

If we confess our sins, he is faithful and just to forgive us our sins and to cleanse us from all unrighteousness.

Matthew 6:12

And forgive us our debts, as we also have forgiven our debtors.

2 Corinthians 2:10-11

Anyone whom you forgive, I also forgive. Indeed, what I have forgiven, if I have forgiven anything, has been for your sake in the presence of Christ, so that we would not be outwitted by Satan; for we are not ignorant of his designs.

Proverbs 24:17

Do not rejoice when your enemy falls, and let not your heart be glad when he stumbles,

Ungrateful People

Luke 6:35

But love your enemies, and do good, and lend, expecting nothing in return, and your reward will be great, and you will be sons of the Most High, for he is kind to the ungrateful and the evil.

1 Corinthians 4:7

For who sees anything different in you? What do you have that you did not receive? If then you received it, why do you boast as if you did not receive it?

1 Thessalonians 5:16-18

Rejoice always, pray without ceasing, give thanks in all circumstances; for this is the will of God in Christ Jesus for you.

Unity

1 Corinthians 1:10

I appeal to you, brothers, by the name of our Lord Jesus Christ, that all of you agree, and that there be no divisions among you, but that you be united in the same mind and the same judgment.

1 Peter 3:8

Finally, all of you, have unity of mind, sympathy, brotherly love, a tender heart, and a humble mind.

Philippians 2:2

Complete my joy by being of the same mind, having the same love, being in full accord and of one mind.

Colossians 3:14

And above all these put on love, which binds everything together in perfect harmony.

Psalm 133:1

A Song of Ascents. Of David. Behold, how good and pleasant it is when brothers dwell in unity!

2 Corinthians 13:11

Finally, brothers, rejoice. Aim for restoration, comfort one another, agree with one another, live in peace; and the God of love and peace will be with you.

Ephesians 4:3

Eager to maintain the unity of the Spirit in the bond of peace.

Romans 12:4-5

For as in one body we have many members, and the members do not all have the same function, so we, though many, are one body in Christ, and individually members one of another.

Romans 15:6

That together you may with one voice glorify the God and Father of our Lord Jesus Christ.

Romans 12:16

Live in harmony with one another. Do not be haughty, but associate with the lowly. Never be wise in your own sight.

Universe

Hebrews 11:3

By faith we understand that the universe was created by the word of God, so that what is seen was not made out of things that are visible.

Isaiah 40:22

It is he who sits above the circle of the earth, and its inhabitants are like grasshoppers; who stretches out the heavens like a curtain, and spreads them like a tent to dwell in;

Psalm 19:1

To the choirmaster. A Psalm of David. The heavens declare the glory of God, and the sky above proclaims his handiwork.

Job 26:7

He stretches out the north over the void and hangs the earth on nothing.

Psalm 8:3-4

When I look at your heavens, the work of your fingers, the moon and the stars, which you have set in place, what is man that you are mindful of him, and the son of man that you care for him?

John 1:3

All things were made through him, and without him was not any thing made that was made.

Unselfishness

Philippians 2:4

Let each of you look not only to his own interests, but also to the interests of others.

Romans 12:10

Love one another with brotherly affection. Outdo one another in showing honor.

John 13:34

A new commandment I give to you, that you love one another: just as I have loved you, you also are to love one another.

James 5:16

Therefore, confess your sins to one another and pray for one another, that you may be healed. The prayer of a righteous person has great power as it is working.

1 Corinthians 10:24

Let no one seek his own good, but the good of his neighbor.

Untimely Death

Isaiah 57:1-2

The righteous man perishes, and no one lays it to heart; devout men are taken away, while no one understands. For the righteous man is taken away from calamity; he enters into peace; they rest in their beds who walk in their uprightness.

Psalm 118:17

I shall not die, but I shall live, and recount the deeds of the Lord.

Psalm 116:15

Precious in the sight of the Lord is the death of his saints.

Genesis 6:3

Then the Lord said, "My Spirit shall not abide in man forever, for he is flesh: his days shall be 120 years."

Romans 14:8

For if we live, we live to the Lord, and if we die, we die to the Lord. So then, whether we live or whether we die, we are the Lord's.

John 11:25-26

Jesus said to her, "I am the resurrection and the life. Whoever believes in me, though he die, yet shall he live, and everyone who lives and believes in me shall never die. Do you believe this?"

Using Talents

1 Peter 4:10

As each has received a gift, use it to serve one another, as good stewards of God's varied grace:

Romans 12:6

Having gifts that differ according to the grace given to us, let us use them: if prophecy, in proportion to our faith;

1 Peter 4:10-11

As each has received a gift, use it to serve one another, as good stewards of God's varied grace: whoever speaks, as one who speaks oracles of God; whoever serves, as one who serves by the strength that God supplies—in order that in everything God may be glorified through Jesus Christ. To him belong glory and dominion forever and ever. Amen.

1 Timothy 4:14

Do not neglect the gift you have, which was given you by prophecy when the council of elders laid their hands on you.

Romans 12:6-8

Having gifts that differ according to the grace given to us, let us use them: if prophecy, in proportion to our faith; if service, in our serving; the one who teaches, in his teaching; the one who exhorts, in his exhortation; the one who contributes, in generosity; the one who leads, with zeal; the one who does acts of mercy, with cheerfulness.

Using Your Time Wisely

Colossians 4:5

Walk in wisdom toward outsiders, making the best use of the time.

Psalm 90:12

So teach us to number our days that we may get a heart of wisdom.

Ephesians 5:16

Making the best use of the time, because the days are evil.

Usury

Exodus 22:25

"If you lend money to any of my people with you who is poor, you shall not be like a moneylender to him, and you shall not exact interest from him.

Psalm 15:5
Who does not put out his money at interest and does not take a bribe against the innocent. He who does these things shall never be moved.

Proverbs 28:8
Whoever multiplies his wealth by interest and profit gathers it for him who is generous to the poor.

Ezekiel 18:13
Lends at interest, and takes profit; shall he then live? He shall not live. He has done all these abominations; he shall surely die; his blood shall be upon himself.

Ezekiel 22:12
In you they take bribes to shed blood; you take interest and profit and make gain of your neighbors by extortion; but me you have forgotten, declares the Lord God.

Deuteronomy 23:19-20
"You shall not charge interest on loans to your brother, interest on money, interest on food, interest on anything that is lent for interest. You may charge a foreigner interest, but you may not charge your brother interest, that the Lord your God may bless you in all that you undertake in the land that you are entering to take possession of it.

Leviticus 25:36
Take no interest from him or profit, but fear your God, that your brother may live beside you.

Jeremiah 15:10
Woe is me, my mother, that you bore me, a man of strife and contention to the whole land! I have not lent, nor have I borrowed, yet all of them curse me.

Ezekiel 18:8
Does not lend at interest or take any profit, withholds his hand from injustice, executes true justice between man and man,

Utterance

Acts 2:4
And they were all filled with the Holy Spirit and began to speak in other tongues as the Spirit gave them utterance.

2 Peter 1:20-21
Knowing this first of all, that no prophecy of Scripture comes from someone's own interpretation. For no prophecy was ever produced by the will of man, but men spoke from God as they were carried along by the Holy Spirit.

Value

Matthew 10:31

Fear not, therefore; you are of more value than many sparrows.

1 Timothy 4:8

For while bodily training is of some value, godliness is of value in every way, as it holds promise for the present life and also for the life to come.

Psalm 139:14

I praise you, for I am fearfully and wonderfully made. Wonderful are your works; my soul knows it very well.

Acts 20:35

In all things I have shown you that by working hard in this way we must help the weak and remember the words of the Lord Jesus, how he himself said, 'It is more blessed to give than to receive.'"

Psalm 15:1-5

A Psalm of David. O Lord, who shall sojourn in your tent? Who shall dwell on your holy hill? He who walks blamelessly and does what is right and speaks truth in his heart; who does not slander with his tongue and does no evil to his neighbor, nor takes up a reproach against his friend; in whose eyes a vile person is despised, but who honors those who fear the Lord; who swears to his own hurt and does not change; who does not put out his money at interest and does not take a bribe against the innocent. He who does these things shall never be moved.

Philippians 2:3

Do nothing from rivalry or conceit, but in humility count others more significant than yourselves.

1 Peter 1:18-19

Knowing that you were ransomed from the futile ways inherited from your forefathers, not with perishable things such as silver or gold, but with the precious blood of Christ, like that of a lamb without blemish or spot.

Genesis 1:26-27

Then God said, "Let us make man in our image, after our likeness. And let them have dominion over the fish of the sea and over the birds of the heavens and over the livestock and over all the earth and over every creeping thing that creeps on the earth." So God created man in his own image, in the image of God he created him; male and female he created them.

Hebrews 13:5

Keep your life free from love of money, and be content with what you have, for he has said, "I will never leave you nor forsake you."

Mark 12:41-44

And he sat down opposite the treasury and watched the people putting money into the offering box. Many rich people put in large sums. And a poor widow came and put in two small copper coins, which make a penny. And he called his disciples to him and said to them, "Truly, I say to you, this poor widow has put in more than all those who are contributing to the offering box. For they all contributed out of their abundance, but she out of her poverty has put in everything she had, all she had to live on."

Vanity

Proverbs 31:30
Charm is deceitful, and beauty is vain, but a woman who fears the Lord is to be praised.

Psalm 119:37
Turn my eyes from looking at worthless things; and give me life in your ways.

Ecclesiastes 5:10
He who loves money will not be satisfied with money, nor he who loves wealth with his income; this also is vanity.

Ecclesiastes 2:11
Then I considered all that my hands had done and the toil I had expended in doing it, and behold, all was vanity and a striving after wind, and there was nothing to be gained under the sun.

Ecclesiastes 1:2
Vanity of vanities, says the Preacher, vanity of vanities! All is vanity.

1 Samuel 16:7
But the Lord said to Samuel, "Do not look on his appearance or on the height of his stature, because I have rejected him. For the Lord sees not as man sees: man looks on the outward appearance, but the Lord looks on the heart."

Psalm 39:5
Behold, you have made my days a few handbreadths, and my lifetime is as nothing before you. Surely all mankind stands as a mere breath! Selah

1 Timothy 4:8
For while bodily training is of some value, godliness is of value in every way, as it holds promise for the present life and also for the life to come.

Vengeance

Romans 12:19
Beloved, never avenge yourselves, but leave it to the wrath of God, for it is written, "Vengeance is mine, I will repay, says the Lord."

Matthew 5:38-39
"You have heard that it was said, 'An eye for an eye and a tooth for a tooth.' But I say to you, Do not resist the one who is evil. But if anyone slaps you on the right cheek, turn to him the other also.

Ezekiel 25:17

I will execute great vengeance on them with wrathful rebukes. Then they will know that I am the Lord, when I lay my vengeance upon them."

2 Thessalonians 1:6

Since indeed God considers it just to repay with affliction those who afflict you,

Ephesians 4:26-27

Be angry and do not sin; do not let the sun go down on your anger, and give no opportunity to the devil.

Hebrews 10:30

For we know him who said, "Vengeance is mine; I will repay." And again, "The Lord will judge his people."

Leviticus 19:18

You shall not take vengeance or bear a grudge against the sons of your own people, but you shall love your neighbor as yourself: I am the Lord.

Romans 13:4

For he is God's servant for your good. But if you do wrong, be afraid, for he does not bear the sword in vain. For he is the servant of God, an avenger who carries out God's wrath on the wrongdoer.

Revelation 21:8

But as for the cowardly, the faithless, the detestable, as for murderers, the sexually immoral, sorcerers, idolaters, and all liars, their portion will be in the lake that burns with fire and sulfur, which is the second death."

Deuteronomy 32:35

Vengeance is mine, and recompense, for the time when their foot shall slip; for the day of their calamity is at hand, and their doom comes swiftly.'

1 Thessalonians 5:15

See that no one repays anyone evil for evil, but always seek to do good to one another and to everyone.

Psalm 94:1

O Lord, God of vengeance, O God of vengeance, shine forth!

1 Samuel 24:12

May the Lord judge between me and you, may the Lord avenge me against you, but my hand shall not be against you.

Matthew 26:52-54

Then Jesus said to him, "Put your sword back into its place. For all who take the sword will perish by the sword. Do you think that I cannot appeal to my Father, and he will at once send me more than twelve legions of angels? But how then should the Scriptures be fulfilled, that it must be so?"

Verbal Abuse

Matthew 12:36-37
I tell you, on the day of judgment people will give account for every careless word they speak, for by your words you will be justified, and by your words you will be condemned."

Titus 3:10
As for a person who stirs up division, after warning him once and then twice, have nothing more to do with him,

Psalm 34:18
The Lord is near to the brokenhearted and saves the crushed in spirit.

Colossians 3:19
Husbands, love your wives, and do not be harsh with them.

Ephesians 4:29
Let no corrupting talk come out of your mouths, but only such as is good for building up, as fits the occasion, that it may give grace to those who hear.

Proverbs 22:24
Make no friendship with a man given to anger, nor go with a wrathful man,

Ephesians 4:31
Let all bitterness and wrath and anger and clamor and slander be put away from you, along with all malice.

1 Corinthians 7:15
But if the unbelieving partner separates, let it be so. In such cases the brother or sister is not enslaved. God has called you to peace.

Vessels

1 Corinthians 6:19-20
Or do you not know that your body is a temple of the Holy Spirit within you, whom you have from God? You are not your own, for you were bought with a price. So glorify God in your body.

2 Corinthians 4:7
But we have this treasure in jars of clay, to show that the surpassing power belongs to God and not to us.

2 Kings 4:1-7
Now the wife of one of the sons of the prophets cried to Elisha, "Your servant my husband is dead, and you know that your servant feared the Lord, but the creditor has come to take my two children to be his slaves." And Elisha said to her, "What shall I do for you? Tell me; what have you in the house?" And she said, "Your servant has nothing in the house except a jar of oil." Then he said, "Go outside, borrow vessels from all your neighbors, empty vessels and not too few. Then go in and shut the door behind yourself and your sons and pour into all these vessels. And when one is full, set it aside." So she went from him and shut the door behind herself and her sons. And as she poured they brought the vessels to her. When the

vessels were full, she said to her son, "Bring me another vessel." And he said to her, "There is not another." Then the oil stopped flowing. She came and told the man of God, and he said, "Go, sell the oil and pay your debts, and you and your sons can live on the rest."

1 Peter 3:7
Likewise, husbands, live with your wives in an understanding way, showing honor to the woman as the weaker vessel, since they are heirs with you of the grace of life, so that your prayers may not be hindered.

James 4:7
Submit yourselves therefore to God. Resist the devil, and he will flee from you.

2 Timothy 2:20-21
Now in a great house there are not only vessels of gold and silver but also of wood and clay, some for honorable use, some for dishonorable. Therefore, if anyone cleanses himself from what is dishonorable, he will be a vessel for honorable use, set apart as holy, useful to the master of the house, ready for every good work.

1 Thessalonians 4:3-5
For this is the will of God, your sanctification: that you abstain from sexual immorality; that each one of you know how to control his own body in holiness and honor, not in the passion of lust like the Gentiles who do not know God;

Victorious Life

Romans 8:37
No, in all these things we are more than conquerors through him who loved us.

1 Corinthians 15:57
But thanks be to God, who gives us the victory through our Lord Jesus Christ.

1 John 5:4-5
For everyone who has been born of God overcomes the world. And this is the victory that has overcome the world—our faith. Who is it that overcomes the world except the one who believes that Jesus is the Son of God?

Isaiah 41:10-13
Fear not, for I am with you; be not dismayed, for I am your God; I will strengthen you, I will help you, I will uphold you with my righteous right hand. Behold, all who are incensed against you shall be put to shame and confounded; those who strive against you shall be as nothing and shall perish. You shall seek those who contend with you, but you shall not find them; those who war against you shall be as nothing at all. For I, the Lord your God, hold your right hand; it is I who say to you, "Fear not, I am the one who helps you."

Galatians 2:20
I have been crucified with Christ. It is no longer I who live, but Christ who lives in me. And the life I now live in the flesh I live by faith in the Son of God, who loved me and gave himself for me.

Ephesians 6:16

In all circumstances take up the shield of faith, with which you can extinguish all the flaming darts of the evil one;

Romans 12:2

Do not be conformed to this world, but be transformed by the renewal of your mind, that by testing you may discern what is the will of God, what is good and acceptable and perfect.

Galatians 5:16

But I say, walk by the Spirit, and you will not gratify the desires of the flesh.

Romans 6:14

For sin will have no dominion over you, since you are not under law but under grace.

Philippians 2:13

For it is God who works in you, both to will and to work for his good pleasure.

Romans 16:20

The God of peace will soon crush Satan under your feet. The grace of our Lord Jesus Christ be with you.

Victory

Philippians 4:13

I can do all things through him who strengthens me.

John 16:33

I have said these things to you, that in me you may have peace. In the world you will have tribulation. But take heart; I have overcome the world."

1 Corinthians 15:57

But thanks be to God, who gives us the victory through our Lord Jesus Christ.

James 1:12-14

Blessed is the man who remains steadfast under trial, for when he has stood the test he will receive the crown of life, which God has promised to those who love him. Let no one say when he is tempted, "I am being tempted by God," for God cannot be tempted with evil, and he himself tempts no one. But each person is tempted when he is lured and enticed by his own desire.

Psalm 108:13

With God we shall do valiantly; it is he who will tread down our foes.

1 Corinthians 10:13

No temptation has overtaken you that is not common to man. God is faithful, and he will not let you be tempted beyond your ability, but with the temptation he will also provide the way of escape, that you may be able to endure it.

Deuteronomy 20:1-4

"When you go out to war against your enemies, and see horses and chariots and an army larger than your own, you shall not be afraid of them, for the Lord your God is with you, who brought you up out of the land of Egypt. And when you draw near to the battle, the priest shall come forward and speak to the people and shall say to them, 'Hear, O Israel, today you are drawing near for battle against your enemies: let not your heart faint. Do not fear or panic or be in dread of them, for the Lord your God is he who goes with you to fight for you against your enemies, to give you the victory.'

2 Corinthians 12:9-10

But he said to me, "My grace is sufficient for you, for my power is made perfect in weakness." Therefore I will boast all the more gladly of my weaknesses, so that the power of Christ may rest upon me. For the sake of Christ, then, I am content with weaknesses, insults, hardships, persecutions, and calamities. For when I am weak, then I am strong.

Ephesians 6:13

Therefore, take up the whole armor of God, that you may be able to withstand in the evil day, and having done all, to stand firm.

Ephesians 6:10

Finally, be strong in the Lord and in the strength of his might.

Victory in Christ

1 Corinthians 15:57

But thanks be to God, who gives us the victory through our Lord Jesus Christ.

Romans 8:37

No, in all these things we are more than conquerors through him who loved us.

2 Corinthians 2:14

But thanks be to God, who in Christ always leads us in triumphal procession, and through us spreads the fragrance of the knowledge of him everywhere.

Deuteronomy 20:4

For the Lord your God is he who goes with you to fight for you against your enemies, to give you the victory.'

Romans 8:31

What then shall we say to these things? If God is for us, who can be against us?

Philippians 4:13

I can do all things through him who strengthens me.

Romans 6:14

For sin will have no dominion over you, since you are not under law but under grace.

Violence

Psalm 11:5
The Lord tests the righteous, but his soul hates the wicked and the one who loves violence.

Matthew 26:52-54
Then Jesus said to him, "Put your sword back into its place. For all who take the sword will perish by the sword. Do you think that I cannot appeal to my Father, and he will at once send me more than twelve legions of angels? But how then should the Scriptures be fulfilled, that it must be so?"

Proverbs 3:31
Do not envy a man of violence and do not choose any of his ways,

Isaiah 60:18
Violence shall no more be heard in your land, devastation or destruction within your borders; you shall call your walls Salvation, and your gates Praise.

Matthew 5:38-39
"You have heard that it was said, 'An eye for an eye and a tooth for a tooth.' But I say to you, Do not resist the one who is evil. But if anyone slaps you on the right cheek, turn to him the other also.

Romans 13:4
For he is God's servant for your good. But if you do wrong, be afraid, for he does not bear the sword in vain. For he is the servant of God, an avenger who carries out God's wrath on the wrongdoer.

Titus 3:2
To speak evil of no one, to avoid quarreling, to be gentle, and to show perfect courtesy toward all people.

Hebrews 10:30
For we know him who said, "Vengeance is mine; I will repay." And again, "The Lord will judge his people."

1 Timothy 3:3
Not a drunkard, not violent but gentle, not quarrelsome, not a lover of money.

Romans 14:1
As for the one who is weak in faith, welcome him, but not to quarrel over opinions.

Galatians 5:19-21
Now the works of the flesh are evident: sexual immorality, impurity, sensuality, idolatry, sorcery, enmity, strife, jealousy, fits of anger, rivalries, dissensions, divisions, envy, drunkenness, orgies, and things like these. I warn you, as I warned you before, that those who do such things will not inherit the kingdom of God.

Genesis 9:5-6

And for your lifeblood I will require a reckoning: from every beast I will require it and from man. From his fellow man I will require a reckoning for the life of man. "Whoever sheds the blood of man, by man shall his blood be shed, for God made man in his own image.

Virtue

2 Peter 1:5

For this very reason, make every effort to supplement your faith with virtue, and virtue with knowledge,

Philippians 4:8

Finally, brothers, whatever is true, whatever is honorable, whatever is just, whatever is pure, whatever is lovely, whatever is commendable, if there is any excellence, if there is anything worthy of praise, think about these things.

2 Peter 1:5-8

For this very reason, make every effort to supplement your faith with virtue, and virtue with knowledge, and knowledge with self-control, and self-control with steadfastness, and steadfastness with godliness, and godliness with brotherly affection, and brotherly affection with love. For if these qualities are yours and are increasing, they keep you from being ineffective or unfruitful in the knowledge of our Lord Jesus Christ.

Ephesians 4:2

With all humility and gentleness, with patience, bearing with one another in love,

Proverbs 10:9

Whoever walks in integrity walks securely, but he who makes his ways crooked will be found out.

Vision

Habakkuk 2:2-3

And the Lord answered me: "Write the vision; make it plain on tablets, so he may run who reads it. For still the vision awaits its appointed time; it hastens to the end—it will not lie. If it seems slow, wait for it; it will surely come; it will not delay.

Proverbs 29:18

Where there is no prophetic vision the people cast off restraint, but blessed is he who keeps the law.

Joel 2:28

"And it shall come to pass afterward, that I will pour out my Spirit on all flesh; your sons and your daughters shall prophesy, your old men shall dream dreams, and your young men shall see visions.

Jeremiah 29:11

For I know the plans I have for you, declares the Lord, plans for welfare and not for evil, to give you a future and a hope.

Daniel 7:13-14

"I saw in the night visions, and behold, with the clouds of heaven there came one like a son of man, and he came to the Ancient of Days and was presented before him. And to him was given dominion and glory and a kingdom, that all peoples, nations, and languages should serve him; his dominion is an everlasting dominion, which shall not pass away, and his kingdom one that shall not be destroyed.

Amos 3:7

"For the Lord God does nothing without revealing his secret to his servants the prophets.

Acts 18:9

And the Lord said to Paul one night in a vision, "Do not be afraid, but go on speaking and do not be silent,

Jeremiah 23:16

Thus says the Lord of hosts: "Do not listen to the words of the prophets who prophesy to you, filling you with vain hopes. They speak visions of their own minds, not from the mouth of the Lord.

Numbers 12:6

And he said, "Hear my words: If there is a prophet among you, I the Lord make myself known to him in a vision; I speak with him in a dream.

Volunteering

1 Peter 4:10

As each has received a gift, use it to serve one another, as good stewards of God's varied grace:

Galatians 6:10

So then, as we have opportunity, let us do good to everyone, and especially to those who are of the household of faith.

Acts 20:35

In all things I have shown you that by working hard in this way we must help the weak and remember the words of the Lord Jesus, how he himself said, 'It is more blessed to give than to receive.'"

Luke 6:35

But love your enemies, and do good, and lend, expecting nothing in return, and your reward will be great, and you will be sons of the Most High, for he is kind to the ungrateful and the evil.

Luke 12:33-34

Sell your possessions, and give to the needy. Provide yourselves with moneybags that do not grow old, with a treasure in the heavens that does not fail, where no thief approaches and no moth destroys. For where your treasure is, there will your heart be also.

1 Timothy 6:17-19

As for the rich in this present age, charge them not to be haughty, nor to set their hopes on the uncertainty of riches, but on God, who richly provides us with everything to enjoy. They are to do good, to be rich in good works, to be generous and ready to share, thus storing up treasure for themselves as a good foundation for the future, so that they may take hold of that which is truly life.

Proverbs 11:24

One gives freely, yet grows all the richer; another withholds what he should give, and only suffers want.

Ephesians 2:10

For we are his workmanship, created in Christ Jesus for good works, which God prepared beforehand, that we should walk in them.

Matthew 25:35

For I was hungry and you gave me food, I was thirsty and you gave me drink, I was a stranger and you welcomed me,

Colossians 3:23-24

Whatever you do, work heartily, as for the Lord and not for men, knowing that from the Lord you will receive the inheritance as your reward. You are serving the Lord Christ.

Matthew 25:40

And the King will answer them, 'Truly, I say to you, as you did it to one of the least of these my brothers, you did it to me.'

Isaiah 58:10

If you pour yourself out for the hungry and satisfy the desire of the afflicted, then shall your light rise in the darkness and your gloom be as the noonday.

Matthew 9:37

Then he said to his disciples, "The harvest is plentiful, but the laborers are few;

Voting

Deuteronomy 1:13

Choose for your tribes wise, understanding, and experienced men, and I will appoint them as your heads.'

1 Timothy 2:1-2

First of all, then, I urge that supplications, prayers, intercessions, and thanksgivings be made for all people, for kings and all who are in high positions, that we may lead a peaceful and quiet life, godly and dignified in every way.

Proverbs 29:2

When the righteous increase, the people rejoice, but when the wicked rule, the people groan.

Romans 13:1

Let every person be subject to the governing authorities. For there is no authority except from God, and those that exist have been instituted by God.

Vulnerability

2 Corinthians 12:9-10

But he said to me, "My grace is sufficient for you, for my power is made perfect in weakness." Therefore, I will boast all the more gladly of my weaknesses, so that the power of Christ may rest upon me. For the sake of Christ, then, I am content with weaknesses, insults, hardships, persecutions, and calamities. For when I am weak, then I am strong.

James 1:1-27

James, a servant of God and of the Lord Jesus Christ, To the twelve tribes in the Dispersion: Greetings. Count it all joy, my brothers, when you meet trials of various kinds, for you know that the testing of your faith produces steadfastness. And let steadfastness have its full effect, that you may be perfect and complete, lacking in nothing. If any of you lacks wisdom, let him ask God, who gives generously to all without reproach, and it will be given him. ...

James 5:16

Therefore, confess your sins to one another and pray for one another, that you may be healed. The prayer of a righteous person has great power as it is working.

2 Corinthians 6:11-13

We have spoken freely to you, Corinthians; our heart is wide open. You are not restricted by us, but you are restricted in your own affections. In return (I speak as to children) widen your hearts also.

Luke 6:27-36

"But I say to you who hear, Love your enemies, do good to those who hate you, bless those who curse you, pray for those who abuse you. To one who strikes you on the cheek, offer the other also, and from one who takes away your cloak do not withhold your tunic either. Give to everyone who begs from you, and from one who takes away your goods do not demand them back. And as you wish that others would do to you, do so to them. If you love those who love you, what benefit is that to you? For even sinners love those who love them. And if you do good to those who do good to you, what benefit is that to you? For even sinners do the same. And if you lend to those from whom you expect to receive, what credit is that to you? Even sinners lend to sinners, to get back the same amount. But love your enemies, and do good, and lend, expecting nothing in return, and your reward will be great, and you will be sons of the Most High, for he is kind to the ungrateful and the evil. Be merciful, even as your Father is merciful.

Galatians 6:2

Bear one another's burdens, and so fulfill the law of Christ.

John 13:34-35

A new commandment I give to you, that you love one another: just as I have loved you, you also are to love one another. By this all people will know that you are my disciples, if you have love for one another."

Wages

Romans 4:4

Now to the one who works, his wages are not counted as a gift but as his due.

Romans 6:23

For the wages of sin is death, but the free gift of God is eternal life in Christ Jesus our Lord.

James 5:4

Behold, the wages of the laborers who mowed your fields, which you kept back by fraud, are crying out against you, and the cries of the harvesters have reached the ears of the Lord of hosts.

Leviticus 19:13

"You shall not oppress your neighbor or rob him. The wages of a hired servant shall not remain with you all night until the morning.

Jeremiah 22:13

"Woe to him who builds his house by unrighteousness, and his upper rooms by injustice, who makes his neighbor serve him for nothing and does not give him his wages,

1 Timothy 5:18

For the Scripture says, "You shall not muzzle an ox when it treads out the grain," and, "The laborer deserves his wages."

Deuteronomy 24:14-15

"You shall not oppress a hired servant who is poor and needy, whether he is one of your brothers or one of the sojourners who are in your land within your towns. You shall give him his wages on the same day, before the sun sets (for he is poor and counts on it), lest he cry against you to the Lord, and you be guilty of sin.

Malachi 3:5

"Then I will draw near to you for judgment. I will be a swift witness against the sorcerers, against the adulterers, against those who swear falsely, against those who oppress the hired worker in his wages, the widow and the fatherless, against those who thrust aside the sojourner, and do not fear me, says the Lord of hosts.

Waiting on God

Isaiah 40:31

But they who wait for the Lord shall renew their strength; they shall mount up with wings like eagles; they shall run and not be weary; they shall walk and not faint.

Psalm 27:13-14

I believe that I shall look upon the goodness of the Lord in the land of the living! Wait for the Lord; be strong, and let your heart take courage; wait for the Lord!

Lamentations 3:25

The Lord is good to those who wait for him, to the soul who seeks him.

Proverbs 3:5-6

Trust in the Lord with all your heart, and do not lean on your own understanding. In all your ways acknowledge him, and he will make straight your paths.

Isaiah 30:18

Therefore, the Lord waits to be gracious to you, and therefore he exalts himself to show mercy to you. For the Lord is a God of justice; blessed are all those who wait for him.

James 5:7-8

Be patient, therefore, brothers, until the coming of the Lord. See how the farmer waits for the precious fruit of the earth, being patient about it, until it receives the early and the late rains. You also, be patient. Establish your hearts, for the coming of the Lord is at hand.

2 Peter 3:9

The Lord is not slow to fulfill his promise as some count slowness, but is patient toward you, not wishing that any should perish, but that all should reach repentance.

Wake up

Romans 13:11

Besides this you know the time, that the hour has come for you to wake from sleep. For salvation is nearer to us now than when we first believed.

1 Thessalonians 5:5-6

For you are all children of light, children of the day. We are not of the night or of the darkness. So then let us not sleep, as others do, but let us keep awake and be sober.

Isaiah 60:1

Arise, shine, for your light has come, and the glory of the Lord has risen upon you.

Revelation 3:2-3

Wake up, and strengthen what remains and is about to die, for I have not found your works complete in the sight of my God. Remember, then, what you received and heard. Keep it, and repent. If you will not wake up, I will come like a thief, and you will not know at what hour I will come against you.

Ephesians 5:14

For anything that becomes visible is light. Therefore, it says, "Awake, O sleeper, and arise from the dead, and Christ will shine on you."

Proverbs 20:13

Love not sleep, lest you come to poverty; open your eyes, and you will have plenty of bread.

Walking by Faith

2 Corinthians 5:7
For we walk by faith, not by sight.

Proverbs 3:5-6
Trust in the Lord with all your heart, and do not lean on your own understanding. In all your ways acknowledge him, and he will make straight your paths.

Hebrews 11:6
And without faith it is impossible to please him, for whoever would draw near to God must believe that he exists and that he rewards those who seek him.

Romans 10:17
So faith comes from hearing, and hearing through the word of Christ.

Hebrews 11:1
Now faith is the assurance of things hoped for, the conviction of things not seen.

2 Corinthians 4:16-18
So we do not lose heart. Though our outer self is wasting away, our inner self is being renewed day by day. For this light momentary affliction is preparing for us an eternal weight of glory beyond all comparison, as we look not to the things that are seen but to the things that are unseen. For the things that are seen are transient, but the things that are unseen are eternal.

Romans 1:17
For in it the righteousness of God is revealed from faith for faith, as it is written, "The righteous shall live by faith."

War

Ecclesiastes 3:8
A time to love, and a time to hate; a time for war, and a time for peace.

Matthew 24:6
And you will hear of wars and rumors of wars. See that you are not alarmed, for this must take place, but the end is not yet.

Jeremiah 51:20
"You are my hammer and weapon of war: with you I break nations in pieces; with you I destroy kingdoms;

James 4:1-2
What causes quarrels and what causes fights among you? Is it not this, that your passions are at war within you? You desire and do not have, so you murder. You covet and cannot obtain, so you fight and quarrel. You do not have, because you do not ask.

Deuteronomy 20:1-4
"When you go out to war against your enemies, and see horses and chariots and an army larger than your own, you shall not be afraid of them, for the Lord your God is with you, who brought you up out of the land of Egypt. And when you draw near to the battle, the priest shall come forward and speak to the people and shall say to them, 'Hear, O Israel, today you are drawing near for battle against your enemies: let not your heart faint. Do not fear or panic or be in dread of them, for the Lord your God is he who goes with you to fight for you against your enemies, to give you the victory.'

Isaiah 2:4
He shall judge between the nations, and shall decide disputes for many peoples; and they shall beat their swords into plowshares, and their spears into pruning hooks; nation shall not lift up sword against nation, neither shall they learn war anymore.

Warnings Before Destruction

Ezekiel 3:17-19
"Son of man, I have made you a watchman for the house of Israel. Whenever you hear a word from my mouth, you shall give them warning from me. If I say to the wicked, 'You shall surely die,' and you give him no warning, nor speak to warn the wicked from his wicked way, in order to save his life, that wicked person shall die for his iniquity, but his blood I will require at your hand. But if you warn the wicked, and he does not turn from his wickedness, or from his wicked way, he shall die for his iniquity, but you will have delivered your soul.

Proverbs 16:18
Pride goes before destruction, and a haughty spirit before a fall.

Luke 21:28
Now when these things begin to take place, straighten up and raise your heads, because your redemption is drawing near."

Matthew 10:28
And do not fear those who kill the body but cannot kill the soul. Rather fear him who can destroy both soul and body in hell.

Waste

John 6:12
And when they had eaten their fill, he told his disciples, "Gather up the leftover fragments, that nothing may be lost."

Ezekiel 16:49
Behold, this was the guilt of your sister Sodom: she and her daughters had pride, excess of food, and prosperous ease, but did not aid the poor and needy.

Proverbs 18:9
Whoever is slack in his work is a brother to him who destroys.

Wasting Time

Ephesians 5:16-17
Making the best use of the time, because the days are evil. Therefore, do not be foolish, but understand what the will of the Lord is.

Colossians 3:23
Whatever you do, work heartily, as for the Lord and not for men,

Proverbs 6:9-11
How long will you lie there, O sluggard? When will you arise from your sleep? A little sleep, a little slumber, a little folding of the hands to rest, and poverty will come upon you like a robber, and want like an armed man.

Water

John 4:14
But whoever drinks of the water that I will give him will never be thirsty again. The water that I will give him will become in him a spring of water welling up to eternal life."

Isaiah 12:3
With joy you will draw water from the wells of salvation.

Isaiah 44:3
For I will pour water on the thirsty land, and streams on the dry ground; I will pour my Spirit upon your offspring, and my blessing on your descendants.

Ezekiel 36:25
I will sprinkle clean water on you, and you shall be clean from all your uncleannesses, and from all your idols I will cleanse you.

Revelation 22:1
Then the angel showed me the river of the water of life, bright as crystal, flowing from the throne of God and of the Lamb

Revelation 22:17
The Spirit and the Bride say, "Come." And let the one who hears say, "Come." And let the one who is thirsty come; let the one who desires take the water of life without price.

Isaiah 49:10
They shall not hunger or thirst, neither scorching wind nor sun shall strike them, for he who has pity on them will lead them, and by springs of water will guide them.

John 7:37-39
On the last day of the feast, the great day, Jesus stood up and cried out, "If anyone thirsts, let him come to me and drink. Whoever believes in me, as the Scripture has said, 'Out of his heart will flow rivers of

living water.'" Now this he said about the Spirit, whom those who believed in him were to receive, for as yet the Spirit had not been given, because Jesus was not yet glorified.

Water Baptism

1 Peter 3:21
Baptism, which corresponds to this, now saves you, not as a removal of dirt from the body but as an appeal to God for a good conscience, through the resurrection of Jesus Christ,

Acts 2:38
And Peter said to them, "Repent and be baptized every one of you in the name of Jesus Christ for the forgiveness of your sins, and you will receive the gift of the Holy Spirit.

Acts 22:16
And now why do you wait? Rise and be baptized and wash away your sins, calling on his name.'

Mark 16:16
Whoever believes and is baptized will be saved, but whoever does not believe will be condemned.

1 Corinthians 12:13
For in one Spirit we were all baptized into one body—Jews or Greeks, slaves or free—and all were made to drink of one Spirit.

John 3:5
Jesus answered, "Truly, truly, I say to you, unless one is born of water and the Spirit, he cannot enter the kingdom of God.

Galatians 3:27
For as many of you as were baptized into Christ have put on Christ.

Matthew 3:11
"I baptize you with water for repentance, but he who is coming after me is mightier than I, whose sandals I am not worthy to carry. He will baptize you with the Holy Spirit and fire.

Matthew 28:19
Go therefore and make disciples of all nations, baptizing them in the name of the Father and of the Son and of the Holy Spirit,

Wavering

James 1:6
But let him ask in faith, with no doubting, for the one who doubts is like a wave of the sea that is driven and tossed by the wind.

Hebrews 10:23
Let us hold fast the confession of our hope without wavering, for he who promised is faithful.

James 1:3

For you know that the testing of your faith produces steadfastness.

Weakness

2 Corinthians 12:9

But he said to me, "My grace is sufficient for you, for my power is made perfect in weakness." Therefore I will boast all the more gladly of my weaknesses, so that the power of Christ may rest upon me.

Psalm 34:17-20

When the righteous cry for help, the Lord hears and delivers them out of all their troubles. The Lord is near to the brokenhearted and saves the crushed in spirit. Many are the afflictions of the righteous, but the Lord delivers him out of them all. He keeps all his bones; not one of them is broken.

Romans 8:26

Likewise the Spirit helps us in our weakness. For we do not know what to pray for as we ought, but the Spirit himself intercedes for us with groanings too deep for words.

Wealth

Hebrews 13:5

Keep your life free from love of money, and be content with what you have, for he has said, "I will never leave you nor forsake you."

Matthew 6:24

"No one can serve two masters, for either he will hate the one and love the other, or he will be devoted to the one and despise the other. You cannot serve God and money.

1 Timothy 6:10

For the love of money is a root of all kinds of evils. It is through this craving that some have wandered away from the faith and pierced themselves with many pangs.

Matthew 6:19-21

"Do not lay up for yourselves treasures on earth, where moth and rust destroy and where thieves break in and steal, but lay up for yourselves treasures in heaven, where neither moth nor rust destroys and where thieves do not break in and steal. For where your treasure is, there your heart will be also.

Weapons

Matthew 26:52-54

Then Jesus said to him, "Put your sword back into its place. For all who take the sword will perish by the sword. Do you think that I cannot appeal to my Father, and he will at once send me more than twelve legions of angels? But how then should the Scriptures be fulfilled, that it must be so?"

Psalm 144:1

Of David. Blessed be the Lord, my rock, who trains my hands for war, and my fingers for battle;

Weariness

Galatians 6:9
And let us not grow weary of doing good, for in due season we will reap, if we do not give up.

Isaiah 40:29-31
He gives power to the faint, and to him who has no might he increases strength. Even youths shall faint and be weary, and young men shall fall exhausted; but they who wait for the Lord shall renew their strength; they shall mount up with wings like eagles; they shall run and not be weary; they shall walk and not faint.

Matthew 11:28-30
Come to me, all who labor and are heavy laden, and I will give you rest. Take my yoke upon you, and learn from me, for I am gentle and lowly in heart, and you will find rest for your souls. For my yoke is easy, and my burden is light."

Wicked Heart

Jeremiah 17:9
The heart is deceitful above all things, and desperately sick; who can understand it?

Mark 7:21
For from within, out of the heart of man, come evil thoughts, sexual immorality, theft, murder, adultery,

Romans 1:21
For although they knew God, they did not honor him as God or give thanks to him, but they became futile in their thinking, and their foolish hearts were darkened.

Widow

Exodus 22:22-24
You shall not mistreat any widow or fatherless child. If you do mistreat them, and they cry out to me, I will surely hear their cry, and my wrath will burn, and I will kill you with the sword, and your wives shall become widows and your children fatherless.

Psalm 68:5
Father of the fatherless and protector of widows is God in his holy habitation.

1 Timothy 5:3-6
Honor widows who are truly widows. But if a widow has children or grandchildren, let them first learn to show godliness to their own household and to make some return to their parents, for this is pleasing in the sight of God. She who is truly a widow, left all alone, has set her hope on God and continues in supplications and prayers night and day, but she who is self-indulgent is dead even while she lives.

1 Timothy 5:16
If any believing woman has relatives who are widows, let her care for them. Let the church not be burdened, so that it may care for those who are truly widows.

Wife

Proverbs 18:22
He who finds a wife finds a good thing and obtains favor from the Lord.

1 Peter 3:7
Likewise, husbands, live with your wives in an understanding way, showing honor to the woman as the weaker vessel, since they are heirs with you of the grace of life, so that your prayers may not be hindered.

Ephesians 5:25
Husbands, love your wives, as Christ loved the church and gave himself up for her,

Genesis 2:24
Therefore, a man shall leave his father and his mother and hold fast to his wife, and they shall become one flesh.

Ephesians 5:22
Wives, submit to your own husbands, as to the Lord.

Proverbs 14:1
The wisest of women builds her house, but folly with her own hands tears it down.

Hebrews 13:4
Let marriage be held in honor among all, and let the marriage bed be undefiled, for God will judge the sexually immoral and adulterous.

Proverbs 12:4
An excellent wife is the crown of her husband, but she who brings shame is like rottenness in his bones.

Proverbs 19:14
House and wealth are inherited from fathers, but a prudent wife is from the Lord.

Ephesians 5:33
However, let each one of you love his wife as himself, and let the wife see that she respects her husband.

Proverbs 21:9
It is better to live in a corner of the housetop than in a house shared with a quarrelsome wife.

Will of God

Romans 12:2

Do not be conformed to this world, but be transformed by the renewal of your mind, that by testing you may discern what is the will of God, what is good and acceptable and perfect.

1 Thessalonians 5:18

Give thanks in all circumstances; for this is the will of God in Christ Jesus for you.

1 Peter 2:15

For this is the will of God, that by doing good you should put to silence the ignorance of foolish people.

1 Thessalonians 4:3

For this is the will of God, your sanctification: that you abstain from sexual immorality;

Matthew 6:10

Your kingdom come, your will be done, on earth as it is in heaven.

John 7:17

If anyone's will is to do God's will, he will know whether the teaching is from God or whether I am speaking on my own authority.

Ephesians 5:17

Therefore, do not be foolish, but understand what the will of the Lord is.

2 Peter 3:9

The Lord is not slow to fulfill his promise as some count slowness, but is patient toward you, not wishing that any should perish, but that all should reach repentance.

Jeremiah 29:11

For I know the plans I have for you, declares the Lord, plans for welfare and not for evil, to give you a future and a hope.

Hebrews 10:36

For you have need of endurance, so that when you have done the will of God you may receive what is promised.

Winning Souls for Christ

1 Corinthians 9:19-23

For though I am free from all, I have made myself a servant to all, that I might win more of them. To the Jews I became as a Jew, in order to win Jews. To those under the law I became as one under the law (though not being myself under the law) that I might win those under the law. To those outside the law I became as one outside the law (not being outside the law of God but under the law of Christ) that I might win those outside the law. To the weak I became weak, that I might win the weak. I have become all things to all people, that by all means I might save some. I do it all for the sake of the gospel, that I may share with them in its blessings.

Mark 16:15

And he said to them, "Go into all the world and proclaim the gospel to the whole creation.

Proverbs 11:30

The fruit of the righteous is a tree of life, and whoever captures souls is wise.

John 15:16

You did not choose me, but I chose you and appointed you that you should go and bear fruit and that your fruit should abide, so that whatever you ask the Father in my name, he may give it to you.

Acts 1:8

But you will receive power when the Holy Spirit has come upon you, and you will be my witnesses in Jerusalem and in all Judea and Samaria, and to the end of the earth."

Wisdom

James 1:5

If any of you lacks wisdom, let him ask God, who gives generously to all without reproach, and it will be given him.

James 3:17

But the wisdom from above is first pure, then peaceable, gentle, open to reason, full of mercy and good fruits, impartial and sincere.

Proverbs 1:7

The fear of the Lord is the beginning of knowledge; fools despise wisdom and instruction.

Ephesians 5:15-17

Look carefully then how you walk, not as unwise but as wise, making the best use of the time, because the days are evil. Therefore do not be foolish, but understand what the will of the Lord is.

Proverbs 19:20

Listen to advice and accept instruction, that you may gain wisdom in the future.

Proverbs 12:15

The way of a fool is right in his own eyes, but a wise man listens to advice.

Proverbs 10:23

Doing wrong is like a joke to a fool, but wisdom is pleasure to a man of understanding.

Colossians 3:16

Let the word of Christ dwell in you richly, teaching and admonishing one another in all wisdom, singing psalms and hymns and spiritual songs, with thankfulness in your hearts to God.

Proverbs 18:15

An intelligent heart acquires knowledge, and the ear of the wise seeks knowledge.

Proverbs 2:6

For the Lord gives wisdom; from his mouth come knowledge and understanding;

Psalm 111:10

The fear of the Lord is the beginning of wisdom; all those who practice it have a good understanding. His praise endures forever!

Wise Counsel

Proverbs 12:15

The way of a fool is right in his own eyes, but a wise man listens to advice.

Proverbs 11:14

Where there is no guidance, a people falls, but in an abundance of counselors there is safety.

Proverbs 15:22

Without counsel plans fail, but with many advisers they succeed.

Proverbs 19:20-21

Listen to advice and accept instruction, that you may gain wisdom in the future. Many are the plans in the mind of a man, but it is the purpose of the Lord that will stand.

Proverbs 24:6

For by wise guidance you can wage your war, and in abundance of counselors there is victory.

Witchcraft

Leviticus 19:31

"Do not turn to mediums or necromancers; do not seek them out, and so make yourselves unclean by them: I am the Lord your God.

Exodus 22:18

"You shall not permit a sorceress to live.

Leviticus 20:27

"A man or a woman who is a medium or a necromancer shall surely be put to death. They shall be stoned with stones; their blood shall be upon them."

Revelation 21:8

But as for the cowardly, the faithless, the detestable, as for murderers, the sexually immoral, sorcerers, idolaters, and all liars, their portion will be in the lake that burns with fire and sulfur, which is the second death."

Leviticus 20:6

"If a person turns to mediums and necromancers, whoring after them, I will set my face against that person and will cut him off from among his people.

Witnessing

1 Peter 3:15

But in your hearts honor Christ the Lord as holy, always being prepared to make a defense to anyone who asks you for a reason for the hope that is in you; yet do it with gentleness and respect,

Mark 16:15-16

And he said to them, "Go into all the world and proclaim the gospel to the whole creation. Whoever believes and is baptized will be saved, but whoever does not believe will be condemned.

Colossians 4:6

Let your speech always be gracious, seasoned with salt, so that you may know how you ought to answer each person.

Matthew 5:16

In the same way, let your light shine before others, so that they may see your good works and give glory to your Father who is in heaven.

Romans 1:16

For I am not ashamed of the gospel, for it is the power of God for salvation to everyone who believes, to the Jew first and also to the Greek.

Matthew 28:18-20

And Jesus came and said to them, "All authority in heaven and on earth has been given to me. Go therefore and make disciples of all nations, baptizing them in the name of the Father and of the Son and of the Holy Spirit, teaching them to observe all that I have commanded you. And behold, I am with you always, to the end of the age."

Acts 1:8

But you will receive power when the Holy Spirit has come upon you, and you will be my witnesses in Jerusalem and in all Judea and Samaria, and to the end of the earth."

Work

Colossians 3:23

Whatever you do, work heartily, as for the Lord and not for men,

Proverbs 16:3

Commit your work to the Lord, and your plans will be established.

1 Corinthians 10:31

So, whether you eat or drink, or whatever you do, do all to the glory of God.

Proverbs 18:9

Whoever is slack in his work is a brother to him who destroys.

Genesis 2:15

The Lord God took the man and put him in the garden of Eden to work it and keep it.

Ephesians 4:28

Let the thief no longer steal, but rather let him labor, doing honest work with his own hands, so that he may have something to share with anyone in need.

Worry

Philippians 4:6-7

Do not be anxious about anything, but in everything by prayer and supplication with thanksgiving let your requests be made known to God. And the peace of God, which surpasses all understanding, will guard your hearts and your minds in Christ Jesus.

Proverbs 12:25

Anxiety in a man's heart weighs him down, but a good word makes him glad.

Matthew 6:33-34

But seek first the kingdom of God and his righteousness, and all these things will be added to you. "Therefore do not be anxious about tomorrow, for tomorrow will be anxious for itself. Sufficient for the day is its own trouble.

Philippians 4:13

I can do all things through him who strengthens me.

Matthew 11:28-30

Come to me, all who labor and are heavy laden, and I will give you rest. Take my yoke upon you, and learn from me, for I am gentle and lowly in heart, and you will find rest for your souls. For my yoke is easy, and my burden is light."

1 Peter 5:6-7

Humble yourselves, therefore, under the mighty hand of God so that at the proper time he may exalt you, casting all your anxieties on him, because he cares for you.

John 14:27

Peace I leave with you; my peace I give to you. Not as the world gives do I give to you. Let not your hearts be troubled, neither let them be afraid.

Womb

Isaiah 49:5

And now the Lord says, he who formed me from the womb to be his servant, to bring Jacob back to him; and that Israel might be gathered to him— for I am honored in the eyes of the Lord, and my God has become my strength—

Jeremiah 1:4-5

Now the word of the Lord came to me, saying, "Before I formed you in the womb I knew you, and before you were born I consecrated you; I appointed you a prophet to the nations."

Isaiah 44:24

Thus says the Lord, your Redeemer, who formed you from the womb: "I am the Lord, who made all things, who alone stretched out the heavens, who spread out the earth by myself,

Luke 1:44

For behold, when the sound of your greeting came to my ears, the baby in my womb leaped for joy.

Isaiah 49:1

Listen to me, O coastlands, and give attention, you peoples from afar. The Lord called me from the womb, from the body of my mother he named my name.

Psalm 22:9-10

Yet you are he who took me from the womb; you made me trust you at my mother's breasts. On you was I cast from my birth, and from my mother's womb you have been my God.

Galatians 1:15

But when he who had set me apart before I was born, and who called me by his grace,

Luke 1:41

And when Elizabeth heard the greeting of Mary, the baby leaped in her womb. And Elizabeth was filled with the Holy Spirit,

Women

Titus 2:3-5

Older women likewise are to be reverent in behavior, not slanderers or slaves to much wine. They are to teach what is good, and so train the young women to love their husbands and children, to be self-controlled, pure, working at home, kind, and submissive to their own husbands, that the word of God may not be reviled.

Proverbs 14:1

The wisest of women builds her house, but folly with her own hands tears it down.

Word of God

Hebrews 4:12

For the word of God is living and active, sharper than any two-edged sword, piercing to the division of soul and of spirit, of joints and of marrow, and discerning the thoughts and intentions of the heart.

Matthew 4:4

But he answered, "It is written, "'Man shall not live by bread alone, but by every word that comes from the mouth of God.'"

2 Timothy 3:16
All Scripture is breathed out by God and profitable for teaching, for reproof, for correction, and for training in righteousness,

Ephesians 6:17
And take the helmet of salvation, and the sword of the Spirit, which is the word of God,

John 1:1
In the beginning was the Word, and the Word was with God, and the Word was God.

Isaiah 55:11
So shall my word be that goes out from my mouth; it shall not return to me empty, but it shall accomplish that which I purpose, and shall succeed in the thing for which I sent it.

1 Thessalonians 2:13
And we also thank God constantly for this, that when you received the word of God, which you heard from us, you accepted it not as the word of men but as what it really is, the word of God, which is at work in you believers.

Luke 11:28
But he said, "Blessed rather are those who hear the word of God and keep it!"

Psalm 119:105
Your word is a lamp to my feet and a light to my path.

Workaholic

Hebrews 13:5
Keep your life free from love of money, and be content with what you have, for he has said, "I will never leave you nor forsake you."

Psalm 127:1-2
A Song of Ascents. Of Solomon. Unless the Lord builds the house, those who build it labor in vain. Unless the Lord watches over the city, the watchman stays awake in vain. It is in vain that you rise up early and go late to rest, eating the bread of anxious toil; for he gives to his beloved sleep.

Worship

John 4:24
God is spirit, and those who worship him must worship in spirit and truth."

Psalm 95:6
Oh come, let us worship and bow down; let us kneel before the Lord, our Maker!

Romans 12:1

I appeal to you therefore, brothers, by the mercies of God, to present your bodies as a living sacrifice, holy and acceptable to God, which is your spiritual worship.

John 4:23

But the hour is coming, and is now here, when the true worshipers will worship the Father in spirit and truth, for the Father is seeking such people to worship him.

Colossians 3:14-17

And above all these put on love, which binds everything together in perfect harmony. And let the peace of Christ rule in your hearts, to which indeed you were called in one body. And be thankful. Let the word of Christ dwell in you richly, teaching and admonishing one another in all wisdom, singing psalms and hymns and spiritual songs, with thankfulness in your hearts to God. And whatever you do, in word or deed, do everything in the name of the Lord Jesus, giving thanks to God the Father through him.

Isaiah 12:5

"Sing praises to the Lord, for he has done gloriously; let this be made known in all the earth.

Hebrews 13:15

Through him then let us continually offer up a sacrifice of praise to God, that is, the fruit of lips that acknowledge his name.

Luke 4:8

And Jesus answered him, "It is written, "'You shall worship the Lord your God, and him only shall you serve.'"

Psalm 29:2

Ascribe to the Lord the glory due his name; worship the Lord in the splendor of holiness.

Wrath of God

Romans 1:18

For the wrath of God is revealed from heaven against all ungodliness and unrighteousness of men, who by their unrighteousness suppress the truth.

John 3:36

Whoever believes in the Son has eternal life; whoever does not obey the Son shall not see life, but the wrath of God remains on him.

Romans 12:17-21

Repay no one evil for evil, but give thought to do what is honorable in the sight of all. If possible, so far as it depends on you, live peaceably with all. Beloved, never avenge yourselves, but leave it to the wrath of God, for it is written, "Vengeance is mine, I will repay, says the Lord." To the contrary, "if your enemy is hungry, feed him; if he is thirsty, give him something to drink; for by so doing you will heap burning coals on his head." Do not be overcome by evil, but overcome evil with good.

Ezekiel 25:17

I will execute great vengeance on them with wrathful rebukes. Then they will know that I am the Lord, when I lay my vengeance upon them."

Isaiah 26:21

For behold, the Lord is coming out from his place to punish the inhabitants of the earth for their iniquity, and the earth will disclose the blood shed on it, and will no more cover its slain.

Nahum 1:2-6

The Lord is a jealous and avenging God; the Lord is avenging and wrathful; the Lord takes vengeance on his adversaries and keeps wrath for his enemies. The Lord is slow to anger and great in power, and the Lord will by no means clear the guilty. His way is in whirlwind and storm, and the clouds are the dust of his feet. He rebukes the sea and makes it dry; he dries up all the rivers; Bashan and Carmel wither; the bloom of Lebanon withers. The mountains quake before him; the hills melt; the earth heaves before him, the world and all who dwell in it. Who can stand before his indignation? Who can endure the heat of his anger? His wrath is poured out like fire, and the rocks are broken into pieces by him.

Psalm 7:11

God is a righteous judge, and a God who feels indignation every day.

Matthew 10:28

And do not fear those who kill the body but cannot kill the soul. Rather fear him who can destroy both soul and body in hell.

Youth

1 Timothy 4:12

Let no one despise you for your youth, but set the believers an example in speech, in conduct, in love, in faith, in purity.

Ecclesiastes 11:9

Rejoice, O young man, in your youth, and let your heart cheer you in the days of your youth. Walk in the ways of your heart and the sight of your eyes. But know that for all these things God will bring you into judgment.

Jeremiah 1:4-8

Now the word of the Lord came to me, saying, "Before I formed you in the womb I knew you, and before you were born I consecrated you; I appointed you a prophet to the nations." Then I said, "Ah, Lord God! Behold, I do not know how to speak, for I am only a youth." But the Lord said to me, "Do not say, 'I am only a youth'; for to all to whom I send you, you shall go, and whatever I command you, you shall speak. Do not be afraid of them, for I am with you to deliver you, declares the Lord."

Ecclesiastes 12:1

Remember also your Creator in the days of your youth, before the evil days come and the years draw near of which you will say, "I have no pleasure in them";

Psalm 119:9

How can a young man keep his way pure? By guarding it according to your word.

2 Timothy 2:22

So flee youthful passions and pursue righteousness, faith, love, and peace, along with those who call on the Lord from a pure heart.

1 Corinthians 10:13

No temptation has overtaken you that is not common to man. God is faithful, and he will not let you be tempted beyond your ability, but with the temptation he will also provide the way of escape, that you may be able to endure it.

Ephesians 6:1-4

Children, obey your parents in the Lord, for this is right. "Honor your father and mother" (this is the first commandment with a promise), "that it may go well with you and that you may live long in the land." Fathers, do not provoke your children to anger, but bring them up in the discipline and instruction of the Lord.

Jeremiah 29:11

For I know the plans I have for you, declares the Lord, plans for welfare and not for evil, to give you a future and a hope.

Proverbs 23:26

My son, give me your heart, and let your eyes observe my ways.

Ephesians 4:29

Let no corrupting talk come out of your mouths, but only such as is good for building up, as fits the occasion, that it may give grace to those who hear.

Psalm 144:12

May our sons in their youth be like plants full grown, our daughters like corner pillars cut for the structure of a palace;

Zeal

Romans 10:2
For I bear them witness that they have a zeal for God, but not according to knowledge.

Revelation 3:19
Those whom I love, I reprove and discipline, so be zealous and repent.

Romans 12:11
Do not be slothful in zeal, be fervent in spirit, serve the Lord.

Titus 2:14
Who gave himself for us to redeem us from all lawlessness and to purify for himself a people for his own possession who are zealous for good works.

Isaiah 59:17
He put on righteousness as a breastplate, and a helmet of salvation on his head; he put on garments of vengeance for clothing, and wrapped himself in zeal as a cloak.

Zodiac Signs

Jeremiah 27:9
So do not listen to your prophets, your diviners, your dreamers, your fortune-tellers, or your sorcerers, who are saying to you, 'You shall not serve the king of Babylon.'

Micah 5:12
And I will cut off sorceries from your hand, and you shall have no more tellers of fortunes;

Deuteronomy 18:10-12
There shall not be found among you anyone who burns his son or his daughter as an offering, anyone who practices divination or tells fortunes or interprets omens, or a sorcerer or a charmer or a medium or a necromancer or one who inquires of the dead, for whoever does these things is an abomination to the Lord. And because of these abominations the Lord your God is driving them out before you.

John 14:6
Jesus said to him, "I am the way, and the truth, and the life. No one comes to the Father except through me.

Jeremiah 10:2
Thus says the Lord: "Learn not the way of the nations, nor be dismayed at the signs of the heavens because the nations are dismayed at them,

Made in the USA
Columbia, SC
02 January 2023

75352459R00254